COUNTERMEASURES, THE INTERNATIONAL LEGAL SYSTEM, AND ENVIRONMENTAL VIOLATIONS

Countermeasures, the International Legal System, and Environmental Violations

When Two Wrongs Make a Right for the Environment

Hjörtur B. Sverrisson

CAMBRIA
PRESS
Amherst, New York

Printed in the United States of America

Requests for permission should be directed to:
permissions@cambriapress.com, or mailed to:
Cambria Press
20 Northpointe Parkway, Suite 188
Amherst, NY 14228

Library of Congress Cataloging-in-Publication Data

Sverrisson, Hjörtur Bragi.

Countermeasures, the international legal system, and environmental violations : when two wrongs make a right for the environment / by Hjörtur Bragi Sverrisson.

p. cm.

Includes bibliographical references and index.

ISBN 978-1-60497-540-6 (alk. paper)

1. Offenses against the environment. 2. International offenses. 3. Self-defense. 4. Justification (Law) 5. Sanctions (International law) 6. Environmental law, International. I. Title.

K5278.S94 2008

341.5'82—dc22

2008020172

To Melanie and my parents
for their patience and support

Table of Contents

Acknowledgments **xiii**

Abbreviations **xv**

Introduction and Main Findings **1**

(a) Opening Remarks: When Two Wrongs Make a Right 1
(b) A Prelude to the Law of Countermeasures 2
(c) Use of Countermeasures in Defense of Environmental Interests of States 5
(d) Organization of This Book and Its Main Findings 6
(e) Final Remarks 10

Part I: Countermeasures, Sovereignty, and the International Legal System **13**

Chapter 1: Introduction and Organization **15**

Chapter 2: Sovereignty and the Incompleteness of International Law **21**

(a) Introduction and Purpose 21
(b) Sovereignty 22
(c) The Incompleteness of International Law and Nonjusticiable Disputes 32
(d) Conclusions 42

Chapter 3: Unilateral Acts of States or International Organizations Not Addressed in This Book **51**

(a) Introductory Note 51
(b) Suspension of International Development Projects 52

(c) Security Council Resolutions 53
(d) Self-Defense 55
(e) Acts of Necessity 55

Chapter 4: The Concept of Countermeasures and the Teachings of Highly Qualified Publicists 67

(a) Introduction 67
(b) Retorsion 70
(c) Reprisals 72
(d) Reciprocity 75
(e) Other Views on Countermeasures 78

Chapter 5: Countermeasures and International Tribunals 87

(a) *The Naulilaa Case*, 1928 (*Portugal v. Germany*) 87
(b) *Fishery Jurisdiction Case*, 1974 (*United Kingdom v. Iceland*) 89
(c) *Air Service Agreement Case*, 1978 (*France v. United States*) 92
(d) The *Hostage Case*, 1980 (*United States v. Iran*) 96
(e) The *Gabcikovo-Nagymaros Project*, 1997 (*Hungary v. Slovakia*) 99

Chapter 6: Final Remarks 107

Part II: The Elements of Countermeasures: Requirement and Obstacles **111**

Chapter 7: Introduction and Organization 113

Chapter 8: Considerations Regarding the Legality of Prospective Countermeasures 117

(a) The Purpose of Countermeasures and Its Effects on the Legality of Countermeasures 117
(b) Establishing the Violation: Actual Unlawfulness or Reasonable State's View? 123
(c) The Imminence of the Violation, Anticipatory Countermeasures 128
(d) Injured States, Violations *Erga Omnes*, and Collective Countermeasures 129
(e) Countermeasures: A Remedy for States Only 139

Chapter 9: Procedural Conditions for Countermeasures 149
(a) Introduction 149
(b) Requesting the Responsible State to Fulfill Its Obligation 150
(c) Duty to Notify the Responsible State of the Prospective Countermeasures and to Offer Negotiations 154

Chapter 10: Considerations Related to the Taking of Countermeasures 167
(a) Interests Against Which Countermeasures Can Be Directed and Prohibited Countermeasures 167
(b) Proportionality 173

Chapter 11: Conditions That Might Preclude Countermeasures 189
(a) Introduction 189
(b) Ongoing Negotiations 189
(c) Access to an International Court or Tribunal or Other Effective Dispute Resolution Mechanism 193
(d) Dispute Already Submitted to an International Court or Tribunal 196

Chapter 12: Final Remarks on the Concept of Countermeasures **213**

Part III: Countermeasures and Environmental Threats: Case Studies **219**

Chapter 13: Introduction **221**

Chapter 14: Case Studies: Fisheries **225**

(a) Introduction 225
(b) The Applicable Law on High Seas Fisheries 226
(i) *UNCLOS* 226
(ii) The *Fish Stocks Agreement* 227
(c) Norway/Iceland Loophole Dispute: The *Már Case* 229
(i) Summary 229
(ii) Facts and Analysis 230
(iii) Additional Analysis Related to the Elements of Countermeasures 238
(d) Canada/EC Halibut Dispute: *The Estai Case* 240
(i) Summary 240
(ii) Facts and Analysis 241
(iii) Additional Analysis Related to the Elements of Countermeasures 246

Chapter 15: Case Studies: Trade-Related Countermeasures **263**

(a) Introduction 263
(b) The World Trade Organization and Dispute Settlements 265
(i) General Overview 265
(ii) Jurisdiction 271
(iii) Applicable Law 274

(iv) Priority and Proportionality 281
(v) A Fusion of Article XX and the Countermeasures Doctrine? 284
(c) *The Tuna Dolphin Case of 1991* (*Tuna I*) 286
(i) Summary 286
(ii) Facts and Analysis 287
(iii) Concluding Remarks 292
(d) *The Tuna Dolphin Case of 1994* (*Tuna II*) 292
(i) Summary 292
(ii) Facts and Analysis 293
(iii) Concluding Remarks 297
(e) The *Shrimp/Turtle Case of 1998 and 2001* 297
(i) Summary 297
(ii) Facts and Analysis: *Shrimp/Turtle I* 298
(iii) Facts and Analysis: *Shrimp/Turtle II* 305
(iv) Additional Analysis Relating to the Elements of Countermeasures 310
(f) Highly Migratory Fish Stocks: Chile/EC Swordfish Dispute 314
(i) Summary 314
(ii) Facts and Analysis 314
(iii) Concluding Remarks 319

Chapter 16: Conclusions on Case Studies **337**

General Conclusions **339**

Bibliography **345**
Treaties and International and Domestic Documents (Chronological Order) 345
(a) Multilateral Instruments 345
(b) Other Treaties 352
(c) International Courts or Arbitration 353

(i) Permanent Court of International Justice, 1920–1946 353
(ii) International Court of Justice, 1946– 353
(iii) International Tribunal for the Law of the Sea, 1997– 355
(iv) GATT Panel Decisions, WTO Panel, and Appellate Body Decisions 356
(v) European Court of Justice 357
(vi) International Arbitration (Various Sources) 358
(d) Other International Decisions or Documents 359
(i) International Law Commission Documents 359
(ii) WTO Documents 360
(iii) Other Documents From International Organizations 361
(e) Domestic Decisions and Documents 363
(i) Domestic Judicial Decisions (U.S. Courts) 363
(ii) Domestic Legislation 363
Books, Journals, Reports, and News (Alphabetical Order) 364
(a) Newspapers and News Services 364
(b) Books and Journals 369

Index **393**

ACKNOWLEDGMENTS

This book could not have been written without the inspiration and support from Ambassador Ambler H. Moss, Professor Bernard H. Oxman, Dr. Joaquin Roy, and Dr. Daniel Suman. I would like to express my sincere gratitude to them. I would also like to thank the staff of the Department of International Studies and the School of Law for their support during the time of my studies at the University of Miami—in particular, Steve Ralph and Dr. Andy Gomez for their encouragement, as well as navigation around red tape and administrative challenges.

To my fellow students, I am grateful for the intellectual debates, the different perspectives, and the good company. My family, in particular my wife, I thank for the patience and support that kept me going.

Lastly, I would like to thank Ambassadors Charles and Sue Cobb whose initial funding made this journey possible.

ABBREVIATIONS

CAB	Civil Aeronautics Board
CCMS	NATO Committee for Challenges of Modern Society
CITES	Convention on International Trade in Endangered Species
DSB	Dispute Settlement Body (WTO)
DSU	Dispute Settlement Understanding (WTO)
EC	European Community
ECJ	European Court of Justice
ECR	European Court Reports
EFTA	European Free Trade Association
EEA	European Economic Area
EEZ	Exclusive Economic Zone
EFZ	Exclusive Fishery Zone
ESA	EFTA Surveillance Authority
EU	European Union
FAO	United Nations Food and Agriculture Organization
FCCC	Framework Convention of Climate Change

GATT	General Agreement on Tariffs and Trade
ICCAT	International Commission for the Conservation of Atlantic Tunas
ICJ	International Court of Justice
ILC	International Law Commission
ILM	International Legal Materials
ILR	International Law Reports
IMCO	Inter-Governmental Maritime Consultative Organization
IMF	International Monetary Fund
IMO	International Maritime Organization
ITLOS	International Tribunal for the Law of the Sea
LNTS	League of Nations Treaty Series
MDB	Multinational Development Bank
MEA	Multilateral Environmental Agreement
MMPA	Marine Mammal Protection Act
NAFO	Northwest Atlantic Fisheries Organization
NEAFC	Northeast Atlantic Fisheries Commission
NATO	North Atlantic Treaty Organization
OAS	Organization of American States
OECD	Organisation for Economic Co-operation and Development
OJ	Official Journal of the European Communities
OSCE	Organization for Security and Co-operation in Europe
OPSAR	Convention for the Protection of the Marine Environment of the Northeast Atlantic
PCIJ	Permanent Court of International Justice
Stat.	United States Statues at Large
TIAS	United States Treaties and other International Acts Series
UN	United Nations
UNCED	United Nations Conference on Environment and Development
UNCLOS	United Nations Convention on the Law of the Sea
UNDP	United Nations Development Programme

UNECE	United Nations Economic Commission for Europe
UNEP	United Nations Environmental Programme
UNRIAA	United Nations Reports of International Arbitral Awards
UNTS	United Nations Treaty Series
UTA	Union de Transports Aériens
WTO	World Trade Organization

Countermeasures, the International Legal System, and Environmental Violations

Introduction and Main Findings

(A) Opening Remarks: When Two Wrongs Make a Right

My parents and, later, my wife diligently tried to teach me that two wrongs do not make a right. Although I generally agree with the notion, it might not be true in all instances. One of such instances is the *countermeasures doctrine*. It permits a state that is a victim of an international wrong to commit another international wrong in order to remedy the situation. Thus, two wrongs can make a right.

In an anarchical society of independent states, unilateral measures play an important role. Fortunately, this does not mean that most states act unilaterally most of the time. On the contrary, cooperation is the keyword in most areas of international relations and international law. However, unlike most developed domestic legal systems, the international legal system is not equipped with a comprehensive judicial system or effective enforcement system. Therefore, when violations occur, they are often resolved by communication between states, diplomatic maneuvers, or other amicable means. This also applies to environmental issues; it is probably true that most environmental concerns are resolved in a concerted and cooperative manner between states and interested parties.

However, this is not always the case. States have and will continue to take unilateral measures to enforce environmental policies they believe are beneficial for the condition of the environment or for other political or economic reasons. Many of these unilateral measures are legal per se either because they do not affect rights owed to other states, or because they are directly authorized by the relevant regime as derogation from its general obligations or as part of its enforcement mechanism. The countermeasures doctrine addresses the legality of one of many categories of unilateral measures, namely, those that are not directly justified by the relevant regime but seek their justification in the customary international law of countermeasures.

(B) A Prelude to the Law of Countermeasures

Countermeasures can be defined as any unilateral measures taken by states as a response to hostile or unfriendly acts of another state regardless of whether the unilateral measures taken are legal per se or require a special justification. Such approach, which might be suitable for consideration of the political justification of the measures or for analysis under theories of international relations, is too broad to be of any use for legal analysis. In other words, there is no need to analyze the legality of measures that are already legal. As this book's main topic is the legal analysis of the countermeasures doctrine, it is logical to use the concept in a narrow meaning, covering only unilateral measures that are illegal per se but are justified as a response to an internationally wrongful act of another state. This approach is also in line with international jurisprudence, mainstream scholarly writing, and the work of the International Law Commission (ILC) on state responsibility.

The following definition of countermeasures is, therefore, suggested:

> Countermeasures are unilateral acts of states taken by an injured state against an offending state in order to induce the latter to cease a violation of an international legal obligation it owes to the injured state and/or pay reparation. Countermeasures, which are illegal per se, are legally justified as a response to a prior breach by the offending state. Countermeasures have to be proportionate to the harm done and what is required to further their legitimate purpose. Countermeasures have to be preceded by a communication from the injured state to the offending state, offering negotiation and requesting the latter to cease the violation.

This definition needs an explanation. First, countermeasures can only be taken in response to a violation of an international obligation,[1] which the offending state owes to the injured state. This means, for example, that anticipatory countermeasures are not permitted; the violation has to have occurred prior to the countermeasures. This also means that countermeasures cannot be taken to enforce an environmental policy, no matter how well the policy is based in international law, unless taken in response to a violation of an international obligation. Violation of domestic laws of the injured state does not justify countermeasures, even if the violation can be attributed to a state and is committed within the territory of the injured state. If the act cannot be argued as a violation of international obligations, countermeasures cannot be justified. See further discussion in part II, chapter 8.

Second, a number of unilateral acts fall outside the concept of countermeasures. Among them are acts taken in response to unfriendly, or even illegal, acts of states but do not require a legal justification, as they are legal per se. For example, a decision taken by one state to reduce cultural cooperation with another state because of poor compliance with environmental standards by the latter falls outside the concept of countermeasures. Another example is a decision of one state to not recognize judgments of another state because the latter no longer adheres to that practice. Thus, it is only when the unilateral measure is illegal per se that states have a real reason to invoke the countermeasures doctrine. This issue will be further discussed in part I, chapter 3.

Third, this definition suggests that the players in the game of countermeasures can only be states. It is quite possible to imagine that an international organization could resort to countermeasures against another organization or a state; arguably, such acts could become an increased possibility with the rising level of rights and obligations that international organizations are given. Such unilateral measures raise a number of issues that might distract the analysis from its core issues. Therefore, unilateral measures of international organizations are kept out of the discussion in this book. Also, the classical concept of reprisals, which is, in a way, the mother of the countermeasures doctrine,[2] permitted private individuals who were duly authorized by the injured state to resort to countermeasures against other states on the injured state's behalf. However, these types of reprisals are no longer a part of contemporary law on countermeasures. See further discussion on this issue in part II, chapter 8.

Fourth, countermeasures have to comply with the principle of proportionality. Although legal authors and international jurisprudence do not give precise guidelines on this issue, the principle generally requires countermeasures to be proportionate to the following: the harm caused by the internationally wrongful act, the legal principles that the wrongful act infringes, and the amount of effort needed to acquire the legitimate objectives of the countermeasures, that is, to induce the offending state to comply with its international obligation and/or pay reparation. The principle of proportionality of countermeasures will be discussed further in part II, chapter 10.

According to this preliminary discussion, countermeasures are measures that would be in violation of an international obligation without special legal justification. An example of countermeasures in the environmental field is if an injured state freezes assets belonging to an offending state because of environmental harm the latter caused the former by a violation of its international environmental obligations. Another example is trade restrictions that violate a bilateral trade agreement or World

Trade Organization (WTO) obligations taken in response to similar violations against environmental rights.

The right of countermeasures is partly based on the assumption that a sovereign state has an inherent right to self-preservation to prevent violations of international obligations that deprive it of peaceful enjoyment of its legal rights. It is partly based on the fact that there is no supranational institution with broad powers to enforce international law; the enforcement is still largely in the hands of the sovereign states. The ILC suggested that countermeasures be seen as "a form of self-help, which responds to the position of the injured State in an international system in which the impartial settlement of disputes through due process of law is not yet guaranteed."[3] Even when such a dispute settlement mechanism is present, states often choose not to refer their disputes to a third party; arguably, all states have the propensities "to refuse to accept any higher authority."[4] Because the use of countermeasures infringes legal rights belonging to other sovereign states, it might be said that the countermeasures doctrine represents the fault lines of the Westphalian state system, a collision between the international legal order and the exercise of sovereign state powers. Because of the constraints of the Westphalian state system, one might say that attempts by a state to interfere with actions of another are attempts to create cracks in the system. Such assertion is, however, mistaken; unilateral acts of states, including countermeasures, are an inherent part of the system. They are woven into the fabric of relations between the sovereign states, an indispensable part of the dynamic of the international system, and an important source of changes within it.

(c) Use of Countermeasures in Defense of Environmental Interests of States

In the past 3 decades or so, environmental interests have received increased attention by states. Perhaps this is because of advances in science, increased awareness about relations between the environment and public health, the emergence of acceptable alternatives to environmentally harmful practices, or general economic development, which increases pollution and pressure on natural resources and provides wealth to counter such pollution and pressures. States have attempted to improve the environmental situation of the planet through concerted efforts, bilaterally or through regional or international organizations. The main goal of such efforts has been to set policies, decide on cooperation, share information, transfer technology, and so forth. Occasionally, such efforts result in setting legally binding standards or obligations. Unfortunately, such obligations are seldom accompanied by an effective adjudication or enforcement mechanism. With the growing number of international legally binding obligations in the field of the environment, increased stress on limited natural resources, and growing general concerns about environmental issues, the need for effective remedies to address violations of international environmental obligations become ever more crucial. It is against this background, in particular the absence of an effective adjudication and enforcement mechanism, that this book addresses the use of countermeasures as a remedy against such violations.

Certainly, unilateral measures, such as countermeasures, are not an equally attractive choice for all states regardless of military or economic capabilities. Undoubtedly, unilateral measures favor the strong against the weak. The law of countermeasures is, however, not designed to benefit only powerful states. Its checks and balances somewhat negate the difference between capabilities.

(D) ORGANIZATION OF THIS BOOK AND ITS MAIN FINDINGS

In addition to this introduction, this book is divided into three parts, each containing several chapters. The introduction not only has the role of introducing but also of concluding, as it reproduces the main conclusions from each part. Even though the introduction is not intended to be a short version of the book, it serves as a summary of its main findings, as well as a roadmap for those who are interested in reading further than these introductory pages.

Part I addresses the foundations of unilateral measures: the concept of sovereignty, the limitation of international law, and the tensions between these two forces when they shape the landscape of international relations. The part also puts countermeasures in its legal context, that is, the context of unilateral acts of states. It examines the flora of unilateral measures and where countermeasures belong in that chaotic structure.

Some authors suggested that the concept of sovereignty is a mistaken one and that its role in the international system is over bloated.[5] Nevertheless, its underlying principles are arguably a shaping force in international relations—a resilient restraint on the development of international law. The scholarly debate suggests that state sovereignty is the basis for a state's right to take unilateral measures, whereas international law limits this right. However, under the countermeasures doctrine, a state can go beyond the limits of sovereignty and exercise rights they otherwise would not have.

In part I, the countermeasures doctrine begins to form. This part suggests that the doctrine only includes measures that require a special justification to be legal. Other unilateral measures might require a political justification, but the determination whether the measures taken are, in fact, politically justifiable is outside the scope of this book. Among such measures are sanctions authorized by the United Nations Security Council. They cannot be seen as countermeasures, even if they are taken in response to violations of international obligations; their immediate justification is sought in the *UN Charter* and the authority of the Council to adopt resolutions binding upon all United Nation (UN) member states.

In part II, the elements of the countermeasures doctrine are analyzed. It is divided into four main chapters. The first chapter (chapter 8) examines certain considerations related to the basis for the legality of countermeasures, such as the presence of a prior breach. The second chapter discusses certain procedural requirements states have to fulfill before countermeasures are taken. Then the issues of proportionality and prohibited countermeasures, that is, what acts cannot be justified as countermeasures, are addressed. The last substantive chapter of part II examines conditions under which some theories might preclude the legality of countermeasures.

There is no doubt that countermeasures can put in motion forces that are destructive for the international system. Therefore, countermeasures have to be exercised with caution and with full respect for their limitations and restrictions. Their justification is sought in the imperfection of the international system, that is, the lack of effective adjudication mechanism associated with equally effective enforcement mechanism. In such a system of international law, "the risk of countermeasures may actually be the only effective deterrent to the commission of internationally wrongful acts."[6]

Part II clarifies the countermeasures doctrine by addressing the individual elements of it. This part suggests that the doctrine's primary element is the presence of a prior violation of an international obligation owed to the state taking the countermeasures, attributable to another state or states. Although states other than the one directly injured by the violations can take countermeasures, their authority to take such measures is somewhat in proportion to the injury and much more limited than the right of the directly injured state to resort to such measures.

This part also suggests that prior to taking countermeasures, the injured state has to comply with certain procedural requirements, such as requesting the offending state to comply with its obligations and/or pay reparation, notifying the responsible state of the prospective countermeasures, and offer negotiation.

Part II suggests that even if the right to resort to countermeasures has been established, the means and methods are not unlimited. First, the injured state is precluded from violating certain obligations. Among them are the ban against the use of force under the *UN Charter*, fundamental human rights, prohibition of reprisals against protected persons under humanitarian law, and peremptory norms of international law. In addition to an absolute ban against certain methods, the principle of proportionality also restricts the means chosen by the state. This means that the measures taken should be proportionate to the injury suffered and the rights in question, as well as what is necessary to obtain the legitimate objectives of the measures. It must be noted that the determination of proportionality is not a precise science. Therefore, a certain approximation is sufficient in order to find countermeasures to be proportionate.

Finally, various scholars and governments have suggested that the presence of alternative methods of dispute resolutions can eliminate, reduce, or delay the right to resort to countermeasures. This book questions such approaches. It opines that an ongoing good faith negotiation and access to a binding dispute settlement mechanism do not prevent an injured state from taking countermeasures. However, in the event and to the extent that the dispute settlement mechanism provides an effective remedy for the injured state, capable of providing comparable results and guarantees as countermeasures, the injured state's right to take countermeasures might be restricted.

There is no doubt that the elements of countermeasures are and will be a matter of significant debate. Part II concludes by suggesting that the international system needs a regime of countermeasures because its ability to resolve international disputes and enforce such settlements is underdeveloped.

Part III examines six cases where states resorted to unilateral measures in order to protect environmental interests. The cases are divided into two sets. The first set contains two cases regarding unilateral measures taken by coastal states in response to alleged violations of international obligations related to the exploitation of straddling fish stocks. In all of the cases in the second set, the question of the legality of the measures taken was submitted to a WTO panel.

These cases reveal a number of problems and opportunities for the application of the countermeasures doctrine. The one problem that stands out is endemic in the environmental regime—the lack of clear substantive legal obligation to conserve and protect the environment. It is also notable that the cases, which seem compatible to the countermeasures doctrine, involve the law of the sea, which is probably the most comprehensive regime related to the environment.

Five of the six cases are argued in a legal framework that seems, on the surface, not particularly susceptible to the countermeasures doctrine, that is, the WTO framework and the *EEA* framework. However, on a more positive note for the countermeasures doctrine, this book argues that when analyzing the applicability of and compliance with WTO rules, WTO panels have to take into consideration whether a violation of obligations under WTO-covered agreements can be justified with reference to the countermeasures doctrine.

(E) FINAL REMARKS

The most favorable legal environment for the countermeasures doctrine is where the substantive international obligation is clear, but effective remedies are scarce. The international legal system, however, contains a much broader spectrum of scenarios. On one side is the situation when the substantive obligation is lacking, and countermeasures are, therefore, not the appropriate remedy because the primary element of countermeasures, that is, the presence of prior violation of an international obligation, is absent. As some of the case studies in part III show, this is often the case within the environmental regime. On the other side is when the substantive rule is clear and the regime provides an effective remedy. Then, unilateral acts justified as countermeasures might not be legally acceptable. Such is the situation within the European Union (EU) with regard to violations of EU law[7] and, to a certain extent, the WTO.[8] Countermeasures exist in the space in between these two edges, where the international community has agreed on, positively or passively, certain primary obligations without providing the necessary effective remedies.

The legal requirements for countermeasures need to be approached with due respect; they are not to be taken lightly or referred to simply as nonbinding guidelines. One must remember that frustration, emotion, domestic politics, sovereign identity, and the need to show resolve are all a recipe for unlawful countermeasures and are also, often, the underlying cause for such measures. As such conditions often precede the taking of countermeasure, the overall situation might not represent the injured state's finest hour. Consequently, the environment for a solid and politically detached legal analysis regarding the flora of permissible measures might not be the most favorable. However, the decision to take countermeasures cannot be a spontaneous one; it has to be meticulously analyzed, and proper steps have to be taken before such measures are used. Only then can the countermeasures doctrine form the basis for a legal and legitimate unilateral enforcement of international law.

ENDNOTES

1. This book uses the term "international obligation" in the same meaning as "international legal obligation," thus excluding purely political or moral obligations.
2. The traditional concept of reprisals is as good as identical to the concept of countermeasures as it is used by the International Law Commission in its work on state responsibility. See, for example, *Report of the International Law Commission of the Work of Its Forty Fourth Session* (4 May–24 July 1992), UN doc. A/47/10, International Law Commission Yearbook 1992, vol. II (part 2), (hereafter referred to as *ILC 1992 Report*), pp. 21–22, paras. 139–140 and *Third Report on State Responsibility by Mr. Gaetano Arangio-Ruiz, Special Rapporteur*, Yearbook of the International Law Commission 1991, vol. II (part 1), UN doc. A/CN.4/440 and add. 1 (hereafter referred to as *Third Report 1991 (Arangio-Ruiz)*), p. 12, para. 27.
3. *Report of the International Law Commission on the Work of Its Fifty Third Session* (23 April–1 June 2001 and 2 July–10 August 2001), UN doc. A/56/10, Yearbook of the International Law Commission 2001, vol. II (part 2), (hereafter referred to as *ILC 2001 Report*), p. 136, para. 2 of the commentary to article 52.
4. *Third Report 1991 (Arangio-Ruiz)*, para. 3, p. 7.
5. See, for example, Louis Henkin, *International Law: Politics and Values*, Martinus Nijhoff Publishers, Dordrecht, Boston, London, 1995, pp. 8–10. See also the discussion in part I, chap. 2.
6. *State Responsibility: Comments and Observations Received from Governments*, International Law Commission, Fiftieth session, Geneva, 20 May–12 June 1998, New York, 27 July–14 August 1998, UN doc. no. A/CN.4/488, 25 March 1998, p. 114.
7. See, for example, endnote 3 of chap. 3.
8. Countermeasures of WTO-member states against violations of a WTO obligation have to be authorized by the WTO Dispute Settlement Body. See discussion in part III, chap. 15 (b).

Part I

Countermeasures, Sovereignty, and the International Legal System

Law is politics...made for political ends to promote political values.

—Louis Henkin, *International Law, Politics and Values* (1995)[1]

Chapter 1

Introduction and Organization

E. H. Carr wrote that international law "cannot be understood independently of the political foundation on which it rests and the political interests which it serves."[2] Part I, in this spirit, focuses on the foundations on which the international legal system is built—namely, sovereignty and the limitations of international law.

In this part, the concept of sovereignty, as writers throughout the last few centuries have viewed it, is addressed. Sovereignty and international law are two intertwined concepts that not only limit each other but also have to survive in coexistence. The idea of unilateral measures is about the exercise of sovereign rights of states. However, such measures are limited and governed by international law. A study of the nature of countermeasures, as one of many forms of unilateral measures, is inherently linked to the notion of sovereignty and balance between the appropriate exercise of sovereign rights and the interests of the international system that limits that right. Therefore, the topic of chapter 2 is correctly placed here at the beginning of this book.

There is no doubt that the states' duty to settle disputes between them by amicable means is a part of the corpus of international law. The tenor of the *Charter of the United Nations* (*UN Charter*) confirms this, as well as numerous bilateral and multilateral treaties on amity and cooperation. Article 2(3) of the *UN Charter* reads, "All Members shall settle their international disputes by peaceful means in such a manner that international peace and security, and justice, are not endangered."[3]

The *UN Charter* also outlaws the use of force, except for cases of self-defense; operations warranted by the Security Council; and a member state's right to maintain or establish order within its territory.

The international legal system does not contain a complete web of remedies or enforcement mechanism when the law is broken. Elisabeth Zoller wrote in 1984 that "[i]n the international legal order, ...unilateral remedies are the norm, and each state has to rely first on its own forces."[4] As the *S.S. Lotus Case* suggested,[5] states have wide latitude to exercise their sovereignty, where such exercise is not limited by international law. Therefore, the first point of examination when states take unilateral measures is whether the measures violate international law. If the unilateral measures do not violate a legal obligation of the state taking the measures, then it needs no legal justification; however, it might require a political one. Such unilateral acts are not countermeasures as this book views the concept.

L. Oppenheim, as many authors before and after him, divided unilateral acts into a few categories. Oppenheim's most important methods of unilateral acts were retorsion, reprisal, pacific blockade, and intervention.[6] These distinctions built on the different methods of the unilateral acts. Others divided unilateral acts differently. For example, Zoller's writings provided us with a distinction between retorsion, reprisal, and reciprocity.[7]

As for Oppenheim's distinction between different types of unilateral acts, Zoller's distinction is relevant for limiting the scope of the analysis in this book, which, as indicated earlier, only focuses on unilateral acts that require a special justification for their legality and not the ones that only require a political justification. Samuel Freiherr von Pufendorf argued in 1672 that self-defense is included in the right to self-preservation. There were, however, two types of self-defense: one that hurts the offender and one that did not hurt the offender. Pufendorf contended that the latter was blameless and the former required a certain justification.[8] This line of thought catches the distinction between what is referred to in this study as countermeasures and other kinds of unilateral measures. Countermeasures need a special justification to be legal measures.

Various rules prescribe the options that states have, collectively or unilaterally, to protect its interests. Under the *United Nations Conventions on the Law of the Sea of 1982* (*UNCLOS*),[9] coastal states can arrest foreign fishing vessels that are fishing illegally within the exclusive economic zone. Under the General Agreement on Tariffs and Trade (GATT),[10] states can restrict trade for the purpose of environmental protection and for security reasons.[11] These actions are not necessarily countermeasures under the definition used within this book. They are legal actions per se, integrated in the structure of the relevant regime. The right to take some of these measures is invoked by illegal acts of states or their subjects, and in such cases, they resemble countermeasures. Their illegality is, however, often based on domestic legislation only, not international law. Countermeasures, as this concept is used in this book, go one step further. Their life is outside the regime in what might be called a gray area of self-help. Such measures would not have to be justified under Article XX of GATT 1994 or as enforcement of rights under *UNCLOS*; they would seek their justification in the law of countermeasures.

The reasons for resorting to countermeasures can certainly be various. The need to make a point and the need to press for discontinuance on the injuring act, reparation, and punitive reasons are just a few of the purposes for unilateral actions against the offending state. Oppenheim used the phrase "compulsive means of settlement of state differences" for unilateral acts of states.[12] This terminology derives from the purpose he ascribed to unilateral acts: "compelling another state to declare that it is ready to settle the difference in the manner desired."[13]

The remainder of this part will discuss the legal framework of unilateral acts of which countermeasures are a part. Chapter 3 discusses a number of acts of states, unilateral or not, that fall outside of the scope of this book. This book views countermeasures as one of many unilateral acts of states. Thus, not all unilateral acts are countermeasures, and not all unilateral measures require a special legal justification; some are perfectly legal per se, and some live and breathe in a legal vacuum where political consideration is the sole judge of the appropriateness of such measures. Chapter 4 analyzes the writing of many authoritative scholars, including many of the classical ones. Although the focus of this book is on how contemporary international law describes the concept of countermeasures, a review of the classical writers is necessary to acquire a deeper understanding of the fundamentals of unilateral measures. In chapter 5, this book reviews international cases that are relevant to the discussion of countermeasures.

Endnotes

1. Louis Henkin, *International Law: Politics and Values*, Martinus Nijhoff Publishers, Dordrecht, Boston, London, 1995, p. 4.
2. E. H. Carr, *The Twenty Years' Crisis, 1919–1939: An Introduction to the Study of International Relations*, Macmillan and Co., London, 1939, p. 179.
3. *Charter of the United Nations*, concluded at San Francisco 26 June 1946, entered into force 24 October 1945 (hereafter referred to as the *UN Charter*), 59 Stat. 1031, T.S. 993, 3 Bevans 1153, article 2(3).
4. Elisabeth Zoller, *Peacetime Unilateral Remedies: An Analysis of Countermeasures*, Traditional Publishers, New York, 1984, p. 4.
5. *The Case of the S.S. Lotus* (France v. Turkey), Permanent Court of International Justice, judgment of 7 September 1927, P.C.I.J. Ser. A, No. 10; see in particular at 18–19.
6. L. Oppenheim, *International Law*, vol. II, 7th ed., edited by H. Lauterpacht, Longmans, Green, and Co., London, New York, Toronto, p. 132.
7. See Elisabeth Zoller, *Peacetime Unilateral Remedies*, part I, chap.1 in her book.
8. Samuel Freiherr von Pufendorf, *Of the Law of Nature and Nations*, translated from Latin, printed by L. Lichfield, Oxford, 1703, book II, chap. V, § I, p. 140.
9. *United Nations Convention on the Law of the Sea*, concluded at Montego Bay 10 December 1982, entered into force 16 November 1994, 1833 U.N.T.S. 3, reprinted in 21 I.L.M. 1261 (1982).
10. *General Agreement on Tariffs and Trade*, annex 1A to the *Marrakesh Agreement Establishing the World Trade Organization*, concluded at Marrakesh 15 April 1994, entered into force 1 January 1995, 1867 UNTS 3, reprinted in 33 ILM 15 (1994). The *General Agreement on Tariffs and Trade* was initially opened for signature on 30 October 1947, 55 UNTS 187 (hereafter referred to as GATT 1994 or GATT 1947 in a context prior to the establishment of the WTO).
11. GATT 1994, articles XX and XXI.
12. L. Oppenheim, *International Law*, vol. II, 7th ed., p. 132.
13. Ibid., p. 133.

Chapter 2

Sovereignty and the Incompleteness of International Law

> No doubt 'the nature' which we ascribe to a thing is never more than a projection of the mind…
>
> —Bertrand de Jouvenel, *Sovereignty: An Inquiry into the Political Good* (1955)[1]

(a) Introduction and Purpose

Any right of a state to act or to play a role in the international society is based on the assumption that the state is a sovereign entity. Sovereignty can be described as the state's power and capabilities to control its territory and exercise such control, as well as the right and ability to conduct relations with other states. It can be argued that with the creation of the Westphalian state system, the alleged right of a state to largely do whatever it pleases to protect its interests was partly surrendered to the international society, whose role is to protect or, at least, promote protection of these interests.[2]

With the development of sovereignty and the international system into something that might already be called a post-Westphalian system, the sphere of international law has been broadened and the sovereignty of the state has been reduced. The wider the sphere of international law is and the narrower and more restricted the exercise of state sovereignty is, the less space there is for unilateral measures. Europe, which in the 1600s was the birthplace of a new state system, is perhaps taking the lead role again with the European integration and the creation of a new system of states that might be called the Brussels state system. Such a system, arguably, eliminates—or at least substantially reduces—the right of one member state to take countermeasures against another member state to compel the latter to comply with an obligation under community law.[3] This results from both (a) the growingly extensive supranational system to which disputes between the member states can be submitted, and (b) the number of procedural and substantive rules guiding the resolution of such disputes.

The anarchical international system of states is lacking such supranational institutions except, perhaps, in the case of the Security Council. Unilateral measures are, therefore, an inherent part of the international system and even sometimes a substantial driving force for changes in the system.

Thus, before countermeasures can be discussed, the concept of sovereignty must be briefly explained. For the same reason, the limits of international law and judicial process in international law should also be touched upon. The remainder of this chapter focuses on these topics. Certainly, the intention is not to thoroughly analyze these concepts; it is rather to shed a light on some basic foundations of the international legal system and to serve as a prelude to the following chapters.

(B) SOVEREIGNTY

It has frequently been said that the *S.S. Lotus Case*[4] set forth the rule that states have power to do anything, provided that their actions do not violate an established rule of international law. According to that interpretation, states' exercising of their sovereign rights in international territory is limited only by international law. Others question this assertion and believe that the territorial jurisdiction of states, the prerequisite for exercising any power in international law, is derived from the international legal order.[5] The argument is that territorial jurisdiction is a phenomenon that cannot be decided unilaterally by states; therefore, it has to be given to them by the system. Nevertheless, if it is accepted that the international system was created by independent entities at Westphalia in 1648, it follows that the power and authority of such entities was only limited by what they accepted. Arguably, this debate is too abstract to have any bearing in reality. However, whatever might have been true at the genesis of the international system, there are hints that the balance between the powers of the sovereign state and the international system has changed, favoring the latter.

It can be disputed when sovereignty as we know it today was first formulated. It can be argued that it was in the end of the sixteenth century, largely taken from Jean Bodin's 1576 writings, *Les Six Livres la République*.[6] Bodin emphasized that sovereignty is the perpetual power of the monarch in contrast to power given to someone for a certain period of time, such as the power of a governor.[7] Bodin did not believe that an authority chosen by the people to rule for a certain period of time, such as a lieutenant prince or archons,[8] was sovereign because of the time limits of the authority's power.[9] Furthermore, Bodin said that sovereignty was "not limited, either in power, or in function."[10] As such, the sovereign did not have to answer to the people, not even after stepping down from office.[11] Bodin, however, made two exceptions from the absolute power of the sovereign: the law of God and the law of nature. This gives modern readers a certain room for a dynamic interpretation of Bodin's concept of sovereignty. This is also important when trying to understand his ideas in the times of a theological-political environment.

Bodin's ideas of sovereignty did not monopolize the discussion of sovereignty in the sixteenth and seventeenth centuries. Among other opinion makers on this issue was Thomas Hobbes. In L. Oppenheim's view, Hobbes did not believe in the limitation that religion imposed upon the sovereign prince. He went further arguing that no power was above the sovereign and the sovereign could do whatever he pleased. Pufendorf was, however, a bit more modest; he said that constitutional restrains could limit the power of a sovereign. The sovereign was, however, still the supreme power within the state.[12]

Bodin's and Hobbes' ideas of sovereignty, that sovereigns have perpetual and absolute power over their citizens and subjects, have only a little resemblance to modern concepts of sovereignty. Bodin concentrated on what the modern theorist Stephen D. Krasner called "domestic sovereignty," that is, "formal organization of political authority within the state and the ability of public authorities to exercise effective control within the borders of their own polity."[13] Furthermore, Bodin did not really discuss the connection between sovereignty and intervention of another monarch. This was the subject of the peace agreement made at Westphalia in 1648 after the Thirty Year War. Sovereignty then became a political fact and, later, developed into a rule of law.[14]

The creation of international legal order has been attributed to the peace treaty signed at Westphalia in 1648.[15] John Westlake wrote that with the *Treaty of Westphalia* "[i]nternational law was born."[16] First, there was a general consensus that states had a duty not to take the law into their own hands. Second, "there was a general agreement as to where the rules that define those duties were to be looked for."[17] Third, an injured state now had expectation of support from the international community to acquire reparation.[18]

Marking the end of the Thirty Year War, the *Treaty of Westphalia* created a structure for a relationship between states with variable levels of independence. Creation of territorial sovereignty, the notion of nonintervention, and the concerns of the international system about violation of what later would be called international law were the cornerstones of the treaty. Accordingly, the discussion on sovereignty changed its focus from the role of the sovereign as the almighty ruler to the rights and responsibilities of the state as an entity with internal institutions and, more importantly, a unit within the international system.

Georg Friedrich von Martens[19] emphasized the supremacy of state power. He wrote in 1789, "For a state to be entirely free and sovereign, it must govern itself, and acknowledge no legislative superior but God."[20] For Martens, the supremacy of state power was, however, not an absolute value. Even if a state was under the protection of other states, it did not deprive that state of its sovereignty.[21] Martens accepted different types of sovereignty depending on whether it was a royal state or not.[22] He also discussed different levels of supremacy and what he called demi-sovereign states, such as the states of the German Empire.[23]

In Martens' writings, one can sense a support for certain distinctions of sovereignty depending on the size of the state. However, Martens believed that such distinctions were not based on the law, but rather on facts.[24] These ideas can be translated into the modern legal thinking of the difference between legal status and political status of a state in the international system. Another trace of the idea of different levels of sovereignty, also depending on the size of the state, can be found in an answer provided by an attorney in the United States War Department when he was asked to prepare a memo for President Wilson, explaining whether the U.S. invasion of Veracruz in 1914 was an act of war. The attorney, Felix Frankfurter, who later became a justice in the U.S. Supreme Court, said to the general who requested the memo that the answer, although not appropriate in a memo, was simple; "[i]t would be an act of war against a great nation; it isn't against a small nation."[25] As Martens suggested, this line of thinking represents political values that cannot be equated to legal values. It could, therefore, be assumed that political dimensions and levels of sovereignty can be different from legal ones.

Another early writer, Emmerich de Vattel, viewed sovereignty as the heart of the state. He argued that sovereignty is the "public authority, which commands in civil society, and orders and directs what each is to perform, to obtain the end of its institution."[26] Vattel's notion of sovereignty focuses on control over the state's territory and its subjects.

In the mid 1800s, Henry Wheaton defined sovereignty as "the supreme power by which any State is governed."[27] A sovereign state was, according to Wheaton, "any nation or people, whatever may be the form of its internal constitution, which governs itself independently of foreign powers."[28] The focus of his definition is on both domestic powers and the existence of the state in the international society. To describe this difference, Wheaton distinguished between internal and external sovereignty, where the latter one deals with relations to other political societies and is regulated by international law.[29] Just like Martens, Wheaton admitted that there are different degrees of sovereignty.[30]

Similar to the opinions of Pufendorf,[31] Wheaton indicated that he saw the right to self-defense as a part of the absolute right to self-preservation. However, this absolute right might in his mind not have been so absolute because Wheaton, in what might have been an internal contradiction in his work, also realized the relativity of the state's right. He argued that a state can exercise its sovereignty as long as it does not interfere with another state's exercise of its own.[32] In the late 1800s, Theodore D. Woolsey wrote that sovereignty related to the uncontrolled exclusive exercise power of the state; that is, both of the power of entering into relations with other states, and of the power of governing its own subjects. This power is supreme within a certain territory, and supreme over its own subjects wherever no other sovereignty has jurisdiction.[33] T. J. Lawrence wrote on a similar note that sovereignty has two faces, the internal and the external—it is the power to deal with internal affairs, as well as the power to deal with foreign affairs.[34]

John Westlake wrote that nations are

> regarded as persons living in a state of nature, nations are naturally equal as men are naturally equal; a small nation is as much a nation as a large one, just as a dwarf is as much a man as a giant; it is therefore natural or necessary that all nations have the same rights and the same obligations, as much and no more being allowed to one nation as to another.[35]

Westlake's arguments are for the equal legal status of states; he did not address the political unequal distribution of capabilities between states or how it restrains the otherwise equal legal rights of states.

Westlake's metaphor of persons as states is more than just a figure of speech. He saw men as the ultimate members of the international society and states as its immediate members. Therefore, he dived under the surface of the state as an entity and argued that the state is only the collective form of a group of people. He wrote, "[t]he duties and rights of states are only the duties and rights of men who compose them."[36] Despite these liberal ideas about the nature of the state and its place in the international system, Westlake was more rigid when it came to the notion of sovereignty. As many of his predecessors, he did not see sovereignty in degrees. He argued that you either have it or not.

> A group of men is fully sovereign when it has no constitutional relations making it in any degree dependent on any other group: if it has such relations, so much of sovereignty as they leave it is a kind or degree of semi-sovereignty, though the constitution may not call it by that name.[37]

The complete independence from another group was an important element of sovereignty; dependency on another group affecting the exercise of foreign relations of a state could be fatal for the latter's entitlement to be called sovereign.[38] Similarly, Hans Morgenthau supported the notion that sovereignty has no degree. He thought of sovereignty as applying to states that are "totally independent of each other" and "recognizing no secular authority above themselves."[39]

Westlake did not see sovereignty of one state as an absolute barrier for another state to take measures for its self-preservation. He argued that while a state's actions within its own territory are justified by its sovereign right to govern the territory, "[w]hen a state employs force in the territory of another state, …the state so acting…must find its justification in some other principle."[40] Westlake called this the principle of self-preservation; it exists just as the right of a natural person to protect oneself.[41]

International relations and international law have come a long way from theories of absolute sovereignty, where the limitation to a state's sovereignty could only be derived from its free will.[42] Already in the interwar years, theories of relative sovereignty gained popularity. They had the idea in common that sovereignty was not unlimited and absolute; it was restrained not only by domestic constitutional concerns like Pufendorf would have argued, but also, as Wheaton had already argued in the 1800s, by other states' sovereignty. The actions taken on the basis of sovereignty had to be compatible to the sovereignty of other states.[43] Some authors went even so far to say that the individual, instead of the state, was the sole subject of international law and that sovereignty was a fiction.[44] Moreover, liberal theories of international relations, globalization, and modernization have attempted to explain the changes in the way states behave in the international society and what the international society tolerates as acceptable behavior of states. In short, leaders of states are, in general, not considered to get their power from God; accordingly, their authority and acts can be questioned at the domestic and the international level.

Many modern writers have criticized the concept of sovereignty and the use of it. One of those writers is Louis Henkin, who wrote in 1995 that the

> pervasiveness of the concept is unfortunate, rooted in mistake, unfortunate mistake. Sovereignty is a bad word, not only because it has served terrible national mythologies; in international relations, and even in international law, it is often a catchword, a substitute for thinking and precision.[45]

Henkin did not restrain himself in his attacks on the concept of sovereignty. He pointed out its original use as an internal concept and not a concept dealing with relations between states. He bluntly condemned states' attempts to use the concept as a shield against international scrutiny and monitoring of international law, especially when the sources of such a law are treaties that the state in question has voluntarily signed.[46] Finally, Henkin suggested that the concept should, at least for legal purposes, be relegated "to the shelf of history as a relic from an earlier era."[47]

Krasner was subtler in his writings about the concept of sovereignty.[48] He divided the concept into four categories, each describing the relevant part of the authority or control that a sovereign state is supposed to have. In addition to the concept of domestic sovereignty (the formal organization of political authority within the state and the ability of public authorities to exercise effective control within the borders of their own polity[49]), Krasner discussed what he called Westphalian sovereignty and international legal sovereignty, as well as interdependence sovereignty. In Krasner's writings, Westphalian sovereignty referred to the "exclusion of external actors from authority structures within a given territory."[50] This is exactly what Henkin criticized as having no place in international relations. International law deals with the parts of sovereignty that states, whether individually or collectively, intentionally or unconsciously, and freely or forced, agree to surrender to the international community. States do not have sovereignty over rights and obligations they have surrendered to the international society. Henkin wrote, "[w]hat they retain is not 'sovereignty' but the remainder of what they ceded to the needs of governance."[51] With this line of thought, one might divide control or authority between the international society and the states without ever referring to a normative phrase, such as "sovereignty."

Krasner's third category of sovereignty, international legal sovereignty, refers to the "practices associated with mutual recognition, usually between territorial entities that have formal juridical independence."[52] Henkin did not see these practices as relevant. He wrote, "[r]ecognition is still in the language of diplomats but it does not belong in the language of law."[53] These different opinions can be traced to the difference between the legal notion of sovereignty and the political one. Henkin downplayed the role of state recognition in the legal arena, whereas Krasner contended it had a role in the political arena.

The fourth category in Krasner's writings is interdependence sovereignty. Interdependence sovereignty focuses on the control of borders and what flows in and out of them, including capital, goods, people, and pollutants.[54] The word "control" must be emphasized here and distinguished from authority. A state might have the authority to enact legislation aimed at controlling cross-border flow but be unable to effectively implement the legislation, that is, to actually control the flow.

Krasner's conclusions on sovereignty are mainly that the international system has always been flexible about the concept of sovereignty and that the system is susceptible for new rules.

> The international system is not like a game of chess. ...Entities that have lacked one or more of the attributes conventionally associated with sovereignty...have operated perfectly well and have sometimes hardly been noticed, moving bishop in a straight line, as it were, without any of the other players protesting.[55]

From a legal standpoint, sovereignty might be best viewed as the state's control and authority that has not been surrendered to the international community. As such, there is no need to view disputes over interventions or scrutiny as a question of sovereignty, rather a question of the scope of the international right or obligation. If a state has agreed to freeze the levels of carbon dioxide release, it has no sovereign right to exceed them. A state that has lost certain rights through the emerging of a rule of customary international law has no sovereign rights to violate that rule. This approach would, however, only tell half of the story. Although states have agreed to be bound by a primary obligation, for example, the obligation to freeze levels of carbon dioxide release, they might not have agreed to any compulsory mechanism to adjudicate or enforce the rule if the obligation is violated. This is where countermeasures might come into play. The all too frequent absence of effective enforcement mechanism calls for a role of unilateral measures.

In the contemporary international state system, a question about sovereignty arises when states are members of international organizations or international treaties, such as environmental treaties. Are they giving up a part of their sovereignty, are they sharing it with other states, or are they simply exercising it? The answer is probably all of the above. By looking at the EU, the answer is not too clear. It is true that states have transferred competencies to the EU, including some that traditionally fall within the sovereignty of states;[56] however, the act of joining the EU was taken by exercising sovereign powers. Some might say that economic restrains of the European integration that was already under way left the states with no effective power as sovereigns to decide whether to join or stay outside of the EU. That is, however, not all true; although staying outside might have been an economically less attractive choice, some states, such as Norway and Switzerland, have to date decided to stay outside the community.[57]

It can be argued that a state that has signed a treaty on reducing the carbon dioxide pollution from their territory has given up a part of its sovereign rights to regulate the amount of such pollution in the environment, inasmuch such regulation violates its obligation under the treaty. This may, however, not be that easy. Depending on the constitution of the state in question, the treaty might not have direct domestic effect (i.e., is not treated as the law of the land) or may not be self-executing (i.e., domestic legislation is required to render the treaty effective in the domestic legal system). At first sight, the state might, therefore, have retained its domestic sovereignty to adopt and implement rules and regulations binding upon persons under its jurisdiction. With the traditionally weak enforcement mechanism and a lack of judicial organs to handle international disputes, this might be true. However, if the violation results in an injury to another state, then the injured state, after fulfilling the necessary requirements, could act unilaterally to compel the violating state to comply with the treaty in question based on the law of countermeasures. Therefore, despite the domestic sovereignty granted to its leaders by its constitution, and despite the weak enforcement system and the lack of compulsory adjudication, the offending state's alleged domestic sovereignty might not be that easy to exercise.

The question of what happens to sovereignty when a state joins an international regime has, however, to be considered in the light of the development of the regime. A convention or a regime into which a state enters voluntarily might evolve into something else, such as a more intrusive institution than the state had in mind in the beginning. A politically weak state might, therefore, be coerced into continuing as a member of the regime without a real chance of bargaining or negotiating the changing conditions to which it has to comply. In such cases, a state, which in the beginning exercised its sovereign power by joining the regime, has lost a part of its sovereignty if its control of the domestic authority that will be transferred to the international regime has been reduced. While any legal positivist could say that an EU state can change its domestic legislation and renounce the rights and duties of the community, such drastic action could lead to a disaster, both economically and politically. The cost would be so great that it is, at this time in history, not even worth discussing further.

It is important not to let the concept of sovereignty define the limits of international law. Although still a politically vibrant concept, legally it might be little more than a myth, a normative concept that unduly restrains our thoughts about the international legal order. But until the jury has come back on that, it can, nevertheless, not be ignored.

(c) The Incompleteness of International Law and Nonjusticiable Disputes

Sovereignty, as we know it today, certainly acts as a political restraint on the enforcement of international law and compulsory adjudication of international disputes. When the international society decides how intrusive its involvement in international environmental disputes can be, it has to delicately balance the political concept of sovereignty and the strength of international environmental law if environmental law is not to lose its credibility. This is, however, a question of politics rather than law. On these lines, it is appropriate to discuss the incompleteness of international law and limitation of judicial process in international law.

Unlike most domestic legal systems that do not ask persons for permission before asserting jurisdiction over them, the international legal system does not make a state subject to jurisdiction of courts or tribunals without the state's consent. Because a state is a sovereign entity, inasmuch its sovereignty has not been surrendered by international treaties or state practice, it is generally considered that it has the final say whether or not to accept such jurisdiction.

There are mainly three methods for a state to accept a jurisdiction of an international tribunal. First, the state can accept a clause in a treaty and, thusly, accept a jurisdiction for disputes arising from the implementation or interpretation of rights or obligations under that treaty. Second, the state can accept a Compromi, a special agreement between disputing states that submits the dispute to an international tribunal. Finally, as prescribed in Article 36 of the Statute of the International Court of Justice, states can accept the jurisdiction of the ICJ over disputes with states that have submitted comparable declarations.[58]

The notion of sovereignty was discussed before as the power of a state to decide on its domestic affairs and to conduct relations with other states. The existence of sovereignty as a sphere of legal authority and control and the states' tendency to maintain it acts as a restraint on the expansion of international law and the power of the international society over states. International law does not cover all aspects of the international society but only the ones that states have surrendered, by agreement or through practice, to the international society. The incompleteness of international law and its lack of capabilities to resolve disputes are, therefore, strongly related to the development of what we call sovereignty.

In the early days of the concept of international law as the world knows it, scholars disputed the limits and capabilities of international law. It is in harmony with what already has been discussed about absolute sovereignty and the thought that states did not have to obey any higher authority. State sovereignty was not to be touched and international law could only be applied to "matters less important than the independence and the vital interests of States."[59] Closely related to this line of thought is the doctrine of limitation of judicial process in international law. This doctrine, as explained by Vattel in the mid 1700s, stated that there had to be a distinction between legal disputes and political disputes. Vattel argued that "every power owes then this respect to the happiness of human society, to appear open to every method of reconciliation, when it relates to interests that are not essential, or that are of small consequence."[60] However, when essential rights of states were threatened, there was no duty to seek peaceful settlements but rather a right to "exhaust its resources, and nobly shed the last drop of its blood."[61] The thought behind such distinction is that when the question is about the continuance of the sovereignty of states, there is no room for legal disputes; every state has to rely on its own power and capabilities.

Half a century later, Wheaton supported a different line of thought. He argued that if it is clear that exercise of sovereign powers "directly affects the security of others,"[62] it is easy to assign the limits of sovereignty. However, when the limits are unclear, such as "where it merely involves a supposed contingent danger to the safety of others,"[63] the question of whether a state had exceeded its powers belongs "rather to the science of politics than of public law."[64] Thus, in an unclear situation, or when the results from a state's actions are unclear, Wheaton suggested that the answer to the question might be beyond the limits of international law. Wheaton's assumption was that international law is primitive law and does not have the ability to address complex problems or disputes. However, Wheaton did not argue his theory of the nonjusticiable disputes on the basis that the law could not handle disputes about "essential rights."

Since this doctrine of nonjusticiable disputes was partly traceable to the incompleteness of international law, it had to follow the development of international law and yield to the expansion of the law into the field of political disputes. Therefore, writers in the early part of the 1900s, formulated the doctrine differently, as Lauterpacht illustrated in the following text.

> If the parties ask merely for the application or interpretation of existing international law, the dispute is a legal one; it is a controversy in which the parties are in dispute as to existing legal rights. If, on the other hand, the parties profess to disregard an existing rule and claim a change in the law, the dispute is a political one; it is a conflict of interest.[65]

The latter dispute was nonjusticiable under this doctrine because it was outside the realm of the law.[66] Lauterpacht was suggesting the third version of the limitation of international law. Whereas Vattel argued that essential rights should be kept out of reach of international law and Wheaton argued that complex disputes should not be touched by international adjudication,

Lauterpacht suggested that if a dispute was, in essence, about a question unresolved by international law, it has to be settled by political means first.

Oppenheim doubted this distinction between legal and political disputes. He said when a claim for a change of existing law is a part of a treaty obligation to settle disputes peacefully or undertaken "in general instruments providing for remedial or legislative action of the organs of the international community," the dispute "properly [falls] within the purview of International Law."[67] Oppenheim and other writers, however, saw international law as necessarily weak and as primitive law, that is, could not become anything else if it was to survive and maintain its credibility.[68] Oppenheim based this assumption on his idea that there "is not, and never will be, a central authority above the several States."[69]

Since Oppenheim wrote this in the early days of the last century, the international legal arena has gone through considerable changes. The establishment of the League of Nations and, later, the UN with the Security Council as a centerpiece has changed the landscape of the international society. The European integration, the emerging norms of protection of human beings and their environment, have, to put it gently, given rise to the thought that Oppenheim's assertion that there is not and never will be a supranational authority is obsolete. Accordingly, it can and should be doubted that international law is and has to be weak law to exist. However, this debate is not over yet. Morgenthau argued that international law is a compromise between various national interests. He wrote, "[i]n order to find a common basis on which all those different national interests can meet in harmony, rule of international law embodied in general treaties must often be vague and ambiguous."[70] He compared international legal systems with domestic legal systems that have courts to adjudicate and agencies to enforce, both of which is more or less missing in the international legal system. As is true for other scholars, Morgenthau's words should be interpreted in the light of his era, that is, the interwar years, World War II, and the cold war years. As such, his era was dominated by conflicts, potential threats, and international relations that were constrained by perceived or real ideological obsessions.

Morgenthau was, however, far from being the only one supporting the doctrine of the nonjusticiability of essential interests of states. Judge Oda, in his dissenting opinion in *Military and Paramilitary Activities in and Against Nicaragua*,[71] argued, as Vattel did much earlier, that politically charged disputes, such as the conflicts between the United States and Nicaragua, might be a nonjudiciable dispute and inadmissible for the court. He argued that disputes about politically sensitive issues, especially if they are related to essential interests of states, should not be admissible in international tribunals.

Judge Oda limited his discussion to cases brought to the court on the basis of the voluntary jurisdiction in Article 36(2)[72] of the *Statute of the Court*.[73] Therefore, his arguments do not address cases where jurisdiction is based on a compromi or provisions in other treaties or conventions between the parties to the dispute (Article 36(1) jurisdiction). Judge Oda argued that by voluntarily accepting the court's jurisdiction of all cases between states, states were not surrendering the right to refuse jurisdiction in cases where essential interests were at stake.[74]

Judge Oda traced the development of international compulsory arbitration for sources for his arguments. He cited comments on drafts of statutes of international arbitrations that emphasized that compulsory adjudication of international disputes will not cover disputes relating to "vital interest, the independence, or the honour of the…Contracting States."[75] Judge Oda also cited a draft from the 1907 Peace Conference in The Hague contemplating establishment of a compulsory international arbitration. The draft, Article 16(a), provided for jurisdiction of a court over disputes of legal nature that diplomacy had not been able to settle, "provided, nevertheless, that they do not affect the vital interests, the independence or the honor of any of the said States and do not concern the interests of other States not involved in the dispute."[76] As Judge Oda pointed out, the draft was never accepted.

In this book, it is doubted that judicial settlement of disputes are inappropriate where vital national interests are at issue or when the dispute is heavily politically charged. The development of the international legal system suggests that this viewpoint is fading, if it is not already obsolete.

There is, however, a subjective element that should be given attention, that is, judicial process might not be appropriate where it is not reasonable to expect that the states involved in the dispute will follow the court's order. Here, the decisive aspect is whether the judicial process offers a solution for the disputants. In the aforementioned case between Nicaragua and the United States, Judge Lachs wrote:

> [I]t becomes clear that the dividing line between justiciable and non-justiciable disputes is one that can be drawn only with great difficulty. It is not the purely formal aspects that should in my view be decisive, but the legal framework, the efficacy of the solution that can be offered, the contribution the judgment may make to removing one more disputes from the overcrowded agenda of contention the world has to deal with today.[77]

It is probably impossible to estimate the likelihood of whether a judgment removes a dispute from the overcrowded agenda of contention. An absence from the court proceedings after the court has ruled it has jurisdiction is an indication that a state will not comply with the courts final judgment.[78] If such absence ought to result in the court's abstention from the dispute, the credibility of the compulsory jurisdiction of the court would suffer. Thus, another criterion has to be found.

In the international system, the political nature and the legal nature of a dispute do not necessarily go hand in hand. A legal solution of a dispute can be found without reasonable expectation of a solution of its political dimension. Certainly, such disparity weakens the international judicial system, but it can also weaken the political strength and viability of the opposing state's position. Therefore, a judgment in a politically charged dispute can have effects, although not necessarily in the way that the operative part of the judgment prescribed. Judge Lachs' words in his dissenting opinion do not, therefore, provide a clear guideline on whether a dispute is justiciable; at best, it presents a point of departure for the legal debate on the issue.

The doctrine of nonjusticiable disputes is not only known in international law, but also it has its relative, arguably not so distant, in domestic law. In the United States, a similar concept is known as the political question doctrine. It deals with certain disputes that are better left in the hands of other branches of government than the judicial branch. In *Baker v. Carr*, the doctrine was explained by Justice Brennan of United States Supreme Court.

> Prominent on the surface of any case held to involve a political question is found a textually demonstrable constitutional commitment of the issue to a coordinate political department; or a lack of judicially discoverable and manageable standards for resolving it; or the impossibility of deciding without an initial policy determination of a kind clearly for nonjudicial discretion; or the impossibility of a Court's undertaking independent resolution without expressing lack of the respect due coordinate branches of government; or an unusual need for unquestioning adherence to a political decision already made; or the potentiality of embarrassment from multifarious pronouncements by various departments on one question.[79]

Similarly, although not under the shield of the political question doctrine, in the field of United States immigration law, the judicial system has not been keen to enter into disputes that touch upon foreign affairs powers of the political branches of government. In *Fong Yue Ting v. United States*, a well-known case in United States jurisprudence, Justice Gray explained the allocation of powers in immigration matters.

> The power to exclude or to expel aliens, being a power affecting international relations, is vested in the political departments of the government, and is to be regulated by treaty or by act of Congress and to be executed by the executive authority according to the regulations so established, except so far as the judicial department has been authorized by treaty or by statute, or is required by the paramount law of the constitution, to intervene.[80]

Whether it is because the issue has directly been assigned to a non-judicial entity, or because there are no "judicially discoverable and manageable standards for resolving" the dispute, it could be inherent in domestic and international legal systems that certain issues are meant to be left outside of reach of the judicial branch or, at least, their role is to remain limited.

These domestic limitations of the judicial process must, however, be distinguished from their relatives in the international arena. The two aforementioned examples establish a limitation of the judicial power within the United States because the subject matter is better suited under the realm of nonjudicial branches of the government, that is, the executive power. In the international system, the executive power has generally not been delegated to the international legal order.[81] With this power still in the hands of the sovereign states, the conflict over turf is not between different branches of the international legal order at the same level; it is between levels, that is, the sovereign states and the international system. The Security Council had previously dealt with a number of cases that were brought before the ICJ. One might argue that if the council decides to "remain seized of the matter" the ICJ would hesitate to assert jurisdiction over a case dealing with the same issue. However, the court has not seen such wording as an obstacle to its jurisdiction.[82]

The court was, however, more conservative when it was asked to examine the legality of actions warranted by the Security Council. In the *Lockerbie Case*,[83] the court rejected Libya's claim to take provisional measures that would be contrary to a Security Council resolution. Libya asked the court to "to enjoin the United States from taking any action against Libya, calculated to coerce or compel Libya to surrender the accused individuals to any jurisdiction outside of Libya."[84] The Security Council had, after submission of the Libyan application to the court, authorized sanctions against Libya for refusing to extradite two Libyan nationals who were suspected of the bombing of a Pan Am aircraft over Lockerbie, Scotland.[85] Under the *Montreal Convention of 1971*,[86] Libya either had to prosecute the perpetrators or extradite them to a country that had jurisdiction under the convention.[87] The court said that since the U.S. and Libya were bound by the Security Council resolution, it could not order provisional measures, which would have, in fact, invalidated the resolution. The court said:

> Whereas both Libya and the United States, ...are obliged to accept and carry out the decisions of the Security Council...; whereas the Court, which is at the stage of proceedings on provisional measures, considers that prima facie this obligation extends to the decision contained in resolution 748 (1992); and whereas, in accordance with Article 103 of the Charter, the obligations of the parties in that respect prevail over their obligations under any other international agreement, including the Montreal Convention.[88]

This passage should not be understood as indicating that the ICJ is reluctant to look into the legality of Security Council resolutions. It is not based on the built-in supremacy of the Security Council within the UN system, but rather, on the supremacy of the obligation under the charter over obligation under other treaties. The court's ruling on the preliminary objections[89] supports this opinion.[90] In that judgment, the court rejected the contention of the United States (preliminary objection) that the Security Council resolution made Libya's claim moot and decided to hear the case on the merits. Thus, the reason for not looking into the Security Council resolution is based on the supremacy clause in Article 103 of the *UN Charter*. It is accordingly doubtful to say that in the international legal system there is any rule comparable to the political question doctrine, preventing the court from reviewing the legality of the Security Council. This certainly does not mean that the international legal order subscribes to any analogy from the *Marbury v. Madison* doctrine.[91] The court could, therefore, look into the legality of the Security Council's resolution and the legal effects of it, but since the resolution would create international legal obligations, its review would be seriously constrained by the supremacy clause in Article 103.[92]

Wheaton indicated that where the rules were not clear, international law would be timid.[93] On a related note, Lauterpacht suggested that a dispute, which is really a demand for changes, might be more suitable for a political solution than resolution according to the rules of international law.[94] Judge Lachs argued that adjudication of an international dispute might not be proper if it is not likely that such resolution will end the dispute in question.[95] These propositions, from different times in history, represent a resilient line of thought, suggesting that where states have not reached a consensus on the substance of a rule and have, therefore, not subjected themselves to a legal obligation, the adjudication of a dispute in such a field is likely to be futile. In the book *International Law and the Environment*, Patricia W. Birnie and Alan E. Boyle wrote:

> [t]he [ICJ] decides cases in accordance with international law. There are limitations on its ability to reform or develop established rules of law, even where states are agreed that change is necessary. Thus in the 1974 *Icelandic Fisheries* case, the Court was able to depart only to some extent from established customary rules but failed to reach a solution acceptable either to the parties or to the international community as a whole...Where the law is less clear, states face substantial uncertainty in submitting the outcome to the Court's jurisdiction, and the Court itself may be unwilling to adjudicate if, as in the *Nuclear Test* cases, there is no consensus on the rules applicable to the dispute. In a subject where legal rules are still developing, and underlying consensus not yet fully established, the role of adjudication is likely to be limited.[96]

It is hardly correct to say that the absence of international legal rules in one area constitutes a legal vacuum. If the existence of such area is established, one could perhaps say that the sovereignty of states prevails and disputes, if any, do not belong to the long arm of international law but rather to international politics. Any act or omission in such issue would be assessed under the domestic laws of each state, and if they differ, the dispute is a political one. Theoretically, this line of thought might work.

However, it is hard to imagine a dispute between states that cannot be assessed and resolved under international law. One must have in mind that international law, even in the absence of treaties and customs, finds its sources in general principles of law and the "teachings of the most highly qualified publicists of the various nations."[97] There are probably always methods and techniques to unravel the legal rule in any particular circumstances. Nevertheless, if the determination of a legal rule requires legal aerobatics or less solid creative legal reasoning, it is less likely that the resulting rule will be precise and credible. This poses a problem not only for international adjudication where the rule has to be interpreted and applied but also for the use of countermeasures because without a credible determination of a violation of an international obligation, the primary element of countermeasures, the presence of a prior violation of an international obligation, might be absent.

(D) CONCLUSIONS

In the modern interdependent world, it is widely accepted that absolute sovereignty has passed away and the international system is moving toward some form of global governance, although, without a formal comprehensive global government. Theories of the incompleteness of international law and the school of thought that argues that international law has to be weak to survive are, however, still alive. The effectiveness and strength of international law against sovereignty, as a force that limits it, depends not only on how many states support the enforcement of the law but also which states. The unequal distribution of capabilities is a keyword in international relations of which international law forms an integral part.[98] A zealous enforcement of international law by an international organization against a nonwilling great power reduces the legitimacy of that law and even the credibility of the international law as a whole, similar to when international law is left without enforcement when such enforcement is likely to change a state's behavior.

It is important to refresh our memory about the origins of sovereignty. It referred to the powers of the monarch over his territory and his subjects. Thus, it was a concept dealing with domestic issues. After Westphalia, it evolved in addition into the ability of states to conduct foreign relations. The Westphalian principle of noninterference is, however, a domestic concept in nature, confirming the authority and control that the sovereign had over his subjects and territory. Sovereignty as a concept in modern international law is about the authority to govern over issues that have not been surrendered to the international legal order by treaty or state practice. Sovereignty in the political meaning deals also with the struggle between domestic powers and the ones of the international society. It is, however, mainly a catch-all phrase for a broad array of issues that can be seen as the cause for this struggle. The concept has, therefore, been used to serve interests based on identity, nationalism, corporate interests, or other domestic issues that are conveniently, but incorrectly, placed under the hat of sovereignty.

The idea of the incompleteness of international law refers mainly to what issues international law can cover and what is left to the sovereign states to decide. The limitation of judicial process in international law limits the role of international law further. The core idea is that even if the issue area is dealt with by international law, political interests demand that disputes in this area are resolved by political means and not by adjudication. As an example, the United States unsuccessfully argued in the *Nicaragua Case* that even if their intervention was, in fact, a violation of international law, the political sensitivity of the issues should render the dispute inadmissible for adjudication.[99] One must remember that the United States did not attend the pleadings on the merits and did, therefore, not elaborate on this argument as much as they could have.

The borders between domestic powers and international powers are certainly unclear. It is, therefore, of little use to come up with a solution on how sovereignty affects or limits the effectiveness and power of international law however well it is argued. After all, sovereignty is what states make of it. It has no sacred meanings or principles that cannot be altered or abandoned if the interests of the rational, egoistic state demand so. It is, therefore, constantly changing. The words of de Jouvenel quoted at the beginning of this chapter express this thought: that sovereignty is not an establishment that plays a role in the international system. It is, rather, a result of the system, a sphere of control and authority that remains in the hands of states because they have not yet surrendered it to the international system.

ENDNOTES

1. Bertrand De Jouvenel, *Sovereignty: An Inquiry into the Political Good*, originally published in 1955 as *De la Souveraineté. A la Recherche du Bien Public*, translated by J. F. Huntington, University of Chicago Press, Chicago, 1957, p. 219.
2. See, for example, John Westlake, *Chapters on the Principles of International Law*, Cambridge University Press, Cambridge, 1894, p. 59.
3. See *Commission v. Luxemburg and Belgium*, case nos. 90 and 91/63, judgment of 13 November 1964, 1964 European Court Reports 625, at 631; *Commission v. Italy*, case no. 52/75, judgment of 26 February 1976, 1976 European Court Reports 277, at 284; *Commission v. France*, case no. 232/78, judgment of 25 September 1979, 1979 European Court Reports 2729, at 2739; and, somewhat, *The Queen v. Ministry of Agriculture, Fisheries and Food*, ex. parte Hedley Lomas (Ireland) Ltd., case no. C-5/94, judgment of 23 May 1996, 1996 *European Court Reports* I:2553. See also discussion on this in Elisabeth Zoller, *Peacetime Unilateral Remedies: An Analysis of Countermeasures*, Traditional Publishers, New York, 1984, p. 113 and *Fourth Report on State Responsibility by Mr. Gaetano Arangio-Ruiz, Special Rapporteur*, UN doc. no. A/CN.4.444 (hereafter referred to as *Fourth Report 1992 (Arangio-Ruiz)*), International Law Commission Yearbook 1992, vol. II, (part 1), pp. 35–36, paras. 98–100.
4. *The Case of the S.S. Lotus* (*France v. Turkey*), Permanent Court of International Justice, judgment of 7 September 1927, P.C.I.J. Ser. A, no. 10; see in particular at 18–19.
5. Elisabeth Zoller, *Peacetime Unilateral Remedies: An Analysis of Countermeasures*, Traditional Publishers, New York, 1984, p. 79.
6. Jean Bodin, *The Six Books of the Commonwealth*, first published in 1576, first translated into English by Richard Knolles, London, 1606, reprinted by Kenneth. D. McRae, Cambridge, Massachusetts, 1962. Before Bodin, the concept of sovereignty (souverain) was known and used in France for an authority, political or not, "which had no other authority above itself." See L. Oppenheim, *International Law*, vol. I, 8th ed., edited by H. Lauterpacht, David McKay Company Inc., New York, 1955, p. 120.
7. Jean Bodin, *On Sovereignty, Four Chapters from The Six Books of the Commonwealth*, edited and translated by Julian H. Franklin, Cambridge, England, 1992, book I, chap. 8, pp. 1–2.

8. Archons ruled in the time of the Athenians for a term of nine or ten years.
9. Jean Bodin, *On Sovereignty, Four Chapters from The Six Books of the Commonwealth*, book I, chap. 8, pp. 4–5.
10. Ibid., p. 3.
11. Ibid.
12. Hobbes and Pufendorf, as cited in L. Oppenheim, *International Law*, vol. I, 8th ed., edited by H. Lauterpacht, David McKay Company Inc., New York, 1955, p. 121.
13. Stephen D. Krasner, *Sovereignty: Organized Hypocrisy*, Princeton University Press, 1999, p. 4.
14. Hans Morgenthau, *Politics among Nations*, p. 328.
15. See, for example, Ibid., p. 294.
16. John Westlake, *Chapters on the Principles of International Law*, Cambridge University Press, Cambridge, 1894, p. 59.
17. Ibid.
18. Ibid. On a detailed description of the causes of the Thirty Year War and how it resulted in the *Treaty of Westphalia*, see, for example, John Hosack, *On the Rise and Growth of the Law of Nations, as Established by General Usage and by Treaties*, John Murray, London, 1882.
19. Georg Friedrich von Martens should not be confused with Fyodor Fyodorovich Martens, another renowned legal scholar and the author of the so-called Martens Clause from the Peace Conference in The Hague in 1899.
20. Georg Friedrich von Martens, *A Compendium of the Law of Nations*, originally published in 1795, translated by William Cobbet, Cobbet and Morgan, Pall-Mall, London, 1802, p. 23.
21. Ibid., p. 24.
22. Ibid., pp. 29–30.
23. Ibid., p. 31.
24. Ibid., p. 24, endnote, citing de Leibnitz, *Cæsarini Furstenerii Suprematu Principum*, chap. 12.
25. Harlan B. Phillips (ed.), *Felix Frankfurter Reminisces*, Secker & Warburg, London, 1960, p. 60.
26. Emmerich de Vattel, *The Law of Nations* or *Principles of the Law of Nature, Applied to the Conduct and Affairs of Nations and Sovereigns*, originally published in 1757, Simeon Butler, Northampton, Massachusetts, 1820, book I, chap. IV, § 38, p. 69.
27. Henry Wheaton, *Elements of International Law*, Lea and Blanchard, Philadelphia, Pennsylvania, 1846, p. 55.
28. Ibid., p. 66.

29. Ibid., p. 55.
30. Ibid., p. 66.
31. See Samuel Freiherr von Pufendorf, *Of the Law of Nature and Nations*, translated from Latin, printed by L. Lichfield, Oxford, 1703, book II, chap. V, § I, p. 140.
32. Henry Wheaton, *Elements of International Law*, p. 102.
33. Theodore D. Woolsey, *Introduction to the Study of International Law*, 5th ed., Charles Scribner's Sons, New York, 1879, p. 35.
34. T. J. Lawrence, *The Principles of International Law*, 4th ed., Macmillan and Co., London, 1911, p. 56.
35. John Westlake, "The Equality and Independence of States" in *The Collected Papers of John Westlake on Public International Law*, edited by L. Oppenheim, Cambridge University Press, Cambridge, 1914, p. 86, citing Wolff, Jus Gentium, sections 16–18 and Vattel, "Le Droit des Gens," sections 18 and 19 of the *Préliminaires*.
36. John Westlake, "The Principles of International Law" in *The Collected Papers of John Westlake on Public International Law*, edited by L. Oppenheim, Cambridge University Press, Cambridge, 1914, p. 78.
37. John Westlake, "The Equality and Independence of States, at 87.
38. See Ibid., at 88.
39. Hans Morgenthau, *Politics among Nations*, p. 294.
40. John Westlake, "International Rights of Self-Preservation" in *The Collected Papers of John Westlake on Public International Law*, edited by L. Oppenheim, Cambridge University Press, Cambridge, 1914, p. 111.
41. Ibid., at 112–113.
42. See Djura Nincic, *The Problem of Sovereignty in the Charter and the Practice of the United Nations*, pp. 6–7. See also Henry Wheaton, *Elements of International Law*, p. 102.
43. Djura Nincic, *The Problem of Sovereignty in the Charter and the Practice of the United Nations*, p. 9.
44. See Ibid., p.11, citing George Stelle, *Precis du Droit des Gens*, p. 10 and Duguit, *L'Etat, le Droit Objectif et la Loi Positive*, T. I. 1901 and *L'Etat, les Gouvernants et les Agents*, T. II, 1903. See also Westlake, "The Principles of International Law," p. 78, on men as the ultimate members of the international society.
45. Louis Henkin, *International Law: Politics and Values*, Martinus Nijhoff Publishers, Dordrecht, Boston, London, 1995, p. 8.
46. Ibid., p. 9.
47. Ibid., p. 10.

48. See Stephen D. Krasner, *Sovereignty: Organized Hypocrisy*, Princeton University Press, 1999. See also Stephen D. Krasner (ed.), *Problematic Sovereignty: Contested Rules and Political Possibilities*, Columbia University Press, New York, 2000.
49. Stephen D. Krasner, *Sovereignty: Organized Hypocrisy*, Princeton University Press, 1999, p. 4.
50. Ibid., pp. 3–4.
51. Louis Henkin, *International Law: Politics and Values*, p. 10.
52. Stephen D. Krasner, *Sovereignty: Organized Hypocrisy*, pp. 3–4.
53. Louis Henkin, *International Law: Politics and Values*, p. 10.
54. Stephen D. Krasner, *Sovereignty: Organized Hypocrisy*, pp. 3–4.
55. Ibid., p. 229.
56. Hans Morgenthau seemed to define sovereignty as a supreme law-giving and law-enforcing power of a state (Hans Morgenthau, *Politics among Nations*, pp. 331–333). It is true that the states of the European Union have transferred a great deal of their competencies, including some of their legislative and judicial power, to institutions of the EU. Furthermore, the power to make international agreements has also, in some fields, been surrendered to the EU, but this power is a part of the traditional definition of a state. With the development of the EU in mind, one might suggest that the definition of a sovereign state is in dire need of an overhaul.
57. Norway is, along with Iceland and Lichtenstein, a party to the *Agreement on the European Economic Area*, which gives the country a number of the rights it would enjoy as a member of the European Union. Furthermore, Switzerland has signed and ratified seven bilateral agreements with the EU, giving the country similar rights as Norway has within the EU.
58. See *Statute of the International Court of Justice*, concluded at San Francisco 26 June 1946, entered into force 24 October 1946, 59 Stat. 1055, T.S. 993, 3 Bevans 1179.
59. H. Lauterpacht, *The Function of Law in the International Community*, Clarendon Press, Oxford, 1933, p. 7.
60. Emmerich de Vattel, *The Law of Nations* or *Principles of the Law of Nature*, book II, chap. XVIII, § 332, p. 345.
61. Emmerich de Vattel, *Le Droit des Gens* or *Principes de la Loi Naturelle, Appliqués à la Conduite et aux Affaires des Nations et des Souverains* (1758), book II, chap. XVIII. Fenwick's translation of 1916 *Classics of International Law*, cited in H. Lauterpacht, *The Function of Law in the International Community*, pp. 8–9. In Vattel's writings used for this book, the language is "It [the republic] will not even attempt to wait the method

of conference on so odious a pretension: It will bring into this quarrel all its efforts, its last resources, and all the best blood it is capable of shedding." See Emmerich de Vattel, *The Law of Nations* or *Principles of the Law of Nature*, book II, chap. XVIII, § 332, p. 345.

62. Henry Wheaton, *Elements of International Law*, p. 102.
63. Ibid., pp. 102–103.
64. Ibid., p. 103.
65. H. Lauterpacht, *The Function of Law in the International Community*, p. 17.
66. Ibid., pp. 351–352.
67. L. Oppenheim, *International Law*, vol. II, 7th ed., edited by H. Lauterpacht, David McKay Company Inc., New York, 1952, p. 6.
68. See a similar school of thought in H. Lauterpacht, *The Function of Law in the International Community*, p. 405, citing the work of Oppenheim, Holland, Zitelmann, and De Louter.
69. Ibid., p. 404, citing Oppenheim, *International Law*, vol. I, 8th ed., p. 288.
70. Hans Morgenthau, *Politics among Nations*, p. 299.
71. *Military and Paramilitary Activities in and Against Nicaragua* (merits) (*Nicaragua v. United States of America*), International Court of Justice, judgment of 27 June 1986, 1986 I.C.J. 14, at 219, para. 15 et seq.
72. State declaration accepting the compulsory jurisdiction of the court.
73. *Statute of the International Court of Justice*, see supra endnote 58 of this chapter.
74. *Military and Paramilitary Activities in and Against Nicaragua*, dissenting opinion by Judge Oda, 1986 I.C.J. 14, at 236, para. 48. In contrast, the *Hostage Case* of 1980 was not based on reciprocal declaration according to article 36(2), and Judge Oda's opinion had no direct bearing on the correctness of the decision of the court not to entertain Iran's assertion of nonjusticiability based on a politically charged underlying dispute.
75. *Military and Paramilitary Activities in and Against Nicaragua*, dissenting opinion by Judge Oda, 1986 I.C.J. 14, at 224, para. 25, citing *British and Foreign State Papers*, vol. XCVI, p. 35.
76. *Military and Paramilitary Activities in and Against Nicaragua*, dissenting opinion by Judge Oda, 1986 I.C.J. 14, at 222, para. 22.
77. Ibid., separate opinion by Judge Lachs, 1986 I.C.J. 14, at 168.
78. See, for example, the *Fisheries Cases* of 1974 (*U.K. v. Iceland*), the *Hostage Case* of 1980 (*United States v. Iran*), and the *Nicaragua Case of 1986* (*Nicaragua v. United States*). In these cases, the respondent refused to accept the jurisdiction of the International Court of Justice, did not attend the pleadings on the merits, and, in none of the cases, did the respondent comply with the judgment.

79. *Baker v. Carr*, 369 U.S. 186 (1962), at 217, 82 S.Ct. 691, at 710.
80. *Fong Yue Ting v. United States*, 149 U.S. 698 (1893), at 713, 13 S.Ct. 1016, at 1022.
81. One exception is, however, the powers of the Security Council over issues that threaten international peace and security.
82. See, for example, *Military and Paramilitary Activities in and Against Nicaragua*, 1986 I.C.J. 14 and *United States Diplomatic and Consular Staff in Tehran* (*United States of America v. Iran*), International Court of Justice, judgment of 24 May 1980, 1980 I.C.J. 3.
83. *Questions of Interpretation and Application of the 1971 Montreal Convention Arising from the Aerial Incident at Lockerbie* (provisional measures) (*Libyan Arab Jamahiriya v. United States of America*), International Court of Justice, order of 14 April 1992. 1992 I.C.J. 115. See also identical case against the United Kingdom, 1992 I.C.J. 3.
84. Ibid., at 119, para. 11.
85. *Security Council Resolution no. 883* (1993), UN doc. S/RES/883 (1993), 11 November 1993.
86. *Montreal Convention for the Suppression of Unlawful Acts Against the Safety of Civil Aviation*, concluded at Montreal on 23 September 1971, entered into force on 26 January 1973, 974 U.N.T.S. 177, articles 5–7.
87. Ibid., article 7.
88. *Questions of Interpretation and Application of the 1971 Montreal Convention Arising from the Aerial Incident at Lockerbie*, at 126, para. 42.
89. *Questions of Interpretation and Application of the 1971 Montreal Convention Arising from the Aerial Incident at Lockerbie* (preliminary objections) (*Libyan Arab Jamahiriya v. United States of America*), International Court of Justice, judgment of 27 February 1998, 1998 I.C.J. 114.
90. See also *United States Diplomatic and Consular Staff in Tehran*, 1980 I.C.J. 3, at 23, para. 43.
91. *Marbury v. Madison*, 5 U.S. (1 Cranch) 137 (1803). This case established a doctrine allowing a judicial review of acts of the U.S. Congress.
92. On the interaction between ICJ and the Security Council, see Jose E. Alvarez, "Judging the Security Council," *American Journal of International Law* 90 (1996): 1.
93. Henry Wheaton, *Elements of International Law*, p. 103.
94. H. Lauterpacht, *The Function of Law in the International Community*, p. 17.
95. *Military and Paramilitary Activities in and against Nicaragua*, separate opinion by Judge Lachs, 1986 I.C.J. 14, at 168.
96. Patricia W. Birnie and Alan E. Boyle, *International Law and the Environment*, Clarendon Press, Oxford University Press, Oxford, New York, 1992, p. 185.

97. *Statute of the International Court of Justice*, article 38(1)(d).
98. See, for example, Poul R. Viotti and Mark V. Kauppi, *International Relations Theory, Realism, Pluralism, Globalism, and Beyond*, 3rd ed., Allyn and Bacon, Boston, 1999, p. 71 and Kenneth N. Waltz, *Theory of International Politics*, McGraw-Hill Inc., New York, 1979, p. 97.
99. *Military and Paramilitary Activities in and Against Nicaragua* (jurisdiction), (Nicaragua v. United States of America), International Court of Justice, Judgment of 26 November 1984, 1984 I.C.J. 392, at 429 et seq., para. 84 et seq.

CHAPTER 3

UNILATERAL ACTS OF STATES OR INTERNATIONAL ORGANIZATIONS NOT ADDRESSED IN THIS BOOK

(A) INTRODUCTORY NOTE

Apart from countermeasures, there is a flora of international measures, which at least on their surface appear to be unilateral. Many of these measures are in response to acts that could be a breach of a legal obligation, international or not, or behavior in breach of political or moral obligations. The fact that unilateral measures are taken in response to such breaches does not on its own make them countermeasures. To better clarify this distinction, it might be helpful to discuss briefly such unilateral measures. Among them are measures based on resolutions adopted by the Security Council, measures justified as acts of necessity, and self-defense, as well as other measures taken by states that are not illegal per se but could be in response to an illegal or unwanted situation, such as refusal to provide development aid already offered.

(B) Suspension of International Development Projects

A number of international development projects provide a vital assistance to the livelihood of many underdeveloped territories. A decision of the donor state to suspend or cancel such a project in response to acts or inactions of the receiving state is generally not countermeasures even if the acts or inactions in question violate international obligations that the receiving state owes to the donor state. This is because the obligation to provide the development aid would generally not constitute an international legal obligation. Thus, a decision of the EU not to grant aid money to a road-building project in Honduras might be justified by the lack of democratic processes within the Honduran government. It might even be canceled for a much less important reason. The result might have serious effects for those communities in Honduras that were intended to benefit from the project. Canceling or scaling down the project might, therefore, be utterly disproportionate, decided without any warning or consultation with the Honduran authorities or without giving them a reasonable time to improve the situation that caused the cancellation. The EU, in absence of an international legal obligation to provide the aid, would not be held internationally liable for deaths, injury, or economic coast resulting from the fact that the road was never built. Its liability would be a political one. Even if the decision to cancel the aid project would have been taken as a response to an illegal act of the receiving government, it would still not be countermeasures unless the act of canceling requires a justification under international law.[1]

Similarly, multinational development banks (MDBs) engage in numerous activities of economic nature. Their decision to withdraw or cancel a project can be made as a response to an act of a state that is a violation of a legal rule or politically deplorable. The lending agreement between the receiving state and the relevant MDB would, in most cases, be the source of rules applicable to that particular project. It might, for example, contain clauses demanding improvement of environmental practices as a condition for the lending. The MDB might cite a violation of such a requirement as a reason for canceling the loan or altering its conditions. However, such a measure would generally not constitute a countermeasure unless the obligation that the receiving state owes to the MDB would be considered an international legal obligation and not merely a private contractual obligation; and the measures taken by the MBD would go beyond the contractual remedy authorized in the documents relevant to the project.

(c) Security Council Resolutions

The UN Security Council deserves some attention here. In theory, the council is an executive body responsible for maintaining peace and international security. However, when working as a whole and dealing with international peace and security, it is truly the world government, a sole tribunal, and the highest legislator. Since the Security Council defines what is of its concern, that is, what is a threat to international peace and security, its competence can be quite broad. Theoretically, environmental issues can, therefore, be considered by the Security Council, especially when environmental degradation threatens political stability and, therefore, the peace.

The Security Council makes decisions by adopting resolutions. To pass, they require affirmative votes of nine member states. According to Article 27 of the *UN Charter*, the five permanent members of the council have a right to veto any decision, with the exception of procedural matters.[2] This right basically prevents the council from making decisions unfavorable to the interests of the permanent members.

The Security Council's resolutions are an independent source of international law and can even put aside international treaties.[3] A resolution that orders a certain distribution of drinking water, for example, demands that a state closes a nuclear power reactor, or requests that a state stop digging irrigation canals that deprive other states of water for agriculture, has the status of a legally binding order according to Article 25 of the *UN Charter*.

The role of the Security Council is described in chapters 5 to 7 in the *UN Charter*. According to Article 24 of the charter, its primary responsibilities are the maintenance of international peace and security.[4] Article 39 of the charter gives the Security Council authority to determine

> the existence of any threat to the peace, breach of the peace, or act of aggression and shall...decide what measures shall be taken in accordance with Articles 41 and 42, to maintain or restore international peace and security.[5]

Article 41 deals with measures that do not include the use of force. Examples of Article 41 measures are economic sanctions, embargos, and communication interruptions, as well as severances of diplomatic relations.[6] The Security Council is supposed to use such measures prior to resorting to the use of force except when it deems such measures to be inadequate.[7]

Being a permanent member of the Security Council is an excellent opportunity to exercise power politics to the extreme. A permanent member can never be sanctioned or threatened with measures provided for in Article 41 or 42 of the charter against its will. For example, if a case is brought against a permanent member before the ICJ for violations of international law and the permanent member loses, enforcement can be quite problematic because it is, according to Article 94(2) of the charter, in the hands of the Security Council.[8] The UN system of five permanent members in the Security Council with veto power can, therefore, defeat the spirit of the *UN Charter* without any recourse to international law for the rest of the UN members. Article 24(2) of the charter provides, however, that "in discharging these duties the Security Council shall act in accordance with the *Purposes and Principle* of the United Nations."[9] Among the "purposes and principles" of the UN is to maintain international peace "in conformity with the principles of justice and international law."[10] When it is, however, the Security Council that sets the standards of justice and international law—as a body with a legislative function with regard to international peace and security—the permanent members along with at least four nonpermanent members are trusted to do what is right with no effective legal restrains. The bottom line is the UN system can never work against a permanent member—only with them or not at all.

A resolution adopted by the Security Council, and taken in response to an internationally wrongful act of another state, is not countermeasures. It does not require a prior violation of international law because it relies on the *UN Charter* as its source of authority. Actions authorized by the Security Council in order to induce a state to comply with its international obligations are, for the same reasons, not countermeasures.

(D) Self-Defense

Related to the authority of the Security Council is the inherent right of a state to self-defense, referred to in Article 51 of the *UN Charter*. This right, which has similar roots as countermeasures, authorizes a state to use force against another state "if an armed attack occurs against [it]."[11] The emergence of theories of environmental security, which see threats against the environment as a threat against the security of the state or its people, makes the notion of self-defense against environmental threats an interesting topic, however, not a topic of this book. Besides, theories of environmental security are barely developed enough or sufficiently accepted to make this combination ripe for any serious analytical study. Also, there would be a myriad of additional considerations that would have to be discussed and analyzed, thus, it is better left for others.

(E) Acts of Necessity

Countermeasures also have a certain resemblance to acts of necessity. The notion of acts of necessity, acts that violate international obligation but are justified due to necessity, is arguably more related to countermeasures than self-defense. It might, therefore, be quite appropriate also to discuss how unilateral measures to protect the environment can be precluded from wrongfulness by qualifying as such acts. However, as is true about self-defense, this would open up a world of considerations different from the ones that this book deals with. It is, therefore, not the topic of this book.

Nevertheless, it is appropriate to discuss briefly the main elements of such measures. The ILC suggested in Article 25 of its *2001 Draft Articles*[12] that necessity can be a justification for otherwise illegal unilateral acts. Article 25 reads as follows:

> 1. Necessity may not be invoked by a State as a ground for precluding the wrongfulness of an act not in conformity with an international obligation of that State unless the act:
>
>   a. Is the only way for the State to safeguard an essential interest against a grave and imminent peril; and
>   b. Does not seriously impair an essential interest of the State or States toward which the obligation exists, or of the international community as a whole.
>
> 2. In any case, necessity may not be invoked by a State as a ground for precluding wrongfulness if:
>
>   a. The international obligation in question excludes the possibility of invoking necessity; or
>   b. The State has contributed to the situation of necessity.[13]

As this text indicates, the striking difference between acts of necessity and countermeasures is that a prior illegal act of another state is not required for an act to be justified under the acts of necessity doctrine. As will be mentioned later,[14] anticipatory countermeasures are not permitted, as the prior breach requirement is not fulfilled. In such circumstances, a state that is faced with an imminent environmental peril could perhaps justify acts that otherwise would be illegal as acts of necessity. The ILC wrote in its commentary to the *2001 Draft Articles*:

> The plea of necessity is exceptional in a number of respects… . It arises where there is an irreconcilable conflict between an essential interest on the one hand and an obligation of the State invoking necessity on the other. These special features mean that necessity

> will only rarely be available to excuse non-performance of an obligation and that it is subject to strict limitations to safeguard against possible abuse.[15]

State of necessity was apparently the main justification for the bombing of the Liberian oil tanker *Torrey Canyon*, which struck aground of the coast of the United Kingdom in March 1967, however, outside its territorial waters. The incident and its legal implications were described in a 1980 report of the ILC, in the commentary to Article 33 of its *Draft Articles on State Responsibility*.[16] The tanker started leaking large quantities of its 117,000 ton cargo of crude oil. After several attempts to rescue the ship and reduce the damage, including using detergent to disperse the oil and assisting the salvage company hired by the ship owner to refloat the vessel, the United Kingdom decided to blow it up to burn up the oil that was threatening the marine environment and the English coast.[17] The British government "stressed the existence of a situation of extreme danger and claimed that the decision to bomb the ship had been taken only after all other means had failed."[18] The ILC concluded,

> It seems to the Commission that, even if the ship owner had not abandoned the wreck and even if he had tried to oppose its destruction, the action taken by the British Government would have had to be recognized as internationally lawful because of a state of necessity.[19]

The doctrine of acts of necessity gained further credibility when the ICJ applied it in the *Gabcikovo-Nagymaros Project* in 1997.[20] The facts of the case in short are that on 16 September 1977, Hungary and Czechoslovakia[21] signed a treaty on the construction and operation of a system of locks on the Danube River.[22] The treaty dealt with a joint investment between these two countries aimed at production of hydroelectricity, navigation, and flood protection. The parties to the treaty also undertook to protect the quality of the river water and the surrounding environment from harmful consequences of the implementation of the treaty.[23]

The main projects of the treaty were the Gabcikovo System of Locks combined with a bypass canal and a 720 MW hydroelectric power plant within Slovak territory and the Nagymaros System of Locks and a 158 MW hydroelectric power plant within the Hungarian territory. Other parts of the project included the Dunakiliti Dam in Hungarian territory, the Dunakiliti-Hrusov head-water installations in Hungarian and Slovak territory, a number of flood control works, deepening of the river bed, and restoration of vegetation.

According to an agreement on mutual assistance between the parties[24] associated with the *1977 Treaty*, the project was supposed to be completed in 1991.[25] In 1983, the parties agreed to slow down the constructions and to complete it in 1995.[26] Later, in 1989, the parties decided to speed up the project again and have it finished in 1994.[27]

During political and economic unrest in Eastern Europe, doubts arose—especially in Hungary—of the economical feasibility of the project, as well as its environmental impact.[28] Consequently, the project generated intense criticism in Hungary, and in May 1989, the Hungarian government decided to suspend the project within its territory, pending environmental studies.[29] The reasons given were a lack of scientific knowledge of the impact of the Nagymaros part of the project and that "the risk of constructing the Barrage System in accordance with the original plan cannot be considered acceptable."[30] Despite willingness of the Czechoslovakian government to amend the completion date and other items, negotiations proved futile. On 27 October 1989, the Hungarian government decided to abandon the Nagymaros part of the project and maintain the Dunakiliti Dam at status quo. In November 1989, dramatic political changes took place in Czechoslovakia and Hungary. A new government that took over in Hungary declared the project a mistake.[31] The new Czechoslovakian president called the project a "totalitarian, gigomaniac monument which is against nature."[32] However, the Czechoslovakian position was to modify the treaty but not cancel the project.[33]

The Hungarian government claimed a "state of ecological necessity" as a reason for not continuing with the project.[34] The Dunakiliti part of the project would lead to changes in groundwater level and quality. As for surface water, risk of eutrophication would arise. The results would be that the fluvial flora and fauna "would have been condemned to extinction."[35] Hungary argued that if the Nagymaros Dam was to be built, it would result in deterioration of the quality of the river water of the Danube. In addition, the operation of the Gabcikovo power plant would have caused "significant daily variations in the water level in the reservoir upstream, which would have constituted a threat to aquatic habitants in particular."[36] The Nagymaros Dam would also put at risk or diminish the yield of the riverbank wells that provided two thirds of Budapest's freshwater.[37]

The Slovak government rejected that a state of ecological necessity was present in the situation. In addition, it doubted that ecological necessity could, under the law of state responsibility, "constitute a circumstance precluding the wrongfulness of an act."[38]

The case came before the International Court of Justice on 2 July 1993 as a result of an agreement between Hungary and Slovakia to submit the dispute to the court. After addressing a few of the parties less relevant arguments, the court proceeded to answer the question if Hungary was entitled to suspend and subsequently abandon its part of the Gabcikovo-Nagymaros project. In short, the answer was in the negative.

Before it came to that conclusion, the court addressed the concept of state of necessity. The parties had agreed that the *1980 Draft Articles on the International Responsibility of States*, drafted by the ILC, should be the basis for the evaluation. In addition, the court said that state of necessity as a ground for precluding a wrongfulness of an act was recognized by customary international law. It also noted that such grounds could only apply in exceptional circumstances and "the State concerned is not the sole judge of whether those conditions have been met."[39]

The court then went on and said,

> In the present case, the following basic conditions set forth in Draft Article 33 are relevant: it must have been occasioned by an '*essential interest*' of the State which is the author of the act conflicting with one of its international obligations; that interest must have been threatened by a '*grave and imminent peril*'; the act being challenged must have been the '*only means*' of safeguarding that

> interest; that act must not have '*seriously impair[ed] an essential interest*' of the State towards which the obligation existed; and the State which is the author of that act must not have '*contributed to the occurrence of the state of necessity*'. Those conditions reflect customary international law.[40]

The court cited the work of the ILC and the *Nuclear Weapons Case*[41] of 1996 and concluded quickly and without any complex deliberation that Hungary's environmental interests could be essential interests within the meaning of Article 33 of the *1980 Draft Articles*.[42] The presence of essential interests under the court's view does not require a threat to the existence of a state. Citing previous work of the ILC, the court accepted that a grave danger to the ecological preservation of a part of a state's territory could constitute essential interests of a state. The court also noted that environmental interests have only recently entered the sphere of states' essential interests.[43]

The court thereafter analyzed the term of grave and imminent peril. In the court's view, "peril" had to be more than possible or perceived to fulfill the requirement of immediacy. However, the court noted

> [t]hat does not exclude...that a 'peril' appearing in the long term might be held to be 'imminent' as soon as it is established...that the realization of that peril, however far off it might be, is not thereby any less certain and inevitable."[44]

After elaborating on these general requirements for the state of necessity, the court turned to the facts of the case. First, it addressed the Nagymaros part of the project. Hungary argued that it would cause serious fresh water problems in terms of quality and quantity. The court, however believed that the dangers from the upstream reservoir were long term in nature and uncertain and would depend on how the Nagymaros part of the project would have been operated. In relation to the upstream reservoir, the court could not find a condition constituting a grave peril. In addition, because of the uncertainties of how the parties would operate the Nagymaros Dam, the peril was not imminent.[45] In relation to the effect of construction downstream of the Nagymaros

Dam that allegedly caused a risk of freshwater shortage in Budapest, the court pointed out that Hungary had already deepened the riverbed to extract building materials and the depth of the river already fulfilled the *1977 Treaty* requirements. The concerns of Hungary were, however, more complex than this. In what might be interpreted as an attempt to avoid analyzing the problem further, the court said that even if these freshwater problems constituted a grave and imminent peril, Hungary had other means of preventing the harm than to abandon the project altogether, such as discharging gravel into the river or "processing the river water in an appropriate manner."[46] The court seems to be suggesting that the cost of the suggested measures in proportion to the decision to suspend the Gabcikovo-Nagymaros project does not justify the latter.

With regard to the Gabcikovo part of the dispute, the court focused on the uncertainty of the scientific data and that the alleged injury was a result of a slow, natural process. A report from June 1989 by an ad hoc committee of the Hungarian Academy of Science stated, "[b]ecause of the complexity of the ecological processes and lack of the measured data and the relevant calculations the environmental impacts cannot be evaluated."[47]

Because of this uncertainty about the nature and extent of the threat, the court held that Hungary had not shown that the requirement of imminence of the peril in question for invoking state of necessity as a justification for suspending the *1977 Treaty* was met. It also played a role in the court's decision that it believed that other, more proportionate measures were available to Hungary.[48] The uncertainty related to the evaluation of scientific evidence and the translation of such evidence into legal evidence or arguments apparently constituted a problem for the court. The court could, therefore, not say with certainty what ecological damage was a result of human-inflicted changes and what derived from natural development. Also, the court did not seem to be certain what environmental damage could be averted by Hungary. It must be noted that the court said that it was not necessary to determine which side is scientifically better founded.[49]

As said before, the notion of acts of necessity as a justification for otherwise illegal acts are not to be analyzed further in this book. However, it raises interesting issues with regard to responses to environmental perils where legal remedies are few and far between and, in particular, when countermeasures are not available because the environmental interests are not protected by international law.

Endnotes

1. See also *Fourth Report 1992 (Arangio-Ruiz)*, Yearbook of the International Law Commission 1992, vol. II (part 1), p. 32, para. 82, where the possibility that development cooperation cannot be infringed by way of countermeasures is rejected.
2. In the *UN Charter*, the word "veto" is, however, not used. The text says that "concurring votes" of the permanent members of the Security Council are needed to adopt a resolution. When North Korea invaded South Korea in June 1950, the USSR representative in the Security Council had been boycotting the council to protest its decision to let Taiwan represent China as a permanent member. When the council voted on *Resolution 83 (1950)* (*Security Council Resolution no. 83 [1950]*, UN doc. S/1511, 27 June 1950), dealing with taking military action against North Korea, the USSR was not there to vote against or with the resolution. Instead of using the plain text of the charter, the council interpreted article 27 (rightfully or not) as requiring a direct veto to block a resolution. The resolution was therefore adopted in the absence of the Soviet representative and without the "concurring vote" the article requires. Since then, it has not been seriously disputed that a permanent member has to vote against a resolution to block it.
3. According to article 25 of the *UN Charter*, member states of the United Nations are required to accept and carry out resolutions adopted by the Security Council. If this duty is analyzed under the supremacy provision in article 103 of the *UN Charter*, it is most likely safe to assume that a Security Council resolution can override a right or obligation established by a treaty. See also *Questions of Interpretation and Application of the 1971 Montreal Convention Arising from the Aerial Incident at Lockerbie* (preliminary objections) (*Libyan Arab Jamahiriya v. United States of America*), International Court of Justice, judgment of 27 February 1998, 1998 I.C.J. 114.
4. *UN Charter*, article 24.
5. Ibid., article 39.
6. Ibid., article 41.
7. Ibid., article 42.
8. Ibid., article 94(2).
9. Ibid., article 24(2), italics added.
10. Ibid., article 1(1).
11. Ibid., article 51.

12. *2001 Draft Articles on State Responsibility*, (hereafter referred to as *2001 Draft Articles*), *Report of the International Law Commission on the Work of Its Fifty Third Session*, (23 April–1 June 2001 and 2 July–10 August 2001), UN doc. A/56/10, Yearbook of the International Law Commission 2001, (hereafter referred to as *ILC 2001 Report*), p. 26 et seq. The *2001 Draft Articles* and the work of the International Law Commission on this issue will be discussed later in this book.
13. *2001 Draft Articles*, article 25.
14. See part II, chap. 8.
15. *ILC 2001 Report*, p. 80.
16. *Report of the International Law Commission on the Work of Its Thirty Second Session (5 May to 25 July 1980)* (hereafter referred to as *ILC 1980 Report*), Yearbook of the International Law Commission 1980, vol. II, (part 2), p. 39, para. 15 of the commentary to article 33.
17. *ILC 1980 Report*, p. 39, para. 15 of the commentary to article 33.
18. Ibid.
19. Ibid.
20. *Gabcikovo-Nagymaros Project* (*Hungary v. Slovakia*), International Court of Justice, judgment of 25 September 1997, 1997 I.C.J. 7.
21. In January 1993, Czechoslovakia was divided into Slovak Republic and Czech Republic. The Danube River is now in the territory of the Slovak Republic.
22. *Treaty Concerning the Construction and Operation of the Gabcikovo-Nagymaros System of Locks*, concluded at Budapest on 16 September 1977, entered into force on 30 June 1978, (*Hungary-Czechoslovakia*), 1109 U.N.T.S. 235.
23. *Gabcikovo-Nagymaros Project*, 1997 I.C.J. 7, at 17–18, para. 15.
24. *Agreement Between the Government of the Czechoslovak Socialist Republic and the Government of the Hungarian People's Republic Concerning Mutual Assistance in the Construction of the Gabcikovo-Nagymaros System of Locks*, signed on 16 September 1977, entered into force on 30 June 1978, (hereafter referred to as the *Mutual Assistance Agreement*), 1724 U.N.T.S. 119.
25. *Mutual Assistance Agreement*, article 1(1).
26. *Protocol Amending the Agreement Between the Government of the Czechoslovak Socialist Republic and the Government of the Hungarian People's Republic Concerning Mutual Assistance in the Construction of the Gabcikovo-Nagymaros System of Locks*, concluded on 10 October 1983, entered into force on 7 February 1984, 1724 U.N.T.S. 124 (hereinafter called the *1983 Protocol*).

27. *Protocol Amending the Agreement Between the Government of the Czechoslovak Socialist Republic and the Government of the Hungarian People's Republic Concerning Mutual Assistance in the Construction of the Gabcikovo-Nagymaros System of Locks*, concluded and entered into force on 9 February 1989, 1724 U.N.T.S. 128 (hereinafter called the *1989 Protocol*).
28. *Gabcikovo-Nagymaros Project*, 1997 I.C.J. 7, at 31, para. 32.
29. Ibid. at 31–32, paras. 32–33.
30. Letter dated June 24, 1989, from the Hungarian deputy prime minister to the Czechoslovakian deputy prime minister, cited in *Gabcikovo-Nagymaros Project*, at 32, para. 35.
31. *Gabcikovo-Nagymaros Project*, at 34, para. 38.
32. Ibid., at 34, para. 38.
33. Ibid., at 34, para. 38.
34. Ibid., at 36, para. 40.
35. Ibid., at 35, para. 40.
36. Ibid., at 36, para. 40.
37. Ibid., at 36, para. 40.
38. Ibid., at 37, para. 44.
39. Ibid., at 40, para. 51.
40. Ibid., at 40–41, para. 52, italics added.
41. *Legality of the Threat or Use of Nuclear Weapons*, International Court of Justice, Advisory Opinion of 8 July 1996, 1996 I.C.J. 226.
42. *Gabcikovo-Nagymaros Project*, at 41, para. 53.
43. Ibid., at 41, para. 53.
44. Ibid., at 42, para. 54.
45. Ibid., at 42–43, para. 55.
46. Ibid., at 43, para. 55.
47. Report dated 23 June 1989, by the ad hoc committee of the Hungarian Academy of Science, cited in *Gabcikovo-Nagymaros Project*, at 44, para. 56.
48. *Gabcikovo-Nagymaros Project*, at 45–46, para. 57.
49. Ibid., at 42, para. 54.

Chapter 4

The Concept of Countermeasures and the Teachings of Highly Qualified Publicists

(a) Introduction

It is certainly true that the definition used in this book is not the only definition of countermeasures, although it is quite arguably the mainstream approach. Some would like to include measures that do not require a justification based on a prior breach. For example, Louis Henkin et al. seemed to include the concept of retorsion in the countermeasures doctrine. Retorsions are unilateral acts that are generally permissible without a prior breach by the offending state.[1] The decision to present a narrow definition of the concept of countermeasures is taken here for a simple reason: any intellectual discussion about the legality of countermeasures is of little use if taking the measures does not raise questions about their legality but merely about their political feasibility. The approach chosen in this book is, therefore, to make sense out of a concept that has sometimes been used to describe various unilateral measures taken by states in a somewhat inconsistent and unstructured manner.

Unilateral measures in one way or another have been known throughout history. It is reasonable to assume that people have, from the outset, used nonfriendly means to retaliate for wrongs committed against them. From the writing of Hugo Grotius on just war to the modern *International Law Commission Reports on State Responsibility*, scholars have tried to explain how states can react unilaterally to wrongs committed against them. Some of the early writers thought of reprisals or countermeasures as forcible,[2] as well as nonforcible measures. Because the former might not always be permitted under contemporary law of countermeasures, not all of their thoughts on the notion of reprisals are perfectly applicable to the discussion here on the countermeasures doctrine. Also, some forcible measures might require caution or preparation before such measures are taken, caution that might not be necessary if the nature of the countermeasures is less forceful than the author had in mind. This difference between the rules applicable to forcible and nonforcible reprisals is, nevertheless, small and blurred. Omer Yousif Elagab, a renowned scholar in this field, suggested:

> [T]he conditions governing the right of resort to forcible and nonforcible reprisals were basically the same. Thus, although forcible reprisals have been outlawed, the same conditions of legality that hitherto existed will continue to apply with equal validity to nonforcible reprisals.[3]

The tribunal in the *Air Service Agreement Case* seemed to agree with this line of thought when it suggested that a state can resort to countermeasures, "within the limits set by the general rules of international law pertaining to the use of armed force..."[4] Other writers have not suggested that there is a difference between the law of forcible and nonforcible countermeasures. A hint of an exception from that silence might be found in the arguments set fourth by the United States in the *Air Service*

Agreement Case where the United States argued that "when alternative means of satisfaction exist," the ban against countermeasures "applies to armed reprisals only."[5] The tribunal did not comment on this difference. Therefore, the writings of classical scholars will generally be seen as applicable to the contemporary doctrine of countermeasures, with the main exception that the use of force is not permitted.

An early writer, von Martens, explained the right of forcible means in the following way:

> In case of difference between two sovereigns, he who complains of a violation of his natural or positive rights, ought, unless his pretensions be of an indisputable nature, to begin by sufficiently proving those rights, as well as the violation of them complained of. This done, if he cannot obtain due satisfaction by amicable means, or if he foresees that it would be useless to try such means, he may, if he does not choose to renounce satisfaction altogether, have recourse to forcible means, whether it be in defence or pursuit of his rights. Forcible means are, indeed, in such case, the only ones that are left to sovereigns who acknowledge no judge or superior.[6]

This passage explains the concept in a manner comparable to the way chosen in this book. From the passage, one can point out three important attributes of the concept of countermeasures. First, the dispute in question has to be between states. This means that individuals acting in their own capacity cannot be seen as actors in the regime of countermeasures.

The second attribute inferred from Martens' passage is that the injured state has to be able to point at a violation of its rights. This is one of the core requirements for countermeasures, its primary element. Without it, countermeasures cannot be justified.

Martens' third attribute is that the injured state has to make an attempt to resolve the dispute by amicable means and has to have been unable to obtain satisfaction by such means. Countermeasures are generally a last resort or, at least, not the primary tool in foreign relations. Marten's suggestion is that in most cases a reasonable demand must be made before states take potentially destabilizing actions, such as countermeasures, and is arguably a part of the general duty to resolve international disputes by amicable means. However, as the United States argued in the *Air Service Agreement Case*,[7] the requirement of using all alternative means might be less strict when the countermeasures taken are less intrusive. As will be discussed further later, the contemporary countermeasures doctrine does generally not require injured states to exhaust all amicable means, such as negotiation, conciliation, or arbitration, prior to resorting to countermeasures. This difference between Marten's writings and the contemporary doctrine might also be traced to the principle of proportionality rather than to a distinction between forcible or nonforcible measures.

One must be mindful that countermeasures do not live in a vacuum. They form a part of a larger structure of unilateral measures taken by states during peacetime. It is helpful for the understanding of countermeasures to discuss and explain two different categories of measures that states take unilaterally against other states: retorsions and reprisals. As the concept of countermeasures is used here, retorsions fall outside of the concept. The term reprisals has, however, been used for responses to illegal acts of other states and, provided that they fulfill certain requirements, generally correspond to what contemporary international law calls countermeasures.[8]

Many authors have analyzed these two concepts in the flora of unilateral acts of states. A good number of them have added other types of acts, such as pacific blockade and intervention, as well as reciprocity.[9] Such qualification serves little purpose other than to discuss different methods of compelling states to change their behavior but does not address the difference between measures that have to be justified as being a response to a prior internationally wrongful act and those whose validity is measured in political terms.

(B) RETORSION

Among the modern authors who have discussed countermeasures is Zoller. In 1984, her book, *Peacetime Unilateral Remedies: An Analysis of Countermeasures*, shed an important light on the legal environment of nonforceful unilateral remedies. Zoller recognized the landscape from which countermeasures rise, that is, the framework of unilateral remedies. She discussed several types of peaceful unilateral remedies, including retorsions and reprisals. According to Zoller, retorsion is "an unfriendly but nevertheless lawful act by the aggrieved party against the wrongdoer."[10] Since it is a legal act per se, it does not require a special legal justification. It is, therefore, a response that can be used when one state treats another state in a manner less friendly than the latter had hoped.

Certainly, Zoller did not invent the concept of retorsion out of the blue; it is an offspring of earlier legal minds. In the late 1800s, Woolsey wrote that retorsion is an act resorted to when a nation "has failed in comity or politeness."[11] Hall wrote on similar notes and saw retorsion as an answer to an unfriendly but legal act of another state.[12] Despite the fact that retorsions are not illegal acts, Hall argued that "urgent necessity" was required for such acts.[13] It is, however, apparent from Hall's writings that the question of whether that requirement was fulfilled would be a political question rather than a legal one. Hall saw retorsions as reciprocal acts in nature. He argued that it "consists in treating the subject of the state giving provocation in an identical or closely analogous manner with that in which the subjects of the state using retorsion are treated."[14] Other authors do not generally require that retorsions be in a reciprocal form. Another early twentieth-century writer, Thomas E. Holland, wrote that retorsion referred to "retaliation for unequal or unfair treatment by a State still acting with its strict rights…as opposed to illegal acts."[15] Oppenheim defined retorsion as "the technical term for retaliation for discourteous, or unkind, or unfair and inequitable acts by acts of the same or a similar kind."[16] Retorsion is, therefore, according to Oppenheim, not to restore legal inequality but rather a response to political acts that "involve discourtesy or unfriendliness to another state."[17] Although Oppenheim did not see retorsion as a response to an illegal act, he seemed to assume that retorsion needs a special justification. However, such justification would not necessarily be a legal one but rather a political justification.[18] Henkin followed the majority of writers who view retorsion as a political act rather than a legal one.

According to Henkin, retorsion describes measures that generally are legally permissible but are taken in response of another state's offense.[19] Willem Riphagen, a former special rapporteur of the ILC, mentioned, as an example of retorsion, suspension of diplomatic relations. Since there is no international legal obligation to establish or maintain diplomatic relations, states can severe or discontinue such relations.[20]

The concept of retorsion is more and less harmonious in the literature, and most authors see the concept of retorsion in a manner similar to the one the previous text described. There are, however, slight variations.[21] Westlake, for example, who discussed the concept in relations to acts in war, saw retorsion as an act by an injured state "in order to compensate himself for the damage which he has suffered and to deter his enemy from continuing or repeating the offence."[22] Under this light, retorsion might be viewed as an act taken as a response to an illegal act and requires such justification. Such conclusion is most likely an incorrect description of Westlake's writings. First, Westlake was discussing the concept as a part of permissible responses to warlike acts as opposed how others have viewed the term as acts less of war. The underlying assumptions are, therefore, different, which could explain the different approach. Second, in a war situation, states can target and destroy people and property without being held legally responsible for the act. It is, therefore, not correct to assume that Westlake saw retorsion as a response to an illegal act. The act triggering the retorsion might just as well be legal under the law of war.

Up to a certain extent, retorsions live and breathe in the incompleteness of international law where no unambiguous rules of international law prohibit the remedy. As such, it is the unregulated behavior of states where only the rules of politics, comity, and international politeness are the proper measurement for the acceptability of the act.

(c) Reprisals

Unlike retorsions, which do not require a legal justification, reprisals are illegal acts of states that can be justified as being a response to an internationally wrongful act of another state. Reprisals are often seen as acts of self-help, aimed at restoring justice. Oppenheim saw a reprisal as an "act, otherwise illegal, performed by a State for the purpose of obtaining justice for an international delinquency by taking the law into its own hands."[23] Vattel explained reprisals on similar notes 200 years earlier. He wrote, "[w]hen a nation cannot obtain justice, either for a loss or an injury, it has a right to do itself justice."[24]

Zoller argued, "[r]eprisals involve nonperformance of an obligation under international law as a response to a breach of international law by another state."[25] Henkin et al. somewhat supported this approach in a popular textbook on international law, suggesting that reprisals refer to "a countermeasure that would be unlawful if not for the prior illegal act of the state against which they were taken."[26] Hall also wrote on similar notes, much earlier. He saw reprisals as a response to a violation of international law.[27] Reprisals consisted of seizure of property belonging to the offending state or individuals or suspension of treaty obligation with the intention to compel the offending state to grant redress.[28]

The difference between retorsions and reprisals is clear according to the previous descriptions. Retorsions do not live in the structured web of legal arguments but rather the less-structured world of political feasibility. This does certainly not mean that rules of the political game do not apply to reprisals. Just like retorsions, reprisals are an act of states and do, therefore, affect international relations. The unequal distribution of capabilities among the various states plays no less of a role when states decide on resorting to reprisals than when they resort to retorsions.

Some authors have distinguished between retorsions and reprisals in a different manner. For example, Woolsey argued in 1879 that reprisals differed from retorsion not because retorsions were by nature legal acts whereas reprisals are not but, rather, because reprisals are measures of coercive character while retorsions are of reciprocal nature.[29] This needs some further explanation. Woolsey argued that reprisals are coercive measures to compel the offending state to repair the wrong. Reprisals are, therefore, not the last say in the dispute but a method of getting the other state to act. Retorsions are, however, measures that "do injury to another, similar and equivalent to that which we have experienced from him."[30] Retorsions are, in Woolsey's mind, measures closely related to what modern writers would call reciprocity.[31] Lawrence wrote in a similar manner and argued that retorsions are measures taken "by adopting towards a state that is acting in an unfriendly, though peaceful manner, a similar line of conduct to that complained of in it."[32] Their approach to the concept of retorsion is presumably derived from Vattel's writings, spelled "retortion" in these, but he saw retorsion as the sovereign's right to respond to maltreatment of the citizens by another nation by declaring, "that he will treat the subjects of that nation in the same manner as his are treated."[33]

It is not clear whether retorsions, as these authors viewed the concept, can include measures of a reciprocal nature that would be illegal but for the prior violation by the offending state. Some of the actions qualified as retorsions by these authors are clearly legal by nature, although they are taken in response to an unfriendly act by another state. However, it is also possible to interpret the words of these authors as they were arguing that retorsions can be illegal acts per se but seek justification in the actions of the offending state. Hall, for example, contends that reprisals and retorsions are "prima facie acts of war."[34] Thus, to justify their use in peace times, exceptional reasons are required.[35]

In the minds of earlier authors, the concept of reprisals has an element of violence. Lawrence, for example, used the term "reprisals" as a generic one, describing pressure that is put on an offending state. He argued that reprisals are of a violent nature but still short of a war.[36] Holland wrote in the same manner and argued that the essence of reprisals "is that they are hostile acts committed in time of peace."[37] Hall argued that, although reprisals are violent in nature, their means are, in fact, peaceful, that is, they are an option short of war. Reprisals can, therefore, be justified as a proportionate alternative to acts of war.[38] Henkin et al. wrote that reprisals can be nonforcible, although, traditionally, they involve the use of force.[39] Zoller also recognized the connection between reprisal and violence. She accepted that reprisals were traditionally used in connection with violent countermeasures. However, the modern concept of reprisals is "a sort of a by-product of war…a kind of a legal conflict which has superseded war."[40] The modern concept of reprisals is, therefore, a sort of a war fought with legal arguments rather than by military means.[41]

It is not widely suggested that reprisals have to be reciprocal, that is, that the response has to be related to the same treaty or legal obligation that was violated. Hall, for example, argued that reprisals were normally reciprocal but this was not necessary.[42] In the writings of many others, the authors apparently assume that reprisals do not have to be reciprocal.[43] However, some authors have discussed the notion of reciprocal means of countermeasures. It is proper to give this line of thought a space next.

(d) Reciprocity

It can be argued that reciprocity is not an independent category of unilateral acts but rather a method of such acts. A rule of comity, not a legal obligation, relating to the mutual recognition of judgments and their enforcement is often based on reciprocity, that is, expectations that both states act in the same manner. If one state would refuse to recognize judgments from the other state, the latter one could respond in the same manner. This could be called retorsion by reciprocal means.[44] If the obligation to recognize judgments would be based on a treaty, the same measure could be called a reprisal by reciprocal means. Reciprocal retorsion describes a political act that is not a violation of a legal obligation or necessarily a response to such violation. It is, therefore, of little importance for the discussion here. Reprisal by reciprocal means can, however, have the characteristics of countermeasures, for example, if they are taken in response to illegal acts.

As Zoller argued, reciprocal measures build on the assumption that compliance of one state with the rules of international law hinges on the compliance of another.[45] Zoller saw reciprocity as either positive or negative. A positive reciprocity is a situation when a state does something for another state expecting that the benefiting state will react in the same manner. Reciprocity is negative when a state reacts to an already-taken measure.[46] The positive reciprocity is not important for the discussion on countermeasures because it addresses state actions that create a certain situation instead of reacting to a situation. Negative reciprocity is only relevant here so long as it is a response to an illegal act of another state. Zoller's discussion of reciprocity goes, therefore, well outside the borders of what this book calls countermeasures; she is clearly addressing a wide array of unilateral acts that have various objectives.

Zoller contended that there is a difference between reprisals and reciprocity. According to her, reciprocity allows derogation from a legal obligation similar to the obligation that the measure is supposed to counter. Reprisals, however, "consist in the non-performance of a different rule."[47] A support for this assertion, that reprisals cannot be reciprocal measures, is hard to find in the literature. For example, the term "reprisals" was used in the *Air Service Agreement Case* for an action that was clearly reciprocal in nature.[48]

Zoller argued that reciprocity can only be used to establish a legal situation. She took, as an example, the Iran hostage crisis in 1979 to 1980. The U.S. could not have taken Iranian diplomats hostage to retaliate for the hostage situation in Teheran.[49] In a similar manner, it can be argued that a state that has been injured because of radioactive waste dumped in its territorial sea cannot dump the equal amount of similar waste in the territorial sea of the wrongdoing state. Although both of these suggestions are correct,[50] Zoller might have been slightly inaccurate when she rejected reciprocity that establishes an illegal situation. In fact, Zoller mentioned an example of a reciprocity that results in an illegal situation. She wrote:

> If two states agree by a treaty of establishment to grant each other's nationals access to their courts without providing security for costs...and if one party does not comply with this provision, the other party may also not apply the same provision.[51]

Such a situation is generally illegal; it is a reciprocal violation of a treaty that is in force between these two countries. Also, it is perhaps more accurate to view the examples about the hostage crisis and the radioactive waste as an example of the limitation of reciprocity as unilateral measures. It is widely accepted that reciprocity, just as countermeasures, has to respect the inviolability of persons possessing diplomatic or consular rights.[52] An illegal arrest of persons protected by diplomatic immunity can, therefore, not be a justification for reciprocal measures that deprive another person in a similar situation of his or her freedom. The ban against the dumping of radioactive waste in the territorial waters of another state deals with a different issue. The restrictions of or ban against the dumping of radioactive waste is not only for the protection of rights belonging solely to the injured state, but also it is to protect the rights that are also vested in the global community. Therefore, such actions would not be designed to remedy the situation but rather aggravate it by creating a comparable and possibly irreversible harm to the interest that international law is designed to protect. The reciprocal measures would, therefore, adversely affect rights of states that are not accountable for the initial violation. Such reciprocal measure would, therefore, not qualify as countermeasures not only because it injures a third state but also because such action would be disproportionate. As stated earlier, these reciprocal reprisals are not illegal because they establish or maintain an illegal situation; they are illegal because they do not meet a number of other requirements for countermeasures.

Zoller argued that reciprocity had to be identical or equivalent to the initial offence.[53] Reciprocity by identity is to establish identical conditions between the two states. Since identical reciprocal measures are not always available or appropriate, the question arises whether nonidentical reciprocal measures can be taken. At first sight, it seems odd to discuss the concept of reciprocity without identical measures. Zoller agreed that under such circumstances it is more complicated to resort to reciprocity. However, she suggested that reciprocity could be appropriate measures if an equal value or equal meaning can be established.[54]

It is suggested here that reciprocity is not an independent category of unilateral measures. It is a method of such measures that can fall into both categories of unilateral acts of states, reprisals and retorsions. The concept has, therefore, little direct explanatory power for the discussion in this book. Nevertheless, by resorting to reciprocal measures the state so acting is greatly increasing the chances that the unilateral measures will be deemed proportional whether the measurement is of political or legal nature.

(E) OTHER VIEWS ON COUNTERMEASURES

Countermeasures have been discussed by more than renowned scholars on their own accounts. Domestic sources, such as the United States' *Restatement of the Law* and international sources, such as the work of the ILC, shed a valuable light on the concept of countermeasures.

The *Restatement of the Law* codifies certain views of American legal scholars about United States law, as well as international law. The restatement (third) deals with foreign relations law of the United States. Although not a legally binding document in the United States and certainly not internationally, the restatement has a great persuasive weight within the U.S. legal system and possibly wider effects. The restatement (third) deals with countermeasures and accepts that certain state actions of self-help are compatible with international law. The restatement reads:

1. Subject to Subsection (2), a state victim of a violation of an international obligation by another state may resort to countermeasures that might otherwise be unlawful, if such measures

   a. are *necessary* to terminate the violation or prevent further violation, or to remedy the violation; and
   b. are *not out of proportion* to the violation and the injured suffered.

2. The threat or use of force in response to a violation of international law is subject to prohibition on the threat or use of force in the *United Nations Charter*, as well as Subsection (1).[55]

According to the restatement, the right to take countermeasures that otherwise would be unlawful is constrained by three main conditions: the existence of a previous violation of international law, the necessity requirement, and the requirement of proportionality. It must be noted that the restatement refers to "countermeasures that might otherwise be unlawful,"[56] suggesting that countermeasures might be legal per se. However, to justify otherwise unlawful countermeasures, the condition of a prior breach has to be present. As stated before, this book uses the term "countermeasures" in a narrower meaning than in the restatement.

The ILC has published reports relevant to the discussion on countermeasures and their legality. The work of the ILC will be discussed and analyzed later in this book in relation to the different elements of countermeasures. It is, however, sensible to discuss briefly the basics of the ILC work on countermeasures in this chapter.

The ILC was established on 21 November 1947 by the UN General Assembly during its second session by *Resolution 174(II)*.[57] The commission had certain roots in Article 13(1) of the *UN Charter*, which ordered the General Assembly to "initiate studies and make recommendations for the purpose of…encouraging the progressive development of international law and its codification."[58] The ILC has drafted numerous conventions that have been signed and ratified. Among them are the *Vienna Convention on the Law of Treaties of 1969,*[59] *Vienna Convention on Diplomatic Relations of 1961,*[60] the Geneva conventions related to the law of the sea of 1958,[61] and the *Rome Statute of the International Criminal Court of 1998*[62] just to mention a few. Reports or draft articles produced by the ILC or its special rapporteurs are not binding international law as such but are, however, a significant authority on international law. They have been used by international bodies such as the International Court of Justice and WTO panels as evidence of the existence of certain rules of customary international law or as a support for interpretation of treaty obligations.[63]

As a part of the commission's extensive reports on state responsibility and the accompanied draft articles, the ILC has discussed countermeasures as one of the conditions that can exempt an act from wrongfulness.

The 52nd and 53rd sessions of the ILC[64] continued to produce a substantial volume of documents on state responsibility, many of which are highly relevant and authoritative for the discussion on countermeasures.[65] The final version of the *Draft Articles on State Responsibility,*[66] *2001 Draft Articles*, was produced during the 53rd session. They slightly amended the draft articles from the year before, the *2000 Draft Articles.*[67] Although recognized as a compromise description of the customary international law on state responsibility, it is unlikely that the draft articles will be incorporated in an international convention in the near future. Instead, it appears that they will be left to mature by practice of states and international tribunals.[68]

The concept of internationally wrongful acts is defined in Article 2 of the *2001 Draft Articles*. Under that definition, an international wrongful act of a state is a conduct consisting of either action or omission, which is attributable to the state under international law, and constitutes a breach of an international obligation of the state.[69] According to the *2001 Draft Articles*, the wrongfulness of such an act can, however, be precluded if certain conditions are met. These conditions are consent of the victim state,[70] force majeure,[71] and distress.[72] In addition to these conditions, self-defense,[73] the resort to countermeasures,[74] and the state of necessity[75] can preclude an act from wrongfulness.

Article 22 of the *2001 Draft Articles* has the title *Countermeasures in Respect of an Internationally Wrongful Act.* Its text is as follows:

> The wrongfulness of an act of a State not in conformity with an international obligation towards another State is precluded if and to the extent that the act constitutes a countermeasure taken against the latter State in accordance with chapter II of Part Three.[76]

Article 49 defines the object and limits of countermeasures. It reads:

1. An injured State may only take countermeasures against a State which is responsible for an internationally wrongful act in order to induce that State to comply with its obligations under Part 2.

2. Countermeasures are limited to the nonperformance for the time being of international obligations of the State taking the measures towards the responsible State.
3. Countermeasures shall, as far as possible, be taken in such a way as to permit the resumption of performance of the obligations in question.[77]

The use of the concept of countermeasures in these articles indicates that the ILC sees the rules governing countermeasures as a justification for an act that is otherwise illegal. The commission, therefore, follows the same line of thought as the definition used in this book.

The *2001 Draft Articles* set forth certain qualification for countermeasures. First, the measures have to meet the requirement of proportionality.[78] Second, the measures may not violate certain important rules of international law, such as the ban against use or threat of force, fundamental human rights and humanitarian principles, and peremptory norms, as well as rules pertaining to the inviolability of diplomats and consular agents.[79] Third, countermeasures must be preceded by certain procedural acts, such as a request from the injured state to the offending state to comply with its obligation and an offer from the injured states to negotiate.[80] These suggestions by the ILC are discussed in much more detail later, in particular in part II.

ENDNOTES

1. See Louis Henkin, Richard Crawford Pugh, Oscar Schachter, and Hans Smit, *International Law, Cases, and Materials*, 3rd ed., West Publishing Co., St. Paul, 1993, p. 570.
2. The term "forcible" is not used here for use of force only, which is not permitted as countermeasures, but also less intrusive measures not prohibited under the *UN Charter*.
3. Omer Yousif Elagab, *The Legality of Non-forcible Counter-measures in International Law*, Clarendon Press, Oxford, 1988, p. 68.
4. *Air Service Agreement of 27 March 1946* (*United States v. France*), arbitral decision of 9 December 1978, 54 *International Law Reports* 304 (1978), at 337 para. 81 (hereafter referred to as the *Air Service Agreement Case*), reprinted in 18 UNRIAA 417.
5. Ibid., at 320, para. 18.
6. Georg Friedrich von Martens, *A Compendium of the Law of Nations*, originally published in 1789 in French as *Précis du Droit des Gens Modernes de l'Europe*, translated by William Cobbet, Cobbet and Morgan, Pall-Mall, London 1802, pp. 271–272.
7. *Air Service Agreement Case*, at 320, para. 18.
8. The traditional concept of reprisals is as good as identical to the concept countermeasures as it is used by the International Law Commission in its work on state responsibility. See, for example, *Report of the International Law Commission of the Work of Its Forty Fourth Session*, International Law Commission Yearbook 1992, vol. II (part 2), UN doc. A/47/10, (hereafter referred to as *ILC 1992 Report*) pp. 21–22, paras. 139–140 and *Third Report on State Responsibility by Mr. Gaetano Arangio-Ruiz, Special Rapporteur*, Yearbook of the International Law Commission 1991, vol. II, (part 1), UN doc. A/CN.4/440 and Add. 1, (hereafter referred to as *Third Report 1991 (Arangio-Ruiz)*), p. 12, para. 27.
9. See, for example, L. Oppenheim, *International Law*, vol. II, 7th ed., p. 132; Elisabeth Zoller, *Peacetime Unilateral Remedies: An Analysis of Countermeasures*, p. 15; and Louis Henkin et al., *International Law*, p. 570.
10. Elisabeth Zoller, *Peacetime Unilateral Remedies: An Analysis of Countermeasures*, p. 5.
11. Theodore D. Woolsey, *Introduction to the Study of International Law*, 5th ed., Charles Scribner's Sons, New York, 1879, p. 188.

12. William Edward Hall, *A Treatise on International Law*, 6th ed., Clarendon Press, Oxford, 1909, p. 360.
13. Ibid., p. 361.
14. Ibid., p. 360.
15. Thomas Erskine Holland, *Lectures on International Law*, edited by Thomas Alfred Walker and Wyndham Legh Walker, Sweet & Maxwell, London, 1933, p. 229.
16. L. Oppenheim, *International Law*, vol. II, 7th ed., p. 134.
17. Ibid., p. 134.
18. Ibid., p. 134.
19. See Louis Henkin et al., *International Law*, p. 570.
20. *Fourth Report on the Content, Form, and Degrees of International Responsibility by Mr. Willem Riphagen, Special Rapporteur*, UN doc. A/CN.4/366 and add.1 (hereafter referred to as *Fourth Report 1983 (Riphagen)*), Yearbook of the International Law Commission 1983, vol. II (Part 1), para. 110, p. 21.
21. In addition to John Westlake, see Theodore D. Woolsey, *Introduction to the Study of International Law*, p. 188; T. J. Lawrence, *The Principles of International Law*, 4th ed., Macmillan and Co., London, 1911, pp. 334–335; and Emmerich de Vattel, *The Law of Nations* or *Principles of the Law of Nature*, book II, chap. XVIII, § 341, p. 349.
22. John Westlake, "War" in The *Collected Papers of John Westlake on Public International Law*, edited by L. Oppenheim, Cambridge University Press, Cambridge, 1914, p. 237, at 259.
23. L. Oppenheim, *International Law*, vol. II, 7th ed., p. 136.
24. Emmerich de Vattel, *The Law of Nations* or *Principles of the Law of Nature*, book II, chap. XVIII, § 339, p. 348.
25. Elisabeth Zoller, *Peacetime Unilateral Remedies: An Analysis of Countermeasures*, p. 42.
26. Louis Henkin et al., *International Law*, p. 570.
27. William Edward Hall, *A Treatise on International Law*, p. 360.
28. Ibid., pp. 360–361.
29. Theodore D. Woolsey, *Introduction to the Study of International Law*, pp. 188–189.
30. Ibid., p. 188.
31. See, for example, Elisabeth Zoller, *Peacetime Unilateral Remedies: An Analysis of Countermeasures*, p. 15.
32. T. J. Lawrence, *The Principles of International Law*, 4th ed., Macmillan and Co., London, 1911, pp. 334–335.

33. Emmerich de Vattel, *The Law of Nations* or *Principles of the Law of Nature, Applied to the Conduct and Affairs of Nations and Sovereigns*, Simeon Butler, Northampton, Massachusetts, 1820, book II, chap. XVIII, § 341, p. 349.
34. William Edward Hall, *A Treatise on International Law*, p. 361.
35. Ibid., p. 361.
36. T.J. Lawrence, *The Principles of International Law*, p. 334.
37. Thomas Erskine Holland, *Lectures on International Law*, p. 232.
38. See William Edward Hall, *A Treatise on International Law*, p. 363.
39. Louis Henkin et al., *International Law*, p. 570.
40. Elisabeth Zoller, *Peacetime Unilateral Remedies: An Analysis of Countermeasures*, p. 42.
41. In the Yearbook of the International Law Commission 1991, the commission recognized that many authors had noted that the commission had used the term "countermeasures" "as including the measures traditionally classified as reprisals..." (See *Third Report on State Responsibility by Mr. Gaetano Arangio-Ruiz, Special Rapporteur*, Yearbook of the International Law Commission 1991, vol. II, part 1, (hereafter referred to as *Third Report 1991* (Arangio-Ruiz)), UN doc. A/CN.4/440 and Add. 1, para. 27, p. 12.
42. William Edward Hall, *A Treatise on International Law*, p. 361.
43. See, for example, Elisabeth Zoller, *Peacetime Unilateral Remedies: An Analysis of Countermeasures*, p. 43 and Louis Henkin et al., *International Law*, p. 570.
44. Vattel, Woolsey, and Hall, for example, saw retorsion as reciprocal measures by nature. See Emmerich de Vattel, *The Law of Nations*, book II, chap. XVIII, § 341, p. 349; Theodore D. Woolsey, *Introduction to the Study of International Law*, p. 188; and William Edward Hall, *A Treatise on International Law*, p. 360.
45. Elisabeth Zoller, *Peacetime Unilateral Remedies: An Analysis of Countermeasures*, p. 15.
46. Ibid., pp. 19–20.
47. Ibid., p. 43.
48. See *Air Service Agreement Case*, at 319, para. 17 and at 337, para. 81.
49. Elisabeth Zoller, *Peacetime Unilateral Remedies: An Analysis of Countermeasures*, pp. 26–27.
50. Perhaps for other reasons than to what Zoller refers.
51. Elisabeth Zoller, *Peacetime Unilateral Remedies: An Analysis of Countermeasures*, p. 19.
52. See, for example, Hugo Grotius, *The Rights of War and Peace*, book III, chap. II, § VII, p. 313. The ILC suggested a comparable rule in article

50(2)(b) of the *2001 Draft Articles*. See also discussion on the objects of countermeasures in part II, chap. 10.

53. Elisabeth Zoller, *Peacetime Unilateral Remedies: An Analysis of Countermeasures*, pp. 19–20.
54. Ibid., p. 20.
55. *Restatement of the Law: The Foreign Relations Law of the United States*, vol. 2, American Law Institute Publisher, St. Paul, Minnesota, 1987 (hereafter referred to as *Restatement Third*), § 905, p. 380, italics added.
56. Ibid.
57. See Herbert W. Briggs, *The International Law Commission*, Cornell University Press, Ithaca, NY, 1965, p. 20 and *General Assembly Resolution 174(II)*, UN doc. A/519, 21 November 1947.
58. *UN Charter*, article 13(1).
59. *Vienna Convention on the Law of Treaties*, concluded at Vienna 23 May 1969, entered into force 27 January 1988, 1155 U.N.T.S. 331.
60. *Vienna Convention on Diplomatic Relations*, concluded at Vienna 18 April 1961, entered into force 24 April 1964, 500 U.N.T.S. 95.
61. *Convention on the Territorial Sea and the Contiguous Zone*, concluded at Geneva 29 April 1958, entered into force 10 September 1964, 516 U.N.T.S. 205; *Convention on the High Seas*, concluded at Geneva 29 April 1958, entered into force 30 September 1962, 450 U.N.T.S. 11; *Convention on Fishing and Conservation of the Living Resources of the High Seas*, concluded at Geneva 29 April 1958, entered into force 20 March 1966, 559 U.N.T.S. 285; and *Convention on the Continental Shelf*, concluded at Geneva 29 April 1958, entered into force 10 June 1964, 449 U.N.T.S. 311.
62. *Rome Statute of the International Criminal Court*, concluded at Rome 17 July 1998, entered into force 1 July 2002, doc. A/CONF.183/9.
63. See, for example, *Gabcikovo-Nagymaros Project*, 1997 I.C.J. 7, at 40, para. 50; *Application of the Convention on the Prevention and Punishment of the Crime of Genocide* (*Bosnia and Herzegovina v. Serbia and Montenegro*), International Court of Justice, judgment of 26 February 2007, para. 186; *Mexico—Tax Measures on Soft Drinks and Other Beverages*, report of the panel, WTO doc. WT/DS308/R (7 October 2005), paras. 5.54–5.55; *Brazil—Export Financing Programme for Aircraft*, decision by arbitrators under article 22(6) of *DSU* and article 4(11) of the *SCM Agreement* (*Agreement on Subsidies and Countervailing Measures*), WTO doc. WT/DS46/ARB (28 August 2000), pp. 14–15, para. 3.44; and *European Communities—Regime for the Importation, Sale, and Distribution of Bananas*, decision by arbitrators under article 22(6), WTO doc. WT/DS27/ARB (9 April 1999), p. 38, para. 6.16, note 67.

64. The 52nd session was held in Geneva from 1 May 2000 to 9 June 2000 and 10 July 2000 to 18 August 2000, and the 53rd from 23 April to 1 June and 2 July to 10 August 2001, also in Geneva.
65. See, for example, *Report of the International Law Commission on the Work of Its Fifty Third Session*, (23 April–1 June and 2 July–10 August 2001), UN doc. no. A/56/10, Yearbook of the International Law Commission 2001, (hereafter referred to as *ILC 2001 Report*); p. 1, *Fourth Report on State Responsibility by Mr. James Crawford, Special Rapporteur* (hereafter referred to as *Fourth Report 2001 (Crawford)*), UN doc. A/CN.4/517, 2 April 2001; and *Third Report on State Responsibility by Mr. James Crawford, Special Rapporteur* (hereafter referred to as *Third Report 2000 (Crawford)*), UN doc. A/CN.4/507, Add.1, Add.2, and Add.3, 18 July 2000.
66. *Draft Articles on State Responsibility*, reproduced in *ILC 2001 Report*, see supra endnote 12 of chap. 3, p. 26 et seq. (*2001 Draft Articles*). Although the draft articles are not legally binding, they are generally either evidence of customary international law or indicator of the legal trend.
67. See *Draft Articles on State Responsibility, Report of the Drafting Committee*, UN doc. A/CN.4/600, 21 August 2000 (hereafter referred to as *2000 Draft Articles*).
68. See James Crawford, "The Continuing Debate on a UN Convention on State Responsibility," *International and Comparative Law Quarterly* 54, no. 4 (2005), at 959; *Responsibility of States for Internationally Wrongful Acts*, report of the sixth committee, UN doc. A/62/446, 21 November 2007; and *Responsibility of States for Internationally Wrongful Acts*, resolution adopted by the General Assembly, UN doc. A/RES/62/61, 8 January 2008.
69. *2001 Draft Articles*, article 2.
70. Ibid., article 20.
71. Ibid., article 24.
72. Ibid., article 25.
73. Ibid., article 21.
74. Ibid., article 22.
75. Ibid., article 25.
76. Ibid., article 23.
77. Ibid., article 49.
78. Ibid., article 51.
79. Ibid., article 50.
80. Ibid., article 52.

Chapter 5

Countermeasures and International Tribunals

Disputes in which countermeasures have played a role have come before international tribunals, such as the International Court of Justice. The decisions of these tribunals have impact on the nature and the development of the concept of countermeasures. There are mainly five cases that provide foundations or inspiration for the countermeasures doctrine. These cases are the *Naulilaa Case* from 1928, (*Portugal v. Germany*), *Fishery Jurisdiction Case* from 1974 (*United Kingdom v. Iceland*), *Air Service Agreement of 27 March 1946* from 1978, (*United States v. France*), *United States Diplomatic and Consular Staff in Tehran* from 1980 (*United States v. Iran*), and *Gabcikovo-Nagymaros Project* from 1997 (*Hungary v. Slovakia*).

(a) *The Naulilaa Case*, 1928 (*Portugal v. Germany*)

In 1928, an arbitral tribunal set up under Articles 297–298[1] of the *Treaty of Versailles* decided on a claim from Portugal related to an attack on

Portuguese forts in Mozambique. The decision has been widely cited in the literature on countermeasures and provides a source of law relating to reprisals. Although the case deals with the legality of reprisals involving use of force, it provides important, however brief, guidelines on certain elements of countermeasures, namely, the requirement of a prior internationally wrongful act, the duty to notify the offending state, and the limits that the principle of proportionality sets for the exercise of countermeasures.

In August 1914, German troops attacked the Portuguese fort of Maziua in Mozambique, Africa, which was a Portuguese colony at the time. Germany later accepted responsibility for the attack, which was built on the misunderstanding that Portugal had declared war on Germany.[2] The incident was among a number of smaller events that raised the level of tension between German authorities in South West Africa and Portuguese authorities in Mozambique. During a violent confrontation at the Naulilaa Fort on 19 October 1914, apparently caused by language problems and inadequate translation, three German officers were shot and killed.[3] Even though the shooting took place in a Portuguese controlled territory, German authorities viewed the incident as a violation of the law of nations, justifying six attacks on Portuguese interests in the area as reprisals.[4] Portugal claimed damages resulting from the attacks. In reviewing the responsibility for the attacks, the tribunal rejected Germany's arguments that the Naulilaa incident justified the attacks and held Germany responsible.[5] The reasons that the tribunal gave were threefold. First, there had been no prior violation of international law justifying the attacks; second, Germany had not submitted a notice requesting reparation for the Naulilaa incident; and third, the attacks were disproportional to the Naulilaa incident.[6] With regard to the legality of the Naulilaa incident, the tribunal found the shootings of the German officers and detention to two others permissible under international law, mainly because the shootings took place on a Portuguese territory.[7] On the lack of notice, the tribunal said, "Reprisal is lawful only when preceded by notice which has yielded no satisfactory response."[8] Germany had transmitted a notice about the Naulilaa incident to German radiotelegraph stations that, according to their position, was intended to serve "as a notice to the Portuguese authorities to provide explanations and to hand over the two prisoners."[9] The tribunal held that even if these messages would have been intercepted by the Portuguese authorities, they would not have constituted as a sufficient intergovernmental notice for the purposes of reprisals.[10] Finally, the tribunal addressed what they called "an obvious lack of proportionality between the Naulilaa incident and the six acts of reprisals that followed it."[11]

Arguably, none of these three requirements for reprisals were established or altered by the *Naulilaa Case*; rather, they confirmed rules of reprisals established by earlier writers.

(B) *Fishery Jurisdiction Case*, 1974 (*United Kingdom v. Iceland*)

In a rather hazy legal environment, the government of Iceland decided in 1971 to extend its fishery zone to 50 nautical miles (nm) and to expel all foreign fishing vessels from the area. It was undisputed that foreign vessels had been fishing in the fishing grounds around Iceland for a long time. Furthermore, English, German, and Belgian fishermen depended on these fishing grounds for their survival and for the economic well-being of their costal regions.[12] Before the extension of the fishery zone entered into force in 1972, the British government, along with the German government, referred the matter to the ICJ.

Although the 1958 Conference on the Law of the Sea failed to settle the dispute about the breadth of the territorial sea, the 12-mile fishery zone was generally accepted at the time of the judgment in 1974.[13] In an exchange of notes between Iceland and the United Kingdom from 1961, the states agreed upon a 12-mile fishery zone around Iceland, measured from straight baselines. In return, Iceland agreed not to interfere with British fishing vessels in certain areas within the 12-mile limit in a period of 3 years from the adoption of the settlement.[14] The settlement was, however, not an agreement on the maximum breadth of the fishery zone, and in the notes from the Icelandic government, it seems obvious that the intention of the government was to extend the limits further seaward.[15] According to the settlement, the Icelandic government had to give the United Kingdom a 6-month notice of such extension and, "...in the case of a dispute in relation to such extension, the matter shall, at the request of either party, be referred to the International Court of Justice."[16]

In 1971, the Icelandic government terminated this settlement and revealed its intention to extend the fishery zone to 50 nm.[17] The United Kingdom objected, and on 14 April 1972, before the decision to extend became effective, it referred the dispute to the ICJ. The Icelandic government, however, creatively claimed that after the termination of the settlement, the clause regarding the jurisdiction of the court had also been terminated. However, in a decision of the court from 2 February 1973, the court held that it had jurisdiction and decided to deal with the merits of the case.[18]

One of the measures taken by the government of Iceland to expel foreign fishing vessels was to threaten the vessels with the use of force. In some instances, shots were fired from Icelandic Coast Guard vessels, resulting in damage to fishing vessels from the United Kingdom. In the memorial, the government of the United Kingdom asked the court to adjudge and declare

> that activities by the Government of Iceland, such as are referred to in Part V of this Memorial, that is to say, interference by force or the threat of force with British fishing vessels operating in the said area of the high seas, are unlawful and that Iceland is under an obligation to make compensation therefor to the United Kingdom.[19]

Arguably, these activities were either taken as countermeasures or as enforcement measures for conservation purposes in what the Icelandic government deemed to be within their fishery jurisdiction. Unfortunately, for the judicial discussion, the United Kingdom decided not to pursue this claim.[20]

In addition to the 12-mile fishery zone within which the coastal state could claim exclusive fishery jurisdiction, the court noted that the concept of preferential rights had emerged as a rule of customary international law.[21] The concept originated in a proposal from the Icelandic delegation at the Geneva Conference in 1958. In short, it gave preferential rights to a coastal state that was heavily dependent on fisheries. In a case of a catch limitation, "special consideration should be given to the coastal State whose population is overwhelmingly dependent on the fishing resources in its adjacent waters."[22] The court pointed out that the United Kingdom had "expressly recognized Iceland's preferential right in the disputed waters."[23] However, the intentions of the Icelandic government to exclude all other states from fishing within the 50 miles fishery zone exceeded the concept of preferential rights. These rights gave the coastal state certain priorities but no exclusive rights over the international waters outside the 12-mile fishery zone.[24] The court also looked into the fact that the United Kingdom had a long history of fisheries in the area in question and the economy of some towns in England would be seriously affected if the fisheries would come to an abrupt end.[25] Furthermore, the court took into account that the United Kingdom recognized that conservation of the fish stocks in the area was important not only to Iceland but also to themselves.[26]

Despite the apparent necessity to protect fish stocks in the Iceland area, the court held that Iceland's unilateral actions of prohibiting other states to fish within a 50-mile fishery zone was a violation of international law.[27] However, the United Kingdom did not have unlimited right to fish; it had to take into consideration Iceland's dependency on the fisheries and the conservation of the stocks. Then the court said, "[t]he most appropriate method for the solution of the dispute is clearly that of negotiation."[28]

Although the court admitted that Iceland had preferential rights and vital interests in the sustainability of the fisheries around the island, it did not address Iceland's actions as countermeasures in response to possible violations of its preferential rights. Wherever such approach would have taken this case, the extension of the fishery zone to 50 miles was clearly disproportional to any possible infringements of Iceland's preferential rights. Nevertheless, Iceland's actions against individual trawlers[29] could have been argued as countermeasures, especially if such measures were accompanied with an offer to negotiate a settlement in which Iceland's preferential rights would have been taken into consideration. Iceland, however, went well beyond what could have been considered as a proportional response to possible violations of its preferential rights.

(c) *Air Service Agreement Case*, 1978 (*France v. United States*)

In 1978, the United States and France submitted a dispute regarding the interpretation of the *Air Service Agreement* of 1946[30] to an arbitral tribunal. The facts were that in 1978 Pan Am commenced regular flights to Paris from Los Angeles via London. In London, the passengers changed planes and boarded a smaller plane that was to take them to Paris. French authorities claimed that this exchange of planes, referred to as changes of gauge, was a violation of the *Air Service Agreement*. On 3 May 1978, French authorities ordered a Pan Am plane to return to London after landing at Paris Orly Airport without allowing the passengers to leave the plane or the cargo to be unloaded.[31] On 4 May, the United States proposed that the dispute would be submitted to binding arbitration and Pan Am would be allowed to continue its flights to Paris. France had not responded to that offer when the Civil Aeronautics Board (CAB) issued an order on 9 May requiring Air France and Union de Transports Aériens (UTA) to file all their flight schedules to and from the United States. On 13 May, French authorities agreed in principle to refer the dispute to arbitration. However, they protested the CAB order of 9 May and suggested that negotiations would commence. On 31 May, CAB issued a second order to prevent Air France from operating its flights between Los Angeles and Paris via Montreal until Pan Am would be allowed to resume its flights.[32] The order, which was supposed to come into effect on 12 July, was never implemented because on 11 July the governments of the United States and France agreed to submit the case to an arbitral tribunal.[33]

The tribunal addressed, among other issues, the question if CAB's orders were a violation of international law or could be justified as countermeasures. France argued that since their decision to prohibit the Pan Am flights was not a violation of the *Air Service Agreement*, there was no justification for the reprisals.[34] In addition, France argued that countermeasures may only be used "in the absence of other legal channels to settle the dispute."[35] Furthermore, France argued that the countermeasures lacked the requirement under international law for formal request, that is, there was no formal request from the United States to suspend the flight ban against Pan Am.[36] Finally, French authorities argued that the CAB's orders were disproportionate for two reasons. First, they said that it was a suspension of uncontested rights as countermeasure against suspension of contested rights. Second, they claimed that the economic injury suffered by Air France far outweighed the Pan Am losses.[37]

The United States argued that its actions were "justified under the theory of reprisals and the law of treaties."[38] It rejected the argument that the existence of alternative means of solving the dispute precluded the right to take countermeasures as only relevant in cases of armed reprisals.[39] Also, under such theory, the injuring state would lack the incentive to cooperate and expedite the arbitration proceedings.[40] The United States also rejected France's argument that the measures were disproportionate.[41]

The tribunal laid down its view of the basic rules related to countermeasures. It wrote, "[i]f a situation arises which, in one State's view, results in the violation of an international obligation by another State, the first State is entitled...to affirm its rights through 'counter-measures'."[42] The passage, "in one State's view," indicates that there does not have to be a real violation to invoke the right to countermeasures, that is, that the state's view is sufficient. Although the tribunal does not elaborate further on this issue, an arbitrary decision to view another state's act as a violation does barely fulfill the requirement of prior breach. The "state's view" has to be, as a minimum, based on a reasonable interpretation of international law.[43]

After these preliminary observations, the tribunal addressed the principle of proportionality. It wrote "that judging the 'proportionality' of counter-measures is not an easy task and can at best be accomplished by approximation."[44] The tribunal held that this evaluation would not be complete by only comparing the injury suffered by the airlines. At stake were agreements on a worldwide network of transportation by air. The tribunal clearly saw the alleged violation by French authorities as a part of a much bigger context, that is, the importance of uninterrupted air service. The tribunal argued that in the absence of evidence "sufficient to affirm or reject the existence of proportionality…the Tribunal must be satisfied with a very approximative appreciation."[45] It accordingly accepted the view of the United States that the countermeasures were proportionate.[46] Since there was no *prime facie* evidence of a lack of proportionality, the tribunal, somewhat, shifted the burden of proof onto France.[47] The tribunal's method of evaluating proportionality is not beyond question. It seemed to look at the seriousness of the violation from a very broad perspective, that is, the interests of free air transportation, instead of focusing on the injury suffered by the airlines or the interests of the states resulting from the discontinuance of these particular flights. The dissenting opinion supported this view but added that the tribunal should also have looked into the dispute between the states as a whole instead of focusing on the dispute as was presented to the tribunal.[48] The issue of proportionality will be discussed further in part II, chapter 10.

The tribunal next addressed the question of if the presence of alternative means of solving the dispute, such as negotiation or judicial proceedings, precluded the injured state from resorting to countermeasures. The tribunal answered this question in two steps. It first addressed the effect of negotiation or consultation and then discussed the effects of access to judicial proceedings.

The Air Service Agreement provided for continuing consultation between the parties. The question was, therefore, if the duty to consult meant a prohibition against countermeasures. On that issue, the tribunal said it did "not consider that either general international law or the provisions of the Agreement allow [the tribunal] to go that far."[49] The tribunal believed that countermeasures should be made use of in order to restore equality between the disputing states and encourage negotiation to solve the dispute. Countermeasures should be "a wager on the wisdom, not on the weakness of the other Party."[50] It continued and said it believed it is not possible "to lay down a rule prohibiting the use of counter-measures during negotiations, especially where such counter-measures are accompanied by an offer for a procedure affording the possibility of accelerating the solution of the dispute."[51]

The tribunal was more hesitant when it considered the effects of an access to judicial proceedings on the right to countermeasures. As a starting point, the tribunal did not rule out the possibility that a system of dispute resolution could erase the right to take countermeasures. The tribunal wrote:

> If the proceedings form part of an institutional framework ensuring some degree of enforcement of obligations, the justification of counter-measures will undoubtedly disappear, but owing to the existence of that framework rather than solely on account of the existence of arbitral or judicial proceedings as such.[52]

This can be understood as saying that the enforcement mechanism of the particular regime is a decisive factor whether countermeasures are acceptable or not. The tribunal continued and distinguished between the time when a party has agreed to submit a case to a tribunal and the time when the case is actually before the tribunal. The period preceding the point when the case is before a tribunal is a negotiation period. Therefore, the rule that negotiations do not preclude a state from taking countermeasures is still in effect. The tribunal accordingly stated, "[I]t must be conceded that under present-day international law States have not renounced their right to take countermeasures in such situations."[53]

The tribunal's discussion does not clarify what rules apply from the time the case is before the tribunal and until the tribunal is ready to act by means of interim measures or a final decision. However, it suggested that when a tribunal is ready to act and to the "extent that the tribunal has the necessary means to achieve the objectives justifying countermeasures, it must be admitted that the right of the Parties to initiate such measures disappears."[54]

The tribunal made an interesting point by suggesting that by submitting the dispute to the arbitration, the United States did not renounce their right to take countermeasures. The tribunal said that the implementation of the decision of a tribunal might take time and the United States was taking steps to expedite the proceedings of the arbitration. The tribunal held that under these circumstances the United States had the right to issue the order in question, that is, to prohibit Air France from operating flights between Paris and Los Angeles.[55]

(d) The *Hostage Case*, 1980 (*United States v. Iran*)

On 4 November 1979, the United States embassy in Teheran was taken over by a group of armed people. The Iranian government was not directly involved in the taking of the premises but supported the actions afterward, as well as the continuing detention of the personnel of the embassy, including diplomatic staff.[56]

The United States brought a case before the International Court of Justice on 29 November, claiming that Iran, inter alia, violated a number of articles of the 1961 *Vienna Convention on Diplomatic Relations*, the *1963 Vienna Convention on Consular Relations*, and the *Treaty of Amity, Economic Relations, and Consular Rights* between the United States and Iran.[57]

This case is interesting for the analysis of countermeasures for two reasons. First, it briefly, not explicitly though, looked at the hostage taking as a possible countermeasure against alleged United States espionage or other illegal activities by members of its mission to Iran. Second, the court discussed the rescue operation undertaken unilaterally by the United States as countermeasures. It viewed the rescue operation in an unfavorable light for two reasons. First, the case was under deliberation by the court while it took place; and second, the court had ordered the parties to refrain from any action that might aggravate the situation.

Iran did not recognize the competence of the court to handle the dispute and did not file a memorial. However, the government of Iran submitted a letter explaining its view, claiming that this dispute before the court was merely

> marginal and secondary aspect of an overall problem, one such that it cannot be studied separately, and which involves, inter alia, more than 25 years of continual interference by the United States in the internal affairs of Iran, the shameless exploitation of our country, and numerous crimes perpetrated against the Iranian people, contrary to and in conflict with all international and humanitarian norms.[58]

The court dismissed Iran's assertion that underlying issues outside the competence of the court could preclude the jurisdiction of the court of the issue brought before it. The court said, "no provision of the Statute or Rules contemplates that the Court should decline to take cognizance of one aspect of a dispute merely because that dispute has other aspects, however important."[59]

With regard to jurisdiction, the court found that optional protocols to the *Vienna Conventions on Diplomatic Relations* and on *Consular Relations and the Treaty of Amity, Economic Relations, and Consular Rights* provided sufficient basis for jurisdiction.[60] Previously, the court had addressed the question on the effects of the Security Council resolution regarding the same dispute on the jurisdiction and found that it would not be an "obstacle to the exercise of the Court's jurisdiction."[61]

The court next addressed the responsibility for the actual taking of the embassy and the hostages and found that there was not sufficient information linking the militants to the government of Iran. Iran was accordingly not internationally responsible for the militants' actions of the actual taking of the embassy.[62] However, the court held Iran responsible for not protecting the embassy, including the staff and the archives, and not trying to persuade the militants to abort their operation.[63]

The second phase of the case, the continuing detention of the hostages and occupation of the embassy, was imputed to the Iranian government. The Ayatollah Khomeini had not only approved the militant actions but also encouraged the continuance of them. He also declared that the hostages would be detained until the United States handed over the former Shah, who was in the United States for medical treatment.[64] The court wrote that

> [t]he approval given to these facts by the Ayatollah Khomeini and other organs of the Iranian State, and the decision to perpetuate them, translated continuing occupation of the Embassy and detention of the hostages into acts of that State. The militants, authors of the invasion and jailers of the hostages, had now become agents of the Iranian State for whose acts the State itself was internationally responsible.[65]

According to the court, Iran was, therefore, not only responsible because it failed to protect the embassy and its diplomatic and consular staff but also for the continuing holding of the hostages.

After establishing state responsibility for the situation, the court discussed the substance of the breaches. In short, it found that Iran had violated numerous *Articles of the Vienna Conventions of 1961 and 1963* and the *Treaty of Amity, Economic Relations, and Consular Rights*.[66]

The court then revisited the question of the effects of the underlying political dispute, that is, the 25 years of what Iran called "shameless exploitation of our country."[67] This time it was not for jurisdictional purposes; it could, rather, be interpreted as an analysis of Iran's actions as countermeasures against the alleged United States activities in Iran. The court said that Iran had not provided satisfactory evidence for their assertion that the United States had committed acts "contrary to and in conflict with all international and humanitarian norms."[68] The court went on and said that even if these allegation where true, it could not accept that they could be regarded as a justification for Iran's actions "because diplomatic law itself provides the necessary means of defence against, and sanction for, illicit activities by members of diplomatic or consular missions."[69] Therefore, the remedy provided for in Article 9 of the *Vienna Convention of 1961* and Article 23(1) and 23(4) of the *Vienna Convention of 1963*, that is, to declare a member of a mission a *persona non grata*, are sufficient to protect the receiving country's interests.

If Iran believed that the United States' mission was involved in such illegal activities as it publicly accused it of, a recourse to these remedies would have been the appropriate action.

Although the court did not explicitly address this question as a question of countermeasures, the decision indicates that if a less intrusive remedy is available and sufficient to address the problem at hand, the injured state cannot resort to countermeasures.[70] This approach might also have been influenced by the fact that the measures were directed against diplomatic staff against which, according to classical as well as contemporary scholars, countermeasures cannot be directed.[71]

The other issue relevant to countermeasures is the court's reaction to the rescue operation that the United States attempted in April 1980, when the text of the court's judgment was being finalized. The court said that it

> feels bound to observe that an operation undertaken in those circumstances, from whatever motive, is of a kind calculated to undermine respect for the judicial process in international relations; and to recall that in paragraph 47, 1 B, of its Order of 15 December 1979 the Court had indicated that no action was to be taken by either party which might aggravate the tension between the two countries.[72]

The court did not discuss the legality of the rescue mission, but it indicated that unilateral measures, such as this one, are utterly inappropriate while the case is under deliberation by the court. The latter part of its concerns derives from its express order that the parties should refrain from unilateral acts that would adversely affect the situation. These viewpoints have a bearing on the issue on the effects of submitting a case to a judicial dispute settlement, that is, how it affects the right to resort to countermeasures.

(E) The *Gabcikovo-Nagymaros Project*, 1997 (*Hungary v. Slovakia*)

The facts of this case were discussed previously in relation to acts of necessity. The case is also relevant for the countermeasures doctrine because of certain unilateral measures taken by Czechoslovakia. After Hungary decided to suspend its part of the Gabcikovo-Nagymaros project, Czechoslovakia prepared to continue with its part of the project with the changes consequential to the suspension by Hungary. This new plan was called "Variant C."[73] The court had, in this case, the task of ruling whether these unilateral actions of Czechoslovakia were a violation of international law.

Although Czechoslovakia offered negotiation, Hungary required that Czechoslovakia suspend the work on Variant C until the parties found an alternative solution. It was, however, unacceptable for Czechoslovakia to suspend the project while the countries conducted negotiations.[74] According to Variant C, the Danube was diverted at Cunovo, where both riverbanks were on Slovak territory,[75] some 6 miles upstream of the proposed Hungarian Dunakiliti Dam.[76] In addition, the plan included an overflow dam at Cunovo, a levee between the dam and a bypass canal, and a ship lock, as well as two hydroelectric power plants with a total capacity of 178 GWh.

Hungary claimed that Variant C violated the *1977 Treaty*, other treaties on water management, and general international law.[77] Furthermore, it claimed that an attempt to justify Variant C as countermeasures had to fail, especially because of the requirements of proportionality.[78]

Slovakia argued that their actions were lawful under a "principle of approximate application,"[79] that Hungary's actions made it impossible to implement the *1977 Treaty* according to its text, and that Variant C was the closest possible match to the original solution.[80] Slovakia also claimed it was under an obligation to mitigate its damage suffered by the Hungarian noncompliance with the *1977 Treaty* and was, therefore, obliged to implement Variant C.[81] Finally, Slovakia argued that Variant C could be justified as countermeasures.[82]

The court quickly rejected the approximate application argument and the duty to mitigate damage as arguments for the legality of Variant C. On the former argument, the court said "it could by definition only be employed within the limits of the treaty in question. In the view of the Court, Variant C does not meet that cardinal condition with regard to the *1977 Treaty*."[83] In rejecting the latter argument, the court wrote that

"While this principle might...provide a basis for the calculation for the damages, it could not, ...justify an otherwise wrongful act."[84]

After finding that implementing Variant C was inconsistent with international law, the court addressed the argument of countermeasures. In short, it held that the implementation of Variant C was incompatible with the principle of proportionality. In the court's view, Variant C was in line with certain requirements for countermeasures. First, it was taken in response to an internationally wrongful act and was directed against the state committing that act.[85] Second, Slovakia called upon Hungary to discontinue the wrongful conduct.[86] The justification of Variant C as countermeasures ran into trouble when it came to proportionality, that is, requirement to "commensurate with the injury suffered, taking account of the rights in question."[87] Citing the *River Oder Case* of 1929,[88] modern development of international law and the adoption of the *Convention on the Law of the Non-Navigational Uses of Watercourses of 1997*,[89] the court emphasized the importance of the use of navigable rivers and the equal right of the riparian states.[90] Then the court rejected the Slovak defense based on countermeasures with these words:

> The Court considers that Czechoslovakia, by unilaterally assuming control of a shared resource, and thereby depriving Hungary of its right to an equitable and reasonable share of the natural resources of the Danube—with the continuing effects of the diversion of these waters on the ecology of the riparian area of the Szigetkoz—failed to respect the proportionality which is required by international law.[91]

The *Gabcikovo-Nagymaros Project* is perhaps not a good example for unilateral actions of states related to environmental issues. The dispute was related to a variety of other considerations. The project evolved into an ideological issue when the socialist rule in Eastern Europe began to crumble. Protests against the project might have been a guise for protests against the government and an expression of the underlying political tension. One author said, "In fact, the environmental movement provided one of the few tolerated avenues for opposition to the Communist government."[92] In the spring of 1989, the Hungarian government already had expressed its support for a multiparty government, and environmental issues were soon on every party's platform.[93] In addition, the Danube was a part of the identity of the Hungarian people as the "inspiration for...Hungarian ballades, and folk tales for centuries."[94] The dispute has also its ethnic aspects and may be considered as an expression of ethnic tensions between the Hungarians and Slovaks.[95] The dispute over the dams of Danube was both complex and deep and reached well beyond the four corners of an ecological issue.

Endnotes

1. Articles 297–298 of the *Treaty of Versailles* dealt with property claims against Germany related to their activities in World War I and the determination of such claims.
2. *The Naulilaa Case* (*Portugal v. Germany*), arbitral decision of 31 July 1928, in *Landmark Cases in International Law*, edited by Eric Heinze and Malgosia Fitzmaurice, Kluwer Law International, London, The Hague, Boston, 1998, p. 1266, at 1270. See also original in French in *United Nations Reports of International Arbitral Awards* (*UNRIAA*), vol. II, p. 1011 (1928), at 1017.
3. Ibid., pp. 1275–1276, *UNRIAA*, at 1022–1023.
4. Ibid., p. 1279, *UNRIAA*, at 1026.
5. Ibid., pp. 1279–1280, *UNRIAA*, at 1027.
6. Ibid., pp. 1279–1280, *UNRIAA*, at 1027.
7. Ibid., p. 1280, *UNRIAA*, at 1027.
8. Ibid., p. 1280, *UNRIAA*, at 1027, ("La représaille n'est licite que lorsqu'elle a été précédée d'une sommation restée infructueuse.").
9. Ibid., p. 1279, *UNRIAA*, at 1026.
10. Ibid., pp. 1280–1281, *UNRIAA*, at 1027–1028.
11. Ibid., p. 1281, *UNRIAA*, at 1028, ("disproportion évidente entre l'incident de Naulilaa et les 6 actes de représailles qui l'ont suivi.").
12. *Fishery Jurisdiction Case* (*United Kingdom v. Iceland*), International Court of Justice, judgment of 25 July 1974, 1974 I.C.J. 3, at 28–29, paras. 64–65.
13. Ibid., at 23, para. 52.
14. Ibid., at 13, para. 26.
15. See Ibid.
16. A note from the Icelandic government, cited in *Fishery Jurisdiction Case*, at 13.
17. *Fishery Jurisdiction Case*, at 14, para. 27.
18. Ibid., at 22, para. 46.
19. Ibid., at 7, para. 11.
20. Ibid., at 7, para. 12.
21. Ibid., at 23, para. 52.
22. Ibid., at 24, para. 55.
23. Ibid., at 24, para. 54.

24. Ibid., at 27, para. 62.
25. Ibid., at 28, paras. 62–64.
26. Ibid., para. 66.
27. Ibid., at 29, para. 67.
28. Ibid., at 31, para. 73.
29. Provided, however, that obligations of article 2(4) of the *UN Charter* are not affected.
30. *Air Service Agreement between the United States and France*, concluded 27 March 1946, 139 U.N.T.S. 253, T.I.A.S. 1507, amended by *Exchange of Notes* of 5 April 1960, 458 U.N.T.S. 292, T.I.A.S. 5135.
31. *Air Service Agreement Case*, see supra endnote 4 of chap. 4, 54 I.L.M. 340 (1978), at 310, para. 4.
32. Ibid., at 310–311, paras. 5–8.
33. Ibid., at 311, para. 9.
34. Ibid., at 319, para. 17.
35. Ibid.
36. Ibid.
37. Ibid.
38. Ibid., at 320, para. 18.
39. Ibid.
40. Ibid.
41. Ibid., at 320, para. 18.
42. Ibid., at 337, para. 81.
43. See, for example, *Gabcikovo-Nagymaros Project*, 1997 I.C.J. 7, at 40, para. 51, where the court said that "the State concerned is not the sole judge of whether [conditions justifying act of necessity] have been met." See also part II, chap. 8.
44. *Air Service Agreement Case*, at 338, para. 83.
45. Ibid., at 338, para. 83.
46. Ibid., at 338, para. 83.
47. Ibid.
48. Ibid., at 344.
49. Ibid., at 339, para. 89.
50. Ibid., at 339–340, para. 91.
51. Ibid., at 340, para. 91.
52. Ibid., at 340, para. 94.
53. Ibid., at 340, para. 95.
54. Ibid., at 340, para. 96.
55. Ibid., at 341, paras. 97–99.

56. *United States Diplomatic and Consular Staff in Tehran*, 1980 I.C.J. 3, at 35, para. 74.
57. Ibid., at 6, para. 8.
58. Ibid., at 8, para. 10.
59. Ibid., at 19, para. 36.
60. Ibid., at 24–28, paras. 45–55.
61. Ibid., at 20–24, paras. 39–44.
62. Ibid., at 29, para. 58.
63. Ibid., at 32–33, paras. 67–68.
64. Ibid., at 34, para. 73.
65. Ibid., at 35, para. 74.
66. Ibid., at 35–37, paras. 76–79.
67. Ibid., at 37. para. 81.
68. Ibid., at 37, para. 81.
69. Ibid., at 38, para. 83.
70. It might be argued that the court avoided discussing the overall alleged United States' "shameless exploitation" of Iran as a justification for hostage taking as countermeasures. The remedies provided for in the Vienna conventions of 1961 and 1963 only address remedies against inappropriate behavior of diplomatic and consular staff but not other types or levels of the alleged exploitation. If Iran had managed to prove the alleged exploitation and that it violated the *Treaty of Amity, Economic Relations, and Consular Rights*, the question arises if it could have resorted to other types of countermeasures not directed against diplomatic or consular staff. This is in line with the conclusion of the tribunal in the *Air Service Agreement Case*, where the tribunal hinted that amicable remedies that are narrowly defined might not preclude a state from taking unilateral measures with regard to issues not addressed by the amicable remedy. (See *Air Service Agreement Case*, at 340, para. 96.)
71. See Hugo Grotius, *The Rights of War and Peace*, book III, chap. II, § VII, p. 313 and a comparable rule suggested by the ILC in article 50(2)(b) of the *2001 Draft Articles*.
72. *United States Diplomatic and Consular Staff in Tehran*, at 43, para. 93.
73. *Gabcikovo-Nagymaros Project*, 1997 I.C.J. 7, at 25, para. 23.
74. See Ibid., at 49, para. 64.
75. Ibid., at 49, para. 64.
76. Ibid., at 25, para. 23.
77. Ibid., at 52, para. 70.
78. Ibid., at 52, para. 71.

79. Ibid., at 51, para. 67.
80. Ibid., at 51, para. 67.
81. Ibid., at 51–52, para. 68.
82. Ibid., at 52, para. 69.
83. Ibid., at 53, para. 76.
84. Ibid., at 55, para. 80.
85. Ibid., at 55–56, para. 83.
86. Ibid., at 56, para. 84.
87. Ibid., at 56, para. 85.
88. *Territorial Jurisdiction of the International Commission of the River Oder*, Permanent Court of International Justice, judgment of 10 September 1929, 1929 P.C.I.J. (ser. A) no. 23.
89. *Convention on the Law of the Non-Navigational Uses of Watercourses*, adopted by a United Nations General Assembly Resolution, UN doc. A/RES/51/229, 8 July 1997. Not yet in force.
90. *Gabcikovo-Nagymaros Project*, at 56, para. 85.
91. Ibid., at 56, para. 85.
92. Elizabeth F. Brown, "In Defense of Environmental Rights in East European Constitutions," *University of Chicago Law School Roundtable* 1 (1993), at 196.
93. Ibid., at 196.
94. Ida L. Bostian, "Flushing the Danube: The World Court's Decision Concerning the Gabcikovo Dam," *Colorado Journal of International Environmental Law and Policy* 9 (1998), at 401.
95. Ibid., at 412–413.

Chapter 6

Final Remarks

The concept of sovereignty is perhaps a mistaken one, and perhaps its role in the international system is over bloated. Nevertheless, the perception of the system that this book takes as reality is that sovereignty is a shaping force in international relations, a resilient restraint on the development of international law into spheres that still are under the authority and control of the independent states. The assumption is that state sovereignty is the basis for its right to take unilateral measures, whereas international law limits it. In the case of countermeasures, this remains true but with an important variation, namely, that the doctrine of countermeasures, a doctrine of international law, permits states to go beyond the limits of sovereignty and exercise rights it otherwise would not have. These extended sovereign rights, if they may be called so, are dependent upon certain conditions. These conditions, which were briefly discussed in the introduction and will be more thoroughly analyzed in part II, contain a primary element—the requirement of a prior violation of a state of an international obligation it owes to the state taking the measures. However, because international environmental obligations are often weak and not based on concise legal grounds, the right to resort to countermeasures, the right to go beyond the limits of sovereignty, becomes problematic.

In this part, it is suggested that countermeasures are among various unilateral measures taken by states in the absence of an effective remedy provided by the international system. The writings of scholars who have focused on unilateral measures indicate that there is a consensus, perhaps even a broad one, on the existence of the main elements of the concept of countermeasures; although, as the next part illustrates, their precise formulation remains disputed. Scholars have distinguished not only between various categories of unilateral measures, but also the nature of the measures and their declared objectives. What is relevant, however, for the debate here is whether the measures taken require a special justification to be legal and if that answer is in the negative, such measures do not fall under the concept of countermeasures as it is presented here. Such measures might then, at most, require a political justification, but the determination whether the measures taken are, in fact, politically justifiable is outside the scope of this book. Further, measures that seek their direct justification to reasons other than a prior violation of an international obligation fall outside the concept. Thus, sanctions authorized by the Security Council are not countermeasures, even if the reasons for them are violations of international obligations because their immediate justification is sought in the *UN Charter* and the authority of the council to adopt resolutions binding upon all UN member states. As an example, the sanctions taken by the United Kingdom and the United States against Libya in relation to the latter's role in the Lockerbie bombing could have been seen as countermeasures until the Security Council confirmed them by a resolution.[1] After the adoption of the resolution, the sanctions did not need to be justified by any other reason.

The review of selected international cases where countermeasures have been relevant clearly shows that the concept of countermeasures forms a part of customary international law. It also shows that the conditions for the legality of countermeasures are strict. This is understandable as countermeasures are per se violations of international obligations but justified by the special circumstances surrounding the taking of such measures. The cases reviewed suggest that the concept of countermeasures can be dissected into its elements. The first element and what seems to be an absolute condition for the taking of countermeasures is the presence of a prior violation of an international obligation attributable to the state against which the countermeasures are directed. The second element is that prior to the taking of countermeasures, the injured state has to direct a request to the offending state demanding it ceases the illegal situation. The third element is that countermeasures have to comply with the principle of proportionality, that is, the measures taken have to "commensurate with the injury suffered, taking account of the rights in question."[2] The cases reviewed do not suggest that ongoing negotiations preclude the right to take countermeasures. The same goes for access to a binding third party dispute settlement mechanism, although such procedures could in some circumstances preclude the rights to countermeasures if the body is about to act and such actions are likely to have similar effects as proportionate countermeasures might have.

The following part focuses on analyzing the aforementioned elements of countermeasures.

ENDNOTES

1. *Security Council Resolution no. 883 (1993)*, UN doc. S/RES/883 (1993), 11 November 1993.
2. *Gabcikovo-Nagymaros Project*, at 56, para. 85.

Part II

The Elements of Countermeasures: Requirement and Obstacles

In vain does nature prescribe to nations, as well as to individuals, the care of their self-preservation, and of advancing their own perfection and happiness, if it does not give them a right to preserve themselves from every thing that can render this care ineffectual.

—Emmerich de Vattel, *The Law of Nations* (1757)[1]

CHAPTER 7

INTRODUCTION AND ORGANIZATION

As was discussed in part I, the international system allows states to resort to unilateral measures to protect their own interests, provided that certain conditions are met. These conditions, referred to here as the elements of countermeasures, include the requirement of a prior breach as a justification of countermeasures, certain actions that the injured state has to take prior to resorting to countermeasures, and compliance with the principle of proportionality, as well as conditions that might preclude countermeasures, such as access to an effective remedy.

The elements of countermeasures are not universally agreed upon. As countermeasures live in what some would call a grey area of self-help, a number of issues related to the taking of such measures are subject to controversy. Opinions of states are likely to differ; strong states often prefer little restriction on the taking of countermeasures, whereas weaker states would prefer the opposite. It is the debate between the hawks and the doves. In addition to the writings of scholars and international cases, this part relies heavily on the work of the ILC relating to state responsibility. It is suggested here that the debate within the ILC, including comments that the commission solicited from governments and reports of the rapporteurs, represents a very authoritative source on the elements of countermeasures.

In addition to this short introduction and conclusion, this part is divided into four chapters. In chapter 8, the conditions that can invoke the right to resort to countermeasures, mainly the presence of a violation of an international obligation of a state, are discussed. Chapter 9 focuses on certain procedures that states might have to follow before resorting to countermeasures, including a duty to request the offending state to cease the alleged violations and to offer negotiation. Chapter 10 addresses certain considerations related to the actual taking of the countermeasures, such as against what interest they can be directed and the requirement of proportionality. Finally, chapter 11 discusses whether the presence of alternative methods of dispute resolution, such as open channels of negotiation or access to a binding third party dispute settlement mechanism, affects the right to resort to countermeasures.

Endnote

1. Emmerich de Vattel, *The Law of Nations* or *Principles of the Law of Nature, Applied to the Conduct and Affairs of Nations and Sovereigns*, originally published in 1757, Simeon Butler, Northampton, Massachusetts, 1820, book II, chap. IV, § 49, p. 214.

CHAPTER 8

CONSIDERATIONS REGARDING THE LEGALITY OF PROSPECTIVE COUNTERMEASURES

(A) THE PURPOSE OF COUNTERMEASURES AND ITS EFFECTS ON THE LEGALITY OF COUNTERMEASURES

Generally, the purpose of countermeasures is to compel a state to cease an alleged violation and/or pay reparation. An injured state might also intend to punish the offending state, whether or not such purpose is the primary or secondary reason for taking the measures. The question of what causes one state to take, in peacetimes, potentially destabilizing measures against another state must be answered on a case-to-case basis. Often the causes would be many and diverse, perhaps as many as the persons involved in the decision-making process. This leads, however, to another question—whether the motivation or the purpose affects the determination of the legality of the measures. Or to be more to the point, can countermeasures that are taken for punitive purposes be legal?

Article 49 of the ILC *2001 Draft Articles* suggests that the purpose of countermeasures is to compel the offending state to cease the violation and/or pay reparation. Article 49(1) reads, "An injured State may *only* take countermeasures against a State which is responsible for an internationally wrongful act *in order to induce that State to comply with its obligations* under Part Two."[1] The ILC wrote, "Countermeasures are taken as a form of inducement, not punishment."[2] However, the draft articles do not explicitly exclude countermeasures that have the characteristics of a punishment from being legal.[3] Some authors[4] have argued that punitive countermeasures fall outside the concept of countermeasures not only because they are disproportionate but also because the punitive purpose independently excludes their legality.

Elagab seemed to suggest that countermeasures that are intended to punish are illegal.[5] He distinguished between four different types of motivations for countermeasures. He wrote, "[C]ounter-measures are usually motivated by self-protection, reciprocity, or the desire to induce expeditious settlement of the dispute in question."[6] In addition, he mentioned revenge as a motivation. However, countermeasures "in the absence of any legitimate grievances, but purely as a means of expressing revenge for some extraneous conduct…cannot be regarded as lawful countermeasures since they are not based on any *legally accepted motivation*."[7] Elagab did not suggest a method to determine states' motivation for countermeasures. Therefore, it is not clear if he was suggesting that motivation was a subjective factor, which might require reading into the minds of decision makers, or if the nature of the motivation should the determined by the objective characteristics of the measures taken.

Other authors have linked states' purpose of countermeasures to their legality. Zoller argued that if the purpose of countermeasures is punishment or the measures' results are punitive in nature, they cannot be legal because no state has the authority to punish another.[8] Zoller's position is based on the assumption that "no state is superior to another."[9] She wrote, "Since no subject of law in the international community can be considered as entitled to or even likely to be entitled to more rights than another, there is no legal room for punishment in peacetime international law."[10]

Zoller, however, did not argue that the motivation to punish should have a role in the determination of whether the purpose of the countermeasures is punishment; "[t]he punitive character of a measure depends not on its motives but rather on its effects…"[11] Zoller argued that unilateral measures are punitive in character and, therefore, illegal if they go beyond reciprocity and are final.[12] Punitive countermeasures go farther than putting the parties—the wrongdoing state and the injured state—on an equal footing as the illegal act did not happen. Zoller suggested that if such measures are reversible, they can objectively be viewed as permissible coercive measures,[13] but if the measures are irreversible, that is, final, they do not have the characteristics of coercive measures; if the wrongdoing state would cease the illegal behavior, the measures cannot be withdrawn.[14] On the reversibility of countermeasures, the ILC suggested in its *2001 Draft Articles* that the general rule is that countermeasures have to be reversible, that is, they can be withdrawn when the illegal situation ceases.[15] However, the ILC wrote in its commentary, "The duty to choose measures that are reversible is not absolute."[16] Elagab's writings also support this assertion. He wrote, "The exigencies of a particular situation may dictate the necessity for imposing irreversible counter-measures."[17] Also, Article 49(3) of the *2001 Draft Articles* indicates that irreversible countermeasures are not prohibited. The article reads, "Countermeasures shall, *as far as possible*, be taken in such a way as to permit the resumption of performance of the obligations in question."[18] In the commentary, the ILC wrote, "The phrase 'as far as possible' in paragraph 3 indicates that if the injured State has a choice between a number of lawful and effective countermeasures, it should select one which permits the resumption of performance of the obligations suspended as a result of countermeasures."[19]

The ICJ missed an opportunity to shed light on the requirement of reversibility and its exceptions in the *Gabcikovo-Nagymaros Project*. The court, which found the countermeasures illegal because of failure to meet the proportionality requirement, wrote:

> It is therefore not required to pass upon one other condition for the lawfulness of a countermeasure, namely that its purpose must

> be to induce the wrongdoing State to comply with its obligations under international law, and that the measure must therefore be reversible.[20]

This study agrees with Zoller that the legality of countermeasures should depend on the objective attributes of the countermeasures and their effects and not on the subjective attributes, such as the motivation of the persons who decided to resort to countermeasures. However, the validity of giving the purpose of the measures independent weight in the determination of the legality of the measures must be questioned. It is suggested that other attributes, such as proportionality, which in most cases would lead to a similar conclusion, would be better suited to determine the legality of countermeasures than punitive characteristics of the measures however objectively the characteristics are measured. Further, giving the objectives of the measures such decisive weight in the determination of the legality of the measures might lead the debate down a slippery slope of normative jingles, such as "just" and "unjust" countermeasures. In addition, Zoller's distinction between coercive countermeasures and punitive countermeasures and, therefore, the legality of the countermeasures, rests on the determination whether the measures are final. A decision in the form of countermeasures to halt the import of perishable food is arguably final if the food goes bad while waiting in customs. Lifting the import ban would not repair the damage to the goods. If the import ban goes beyond reciprocity, that is, beyond what is sufficient to make up for the illegal act of the initial wrongdoing state, one could argue that under Zoller's theory, the import ban is an illegal countermeasure because of its punitive character. On the other hand, one could also argue that the import ban was reversible because it can be lifted. This factor, the irrevocability of the measures, would arguably divert the debate from the core elements of countermeasures, such as proportionality and whether the measures are in fact designed to "induce [a state] to comply with its obligations," as the *2001 Draft Articles* requires.[21] When the normative assumptions, that no state has the right to punish another state because all states are equal, that Zoller rests her arguments on are taken into account and questioned, the basis of the suggestion that the purpose of the countermeasures should have weight in the determination of their legality becomes all more feeble. Finally, it must also be pointed out that countermeasures whose motive or purpose is to punish might well induce a state to comply with its obligations. It is, therefore, suggested here that the determination whether a countermeasure is a punishment or not might not be the most suitable factor in the determination of their legality.

Zoller argued also that if the purpose of unilateral measures is reparation, the measures are not only legal as countermeasures, but they also are legal per se and do not require a special justification. She wrote, "...reciprocity is the norm. Such conditions are lawful *per se*; they do not have to be legitimized."[22] Furthermore, "all reciprocating measures having merely a compensatory purpose are lawful *per se*, as their only aim is reparation."[23] Zoller seemed to argue that it is always lawful to take actions that in themselves are only designed to place, and result in placing, the parties in the same situation in which they were prior to the initial illegal act by the offending state. In other words, because of the compensatory purpose of unilateral acts that aim at reparation only, the act is legal per se and should not be seen as countermeasures.[24] The position taken here differs from Zoller's; the legality of the unilateral act of the injured state intended to acquire reparation still hinges on the prior breach of the offending state. Reciprocal measures that are taken to acquire reparation, which without the prior breach are illegal, fall, therefore, within the concept of countermeasures. It then depends on the law of countermeasures whether such reciprocal measures are legal.

Zoller's arguments for giving the purpose of the measures weight in the determination of their legality as countermeasures seems to differ from Elagab's assertion, which seemed to suggest that the motivation to punish can render the measures illegal. She seems to attempt to put an objective measurement on a somewhat subjective factor, that is, the purpose of states' behavior.

The position taken in this study is, therefore, to avoid putting effort into the determination of the motivation or of how imperfect men and women would describe the effect of the measures and instead to focus more on the objective considerations. This does not mean that Zoller's assumption that acts that aim to punish are not legal countermeasures is always wrong. Rather, it would be more accurate to say that if the measure goes beyond a proportionate response, it loses its legal basis because it does not comply with the proportionality requirement and not because of its motives. Accordingly, it is suggested here that countermeasures with punitive character, which in themselves induce the offending state "to comply with its obligation," can qualify as countermeasures, provided they fulfill other requirements of countermeasures, such as proportionality. There is a French saying that goes like this, "one shall not argue over color and taste,"[25] which roughly means that subjective assessment cannot be determined by intellectual debate. Thus, this study suggests that the purpose of countermeasures as punishment does not exclude the measures from being justified as countermeasures.

Grotius wrote on the relations of the purpose of war and its legality that war may "gradually change its nature and its object from the prosecution of a right to the desire of seconding or supporting the aggrandizement of some other power." He argued that despite this change of the motive of the war, it does not become unjust simply because of that.[26] What he means is that the objective attributes alone, not the changing moods of humans, determine whether war is legal or not. Similarly, one has to distinguish between the reason why states resort to countermeasures and their legality. A person whose contractual rights are violated might decide to resort to the remedies permitted in the contract, not because he wants restitution, but mainly because he wants, out of pure malice, to embarrass the offender. It is probably true that under most developed legal systems, the injured person's right to the remedy would seldom hinge on his underlying motive rather then on the objective circumstances and the requirements of the contractual remedy.

(B) Establishing the Violation: Actual Unlawfulness or Reasonable State's View?

Countermeasures, as this study uses the concept, can only be taken as a response to a violation of international law that injures the state taking the countermeasures. Thus, there has to exist a prior violation of an international legal obligation. Countermeasures, as acts that per se violate international law, can only be justified if this requirement is fulfilled.[27] A moral obligation, or an obligation based on comity, often called "imperfect obligation" by earlier writers,[28] is not sufficient to justify countermeasures. Grotius, discussing justification for warlike acts, wrote that a violation of a moral obligation had to be accompanied by a violation of a legal obligation to justify such acts. He wrote, "Thus a person who has conferred a favour, has not, strictly speaking, a *right* to demand a return, for that would be converting an act of kindness into a contract."[29]

The sufficient level of clarity of whether an act is a violation of an international legal obligation is a matter of debate. The lowest level of clarity of the violation is arguably the alleged injured state's reasonable view that the alleged offending state has, in fact, violated international law. This means that the alleged offending state's violation does not have be proven, only that the alleged injured state must believe at the time of the countermeasures that the offending state had violated an international obligation and that the alleged injured state's belief was based on a reasonable interpretation of the law and the facts. Most scholars seem to subscribe to a stricter approach, requiring an absolute violation and thereby rejecting the use of reasonableness or good faith standards.[30]

The tribunal in the *Air Service Agreement Case* arguably relied on the view of the injured states to establish whether a violation has occurred. The tribunal said:

> If a situation arises which, in one State's view, results in the violation of an international obligation by another State, the first State is entitled, within the limits set by the general rules of international law pertaining to the use of armed force, to affirm its rights through 'countermeasures'.[31]

This indicates that it is the legal opinion of the injured state that is the decisive factor whether the requirement of a prior violation has been fulfilled. The tribunal does not indicate that any reasonableness standards should be applied to the injured state's view. Although the tribunal did not explicitly make this connection, it is safe to assume that the tribunal's words tacitly refer to reasonable interpretation as a minimum requirement and not just any view of any injured state. However, it must be noted that the tribunal actually addressed the question whether the practice of transferring passengers to a smaller airplane during transit in London prior to flying to Paris was in compliance with the *Air Service Agreement.* While finding the United States' practice compatible with the agreement, and, therefore, finding that France had violated the agreement, it did not apply any reasonableness standards regarding the violation, that is, it did not look into whether the United States' view that there had been a violation was justified at the time when they announced the countermeasures. Instead, the tribunal objectively determined that there had been a violation.

The well-settled principle of the need of a prior breach of an international obligation was questioned by Lori Fisler Damrosch in her analysis of the *Air Service Agreement Case.*[32] She argued that the *Air Service Agreement Case* could be interpreted as suggesting that a good faith belief that France was is violation would be sufficient to justify countermeasures.[33] Damrosch criticized theories that argue that states resort to countermeasures at their own peril; the uncertainties in the determination whether a prior violation has taken place, are too high. She wrote:

> Putting states at their peril for a wrong guess may well be inadvisable given the present stage of development of international jurisprudence. There is little continuity among persons acting as arbitrators or judges, no appellate body to harmonize the decisions of ad hoc tribunals, not much of a rule of *stare decisis*, and indeed, considerable uncertainty—as compared to national jurisprudence—concerning the very content of the rules to be applied. In short, there is little to facilitate predictability. How, then, can states be 'fairly certain' that an as yet unconstituted tribunal will vindicate their predictions?[34]

Because of this uncertainty, Damrosch suggested that the retaliating state should not be held to the high standard suggested by other authors. She suggested a two-pronged test to measure good faith: the seriousness of the argument that there was, in fact, a violation and the "sincere interest in achieving a prompt and fair resolution of the issue."[35] The main argument for this approach was that states should not be penalized for good faith prediction as to what the unpredictable international legal system would determine at a later stage.[36] Damrosch admitted that there were some dangers associated with adopting this approach that might adversely affect states' incentives to adhere to their obligations.[37]

Elagab wrote that Damrosch's suggestions were highly controversial and might be partly based on a misunderstanding.[38] However, Elagab was willing to entertain an idea of a compromise without seemingly departing from the requirement of an objective violation.[39] He suggested that

> the allegedly aggrieved State should be allowed 'a margin of discretion' when assessing the extent of the counter-measures required by the exigencies of the situation. This would mean that the State in question should enjoy a 'margin of appreciation' in assessing breach as a precipitating factor. Thus, when a Government weights the extent of the countermeasures dictated by an immediate crisis, a reasonable discretion should not be denied.[40]

In the *Gabcikovo-Nagymaros Project*, the issue of necessity was addressed by the ICJ. The court, citing ILC findings, said, "[T]he state of necessity can only be invoked under certain strictly defined conditions which must be cumulatively satisfied; and the State concerned is not the *sole judge* of whether those conditions have been met."[41] This wording indicates, not conclusively though, that states have certain discretion whilst deciding whether conditions for preventive acts based on state of necessity are justified. However, in the following paragraphs in which the court addressed the conditions for state of necessity and whether they have been met, the state discretion is not analyzed any further.[42] It must be noted here that the requirements for state of necessity are different from the ones of countermeasures; but if states were given a margin of discretion when deciding whether the requirements are met, similar arguments might be used with regard to countermeasures.

In a commentary to the *1996 ILC Draft Articles on State Responsibility*, the ILC stated that countermeasures could only be taken in response to conduct that is actually unlawful and "a mere good faith belief on the part of the injured State which turns out not to be well-founded would not be sufficient to justify the taking of countermeasures."[43] The ILC's words seem to indicate that a postevent review of the factors establishing a violation had to be undertaken in order to determine if countermeasures were justifiable. In a more recent commentary to the *2001 Draft Articles*, the ILC confirmed its prior assertion, that a

> State taking countermeasures acts at its peril, if its view of the question of wrongfulness turns out not to be well founded. A State which resorts to countermeasures based on its unilateral assessment of the situation does so at its own risk and may incur responsibility for its own wrongful conduct in the event of an incorrect assessment.[44]

A requirement of an actual violation as a condition for countermeasures does not mean that a tribunal or international competent body has to have decided on the issue. However, this point was raised by Philip Jessup in 1948. He suggested that it was "highly suitable for an international tribunal to pass judgment on the merits of the claim of the state which seeks to free itself from its obligation."[45] Certainly, Jessup's suggestion is desirable to maintain order within the international legal system. However, it must be pointed out that among the reasons for the right to resort to countermeasures is the inability of the international system to adjudicate international disputes and enforce its rulings. Damrosch wrote on this point:

> Tribunals are not always in place to hear disputes or to indicate interim measures of protection; indeed, even when a preexisting agreement calls for arbitration, establishment of the tribunal takes time, and there may be protracted negations over the terms of the *compromis* and the regime to govern the conduct of the parties

> pending the tribunal's decision. If the party allegedly committing the initial breach could enjoy the benefits of its breach without the fear of retaliatory responses during this possibly lengthy period, it would have every incentive to delay submission of the dispute to arbitration and conclusion of the arbitral proceedings.[46]

Vattel wrote that "[t]he law of nations permits reprisals only upon a cause that is evidently just, or for a debt that is extremely clear."[47] Vattel did not analyze this point any further. However, this passage does not seem to leave much room for good faith standards. Arguably, Vattel is suggesting that the breach not only has to objectively exist, but also it has to be beyond doubt. Jessup's suggestion would then have certain basis in Vattel's suggestion.

The position that this study takes is that a state that resorts to countermeasures in good faith does so at its own risk. If the legality of the countermeasures will later be decided by a dispute settlement body, that body must examine the legality of the act that the injured state cites as its justification for the countermeasures. Although the existence of reasonable interpretation in good faith can be determined on the basis of objective factors, opening the door for such leniency can lead to the acceptance of countermeasures against legal acts of states that, at the moment of commission, looked like or had the character of a violation. Such approach might jeopardize the adherence to the rule of law in international relations. Furthermore, the justification of countermeasures might shift its focus to proving that the legal act had the appearance of an illegal act instead of addressing its actual illegality. However, it is not impossible to entertain the thought that factual errors surrounding the situation might render countermeasures legal, even if they otherwise would be illegal because of the absence of an actual illegal act by the offending state. One could think of credible scientific evidence of the harmfulness of certain acts by the offending state that later turned out to be flawed. If the state taking the countermeasures used the best available undisputed scientific methods and communicated its findings to the alleged offending state, which did not object their validity, such conclusion might be justified in exceptional cases.

(c) The Imminence of the Violation, Anticipatory Countermeasures

It is generally accepted that a state cannot resort to countermeasures based solely on fear that another state will violate its obligations resulting in harm. Westlake argued that a military buildup in one country that might later threaten another does not give the latter a right to take actions against the former.[48] He continued and wrote that this applies "so long as an intention to misuse its power cannot be imputed to it on sufficient evidence."[49] Westlake did not further explain the nature of the evidence necessary to justify preemptive self-defense, but he certainly considered this a legally viable option in exceptional cases.

According to Grotius, the violation has to be immediate; any degree of fear is not enough to justify reprisals.[50] Further, Grotius argued that the intention to violate the law is not sufficient; it does not justify reprisals. He wrote:

> Now if any one intend no immediate violence, but is found to have formed a conspiracy to destroy me by assassination, or poison, or by false accusation, perjury, or suborned witnesses, I have no right to kill him. For my knowledge of the danger may prevent it. Or even if it were evident that I could not avoid the danger without killing him; this would not establish my right to do so. For there is every presumption that my knowing it will lead me to apply for the legal remedies of prevention.[51]

Certainly there are good arguments for not responding too hastily to a threat that is perceived to be imminent, even if the intentions of the offender are to violate international law. Due exercise of diplomacy and negotiation, taking advantage of available international mechanism and procedures, could prove to be a better and more proportionate tool. One must note that Westlake and Grotius were commenting on the right to resort to forcible reprisals, including measures that are now prohibited by the *UN Charter*. Arguably the level of caution that states needed to show before such measures were taken is higher than would be necessary for contemporary countermeasures. Nevertheless, contemporary opinions do not seem to depart from the classical ones on this issue, which can only been interpreted as quite negative toward anticipatory countermeasures. Also, international decisions relating to countermeasures, whether forcible or nonforcible, do not indicate that an imminent violation could justify countermeasures.[52]

This rejection of anticipatory countermeasures is by no means surprising, as among the requirements for the legality of countermeasures is a previous breach of an international obligation. The ILC wrote in its commentary to earlier *Draft Articles on State Responsibility* that "[t]he circumstance precluding wrongfulness with which this article is concerned is thus one of those 'countermeasures' which international law regards as legitimate following an internationally wrongful act committed *previously*."[53] The ICJ came to a similar conclusion in the *Gabcikovo-Nagymaros Project*. When discussing countermeasures, the court, citing its earlier decision and the ILC, wrote, "[Countermeasures] must be taken in response to a *previous* international wrongful act of another State…"[54] The conclusion must, therefore, be that anticipatory or preemptive countermeasures are not permitted under international law.[55]

However, as discussed previously, under narrowly defined circumstances unilateral measures taken prior to a breach can be justified under international law pertaining to state of necessity. According to the *ILC 2001 Draft Articles*, such justification can be used if the measures are "the only way for the State to safeguard an essential interest against a grave and imminent peril."[56]

(D) Injured States, Violations *Erga Omnes*, and Collective Countermeasures

The general rule is that only the injured state is permitted to resort to countermeasures.[57] Although this study does not focus on when a state is injured or when a state can invoke state responsibility for a breach of an international obligation in general, it is helpful to examine the notion of an injured state and its limits and how noninjured states can resort to countermeasures. This subchapter first addresses the idea of collective countermeasures, then the notion of an injured state, and lastly, the right of a state that has not suffered a direct injury to resort to countermeasures.

The notion of third party countermeasures, or collective countermeasures, has been disputed and still is today.[58] China, for example, wrote in its response to the *2000 Draft Articles on State Responsibility* that collective countermeasures

> would run counter to the basic principle that countermeasures should and can only be taken by States injured by an internationally wrongful act. More seriously, 'collective countermeasures' could become one more pretext for power politics in international relations, for only powerful States and blocs of States are in a position to take countermeasures against weaker States.[59]

There is no doubt that countermeasures are generally taken in response to a violation affecting interests of the directly injured state. However, despite the words of warning from the Chinese government, a number of good arguments can be made for collective or third party countermeasures. First of all, the effects of a violation of international laws are not always limited to a single state. Although one state might be the primary victim, other states might have various levels of direct interests. This is evident in the field of environmental law; even if a pollution or over-fishing problem might only injure one state, it can later become another state's problem, either directly or indirectly, if not addressed adequately.[60] Second, interests in an interdependent world do not always follow the political boundaries. Even if a state is not directly injured, it might have direct interests in the well-being of the affected state. Security interests or political and economic interests of the injured state might be so intertwined with another state that it feels compelled to take actions against the offending states. Such relationship interests not directly related to the harm in question is arguably a poorer justification for third party countermeasures but not unknown.[61]

Earlier writers expressed their opinion on this issue and were generally negative about the idea of the right of one state to resort to reprisals to protect a third state's interests. Vattel, for example, argued that a nation did not have a right to resort to reprisals for harm done to foreigners, in other words, as a response to an injury to a third state.[62] Martens agreed; he did not accept that states could resort to reprisals for injuries committed against a third state.[63] However, Elagab, citing scholars such as Grotius, Vattel, Hall, Jessup, and Oppenheim, asserted that there "is a long line of doctrinal opinion which maintains that third States may respond to serious breaches of international law pertaining to matters of great importance."[64] This statement might not be entirely accurate; at least some further explanation is required before it can be accepted here.

It is true that Grotius wrote that states did wage wars to protect other states or entities and that he did not question its legality.[65] Furthermore, he wrote that kings "have a right to exact punishment, not only for injuries affecting immediately themselves or their own subjects, but for gross violations of the law of nature and of nations, done to other states or subjects."[66] From the context of this passage,[67] it is clear that Grotius was referring to the right to punish a wrongdoing state, a right that cannot under all circumstances be applied by analogy to countermeasures, which are, under the contemporary literature, not intended to serve as punishment.

As stated previously, Vattel believed that reprisals for the protection of third state's interests were not permitted. However, he argued that against the most serious violations, every state had the right to resort to reprisals. He wrote, "If there be any that makes an open profession of trampling justice under foot, of despising and violating the rights of others, whenever it finds an opportunity, the interests of human society will authorize all others to unite in order to humble and chastize it."[68] Vattel suggested that such measures by the international society should be preceded not only by an in isolated act but also by a "continued conduct, one nations shews that it has evidently this pernicious disposition, and that it considers no right as sacred…"[69] However, Vattel did not see such reaction as a reaction of a third state but rather as response by an injured state. He wrote, "To form and support an unjust pretension is to do an injury, not only to him who is interested in this pretension, but to mock at justice in general, and to injure all nations."[70]

Hall wrote that all states have the right to counter or punish a state that "grossly and patently violated international law in a matter of serious importance."[71] Hall did not explicitly see such a right as deriving from a direct injury; and neither did he mention that this right was in defense of a third state but rather as an injury to the law.[72]

Jessup cited prior writings of legal scholars who argued that threats to peace must concern the international community as a whole. He discussed the right to defend peace in the context of Article 11 of the *Covenant of the League of Nations* and Article 34 and 35 of the *UN Charter*, which are based on the assumption that a threat to peace and international security concerns the international community as a whole. Apart from the threat to peace, Jessup questioned the existence or the reach of a rule under international law that gives a state, not directly injured, an independent right to respond to an offending state.[73]

Oppenheim wrote that a violation of a universally recognized rule of international law would allow all states to react against the violator. Oppenheim did not seem to view such reaction as in defense of a third state and did not elaborate on the exact rationale for his assertion.[74]

Collective protection measures were well-known before the Second World War. However, it was only after that war that such measures systematically became a part of the international political arena.[75] Article 51 of the *UN Charter*, which confirmed the inherent right to self-defense, includes a right of collective self-defense. Oppenheim argued that "in a sense, Article 51 enlarges the right of self-defense as usually understood... by authorizing both individual and collective self-defence."[76] However, Oppenheim should barely be understood as indicating that collective self-defense was illegal before Article 51 but rather that its legal foundations became stronger with the adoption of Article 51.[77] Oppenheim made an interesting point when he argued that the right to take collective measures was not a right to help an ally state and protect its interests; it was a self-interested act designed to protect the rights of the state that takes the measures.[78] He continued and wrote:

> [U]nless such right of collective self-defence is recognised the door is open for piecemeal annihilation of victims of aggression

> by a State or States intent upon the domination of the world. In that sense collective self-defence is no more than rationally conceived individual self-defence.[79]

Although this passage deals with self-defense and the right of a state that is not under armed attack to take measures, this line of thought can be analyzed under the law of countermeasures. This approach focuses not on the interests of the directly injured state but rather on the independent right of the indirectly injured state to protect its interests. It may be inferred from this approach that an indirectly injured state can act without a request from the directly injured state to do so; it can take action independently of the will of the directly injured state.

The ICJ decision in *Nicaragua v. United States*[80] did not support this line of thought. The court said that

> in customary international law, whether of a general kind or that particular to the inter-American legal system, there is no rule permitting the exercise of collective self-defence *in the absence of a request* by the State which regards itself as the victim of an armed attack.[81]

The right to collective self-defense is, according to this passage, not an independent right of the state that watches the "piecemeal annihilation" of their sphere of influence. On the contrary, the injured state has to request the assistance; the view of the state resorting to the measures is not sufficient.[82]

Certainly there are similarities between countermeasures during peacetime and self-defense. There are, however, differences that might question the method of applying this conclusion regarding collective self-defense on collective countermeasures.

The use of armed force as collective self-defense is, in the language of Article 51 of the *UN Charter*, a response to an armed attack. Because of this high level of intrusiveness, the state that is under attack is given the right to defend its interests and secure it from further intrusions. Although constrained by the principle of proportionality and the law of armed conflict, the state acting in self-defense is, therefore, given authority to take unilateral measures of a nature that is generally deemed the most dangerous for peace and security and political stability, that is, to use armed force against another state. This measure is so destabilizing and so contrary to the principles of the international system of states that it must be limited as much as possible. This includes limiting the right of third states to use the armed invasion of the offending state as a justification for its own armed intervention.

This dangerousness is generally on a much lower level when it comes to peacetime countermeasures. Although peaceful countermeasures can have destabilizing effects, such measures are of a different nature from the use of armed force as an act of self-defense. Therefore, it might not be correct to assume that if the right to voluntary collective self-defense is not protected under international law, the same applies to the right to unsolicited collective countermeasures. However, international law does not provide a clear general rule on this issue. Nevertheless, certain indications regarding this issue that might shed a light on the legality of third party countermeasures can be extracted from the *Barcelona Traction Case* and the ILC reports.

The *Barcelona Traction Case*[83] arguably suggests that indirectly injured states do not have the status of an aggrieved party and do, therefore, not have standing to protect their interests. Although the analysis of the ICJ focuses mainly on whether the indirectly injured state has standing before the court, certain conclusions may arguably be drawn from the case, namely, that an indirectly injured state might not have the right to resort to countermeasures against the wrongdoing state. In short, the case dealt with infringement of certain rights of a Canadian company in Spain. The issue of relevance here is whether the Belgian government could have standing based on the fact that many of the shareholders were Belgian subjects. The Belgian government argued it had a right to provide diplomatic protection to these subjects. The court contended

> that the adoption of the theory of diplomatic protection of shareholders as such, by opening the door to competing diplomatic

> claims, could create an atmosphere of confusion and insecurity in international economic relations. ...It might perhaps be claimed that, if the right of protection belonging to the national States of the shareholders were considered as only secondary to that of the national State of the company, there would be less danger of difficulties of the kind contemplated. However, the Court must state that the essence of a secondary right is that it only comes into existence at the time when the original right ceases to exist. As the rights of protection vested in the national state of the company cannot be regarded as extinguished because it is not exercised, it is not possible to accept the proposition that in case of its non-exercise, the national States of the shareholders have a right of protection secondary to that of the national State of the company.[84]

The court accordingly rejected the standing of an arguably indirectly injured state, like Belgium in this case.[85] The conclusion was not absolute as the court suggested that if the primary rights ceased to exist, the secondary rights of the indirectly injured states came into play.[86]

In its 1991 report, the special rapporteur of the ILC questioned the use of concepts such as nondirectly injured states or nondirectly affected states.[87] In the following report, he suggested that such terminology was unacceptable and rejected it in its entirety.[88] He argued that an internationally wrongful act not only resulted in a physical injury but also was, or resulted in, an "infringement of a right, that infringement—whether or not damage has been caused—constituting the injury. ...A State can thus be injured by the breach of an international obligation even if it did not suffer any damage other than the infringements of its right."[89] According to this view, the determination of whether a state is injured ought to rest not only on the physical injury but also on the legal injury. He mentioned, as an example of such a legal injury, a breach of an *erga omnes* obligation such as a violation of an international obligation related to the stratospheric ozone layer; although states would be differently exposed to the danger, the obligation is owed to the international community as a whole, the legal injury would be the same, and "in no case would it be correct to define this difference in terms of a 'direct,' 'less direct,' or 'indirect' juridical injury."[90] According to the special rapporteur, this does not mean, however, that all states have an equal substantive right to obtain redress or reparation. Although all states have suffered a juridical injury, the physical damage differs, resulting in different substantive rights to be recovered from the wrongdoing state. This means that states that do not suffer physical damage might only "be entitled to claim cessation and guarantees of non-repetition, but not pecuniary compensation."[91]

The right to take countermeasures, under this line of thought, depends, then, not on the indirectness of the injury; it is "merely the consequence of the application...of the general rules or principles governing countermeasures, such as the obligation of prior demand for cessation or reparation or prior exhaustion or dispute settlement procedures, and, of course, the requirement of proportionality."[92]

The *2001 Draft Articles* do not follow entirely the line of thought expressed in the ILC's 1992 report on the notion of an injured state. It is notable that the articles do not contain an actual definition of an injured state.[93] However, Article 42 of the *2001 Draft Articles*, which addresses the right of a state to invoke state responsibility as an injured state, provides important hints regarding the definition of an injured state and the distinction from a noninjured state. Those hints indicate that the definition of an injured state is quite narrow.[94] Under Article 42, a state is considered injured if the violated obligation is owed to that state individually,[95] if the state belongs to a group of states to which the obligation is owed and the state is specifically affected,[96] or if the violation is "of such a character as radically to change the position of all the other States to which the obligation is owed with respect to the further performance of the obligation."[97] This narrow definition indicates that a breach of an obligation *erga omnes* does not injure all states; legal or juridical injury is not sufficient to give a state a status of an injured state. However, this does not mean that the *2001 Draft Articles* denies states that only have suffered a juridical injury, as opposed to a physical injury,[98] the rights to invoke state responsibility. Article 48 foresees a right of a noninjured state to invoke state responsibility provided that either of two conditions is met.

The first condition is that the obligation is owed to a group of states, including the state invoking state responsibility, and it "is established for the protection of a collective interest of the group."[99] The wording of the article does not require that the arrangement established has to have the larger part of the international community as members; it can be established by a relatively small group of states. However, it has to be for the protection of collective interests of the group as a whole and "in any event the arrangement must transcend the sphere of bilateral relations of the States parties."[100] In the commentary to Article 48, the ILC mentioned, as an example of such collective interest, environmental interests, or security interests.[101] An agreement between a number of coastal states to reduce fertilizer runoff in order to protect the marine environment might be an example of protection of such collective interests. A state that does not comply with its obligations might not necessarily cause harm to the environment within the Exclusive Economic Zones (EEZ) of all or any of the member states; but any one of them might, however, have the right to raise the issue and demand cessation of the violation as a noninjured state.

The second condition is if the "obligation breached is owed to the international community as a whole,"[102] often referred to as *erga omnes* obligation. The notion of an obligation that is owed to the international community as a whole is not a novelty.[103] It is often traced to the *Barcelona Traction Case*, which, in fact, did little more than to distinguish such obligations from obligations that are owed to particular states. The court suggested that

> an essential distinction should be drawn between the obligations of a State towards the international community as a whole, and those arising vis-à-vis another State in the field of diplomatic protection. By their very nature the former are the concern of all States. In view of the importance of the rights involved, all States can be held to have a legal interest in their protection; they are obligation *erga omnes*.[104]

The court provided little analysis of the elements of an obligation *erga omnes* but mentioned, as an example, acts of aggression and genocide, as well as basic human rights.[105] Later, the ICJ, while dismissing a case that Portugal brought against Australia regarding East-Timor (now Timor Leste) for lack of jurisdiction, the court stated that a breach of the right to self-determination was a breach of an *erga omnes* obligation.[106]

The entitlement of such injured states to substantive rights is, under the *2001 Draft Articles*, limited by the nature of their injury; because they have only suffered a juridical injury, they are only entitled to "cessation of the internationally wrongful act, and assurances and guarantees of non-repetition."[107] In addition, Article 48 suggests that such a state has a right to claim from the responsible state "performance of the obligation of reparation in accordance with the preceding articles in the interest of the injured state or of the beneficiaries of the obligation breached."[108] These limits on the substantive rights of the noninjured state affect their right to resort to countermeasures. A state that does not have a right to reparation cannot resort to countermeasures to compel the wrongdoing state to perform such an obligation. This would be in line with the arguments of the special rapporteur of the ILC in his 1992 report discussed previously.[109] However, under Article 54 of the *2000 Draft Articles*, a noninjured state that can invoke state responsibility could "take countermeasures at the request and on behalf of any State injured by the breach, to the extent that the State may itself take countermeasures..."[110] Article 54 did, however, not authorize a noninjured state to take countermeasures to induce the wrongdoing state to offer assurances and guarantees of nonrepetition. Neither did the article address a general right of a state to resort to countermeasures against a state responsible for a violation of an *erga omnes* obligation.[111]

The ILC, however, in its *2001 Draft Articles*, aborted its attempt to regulate countermeasures taken by a noninjured state. Instead, it included an article that neither authorized nor excluded such measures. Article 54 of the *2001 Draft Article* reads:

> This chapter does not prejudice the right of any State, entitled under article 48, paragraph 1 to invoke the responsibility of

> another State to take lawful measures against that State to ensure cessation of the breach and reparation in the interest of the injured State or of the beneficiaries of the obligation breached.[112]

The ILC explained the reason for this approach by saying that the "the current state of international law on countermeasures taken in the general or collective interest is uncertain."[113] It noted that "State practice is sparse and involves a limited number of States."[114] The ILC concluded by saying:

> At present there appears to be no clearly recognized entitlement of States referred to in article 48 to take countermeasures in the collective interest. Consequently it is not appropriate to include in the present Articles a provision concerning the question whether other States, identified in article 48, are permitted to take countermeasures in order to induce a responsible State to comply with its obligations.[115]

Arguably, the debate on the right of noninjured states in a situation as described in Article 48 of the *2001 Draft Articles* to resort to countermeasures has been reset to the time prior to the *1992 ILC Report* where the notion of indirectly injured states was rejected. A legal framework that rejects the right of such a noninjured state to resort to countermeasure requires the state to show not only legal but also physical harm as a result from the internationally wrongful act. The debate of the legality of such countermeasures might, therefore, make use of concepts, such as indirectly injured or indirectly affected, to form its argument, concepts that were rejected, perhaps for a good reasons, by the ILC over 15 years ago.

(E) Countermeasures: A Remedy for States Only

It is important to note that contemporary international law does not authorize individuals who are not agents of the state to resort to countermeasures on behalf of their state. Earlier in history, when the power of the state in the international arena was weaker, international law accepted the authority of an individual to act on behalf of a state if he or she was so authorized by the state. Vattel argued that whereas reprisals were a tool of the state, the individual could obtain permission to resort to reprisals, that is, the so-called letter of marque.[116] With this permission in hand, the individual could act as the agent of the state and seize whatever property of the offending nation to compensate for his loss. Martens wrote on a similar note that reprisals were only in the hands of the sovereign unless the individual had obtained in advance "*letters of marquee* or of *reprisal*."[117] It is now widely accepted that such semiprivate reprisals are a rule of the past.[118]

ENDNOTES

1. *2001 Draft Articles*, article 49(1), italics added.
2. *Report of the International Law Commission of the Work of Its Fifty Third Session* (23 April–1 June and 2 July–10 August 2001), UN doc. no. A/56/10, Yearbook of the International Law Commission 2001, (hereafter referred to as *ILC 2001 Report*), p. 131.
3. In its comments to the *1996 Draft Articles on State Responsibility* (see *Report of the International Law Commission on the Work of Its Forty Eighth Session* (6 May to 26 July 1996), Yearbook of the International Law Commission 1996, vol. II (part 2), UN. doc. A/51/10), Ireland suggested that the draft articles would clearly state that the right to take countermeasures "does not include the taking of measures of a punitive nature." (State Responsibility, *State Responsibility: Comments and Observations Received from Governments*, UN doc. no. A/CN.4/488, 25 March 1998, p. 118.) The suggested language was neither used in the *2000 Draft Articles* nor the *2001 Draft Articles*. In its comments to the *2000 Draft Articles*, Denmark, on behalf of the Nordic countries, interpreted the language of article 50 as outlawing punitive countermeasures (see *State Responsibility: Comments and Observations Received from Governments*, International Law Commission, fifty third session, Geneva, 23 April–1 June and 2 July–10 August 2001, UN doc. A/CN.4/515, 19 March 2001, p. 77).
4. For example, Elagab and Zoller, as discussed in the following text.
5. Omer Yousif Elagab, *The Legality of Non-forcible Counter-measures in International Law*, Clarendon Press, Oxford, 1988, p. 46.
6. Ibid., p. 44.
7. Ibid., p. 46 (emphasis added).
8. Elisabeth Zoller, *Peacetime Unilateral Remedies: An Analysis of Countermeasures*, Traditional Publishers, New York, 1984, p. 61.
9. Ibid., p. 61.
10. Ibid., p. 59.
11. Ibid., p. 59.
12. Ibid., pp. 57–58.
13. Ibid., pp. 57–58.
14. Ibid., p. 58.
15. *ILC 2001 Report*, p. 131 and *2001 Draft Articles*, article 49(2).
16. *ILC 2001 Report*, p. 131.

17. Omer Yousif Elagab, *The Legality of Non-forcible Counter-measures in International Law*, p. 87.
18. *2001 Draft Articles*, article 49(3), italics added.
19. *ILC 2001 Report*, p. 131.
20. *Gabcikovo-Nagymaros Project* (*Hungary v. Slovakia*), International Court of Justice, judgment of 25 September 1997, 1997 I.C.J. 7, at 56–57, para. 87.
21. *2001 Draft Articles*, article 49(1).
22. Elisabeth Zoller, *Peacetime Unilateral Remedies: An Analysis of Countermeasures*, p. 50.
23. Ibid., p. 51.
24. Ibid., pp. 50–51 and 62. One must remember that Zoller's definition of countermeasures includes only acts that are illegal per se but are justified by the prior violation of the offending state.
25. "Les goûts et les couleurs ne se discutent pas."
26. Hugo Grotius, *The Rights of War and Peace*, originally published in 1625 as *De Jure Belli Ac Pacis*, translated from Latin by A.C. Campell, M. Walter Dunne Publisher, London, New York, 1901, book II, chap. XXII, para. XVII, p. 273.
27. See, for example, *Report of the International Law Commission on the Work of Its Forty Eight Session* (6 May–26 July 1996), UN. doc. no. A/51/10, Yearbook of the International Law Commission 1996, vol. II (part 2), (herafter referred to as the *ILC 1996 Report*), p. 67, *State Responsibility: Comments and Observations Received from Governments*, International Law Commission, fifty third session, Geneva, 23 April–1 June and 2 July–10 August 2001, UN doc. A/CN.4/515, 10 March 2001, pp. 31–32; Hans Kelsen, *Principles of International Law*, 2nd ed., revised and edited by Robert W. Tucker, Holt Rinehart and Winston, Inc, New York, Chicago, San Francisco, Toronto, London, 1966, p. 21; Bin Cheng, *General Principles of Law: As Applied by International Courts and Tribunals*, Stevens & Sons Limited, London, 1953, p. 97; *Naulilaa Case*, p. 1280, UNRIAA, at 1027; and *Gabcikovo-Nagymaros Project*, p. 53, para. 83.
28. See, for example, Thomas Erskine Holland, *Lectures on International Law*, edited by Thomas Alfred Walker and Wyndham Legh Walker, Sweet & Maxwell, London, 1933, p. 229 and Georg Friedrich von Martens, *A Compendium of the Law of Nations*, originally published in 1795, translated by William Cobbet, Cobbet and Morgan, Pall-Mall, London, 1802, p. 272.
29. Hugo Grotius, *The Rights of War and Peace*, book II, chap. XXII, para. XVI, p. 273.
30. See, for example, *Third Report on State Responsibility by Mr. Gaetano Arangio-Ruiz, Special Rapporteur*, (hereafter referred to as *Third Report*

1991 (Arangio-Ruiz)), Yearbook of the International Law Commission 1991, vol. II, part 1, paras. 37–38, p. 14, opting for the stricter approach while discussing the existence of a bona fide approach to the requirement of a previous breach.

31. *Air Service Agreement Case*, see supra endnote 4 of chap. 4, at 337, para. 81.
32. Lori Fisler Damrosch, "Retaliation or Arbitration—or Both? The 1978 United States-France Aviation Dispute," *American Journal of International Law* 74, no. 4 (1980), at 785. Damrosch was the deputy agent for the United States in the *Air Service Agreement Case*.
33. Ibid., at 796.
34. Ibid., at 795.
35. Ibid., at 795.
36. Ibid., at 795.
37. Ibid., at 796.
38. Omer Yousif Elagab, *The Legality of Non-forcible Counter-measures in International Law*, p. 49.
39. Ibid., p. 50.
40. Ibid., p. 50.
41. *Gabcikovo-Nagymaros Project*, at 40, para. 51 (emphasis added).
42. See Ibid., at 40–46, paras. 52–59.
43. *ILC 1996 Report*, p. 67. See also *Third Report on State Responsibility by Mr. James Crawford, Special Rapporteur*, (hereafter referred to as *Third Report 2000 (Crawford)*), addendum, UN doc. no. A/CN.4/507/Add.3, 18 July 2000, p. 5, para. 294.
44. *ILC 2001 Report*, p. 130.
45. Philip C. Jessup, *A Modern Law of Nations: An Introduction*, The Macmillan Company, New York, 1948, p. 152.
46. Lori Fisler Damrosch, "Retaliation or Arbitration—or Both? The 1978 United States-France Aviation Dispute," *American Journal of International* Law 74, no. 4 (1980), at 793–794.
47. Emmerich de Vattel, *The Law of Nations* or *Principles of the Law of Nature*, book II, chap. XVIII, § 343, p. 350.
48. John Westlake, *International Rights of Self-Preservation*, at 121.
49. Ibid., at 122.
50. Hugo Grotius, *The Rights of War and Peace*, book II, chap. I, § V, pp. 77–78.
51. Ibid., p. 78.
52. See, for example, the *Naulilaa Case*, p. 1280, UNRIAA, at 1027; *Gabcikovo-Nagymaros Project*, 1997 I.C.J. 7, at 55–56, para. 83; *Nicaragua Case*, 1986 I.C.J. 14, at 127, para. 249; and the *Air Service Agreement Case*, at 337, para. 81.

53. *Report of the ILC on the Work of Its Thirty First Session* (14 May–3 August 1979), Yearbook of the International Law Commission, vol. II, part 2, 1979 (hereafter referred to as *ILC 1979 Report*), p. 115, para. 2, italics added.
54. *Gabcikovo-Nagymaros Project*, at 55, para. 83 (italics added).
55. See also similar conclusion in Omer Yousif Elagab, *The Legality of Non-forcible Counter-measures in International Law*, pp. 52–55.
56. *2001 Draft Articles*, article 25(1)(a).
57. See, for example, *2001 Draft Articles*, article 49(1). Comments and observations from governments on the *2000 Draft Articles* indicate that there is little consensus on the permissibility of "collective countermeasures" by noninjured states. (See *State Responsibility: Comments and Observations Received from Governments*, UN doc. A/CN.4/515, 19 March 2001, pp. 69–74 and pp. 87–90.
58. For brief overview of state practice in the area, see *ILC 2001 Report*, pp. 137–139.
59. *State Responsibility: Comments and Observations Received from Governments*, UN doc. A/CN.4/515, 19 March 2001, p. 77.
60. If, however, the internationally wrongful act eventually affects such third states directly, such a state would be entitled to take countermeasures as the injured state.
61. See, for example, the *North Atlantic Treaty*, concluded at Washington 4 April 1949, entered into force 24 April 1949, 63 Stat. 2241, T.I.A.S. no. 1964, 4 Bevans 824, article 5; and Nsongurua J. Udombana, "A Question of Justice: The WTO, Africa, and Countermeasures for Breaches of International Trade Obligations," *John Marshall Law Review* 38 (2005), at 1194–1199, justifying collective countermeasures by African states against developed states' trade restrictions.
62. Emmerich de Vattel, *The Law of Nations* or *Principles of the Law of Nature*, book II, chap. XVIII, § 348, pp. 351–352.
63. Georg Friedrich von Martens, *A Compendium of the Law of Nations*, p. 275.
64. Omer Yousif Elagab, *The Legality of Non-forcible Counter-measures in International Law*, p. 58.
65. Hugo Grotius, *The Rights of War and Peace*, book II, chap. XXV, pp. 285–289.
66. Ibid., book II, chap. XX, § XL, p. 247.
67. The passage is in chap. XX of book II, which deals with punishment.
68. Emmerich de Vattel, *The Law of Nations* or *Principles of the Law of Nature, Applied to the Conduct and Affairs of Nations and Sovereigns*, translated from French, printed for Messrs. Berry and Rogers, New York, 1787, book II, chap. V, § 70, p. 250.
69. Emmerich de Vattel, *The Law of Nations*, book II, chap. V, § 70, p. 251.

70. Ibid.
71. William Edward Hall, *A Treatise on International Law*, edited by A. Pearce Higgins, 8th ed., Clarendon Press, Oxford, 1924, p. 65.
72. See Ibid., p. 66.
73. Philip C. Jessup, *A Modern Law of Nations: An Introduction*, pp. 10–12.
74. L. Oppenheim, *International Law*, vol. I, 8th ed., p. 308.
75. See development in collective security regimes, such as article 3 of *the Inter-American Treaty of Reciprocal Assistance* of 1947; articles 4 and 5 of *the North Atlantic Treaty* of 1949; the *Treaty on Social and Cultural Collaboration and Collective Self-Defence* of 1948 (between the Benelux countries, France, and Great Britain); and articles 24 and 25 of the *Charter of the Organization of American States* of 1948.
76. L. Oppenheim, *International Law*, vol. II, 7th ed., p. 155.
77. See also *Military and Paramilitary Activities in and Against Nicaragua* (merits) (*Nicaragua v. United States of America*) International Court of Justice, judgment of 27 June 1986, 1986 I.C.J. 14, at 103, para. 193, "the States represented in the General Assembly regard the exception to the prohibition of force constituted by the right of individual or collective self-defence as already a matter of customary international law."
78. L. Oppenheim, *International Law*, pp. 155–156.
79. Ibid., p. 156.
80. *Military and Paramilitary Activities in and Against Nicaragua*, 1986 I.C.J. 14.
81. Ibid., at 105, para. 199 (italics added).
82. See Ibid., at 104, para. 195.
83. *Barcelona Traction, Light and Power Company, Limited* (*Belgium v. Spain*) International Court of Justice, judgment of 5 February 1970, 1970 I.C.J. 3.
84. Ibid., at 49, para. 96.
85. Ibid., at 51, para. 103.
86. See also Omer Yousif Elagab, *The Legality of Non-forcible Countermeasures in International Law*, p. 56.
87. *Third Report 1991 (Arangio-Ruiz)*, para. 94 et seq., pp. 26–28.
88. *Fourth Report on State* Responsibility by Mr. Gaetano Arangio-Ruiz, Special Rapporteur, UN doc. no. A/CN.4.444 (hereafter referred to as *Fourth Report 1992 (Arangio-Ruiz)*), International Law Commission Yearbook 1992, vol. II, (part 1), para. 127 and paras. 137–138, p. 43 and pp. 45–46, respectively.
89. Fourth Report 1992 (Arangio-Ruiz), para. 129, p. 43.
90. Ibid., para. 135, p. 45.
91. Ibid., para. 144, p. 47.

92. Ibid., para. 146, pp. 47–48. The requirement to exhaust dispute settlement procedures is probably not a part of customary internationally law. After significant opposition from a number of states, the reference to such requirement was removed from the *Draft Articles on State Responsibility* and is not in the *2001 Draft Articles*, see *ILC 2001 Report*, p. 26 et seq.
93. Such definition was in article 40 of the *1996 Draft Articles* but was removed from the *2000 Draft Articles*. See discussion on possible reasons for the removal in *Third Report 2000 (Crawford)*, in particular paras. 82–96, pp. 37–43.
94. See *ILC 2001 Report*, p. 117. The text of article 42 identifying a state as injured is partly tailored after the text of article 60 of the *Vienna Convention on the Law of Treaties* (1155 U.N.T.S. 331), which addresses the termination or suspension of the operation of a treaty as a consequence of its breach. It must be noted that the condition of a material breach for invoking article 60 is not a part of article 42 of the *2001 Draft Articles*.
95. *2001 Draft Articles*, article 42(a).
96. *2001 Draft Articles*, article 42(b)(i).
97. *2001 Draft Articles*, article 42(b)(ii). The text of article 42(b)(ii) is largely taken from article 60(2)(c) of the *Vienna Convention on the Law of Treaties*. The commission's commentary to the draft articles mentioned as examples of such obligation disarmament treaties, nuclear free zones, or "any other treaty where each parties' performance is effectively conditioned upon and requires the performance of each of the others." (See *ILC 2001 Report*, p. 119 and Yearbook of the International Law Commission 1966, vol. II, para. 8, p. 255.)
98. Article 31(2) of the *2001 Draft Articles* indicates that a physical injury (invoking the right to reparation) can be material or moral. This addition is arguably a result of a suggestion from France that moral damage should be included in the definition of an injured state. (See *State Responsibility: Comments and Observations Received from Governments*, UN doc. no. A/CN.4/488, 25 March 1998, p. 95.
99. *2001 Draft Articles*, article 48(1)(a).
100. *ILC 2001 Report*, p. 126.
101. Ibid.
102. *2001 Draft Articles*, article 48(1)(b).
103. See, for example, Vattel's assertion that certain disrespect for the law was an injury to all states, Emmerich de Vattel, *The Law of Nations*, book II, chap. V, § 70, p. 251, endnote 70 of this chapter and associated text.
104. *Barcelona Traction, Light and Power Company, Limited*, at 32, para. 33.

105. Ibid., at 32, para. 34.
106. *East-Timor*, International Court of Justice, judgment of 30 June 1995, 1995 I.C.J. 90, at 102, para. 29. The court wrote, "Portugal's assertion that the rights of peoples to self-determination, as it evolved from the Charter and the United Nations practice, has an *erga omnes* character, is irreproachable."
107. *2001 Draft Articles*, article 48(2)(a). The United States suggested in its comments to the *2000 Draft Articles* that obligation to provide assurances and guarantees of nonrepetition in article 30(b) was not a rule of customary international law. Accordingly, it suggested that the comparable language in article 49 of the *2000 Draft Articles* (article 49 in the *2001 Draft Articles*) should be deleted. The ILC, however, did not change the language. (See *State Responsibility: Comments and Observations Received from Governments*, UN doc. A/CN.4/515, 19 March 2001, pp. 36 and 73.
108. *2001 Draft Articles*, article 48(2)(b).
109. *Fourth Report 1992 (Arangio-Ruiz)*, para. 146, pp. 47–48. See endnote 92 of this chapter and associated text.
110. *2000 Draft Articles*, article 54(1).
111. See comments from the Netherlands in *State Responsibility: Comments and Observations Received from Governments*, UN doc. A/CN.4/515, 19 March 2001, pp. 87–88. However, article 54(2) of the *2000 Draft Articles* permitted countermeasures by noninjured states against serious violations against *erga omnes* obligation.
112. *2001 Draft Articles*, article 54.
113. *ILC 2001 Report*, p. 139.
114. Ibid.
115. Ibid.
116. Emmerich de Vattel, *The Law of Nations* or *Principles of the Law of Nature*, book II, chap. XVIII, § 346, p. 351.
117. Georg Friedrich von Martens, *A Compendium of the Law of Nations*, p. 277.
118. See, for example, L. Oppenheim, *International Law*, vol. II, 7th ed., p. 138.

Chapter 9

Procedural Conditions for Countermeasures

(a) Introduction

When the injured state has established sufficiently that a violation has taken place and has come to the conclusion that countermeasures might be the appropriate response, a question arises: What actions does the injured state have to take before it can resort to countermeasures?

Because countermeasures can be destabilizing for the international system, countermeasures can generally not be the injured state's first choice of action. It is disputed what actions states have to take before countermeasures become a legal option. However, there seems to be a consensus among scholars that certain actions have to be taken prior to resorting to countermeasures, except in cases where the interests of the injured state cannot be preserved without immediate protective measures. Those required actions are mainly a duty to request the offending state to fulfill its obligations under international law, sometimes called a sommation; a duty to request negotiation regarding the dispute; and a duty to inform the offending state of any prospective countermeasures to which the injured state intends to resort.

(B) Requesting the Responsible State to Fulfill Its Obligation

According to the ICJ judgment in the *Gabcikovo-Nagymaros Project*, the injured state must, before resorting to countermeasures, "have called upon the State committing the wrongful act to discontinue its wrongful conduct or to make reparation for it."[1] This requirement was not explicitly in the *1996 Draft Articles* but was implied in Article 47 of said draft articles, the article describing, in general, the right of an injured state to resort to countermeasures.[2] In relation to actions that an injured state has to take prior to countermeasures, a number of states discussed, as a settled rule, the necessity of a demand for cessation of the violation or reparation.[3] From Crawford's *Third Report*, it seems that the requirement of sommation or demand for cessation or reparation was such a well-settled principle of international law that it was not necessary to spell it out in the draft articles.[4] The ILC gave attention to this language of governments and added an explicit requirement of such demand in its revised *2000 Draft Articles*.[5] Under Article 52(1)(a) of the *2001 Draft Articles*, the injured state has a duty to request that the state responsible for the injury fulfils its international obligations.[6]

Although this obligation was not explicitly in the *1996 Draft Articles*, it clearly was not new to the ILC or legal scholars. In the commentary to Article 47 of the *1996 Draft Articles*, the ILC discussed the purpose of a dialogue between the injured state and the offending state after the wrongful act has taken place and how the offending state's answer to the injured state's request for cessation of reparation might affect the need and scope of countermeasures. The discussion presupposes a requirement of such a demand, although it does not explicitly say so. Earlier, Arangio-Ruiz, a former special rapporteur, discussed the concept of sommation. He wrote that state practice in the nineteenth century indicated that sommation or some demand of cessation or reparation was mandatory prior to the use of reprisals or, at least, prior to forceful reprisals.[7] During the interwar years, this practice became more settled as a rule of customary international law. Arangio-Ruiz wrote, "Practice during the period clearly indicates general acceptance of the notion that, under customary international law, an injured State could not lawfully resort to measures without previously making some form of demand for cessation and/or reparation."[8] Although Arangio-Ruiz did not explicitly limit the application of the rule during the period in question to forceful reprisals, the context did not indicate that he saw the rule extending into the sphere of nonforceful reprisals.

In Article 6 of its resolution on reprisals from 1934, the Institute of International Law suggested a rule demanding the injured state to offer the wrongdoer an opportunity to terminate the violation and offer compensation prior to resorting to reprisals.[9] The resolution that dealt with reprisals *en temps de paix* does not, with regard to this requirement, distinguish between forceful and nonforceful countermeasures. In the *Naulilaa Case*, the tribunal said that reprisals are "lawful only when preceded by a *notice* which has yielded no satisfactory response."[10] Later, in the *Air Service Agreement Case*, France claimed that the United States' retaliation "should have been preceded by an unsuccessful formal request, as required by international law."[11] The tribunal in that case did not directly visit this issue—neither its factual nor legal aspects. Its silence about this issue has been called surprising;[12] however, it might be explained with the fact that the states were already negotiating the issue at hand. It is fair to assume that the alleged illegality of the ban on the Pan Am flight and the demand of cessation would have been on the table during that negotiation. Thus, the tribunal might not have seen the need to discuss the obvious.

Many scholars have subscribed to the line of thought that prior demand for cessation and/or reparation is a necessary condition for the legality of countermeasures. Oppenheim argued that reprisals were acceptable only if the injured state could not acquire compensation through negotiation and other friendly means.[13] Although he did not explicitly suggest that a sommation was necessary, it is implied in his words that such measures have to be taken for the right to resort to countermeasures to become active.

Centuries earlier, Vattel emphasized the requirement to demand justice before a state resorts to armed reprisals.

> A sovereign ought to shew in all his quarrels, a sincere desire of rendering justice, and preserving peace. He is obliged before he takes up arms, and after having taken them up also, to offer equitable conditions, and then alone his arms become just against an obstinate enemy, who refuses to listen to justice or to equity.[14]

Vattel argued that reprisals were secondary measures only to be used when justice had been denied and other amicable measures were not available.[15] He also mentioned a few other examples of denial of justice, such as a refusal to hear complaints, rejecting access to tribunals, and unjustified delays of justice. He also wrote that a judgment that was "manifestly unjust and partial"[16] would constitute a denial of justice as well.

Wheaton also suggested that reprisals were acceptable only "in case adequate satisfaction is refused by the offending State."[17] This entails that the injured state has to ask for satisfaction. Woolsey wrote that reprisals are to be used only in "cases of refusal or obstinate delay of justice."[18] As other writers, Woolsey saw reprisals as emergency measures that should be "acted upon only in an extreme case."[19] Furthermore, he argued that "there should be the fullest proof of an intention to deny or to overturn justice."[20]

Included in the requirement of demanding justice, the injured state must give the offending state a reasonable time to cease the violation and offer reparation. Oppenheim, for example, indicated that states must give the wrongdoer a certain time period to offer and provide reparation for the wrong done. The length of this period depends on the imminence of the effects of the violation and its seriousness.[21]

There might be instances where communication between the injured state and the responsible state has been interrupted or is nonexistent because of various reasons. During the 1980 Tehran hostage crisis, the

United States could not formally communicate with Iran because the Iranian government did not want to discuss the fate of the hostages in the embassy or the occupation of the embassy premises. Elagab argued that the court had, in fact, accepted a "constructive demand" from the United States government for termination of the illegal situation. He continued and wrote, "The deduction to be drawn here is that the condition of prior demand will be considered as being fulfilled where appropriate alternative means of intimation have been utilized."[22] A few years earlier, Zoller came to the same conclusion and said that in a situation, like the *Hostage Case*, where "the other party categorically refuses to negotiate…the right to resort to countermeasures may be immediately implemented."[23]

It is possible that, prior to the *Gabcikovo-Nagymaros Project*, the requirement of demand for cessation or reparation prior to countermeasures applied only to armed reprisals. However, the suggestion expressed by the United States in the *Air Service Agreement Case* that France's theory of reprisals, "if correct, applies to armed reprisals only"[24] was apparently not directed against the part of the theory relating to the requirement of demand for cessation or reparation.[25] It seems, therefore, that the ICJ in the *Gabcikovo-Nagymaros Project* only clarified the applicability of this rule, and that it, in fact, had developed into a rule of customary international law much earlier.

The ILC wrote in its commentary to the *2001 Draft Articles* that the "principle underlying the notification requirement is that, considering the exceptional nature and potentially serious consequences of countermeasures, they should not be taken before the other State is given notice of a claim and some opportunity to present a response."[26] Under the *2001 Draft Articles*, the duty to demand that the responsible state fulfills its international obligation seems to be without an exception. The exception to notification and the duty to offer negotiation in Article 52(2) does not apply to the duty to demand compliance and reparation. However, Elagab's and Zoller's analysis of the situation in the *Hostage Case* indicated that this requirement might not be absolute when communication cannot be established or maintained with the offending state. Also, Crawford, special rapporteur of the ILC, seems to have suggested that countermeasures that are "required in order to maintain the status quo," are permitted before the injured states calls "on the responsible State to fulfill its obligations."[27] It is doubtful, however, that any exception from such requirement reaches any further. Arangio-Ruiz, in his analysis of state practice relating to the development of this requirement, argued that although state practice is not in full compliance with the requirement, it

> nevertheless demonstrate[s] the belief of States that, even in cases characterized by a high degree of wrongfulness *and* continuity, and which call for a very *urgent* remedy, resort to measures on the part of the injured State must be preceded, under the law of responsibility, by appropriate demands, *sommations* or intimations.[28]

(c) Duty to Notify the Responsible State of the Prospective Countermeasures and to Offer Negotiations

Notifying the responsible state of the prospective countermeasures is not a clearly accepted practice of states. It is, however, closely related to the sommation requirement and, in a way, additional to that. Although not clear from the international literature, it could be inferred from scholars' general assumptions about countermeasures as a remedy of last resort that injured states are under an obligation to do what is feasible to avoid such remedies. This duty might entail an obligation to indicate its intentions with regard to its reaction to the alleged violation. The ICJ had an opportunity to address this requirement in the *Gabcikovo-Nagymaros Project* but left it untouched. After Hungary suspended work at Nagymaros and Dunakiliti, Slovakia notified Hungary "that it would feel compelled to take unilateral measures if Hungary were to persist in its refusal to resume the works."[29] The court, however, did not cite that notification as a prerequisite for implementing Variant C as countermeasures.

The ILC suggested in its *2001 Draft Articles* that injured states have a duty to notify the offending states about its prospective countermeasures and to offer negotiation. The relevant part of Article 52 reads as follow:

> 1. Before taking countermeasures, an injured State shall:
>
> ...
>
> b. Notify the responsible State of any decision to take countermeasures and offer to negotiate with that State.
>
> 2. Notwithstanding paragraph 1 (b), the injured State may take such urgent countermeasures as are necessary to preserve its rights.[30]

It must be noted that the ILC commentary indicates that the duty under Article 52(1)(b) can be combined with the sommation: the request to cease the illegal situation.[31] This is in line with an earlier report by Arangio-Ruiz who suggested that the sommation and the notification of possible countermeasures should be combined in one communication.[32] The independent value of this duty might, therefore, be questioned; whether the injured state has complied with this obligation might be determined based on the circumstances as a whole and the existence of less formal or less independent communication than the sommation.

The duty to notify the offending state about prospective countermeasures was not specifically questioned by states in their comments to the *2000 Draft Articles*.[33] The general consensus on this rule is in line with the nature of countermeasures as measures of last resort, which suggests that injured states are under an obligation to try to avert the need for such measure, for example, by making their intentions clear. However, if this requirement would be strictly obligatory, it could remove the element of surprise from the coercive power of countermeasures or result in an unacceptable delay for the injured country, which could increase the harmful consequences of the alleged violation. Thus, the ILC suggested in its *2001 Draft Articles* that the duty under Article 52(1)(b) was not absolute; an injured state should be permitted "to take such urgent countermeasures as are necessary to preserve its rights."[34] The ILC added in the commentary to the *2001 Draft Articles* that the wording of the exception in Article 52(2) should be interpreted as including "both [the injured state's] rights in the subject-matter of the dispute and its right to take countermeasures."[35] This means that countermeasures are permissible under Article 52(2) not only because of irreparable harm that might result from the illegal acts but also to ensure that the coercive value of the countermeasures is not lost due to delay associated with the offer to negotiate or the loss of the surprise element. The ILC continued and argued, "Temporary stay orders, the temporary freezing of assets and similar measures could fall within paragraph 2, depending on the circumstances."[36] It seems clear, therefore, that an injured state that intends to resort to countermeasures by freezing the assets of the offending state does not have to announce that decision in advance and does not have to negotiate with the offending state on the modalities of such countermeasures. However, such application of the exception will depend on the mobility of the assets or how easily the offending state can liquidate or transfer them to a territory not under control of the injured state.

Subject to the same exception, the ILC suggested that the injured state should be under an obligation to offer negotiations with the responsible state.[37] Under Article 2(3) of the *UN Charter*, all member states "shall settle their international disputes by peaceful means in such a manner that international peace and security, and justice, are not endangered."[38] Although the provision does not establish an absolute duty to negotiate all disputes, it should not be interpreted only as an encouragement to resolve issues peacefully, but also as an obligation to reserve potentially destabilizing unilateral acts for situations where less intrusive remedies are not likely to produce the necessary results. Vattel wrote that reprisals should be "used between nation and nation to do justice to themselves, when they cannot otherwise obtain it."[39] Vattel, as many others, viewed reprisals as a sort of a last resort, that is, that other less intrusive measures have to be exhausted before them.

This is, however, not an absolute requirement according to Vattel. He wrote:

> It is not always necessary to authorize the having recourse to arms, that all the methods of reconciliation have been expressly rejected; it is sufficient, that there is the utmost reason to believe, that the enemy would not enter into these measures with sincerity; that the issue of them could not be happy, and that a delay could only tend to put the state in greater danger of being oppressed.[40]

Vattel was arguing for a balance between the need for an injured state to take unilateral measures and the need of the international system to be free of potentially destabilizing actions of states. Vattel's words must, of course, be viewed in the light of the ban against the use or threat of force under the *UN Charter* and that countermeasures cannot violate that ban. Vattel's ideas, so interpreted, correspond to the requirement to offer negotiation coupled with the exception.

The duty to offer negotiation developed from a more stringent requirement in the *1996 Draft Articles*, which required states not only to offer negotiation but also to conduct negotiation prior to resorting to countermeasures.[41] The ILC was far from being unanimous on this issue. The commentary to Article 48[42] of the *1996 Draft Articles* reads:

> While the Commission as a whole agreed that negotiations and all other available procedures for the peaceful settlement of disputes should be pursued, there was disagreement as to whether this needed to be prior to the taking of countermeasures. The difficulty here is twofold. First, negotiations or other forms of dispute settlement can be lengthy, and could be almost indefinitely drawn out by a State seeking to avoid the consequences of its wrongful act. Secondly, some forms of countermeasures (including some of the most readily available forms, for example, the freezing of assets) can only be effective if taken promptly.[43]

Despite being aware of this problem and the potential disadvantage it would put the injured state at, the ILC, nevertheless, decided to suggest a provision requiring the injured state to enter into a good faith negotiation prior to resorting to countermeasures.[44] The line of thought was, however, that such provision was not seen as an obstacle to the taking of countermeasures but rather as a provision "making available to the State which is a target of countermeasures an appropriate and effective procedure of resolving the dispute."[45] The central issue is that "full-scale countermeasures should not be taken without an initial attempt to resolve the dispute by negotiation."[46] Although many states supported this formulation,[47] the United Kingdom and the United States rejected this approach. The United Kingdom government wrote that the duty to enter into negotiation prior to the taking of countermeasures or the duty to suspend countermeasures while the disputing parties are engaged in good faith negotiation or other kinds of dispute resolution is not in line with customary international law.[48] The United States, citing the *Air Service Agreement Case*, expressed a similar opinion.[49] Other states supported deleting the requirement of negotiation not necessarily because they were against the principle but because they did not believe that there would be consensus on such provision or because the formulation was confusing.[50] Consequently, the ILC suggested a more lenient requirement in the *2000 Draft Articles*; instead of conducting good faith negotiation, injured states only had to offer negotiation prior to resorting to countermeasures.[51] In addition, an injured state could not take countermeasures, other than "provisional and urgent countermeasures as may be necessary to preserve its rights,"[52] while "negotiations are being pursued in good faith and have not been unduly delayed."[53]

As is true about the duty to notify the offending state about the prospective countermeasures, the duty to offer negotiations was seen positively by most states in their comments to the *2000 Draft Articles*. However, it is not surprising, when debating restrictions on unilateral measures, that a few powerful states argued that the effects of ongoing good faith negotiations on the right to take countermeasures were not a part of customary international law. Japan, for example, aired its concerns about negotiations and their effect on the right to take countermeasures. Japan's comments focused mainly on this temporary ban against countermeasures, along with the possible abuse of the right to take urgent countermeasures.[54] This temporary ban against countermeasures while negotiations were being attempted was also a cause for alarm for Slovakia, the United Kingdom, and the United States.[55] While other states, such as Denmark, the Netherlands, and Spain, supported the effects of good faith negotiations,[56] it was apparent that there was little consensus among states on this issue.[57] Thus, the ban against countermeasures due to ongoing good faith negotiations was not included in the *2001 Draft Articles*. However, the duty to offer negotiation prior to resorting to countermeasures remained as an obstacle to countermeasures in the *2001 Draft Articles*.[58] The duty to offer negotiation came under attack by the United States, which suggested that the duty to offer negotiation and the temporary ban against countermeasures during good faith negotiation contravene international law.[59] However, its supporting arguments only addressed the latter objection; no independent arguments were set forth against the duty to offer negotiation. The United Kingdom also argued against the duty to offer negotiation.[60] It wrote,

> For example, it is clearly not acceptable that the taking of countermeasures in the face of genocide should have to be postponed while the "injured" or "interested" State makes an offer (which a wrongdoing State would no doubt accept with alacrity) to negotiate, or while States engage in negotiations despite the continuation of the killing.[61]

Few would doubt that the exception to the rule, as it is described in Article 52(2),[62] would justify immediate countermeasures under extreme circumstances as the United Kingdom describes. Other doctrines might also be utilized to support an immediate action in such cases. The reason set forth by the United Kingdom for rejecting the duty to offer negotiation is, therefore, not particularly well thought through.

Neither the *Air Service Agreement Case* nor the *Gabcikovo-Nagymaros Project* provided any decisive answers to the question of the duty to offer negotiation prior to resorting to countermeasures. As has been suggested, the parties to the former dispute were already in the process of negotiating and had actually reached an agreement prior to the tribunal's decision. It might not have seen as its role to comment on or even to establish a rule that was not very relevant to the dispute at hand. Accordingly, the tribunal's silence on this issue cannot be taken as an indication that the duty to offer negotiation prior to taking countermeasures was not a rule of customary international law. The silence of the ICJ in the *Gabcikovo-Nagymaros Project* can be explained similarly, but extensive negotiation had taken place between the parties before Slovakia decided to implement Variant C and justify it as countermeasures (see discussion on the *Gabcikovo-Nagymaros Project* in part I, chapter 5).

The remaining issue relating to procedural obstacles to countermeasures is the exception from the duty to notify the offending state of the prospective countermeasures and offer negotiation. As discussed earlier, under the *1996 Draft Articles*, an injured state that was considering resorting to countermeasures was under an obligation to negotiate with the injured state but could resort to interim measures of protection, which were necessary to preserve its rights.[63] A number of powerful states rejected such obstacles to the right to take countermeasures and argued that the duty to negotiate prior to resorting to countermeasures was not a part of customary international law.[64] The ILC subsequently changed the text of the relevant article in the *2000 Draft Articles*. The text of the exception also took some changes; instead of permitting states to resort to interim measures of protection, injured states were permitted to "take such provisional and urgent countermeasures as may be necessary to preserve its rights."[65] The critics of the comparable provision in the *1996 Draft Articles* were not satisfied with this new formulation, which was apparently not intended to limit the responsibilities of the injured state prior to resorting to countermeasures. Their main reasons for their opposition against this provision was an extension of what they had expressed about the duty to offer negotiation, that is, that customary international law did not limit the injured states' right to take countermeasures prior to such an offer to what could be classified as provisional and urgent as is necessary to preserve an injured states' rights.[66] The United Kingdom wrote, "Draft article 53 is so fundamentally flawed as to render the provisions on countermeasures, as currently drafted, wholly unacceptable."[67]

Although the United Kingdom's comments were directed mainly against the obligation to negotiate in good faith and its effects on the right to countermeasures, it was clear that the United Kingdom was not in agreement with the clarity of the provision and the responsibility it put on the injured state. Japan also, in this context, expressed its concerns regarding the lack of clarity and potential for abuse without, however, stating that the exception put too much of a burden on the injured state.[68]

In this study, it is suggested that the ILC has not made a compelling case for the requirement of notification about the prospective countermeasures and the duty to offer negotiation. However, the requirement is in harmony with a main goal of the international legal order—to promote stability and restrict potentially destabilizing unilateral measures. It is also in line with what earlier writers suggested about countermeasures in that they should only be taken when other less destabilizing measures have failed or are not likely to be fruitful. This rule, with its exceptions, is, therefore, a logical restriction on countermeasures, which in themselves violate international law but seek justification in a prior illegal behavior of the offending state. Its precise parameters, however, remain to be set by state practice or jurisprudence.

ENDNOTES

1. *Gabcikovo-Nagymaros Project*, at 56, para. 84.
2. *1996 Draft Articles*, article 47.
3. See comments from France, the United States, Czech Republic, and Germany, *State Responsibility: Comments and Observations Received from Governments*, UN doc. no. A/CN.4/488, 25 March 1998, pp. 119–121.
4. See *Third Report 2000 (Crawford)* addendum, p. 32, para. 357. It must also be pointed out that in the *1996 Draft Articles* the right to resort to countermeasures was conditioned upon various requirements, such as referring the dispute to a settlement procedures and negotiating with the offending state. These guarantees for the offending state were taken out of the *2000 Draft Articles*, raising the need to explicitly stress the need for a sommation.
5. *2000 Draft Articles*, article 53(1).
6. *2001 Draft Articles*, article 52(1)(a).
7. *Fourth Report 1992 (Arangio-Ruiz)*, pp. 8–9, paras. 7–9.
8. Ibid., p. 9, para. 10.
9. L'Institut de Droit International, Le Régime de Représailles en Temps de Paix, *Annuaire de l'Institute de Droit International*, Brussels, 1934, p. 710, ("Dans l'exercice des représailles, l'Etat doit se conformer aux règles suivantes: …Mettre au préalable l'Etat auteur de l'acte illicite en demeure de la faire cesser et d'accorder éventuellement les réparation requises").
10. *Naulilaa Case*, see supra endnote 2 of chap. 4, p. 1280, UNRIAA, at 1027. (La représaille n'est licite que lorsqu'elle a été précédée d'une sommation restée infructueuse.)
11. *Air Service Agreement Case*, see supra endnote 4 of chap. 4, at 319, para. 17.
12. See, for example, Omer Yousif Elagab, *The Legality of Non-forcible Counter-measures in International Law*, p. 68. The ILC in its 2001 report asserts that the tribunal in the *Air Service Agreement Case* stressed "that the injured state must call on the responsible state to fulfil its obligation of cessation and reparation before any resort to countermeasures." (See *ILC 2001 Report*, p. 136, para. 3 of the commentary to article 52 of the *2001 Draft Articles*, citing paras. 85–87 of the tribunal's award.) It is unclear how the words of the cited paragraphs can be interpreted in that manner.
13. L. Oppenheim, *International Law: A Treatise*, vol. II, 7th ed., p. 136.
14. Emmerich de Vattel, *The Law of Nations* or *Principles of the Law of Nature*, book II, chap. XVIII, § 336, p. 347.

15. Ibid. § 350, p. 352. See also Hall, *A Treatise on International Law*, p. 361.
16. Emmerich de Vattel, *The Law of Nations* or *Principles of the Law of Nature*, book II, chap. XVIII, § 350, p. 353.
17. Henry Wheaton, *Elements of International Law*, p. 341.
18. Theodore D. Woolsey, *Introduction to the Study of International Law*, p. 189.
19. Ibid., p. 189.
20. Ibid., p. 189.
21. L. Oppenheim, *International Law*, vol. II, 7th ed., pp. 142–143. See similar line of thought in the *Third Report 200 (Crawford)*, addendum, p. 32, para. 357.
22. Omar Yousif Elagab, *The Legality of Non-forcible Counter-measures in International Law*, p. 69.
23. Elisabeth Zoller, *Peacetime Unilateral Remedies: An Analysis of Countermeasures*, p. 121.
24. *Air Service Agreement Case*, at 320, para. 18.
25. See French claim in *Air Service Agreement Case*, at 320, para. 18 and the United States' comments in *State Responsibility: Comments and Observations Received from Governments*, UN doc. no. A/CN.4/488, 25 March 1998, p. 120, in particular, endnote 97.
26. *ILC 2001 Report*, p. 136, para. 4 of the commentary to article 52.
27. *Fourth Report 2001 (Crawford)*, p. 26, para. 69.
28. *Fourth Report 1992 (Arangio-Ruiz)*, p. 11. para. 15.
29. *Gabcikovo-Nagymaros Project*, at 47, para. 61.
30. *2001 Draft Articles*, articles 52(1)–52(2).
31. See *ILC 2001 Report*, p. 136, para. 5 of the commentary to article 52.
32. *Fourth Report 1992 (Arangio-Ruiz)*, p. 13.
33. See, however, comments from the United Kingdom, which rejected article 53 of the *2000 Draft Articles* (comparable to article 52 of the *2001 Draft Articles*) as a whole, as it does not reflect international law. In its more specific comments where the United Kingdom outlines the problems with article 53, the duty to notify about prospective countermeasures is not criticized. (See *State Responsibility: Comments and Observations Received from Governments*, UN doc. A/CN.4/515, 19 March 2001, pp. 84–85.)
34. *2001 Draft Articles*, article 52(2).
35. *ILC 2001 Report*, p. 136, para. 6 of the commentary to article 52.
36. Ibid.
37. *2001 Draft Articles*, articles 52(1)(b) and 52(2).

38. *UN Charter*, article 2(3). For some literature on the duty to negotiate, see, for example, J.F. O'Connor, *Good Faith in International Law,* Dartmouth, Brookfield, VE, 1991; Teklewold Gebrehana, *Duty to Negotiate: An Element of International Law*, Svenska Institutet för Internationell Rätt, Uppsala, 1978; *Transboundary Environmental Negotiation: New Approaches to Global Cooperation*, edited by Lawrence Susskind, William Moomaw, Kevin Gallagher, Jossey-Bass Publishers, San Francisco, 2002; and Bin Cheng, *General Principles of Law as Applied by International Courts and Tribunals*, Stevens & Sons Limited, London, 1953, p. 105 et seq.
39. Emmerich de Vattel, *The Law of Nations*, book II, chap. XVIII, § 342, p. 349.
40. Ibid., § 334, p. 346.
41. *1996 Draft Articles*, article 48(1).
42. Comparable to article 52 of the *2001 Draft Articles* and article 53 of the *2000 Draft Articles*.
43. *ILC 1996 Report*, pp. 68–69, para. 2 of the commentary to article 48.
44. *1996 Draft Articles*, article 48.
45. *ILC 1996 Report*, p. 69, para. 2 of the commentary to article 48.
46. Ibid.
47. See comments from Denmark, Austria, and France, *State Responsibility: Comments and Observations Received from Governments*, UN doc. no. A/CN.4/488, 25 March 1998, p. 117 and pp. 120–121.
48. *State Responsibility: Comments and Observations Received from Governments*, UN doc. no. A/CN.4/488, 25 March 1998, p. 122.
49. Ibid.
50. See, for example, comments from Ireland and Germany, *State Responsibility: Comments and Observations Received from Governments*, UN doc. no. A/CN.4/488, 25 March 1998, pp. 119–120 and p. 121.
51. *2000 Draft Articles*, article 53(2).
52. See *2000 Draft Articles*, article 53(3).
53. *2000 Draft Articles*, article 53(4).
54. *State Responsibility: Comments and Observations Received from Governments*, UN doc. A/CN.4/515, 19 March 2001, pp. 83–84.
55. Ibid., pp. 84–86.
56. Ibid., pp. 83–84.
57. See also *Fourth Report 2001 (Crawford)*, pp. 25–26, para. 67.
58. See *2001 Draft Articles*, article 52(1)(b).
59. *State Responsibility: Comments and Observations Received from Governments*, UN doc. A/CN.4/515, 19 March 2001, p. 85.
60. Ibid.

61. Ibid.
62. *2001 Draft Article*, article 52(2).
63. *1996 Draft Articles*, article 48(1).
64. See comments by Germany, the United Kingdom, and United States, *State Responsibility: Comments and Observations Received from Governments*, UN doc. no. A/CN.4/488, 25 March 1998, pp. 121–122. It is notable that France, however, suggested that the injured state should "agree to negotiate in good faith" prior to taking countermeasures (See France comments in *State Responsibility: Comments and Observations Received from Governments*, UN doc. no. A/CN.4/488, 25 March 1998, p. 119).
65. *2000 Draft Articles*, article 53(3).
66. See, for example, Unites States' comments in *State Responsibility: Comments and Observations Received from Governments*, UN doc. A/CN.4/515, 19 March 2001, p. 86.
67. Ibid., p. 85.
68. Ibid., pp. 83–84.

Chapter 10

Considerations Related to the Taking of Countermeasures

(a) Interests Against Which Countermeasures Can Be Directed and Prohibited Countermeasures

One of the contested aspects of countermeasures is against which interests countermeasures can be directed. There is little disagreement that countermeasures can be directed against a state, its property, and various interests it might have. An important question is, however, when and up to what extent can countermeasures be directed against citizens of the wrongdoing state and their property.

Early writers concluded that countermeasures could be directed not only against the wrongdoing state but also against citizens of that state. However, opinions on the limitations of subjecting citizens to such measures have differed. Grotius wrote that although it might sometimes be unjust, the subjects of the sovereign can be the objects of the reprisals.[1] He pointed out an important exception: Ambassadors could not be objects of countermeasures.[2] Vattel wrote that reprisals were to be used "between nation and nation."[3] Accordingly, one might prematurely assume that he does not consider that reprisals can be directed against subjects of states, that is, that the property of private citizens, or themselves, can not be seized.[4] However, this would not be the correct interpretation. Vattel wrote, "The goods even of the individuals in their totality ought to be considered as the goods of the nation, in regard to other states."[5] The argument was that the richness of the citizens forms the richness and the power of the nation. The nation has, therefore, direct or indirect interests in the wealth and prosperity of their citizens. When Vattel said "every thing that belongs to the nation is subject to reprisal,"[6] he is clearly referring to the official property of the state, as well as property of its subjects. However, just as Woolsey repeated later,[7] Vattel believed that "the sovereign is to recompense those of his subjects on whom the reprisals fall."[8]

Vattel also supported the legality of arresting individuals belonging to the wrongdoing state as a form of reprisals. Like some other writers, he cited Greek law allowing a citizen whose relative had been assassinated by nationals of another state to arrest up to three such nationals and hold them until justice had been delivered, the assassin punished, or the assassin extradited.[9] Vattel did not explicitly say that this practice was illegal in his time but admitted that it was not common.

On the treatment of persons detained as a method of reprisal, Vattel wrote, "[W]e cannot take their lives, nor inflict any corporal pain upon them."[10] However, it would be justifiable to take lives of those who resist reprisals if necessary.[11] This is in contradiction to Grotius' assertion, which was that a rule allowing intentional killing of those who resisted reprisal could "never be reconciled either to sound religion or morality."[12]

Martens argued that if no reparation is paid, the injured state could seize the property of the wrongdoing state or its subjects. Martens went further and argued that the injured state could seize persons who are subjects of the wrongdoing state. However, the injured state could not take their lives unless it was necessary to prevent further violations and no other means were available.[13]

Wheaton argued that countermeasures could be directed against persons and things that belong to the offending nation until satisfactory reparation is made for the alleged injury.[14] It is not clear if Wheaton meant private persons or only persons who represent the state.

Woolsey argued against making subjects of states or their property the object of reprisals. However, should property of a private citizen be seized as part of reprisal against his state, his society should share his loss.[15] Oppenheim chose not to depart from the teachings of the early writers. He wrote that reprisals can be

> performed against anything and everything that belongs to, or is due to, the delinquent State or its citizens. Ships sailing under its flag may be seized, treaties concluded may be suspended, a part of its territory may be militarily occupied, goods belonging to it, or to its citizens, may be seized, and the like.[16]

Oppenheim also argued that citizens can be objects of reprisals; a state can take citizens of the wrongdoer hostage. He mentioned an example when Prussian authorities arrested two Russian citizens in response to an arrest of a Russian-born Prussian citizen by Russian authorities.[17] Oppenheim emphasized, however, that the treatment of the persons must be humane and the injured state may not treat them as criminals or subject them to punishment.

The ILC suggested in the *2001 Draft Articles* that certain interests are not to be touched by countermeasures. Article 50 of the draft articles reads:

1. Countermeasures shall not affect:
    a. The obligation to refrain from the threat or use of force as embodied in the Charter of the United Nations;
    b. Obligations for the protection of fundamental human rights;
    c. Obligations of a humanitarian character prohibiting reprisals;

d. Other obligations under peremptory norms of general international law.

2. A State taking countermeasures is not relieved from fulfilling its obligations:

   a. Under any dispute settlement procedure applicable between it and the responsible State;
   b. To respect the inviolability of diplomatic or consular agents, premises, archives and documents.[18]

Accordingly, the law of countermeasures cannot be utilized to justify violations of five areas of international obligations: use of force in contravention to the *UN Charter*, fundamental human rights, reprisals under humanitarian law, and peremptory norms, as well as diplomatic and consular inviolability.[19]

Comments from states on Article 51 of the *2000 Draft Articles* indicate that restrictions on countermeasures as described in the article are generally not disputed. Also, it is notable that the Republic of Korea wanted to add a restriction related to environmentally harmful countermeasures. The comments read, "[I]n the light of the growing importance of the environment, the Government of the Republic of Korea would like to see the inclusion of 'obligations to protect the natural environment against widespread, long-term and severe damage'..."[20] The arguments against Article 51 came from the United States and Britain. Neither state disputed that countermeasures cannot involve the use of force in violation of the *UN Charter*. The United States, however, argued that there was no need to repeat this rule in the draft articles because the *UN Charter* "already establishes overriding constraints on behaviour by States."[21] The United States also argued that the manner that Article 51 distinguishes between different categories of international obligation does not reflect customary international law.[22] It further argued that the restrictions in Article 51 were an invitation to confusion as terms such as "fundamental human rights" and "peremptory norms" were not defined in international law.[23] Although no state echoed the United States' concern, the terms "fundamental human rights" and "peremptory norms" require some brief explanations. First, I address the notion of fundamental human rights.

Developments in international human rights law during the latter half of the twentieth century has established a number of limits to the injured states' freedom to chose their own methods of countermeasures. Further, state practice has indicated that countermeasures and other measures of coercion have, up to a certain extent, respected human rights and humanitarian concerns.[24] Whether it is because the states believe they were legally bound to do so, or because respecting certain human needs was a politically attractive choice cannot be determined.

In the commentary to Article 50 of the *2001 Draft Articles*, the ILC explained somewhat the meaning of fundamental human rights in paragraph 1(b). The commission cited the tribunal in the *Naulilaa Case* and a resolution of the International Law Association, which stated that states taking countermeasures had to respect the law of humanity.[25] The commission also cited General Comment 8 (1997) of the Committee on Economic, Social and Cultural Rights, stressing that countermeasures must always "take full account of the provisions of the International Covenant on Economic, Social and Cultural Rights."[26] Article 50 of the *1996 Draft Articles* used the concept of basic human rights. The commentary to Article 50 in the *ILC 1995 Report* explained the meaning of this concept.[27] First, it related to the protection of the humanitarian character of persons who are protected under humanitarian law, as well as humanitarian principles applicable in times of peace.[28] It must be noted that Article 50 of the *2001 Draft Articles* makes a separate mention of humanitarian principles prohibiting reprisals. Thus, arguably, the concept of fundamental human rights in Article 50(1)(b) does not necessarily include pure humanitarian principles. The commentaries in the *ILC 2001 Report* and the *ILC 1995 Report*, however, indicate otherwise.[29] Second, the concept of basic human rights refers to nonderogable human rights. The commission wrote in its 1995 report:

> As a result of its unprecedented development in recent years, the law of human rights provides a minimum standard of humane

> treatment by identifying certain inviolable human rights which may not be suspended of derogated from even in time of war or other public emergencies.[30]

There seems to be a consensus among states and scholars that the right to life, freedom from torture and inhuman treatment, and freedom from slavery belongs to a body of nonderogable rights.[31] In addition, states have, in a number of human right agreements, agreed that certain rights should not be derogated from by anyone.[32] Arangio-Ruiz, a former special rapporteur on state responsibility, said in his report in 1992 that it was not appropriate to enumerate the basic human rights, "which would be immune from countermeasures. Any enumeration would 'crystallize' a rule that must be left open to the evolution of human rights law."[33] It is, however, clear from the text of the article and the ILC literature in general that "less essential" human rights are not immune from countermeasures.[34] Arangio-Ruiz mentioned, as an example, property of foreign nationals located in the territory of the injured state. In his *Third Report on State Responsibility*, he discussed the restraints state should exercise in relation to the taking of property of such foreign nationals without coming to a concrete conclusion.[35] In his *Fourth Report on State Responsibility*, Arangio-Ruiz wrote, "the human rights which should be considered inviolable by countermeasures—the 'more essential' human rights—are not understood to include property rights."[36]

The restrictions on countermeasures described in Article 50(1)(c) of the *2001 Draft Articles*, that is, obligations of a humanitarian character prohibiting reprisals, are taken from Article 60(5) of the *Vienna Convention on the Law of Treaties*.[37] The ILC wrote in its report that these restrictions reflect "the basic prohibition of reprisals against individuals, which exists in international humanitarian law."[38] This protection is, however, not for the benefit of all individuals but only for those who are protected under international humanitarian law.[39]

The prohibition against countermeasures that violate peremptory norms of international law[40] has been somewhat controversial, as already mentioned. This is not due to any assertion that countermeasures can violate peremptory norms but rather because of the uncertainty of the definition of the term.[41] The ILC commentary in the *ILC 2001 Report* is fairly straightforward. The ILC wrote, "Evidently a peremptory norm, not subject to derogation as between two States even by treaty, cannot be derogated from by unilateral action in the form of countermeasures."[42] Since this is evident, the inclusion of this paragraph might not be necessary.[43] The question of the scope of peremptory norms is a matter of debate. The United States argued that apart from "genocide, slavery and torture," the content of peremptory norms "is not well defined or accepted."[44] Whatever is true about the limits of peremptory norms,[45] it is barely advisable to include a list of norms as controversial, as peremptory norms undeniably are in an article on prohibited countermeasures. Instead, the question was left open for arguments in the diplomatic quarters or before international tribunals.

Although Article 50 of the *2001 Draft Articles* is not a law, it indicates that the notion of prohibited countermeasures has wide support in the international community. The law of countermeasures, therefore, can not be utilized to justify any unilateral acts; there are restraints that states will have to respect, limiting their choice of means and methods when taking countermeasures.

(b) Proportionality

The principle of proportionality is a general rule of international law.[46] Moreover, there is a consensus among governments that "the principle of proportionality of countermeasures is a part of customary international law."[47] In relation to the debate in this book, three main rules might be extracted from this principle. First, when resorting to countermeasures, the injured state shall select the least intrusive measure of the available sufficiently effective measures; second, such measure shall be proportionate to the injury suffered; and third, the extent or scope of the measure taken shall be limited to what is necessary to obtain the objective of the countermeasure. The validity of each rule will be the topic of this subchapter.

The rule of proportionality is quite possibly the most important factor in the determination of the legality of countermeasures. It is a comprehensive rule designed to prevent relations between states from deteriorating beyond what is necessary. It encourages a selection of less intrusive measures, such as negotiation, arbitration, or other nondestabilizing measures and, when more intrusive measures are appropriate, to exercise them with the greatest care. The principle thus obliges states that have been injured as a result of an international wrongful act of another state to consider alternative measures to solve the dispute at hand.

The principle of proportionality in relation to unilateral measures taken by states is probably as old as the concept of unilateral measures itself. Vattel wrote in 1789, "Nature gives us no right to have recourse to force, but where mild and pacific methods are ineffectual."[48] He also wrote, "as the law of humanity prescribes to nations no less than to individuals, the mildest measures, when they are sufficient to obtain justice," the sovereign ought to resort to reprisals instead of the more lethal and violent acts of war.[49] Martens argued in a similar manner. He wrote that forcible means could be of various degrees, and a sovereign must "confine himself to the employment of the lowest degree by which he can obtain due satisfaction."[50]

Holland wrote on the proportionality principle as a general rule of international relations that "]t]he duty of Sovereigns is to maintain the rights of their State, and to do this by the gentlest measures."[51] Hall wrote that measures related to states' self-preservation "must evidently be confined within the narrowest limits consistent with obtaining the required end."[52]

Oppenheim suggested that reprisals "must be in proportion to the wrong done, and to the amount of compulsion necessary to get reparation." He cited the German reprisals in relation to the Naulilaa incident as an example of overreaching.[53] Hall wrote on similar notes that reprisals have to be in proportion to the provocation and "not in excess to what is needed to obtain redress."[54] In Oppenheim's and Hall's passage, they both touch upon an important question: in proportion to what? The short answer is that the proportionality principle sets forth a two-point test. First, the countermeasures have to be in proportion to the injury suffered and, second, in proportion to the measures necessary to acquire the legitimate aims. As mentioned earlier, Article 51 of the *2001 Draft Articles* addressed the requirement of proportionality and shed a light on the criteria to which countermeasures have to be proportionate. Article 51 said, "Countermeasures must be commensurate with the injury suffered, taking into account the gravity of the internationally wrongful act and the rights in question."[55]

With regard to the first point, one might ask if the countermeasures have to be in proportion to the actual harm or the potential harm when the harm is not fully realized at the time of the violation. Also, how clear does the extent of the harm have to be to be measured against the proportionality principle? A precise answer to these questions can barely be found in the international jurisprudence. The ILC argued that "what is proportionate is not a matter which can be determined precisely."[56] The nature, character, or quality of the rights in question would be the determining factors rather than indicators of quantitative nature. The *Air Service Agreement Case* might also shed some light on this issue. After stating that assessing the proportionality requirement was a complex process that could at best be approached through approximation, the tribunal suggested that the interests at stake were not only of the airline but also the interests of uninterrupted worldwide air transport. France was unable to prove that the proportionality requirement had not been met. This reasoning might suggest that responses to a minor environmental harm could be argued as proportionate to the potential global environmental interests if the environmental misbehavior that the countermeasures are supposed to discourage will become widespread. This might open up Pandora's Box with regard to countermeasures. By comparing the countermeasures to the potential harm, as opposed to the actual harm in a particular dispute, the tribunal, arguably, misapplied the proportionality principle. However, the tribunal's method was somewhat reinforced in the *Gabcikovo-Nagymaros Project*, where the ICJ determined the proportionality of the countermeasures on the bases of their harm to the rights of all riparian states to enjoy free navigation and use of their common waterways. The court, apparently, used the principle of endangerment instead of the amount of actual harm in this particular case to determine whether the countermeasures were proportionate.[57] There is, however, a slight difference between these two methods that should be noted. The *Air Service Agreement Case* compared the countermeasures with the scope and effects of the initial violations and examined whether the countermeasures were in proportion to the effects of the initial violations to the principle in question. The *Gabcikovo-Nagymaros Project*, however, examined whether the countermeasures disproportionately affected the principle of equal rights of riparian states.

The weight that the tribunal in the *Air Service Agreement Case* gave the principle of uninterrupted air transport can also be seen under the first criterion, that is, the injury suffered, as the injury to the principle refers also to the injury, actual or potential, to the states to which the airlines in question belong.[58] Elagab interpreted the tribunal's words as suggesting that "cognizance should be taken of the serious losses which the United States might have suffered if France's example had been followed by other states with which the United States had similar agreements."[59] He consequently suggested an approach to the proportionality question regarding potential injury in cases of serious breaches of an international obligation. He wrote that in such cases, "proportionality can be determined by taking into consideration not only the immediate injury caused by the breach, but also the potential effects arising from it."[60]

In Article 51 of the *2001 Draft Articles*, the ILC suggested that proportionality should be compared with the injury, taking into account the "rights in question."[61] The phrase "rights in question" was briefly explained by the ILC in its commentary to Article 51. The ILC wrote, "The reference to 'the rights in question' has a broad meaning, and includes not only the effect of a wrongful act on the injured State but also on the rights of the responsible State. Furthermore, the position of other States which may be affected may also be taken into consideration."[62] This passage suggests the proportionality of countermeasures should also be measured with the harm done to the principle in question; however, it does not clearly say if the principle in question is the one that was infringed by the initial violation or the countermeasures.

The Nicaragua Case, which dealt with the use of armed force in a territory of another state, used a somewhat different approach. The court did not include a theory of a "piecemeal inhalation"[63] of the state taking the countermeasure in question or the global interest in preventing cross-border insurgency in the proportionality evaluation. Instead, the court evaluated the proportionality of the United States' actions in the context of the aid received by the Salvadorian armed opposition from Nicaragua and subsequently found that the measures taken by the United States were not proportionate to that aid.[64]

The second point of the proportionality determination refers to what is required to achieve the legitimate aims. Oppenheim wrote that countermeasures have to be proportionate "to the amount of compulsion necessary to get reparation."[65] Arguably, this refers to the means chosen and how they are implemented. As previously discussed, the legitimate purpose of countermeasures is to induce a state to comply with its international obligations.[66] The ILC suggested in its 2001 report[67] that there is a link between the proportionality principle and the aim, as the countermeasures cannot go disproportionately beyond what is necessary to acquire the aim. But, because of the two-point approach, countermeasures that are well within what is proportionate to acquire the aim can be deemed disproportionate because of the first point, that is, that the countermeasures must be proportionate to the harm done. The United States expressed its opinion in its comments to the *1996 Draft Articles* that not enough emphasizes was put on the proportionality between the countermeasures and what was needed to acquire the legitimate aim. The United States wrote, "Proportionality means principally that countermeasures should be tailored to induce the wrongdoer to meet its obligations under international law, and that steps taken towards that end should not escalate but rather serve to resolve the dispute."[68] The United States warned against relying too heavily on a vague concept of gravity of the wrongful act. It argued that countermeasures can arguably go further than the initial illegal act but still be legal.[69] Ireland somewhat supported the United States' argument on the link of the purpose of the countermeasures to the requirement of proportionality, that is, what was needed to induce a state to cease the illegal situation or pay reparation. However, Ireland did not question the reliance on the gravity of the prior wrongful act.[70]

Elagab seemed to come to a conclusion comparable to the one of the United States regarding proportionality to the purpose, that is, to induce a wrongdoing state to cease the illegal situation. He wrote that

> reference may be made to the measures taken by the United States during the hostage crisis. It is submitted that these measures were not disproportionate, since the seriousness of the hostages' detention warranted the employment of countermeasures on a scale sufficient to compel their release. In fact, even more drastic actions could have been taken.[71]

Zoller also suggested that the proportionality in relation to countermeasures is not only about the relation between the breach and the countermeasures but also is about the relation between the countermeasures and their legitimate purpose. Zoller wrote, "countermeasures could be said to respect proportionality when its effects are not disproportionate to the purpose aimed at."[72]

Although the special rapporteur did not suggest a direct link to the purpose of and the necessity for countermeasure in the article on proportionality, he recognized that there was such a link. However, he suggested that this issue should be dealt with in what is now Article 49 of the *2001 Draft Articles*, which describes the right for an injured state to take countermeasures to induce the offending state to comply with its international obligations.[73] He wrote:

> Proportionality is no doubt linked to necessity, in that a clearly disproportionate measure may well be judged not to have been necessary either. But it is also a limitation even on measures which are necessary in the sense that, without them, the target State is unlikely to comply. In every case, a countermeasure must be proportionate to the injury suffered, and this has a function partly independent of the question whether the countermeasure was necessary to achieve a particular result.[74]

These words indicate that, even though there is a link, the need for the measures to induce the wrongdoing state to change its illegal course is limited to the gravity of the initial act. Arguably, the criterion with which the proportionality of the countermeasures is measured has to be seen in its entirety and not by looking at isolated fractions of it. If this position is accepted, there might be instances of violations of international obligations that cannot be legally addressed under the law of countermeasures, that is, when the harm to the injured state and the principle in question is limited and the wrongdoing state is determined not to cease the violation. However, an equitable solution might be found under such circumstances by balancing the interests of the states concerned and the requirements of international legal order. Such solution would, in most cases, suggest that the determination of whether the measures are proportionate requires taking into account the criteria to which countermeasures have to be proportionate as a whole, that is, the injury suffered and the purpose of the measures. The two-point approach could provide the checks necessary to exclude the legality of extreme measures that are not well grounded in the legitimate interests that the measures are designed to protect.

It is immediately visible that the ILC does not use the word "proportionality" in the text of the relevant article. Instead of "proportionate to," the Commission suggested "commensurate with."[75] This language is partly taken from the *Gabcikovo-Nagymaros Project*, which also avoided using the word "proportionality" in its formulation of the principle in that particular case.[76] This language came in new in the *2000 Draft Articles* and is, on the surface, a significant change from the *1996 Draft Articles*.[77] This change was questioned by two states in their comments to the *2000 Draft Articles*, in particular by the United States, which was "concerned that the term 'commensurate' may be interpreted incorrectly to have a narrower meaning than the term 'proportional'."[78] In his fourth report, Crawford, special rapporteur of the ILC, recognized these concerns. However, he did not suggest any changes to Article 50 of the draft articles at this stage but referred the further formulation of the article to the drafting committee.[79] Crawford did not give a clear explanation of the reasons for this change of words. However, he did explain that some governments had proposed "that the requirement of proportionality be more strictly formulated."[80] This proposal was mainly to change the formulation of the requirement from a negative one to a positive one. The change to the phrase "commensurate with" might, therefore, have been a byproduct of the change from a negative formulation to a positive one, as the text in the *Gabcikovo-Nagymaros Project*, from which the positive formulation of proportionality in Article 52 was partly taken, also uses the phrase "commensurate with."[81]

This last point on the negative or positive formulation of the principle of proportionality requires further elaboration. As just mentioned, the principle of proportionality can be formulated in the negative or positive, that is, the principle can state that countermeasures shall not be out of proportion to the criteria (negative formulation) or that the countermeasures shall be proportionate to the criteria (positive formulation). Arguably, there is a slight difference between these formulations. The tribunal in the *Naulilaa Case* used a negative one. The tribunal held that legal scholars disagreed on if reprisals had to be proportionate to the offence.[82] However, it wrote, "Even if we assume that the law of nations does not require the reprisal to be calibrated approximatively to the offence, we must surely consider reprisals *out of all proportion* to the act prompting them to be excessive and thus unlawful."[83] The tribunal in the *Air Service Agreement Case* also used negative formulation. The tribunal wrote that "the measures taken by the United States do not appear to be *clearly disproportionate* when compared to those taken by France."[84] *The Restatement of the Law, Third,* also used a negative formulation of the principle.[85] In the *1996 Draft Articles*, the ILC used the negative formulation.[86] The ILC made it clear, however, that this negative formulation did not mean that some degree of disproportionality was permissible. It wrote, "A countermeasure, which is disproportionate, no matter what the extent, should be prohibited to avoid giving the injured state a degree of leeway that might lead to abuse."[87] The ILC formulation in the *1996 Draft Articles* is narrower than the ones in the *Naulilaa Case* (where the tribunal used the criterion "out of all proportions"), arguably narrower than the one in the *Air Service Agreement Case* (where the tribunal used the criterion "clearly disproportionate"), and possibly close to the meaning of a positively formulated principle. However, the quoted words of the ILC do not mean that there is an accurate formula that can be utilized to determine if countermeasures are proportionate; the ILC accepted the tribunal's view in the *Air Service Agreement Case* "that judging the 'proportionality' of counter-measures is not an easy task and can at best be accomplished by approximation."[88] As stated previously, the reason given for the change from a negative formulation into a positive one is that some governments proposed that the proportionality requirement should be formulated narrower.[89] However, examination of comments and observations of the governments regarding the *1996 Draft Articles* does not indicate that they proposed changing the formulation into a positive one but rather that the article should be reformulated to also include other criteria to which countermeasures should be proportionate.[90]

As the previous paragraphs suggest, international jurisprudence and writings of legal minds do not indicate that the determination of proportionality is a precise science. However, in cases of reciprocal countermeasures, it might be possible to calculate the harm fairly precisely. Under such circumstances, Elagab, while drawing inferences from the words of a former special rapporteur of the ILC, wrote:

> Where a neat calculation of what is regarded as equivalent can be made, then a strict balance between the breach and the reciprocal measures must be maintained. By contrast, where such calculation is not possible it would be sufficient to show that the measures taken do not appear to be manifestly disproportionate to the breach.[91]

Apart from those reciprocal countermeasures that are neatly measurable and taken against neatly measurable illegal acts, countermeasures can rarely, if ever, be compared precisely to the preceding illegal act of the wrongdoing state. Thus, debate on the precise formulation of the proportionality principle in the ILC draft articles might not serve the purpose of clarifying the application of the principle.

This subchapter has suggested that the principle of proportionality of countermeasures is a well-established principle of customary international law. It also proposed that the criteria to which countermeasures have to be proportionate can be divided into two points: the injury suffered[92] and the legitimate aim of the countermeasures. These points should not be viewed in isolation from each other; together they form the fabric that restrains the actions of the injured state.

Endnotes

1. Hugo Grotius, *The Rights of War and Peace*, book III, chap. II, pp. 307–313.
2. Ibid., p. 313. The ILC suggests a comparable rule in article 50(2)(b) of the *2001 Draft Articles.*
3. See Emmerich de Vattel, *The Law of Nation*, book II, chap. XVIII, § 342, p. 349.
4. Ibid., chap. XVIII, § 342, p. 349.
5. Ibid., chap. VII, § 81, p. 225.
6. Ibid., chap. XVIII, § 344, p. 350.
7. Theodore D. Woolsey, *Introduction to the Study of International Law*, p. 189.
8. Emmerich de Vattel, *The Law of Nation*, book II, chap. XVIII, § 345, p. 351 and § 349, p. 352.
9. Ibid., § 351, p. 353.
10. Ibid., § 352, p. 351.
11. Ibid., § 352, p. 354.
12. Hugo Grotius, *The Rights of War and Peace*, book III, chap. II, § VI, p. 312.
13. Georg Friedrich von Martens, *A Compendium of the Law of Nations*, p. 274.
14. Henry Wheaton, *Elements of International Law*, p. 340.
15. Theodore D. Woolsey, *Introduction to the Study of International Law*, p. 189.
16. L. Oppenheim, *International Law*, vol. II, 7th ed., p. 139.
17. Ibid., pp. 139–140.
18. *2001 Draft Articles*, article 50. The article is largely identical to article 51 of the *2000 Draft Articles*.
19. It should be noted that the article does make a distinction between the first four areas and the last one, the inviolability of diplomatic and consular rights. Although the difference is arguably only slight, it seems like the reason why diplomatic and consular rights are protected is not because such rights should never be violated but , rather, to ensure the continuing of channels of communication between the disputing states. See, for example, *ILC 2001 Report*, p. 131, Ireland's comments in *State Responsibility: Comments and Observations Received from Governments*, UN doc. no. A/CN.4/488, 25 March 1998, p. 131 and *Report of the International Law Commission on the Work of Its Forty Forth Session* (4 May–24 July 1992) (herafter referred to as *ILC 1992 Report*), UN doc. no. A/47/10, p. 34, para. 236.

20. *State Responsibility: Comments and Observations Received from Governments*, UN doc. A/CN.4/515, 19 March 2001, pp. 79–80.
21. Ibid., p. 79.
22. Ibid., p. 79.
23. Ibid., p. 79.
24. See, for example, *Fourth Report 1992 (Arangio-Ruiz)*, p. 30, para. 79.
25. *ILC 2001 Report*, p. 132, citing the *Naulilaa Case* at 1026 in UNRIAA (p. 1278 in English translation) and the *Annuaire de l'Institut de Droit International*, vol. 38 (1934), p. 710.
26. *ILC 2001 Report*, p. 132, citing *General Comment 8 (1997)*, UN doc. no. E/C.12/1997/8, 5 December 1997, para. 1.
27. *ILC 1995 Report*, pp. 71–74, paras. 17–25 of the commentary to article 14 of part II, (article 50 of the *1996 Draft Articles* was initially identified as article 14 of part II).
28. *ILC 1995 Report*, pp. 71–72, paras. 17–22. In paras. 20–21, the commentary provides a few examples of state practice of humanitarian principles in relation to reprisals in time of peace.
29. See *ILC 2001 Report*, p. 132 and *ILC 1995 Report*, p. 74, para. 24 of the commentary to article 14 of part II.
30. *ILC 1995 Report*, p. 73, para. 23 of the commentary to article 14 of part II.
31. See, for example, *ILC 1995 Report*, p. 74, para. 23, and endnote 241.
32. See *International Covenant on Civil and Political Rights*, article 4(2); *American Convention on Human Rights*, article 27(2); and the *European Convention for the Protection of Human Rights and Fundamental Freedoms*, article 15(2).
33. *Fourth Report 1992 (Arangio-Ruiz)*, p. 31, para. 81.
34. See, for example, *Fourth Report 2001 (Crawford)*, p. 24, para. 64.
35. *Third Report 1991 (Arangio-Ruiz)*, pp. 33–34, paras. 111–113.
36. *Fourth Report 1992 (Arangio-Ruiz)*, p. 32, para. 83.
37. *ILC 2001 Report*, p. 132.
38. Ibid.
39. See, for example, article 46 of the *Convention for the Amelioration of the Condition of the Wounded and Sick in Armed Forces in the Field*, of 12 August 1949 (First Geneva Convention); article 47 of the *Convention for the Amelioration of the Condition of Wounded, Sick and Shipwrecked Members of Armed Forces at Sea*, of 12 August 1949 (Second Geneva Convention); article 13 of the *Convention Relative to the Treatment of Prisoners of War*, of 12 August 1949 (Third Geneva Convention); article 33 of the *Convention Relative to the Protection of Civilian Persons in Time*

of War, of 12 August 1949 (Fourth Geneva Convention); and article 20 of the *Additional Protocol to the Geneva Conventions of 12 August 1949, and Relating to the Protection of Victims of International Armed Conflicts (Protocol I)*, of 8 June 1977.

40. *2001 Draft Articles*, article 50(1)(d).
41. See United States' comments in *State Responsibility: Comments and Observations Received from Governments*, UN doc. A/CN.4/515, 19 March 2001, p. 79.
42. *ILC 2001 Report*, p. 132, para. 9 in commentary to article 50.
43. See, for example, suggestion in that direction in the *ILC 1995 Report*, p. 74, para. 26.
44. *State Responsibility: Comments and Observations Received from Governments*, UN doc. A/CN.4/515, 19 March 2001, p. 79.
45. The United States listing of peremptory norms did not include the right to self-determination, which was arguably incorporated in the corpus of obligations *erga omnes* by the ICJ in the *Timor Case*. Such inclusion does not automatically mean that the right to self-determination is also a peremptory norm but could be used to support an argument in that direction. (see *East-Timor*, International Court of Justice, judgment of 30 June 1995, 1995 I.C.J. 90, at 102, para. 29.
46. See, for example, Omer Yousif Elagab, *The Legality of Non-forcible Counter-measures in International Law*, p. 93.
47. *Third Report 2000 (Crawford)*, addendum 3, p. 12, para. 308.
48. Emmerich de Vattel, *The Law of Nations*, book II, chap. XVIII, § 331, p. 344.
49. Ibid., book II, chap. XVIII, § 354, p. 354.
50. Georg Friedrich von Martens, *A Compendium of the Law of Nations*, p. 272
51. Thomas Erskine Holland, *Lectures on International Law*, p. 232.
52. William Edward Hall, *A Treatise on International Law*, pp. 266–267.
53. L. Oppenheim, *International Law*, vol. II, 7th ed., p. 141, endnote 1.
54. William Edward Hall, *A Treatise on International Law*, p. 363.
55. *2001 Draft Articles*, article 51.
56. *ILC 2001 Report*, p. 135.
57. *Gabcikovo-Nagymaros Project*, at 56, para. 85.
58. See Elisabeth Zoller, *Peacetime Unilateral Remedies*, p. 134; Omer Yousif Elagab, *The Legality of Non-forcible Counter-measures in International Law*, p. 91; and *Air Service Agreement Case*, dissenting opinion of M. Reuter, at 344–345. Zoller actually argues that the difference between the injury suffered or the injury to the principle is, rather, a difference of degree than of nature.

59. Omer Yousif Elagab, *The Legality of Non-forcible Counter-measures in International Law*, p. 91.
60. Ibid., p. 92.
61. *2001 Draft Articles*, article 51.
62. *ILC 2001 Report*, p. 135, para. 6 of the commentary to article 51.
63. See Oppenheim's argument for third state countermeasures in part II, chap. 8(d). The court did not use, in the proportionality equation, the overall need to contain the political philosophy Nicaragua stood for or to prevent it from spreading to other areas where American interests were at stake.
64. *Military and Paramilitary Activities in and Against Nicaragua*, 1986 I.C.J. 14, at 122, para. 237.
65. L. Oppenheim, *International Law*, vol. II, 7th ed., p. 141, endnote 1.
66. See discussion in part II, chap. 8(a).
67. *ILC 2001 Report*, p. 135, para. 7 of the commentary to article 51.
68. *State Responsibility: Comments and Observations Received from Governments*, UN doc. no. A/CN.4/488, 25 March 1998, p. 127.
69. Ibid., p. 127.
70. Ibid., pp. 125–126.
71. Omer Yousif Elagab, *The Legality of Non-forcible Counter-measures in International Law*, p. 87.
72. Elisabeth Zoller, *Peacetime Unilateral Remedies: An Analysis of Countermeasures*, p. 135.
73. *Third Report 2000 (Crawford)* addendum, p. 28, para. 346.
74. Ibid.
75. The header of the article is, however, *Proportionality*. See *2001 Draft Articles*, article 52.
76. *Gabcikovo-Nagymaros Project*, at 56, para. 85. ("In the view of the court, an important consideration is that the effects of a countermeasure must be commensurate with the injury suffered, taking account of the rights in question.") Arguably, the court might have given the wording more thought if they would have foreseen its later use by the ILC.
77. Article 49 of the *1996 Draft Articles* reads, "Countermeasures taken by an injured state shall not be out of proportion to the degree of gravity of the internationally wrongful act and the effects thereof on the injured state."
78. See comments by Denmark and the United States, *State Responsibility: Comments and Observations Received from Governments*, UN doc. A/CN.4/515, 19 March 2001, p. 80 and p. 82, respectively.
79. *Fourth Report 2001 (Crawford)*, p. 25, paras. 65–66.
80. *Third Report 2000 (Crawford)*, addendum, p. 27, para. 346.

81. See *Gabcikovo-Nagymaros Project*, at 56, para. 85 and *Third Report 2000 (Crawford)*, addendum, pp. 27–28. para. 346. It should also be noted that the ILC has used the phrase "commensurate with" in its prior reports (see, for example, *ILC 1979 Report*, p. 116, para. 5). Same phrase is also used by Omer Yousif Elagab in similar or same meaning as "proportionate to." (See Omer Yousif Elagab, *The Legality of Non-forcible Counter-measures in International Law*, p. 94). See also James Crawford, "The ILC's Articles on Responsibility of States for Internationally Wrongful Acts: A Retrospect," *American Journal of International Law 96* (2002), at 882–883, on the effect of this choice of words.
82. *Naulilaa Case*, p. 1279, UNRIAA, at 1026.
83. Ibid., p. 1281, UNRIAA, at 1028, italics added.
84. *Air Service Agreement Case*, at 338, para. 83, italics added.
85. *Restatement of the Law: The Foreign Relations Law of the United States*, vol. 2, American Law Institute Publisher, St. Paul, Minnesota, 1987, § 905, ("a state victim of a violation of an international obligation by another state may resort to countermeasures that might otherwise be unlawful if such measures...are not out of proportion to the violation and the injured suffered."
86. *1996 Draft Articles*, article 49.
87. *ILC 1995 Report*, p. 65, para. 4 of the commentary to article 13 of part II, (article 49 of the *1996 Draft Articles*). This passage was criticized by the United States government for restricting the use of countermeasures beyond what was customary (*State Responsibility: Comments and Observations Received from Governments*, UN doc. no. A/CN.4/488, 25 March 1998, p. 127).
88. *Air Service Agreement Case*, at 338, para. 83 and *ILC 2001 Report*, p. 135, para. 5 in the commentary to article 51.
89. *Third Report 2000 (Crawford)*, addendum, p. 27, para. 346.
90. *State Responsibility: Comments and Observations Received from Governments*, UN doc. no. A/CN.4/488, 25 March 1998, pp. 124–127.
91. Omer Yousif Elagab, *The Legality of Non-forcible Counter-measures in International Law*, p. 88.
92. Taking into account the account the gravity of the internationally wrongful act and the rights in question.

Chapter 11

Conditions That Might Preclude Countermeasures

(a) Introduction

Westlake argued that the right of one state to resort to reprisals was not absolute. He emphasized that measures that affect other states' sovereignty can only be taken in the absence of other remedies.[1] Countermeasures are, therefore, in his mind, secondary to less intrusive effective remedies provided by the international system. It is now time to give attention to the effects of such less intrusive remedies, such as ongoing negotiation and the presence of judicial remedies, on the right to take countermeasures. Later on, this chapter addresses the legality of countermeasures taken while the underlying dispute is simultaneously under review by an international court or tribunal.

(b) Ongoing Negotiations

Under Article 53 of the *ILC 2000 Draft Articles*, the injured state could not resort to countermeasures while "negotiations are being pursued in good faith and have not been unduly delayed."[2] This was a different approach from the one of the tribunal in the *Air Service Agreement Case* between the United States and France.[3] The tribunal said that the presence of an ongoing negotiation did not preclude the use of countermeasures. However, the tribunal qualified its finding a bit further by adding, "...especially where such counter-measures are accompanied by an offer for a procedure affording the possibility of accelerating the solution of the dispute"[4] This requirement of Article 53 of the *2000 Draft Articles* was a remainder of more comprehensive provisions of the *1996 Draft Articles*, which required the injured state to make use of available amicable dispute resolution procedures and suspend countermeasures while such methods were being explored in good faith.[5] In addition to restrictions on the right to take countermeasures due to ongoing good faith negotiation, the injured state was also obliged to suspend countermeasures if the dispute had been "submitted to a court or a tribunal which has the authority to make decisions binding on the parties."[6] *The Restatement of the Law, Third* suggests an even stricter approach.

> In a dispute between members of an international organization, there may be a requirement that the dispute be submitted to the dispute settlement procedures of the organization, and countermeasures are precluded before that procedure has been concluded or terminated without success.[7]

This passage is set forth in the context of the necessity of countermeasures and seems to argue that countermeasures are not necessary if compulsory dispute settlement procedures are available to the disputing parties. This suggestion would be likely to take some of the teeth out of countermeasures as a viable option in international relations and is in contradiction to the United States' position on this issue as it was presented in the comments to the *1996 Draft Articles*.[8]

Notably, the ILC did not include this contested provision in its *2001 Draft Articles*. As comments from governments show, this is a debated requirement; the ban against countermeasures during good faith negotiations was even less welcomed than the duty to offer negotiations.

The United States wrote in its comments on the *1996 Draft Articles*, "The requirement for prior negotiations may prejudice an injured State's position by enabling a wrongdoing State to compel negotiations that delay the imposition of countermeasures and permit it to avoid its international responsibility."[9] Although this argument is mainly directed against the requirement to conduct negotiation prior to taking countermeasures, this comment is also relevant to the debate on the ban against countermeasures during good faith negotiation because it addressed the possible abuse by the wrongdoing state of such a ban. The United Kingdom aligned itself with the United States and suggested, in its candid comments to the *2000 Draft Articles*, that the article as a whole should be deleted.

> [R]equirements set out in draft Article 53 that negotiations and dispute settlement procedures be pursued in good faith by the responsible State are wholly inadequate as safeguards. It may take a good deal of time to establish bad faith; and it cannot be right to insist that the imposition of countermeasures must be suspended while that time elapses.[10]

Slovakia also expressed its concerns over this formulation; it argued that the

> proposed prohibition or suspension of countermeasures while negotiations are being pursued in good faith would put too much pressure on a State invoking countermeasures; and it should not be forgotten that a State invoking countermeasures is an 'injured State,' injured by a wrongful act of a State towards which countermeasures are aiming.[11]

Japan suggested that this provision would make it too easy for the offending state to avert countermeasures. It wrote, "Since responsible States are likely to accept the offer to negotiate, it seems quite difficult in fact to resort to countermeasures."[12] Other states were either silent or supporting of the ban on countermeasures during good faith negotiations and believed that the right to resort to provisional and urgent countermeasures, as Article 53(3) of the *2000 Draft Articles* authorized, would remedy the possible inconveniences that the ban would cause.[13]

The nature of countermeasures as a coercive tool might shed some light on whether ongoing good faith negotiations do or should prevent resorting to countermeasures. If countermeasures should be precluded in such a situation, a difficult question would become relevant: When is a state conducting good faith negotiations? Also, how much patience must the injured state show the responsible state before it could resort to countermeasures? As is true about good faith negotiation, the purpose of countermeasures is to solve the dispute and establish an equitable situation similar to the one prior to the alleged breach. The threat of countermeasures during the negotiation process might encourage parties to reach a conclusion; it might also frustrate the negotiations. The permissibility of countermeasures during the negotiation process might, therefore, either move the parties closer to the solution or further away. It is necessary not to be caught up in formalism while addressing this issue; the presence or absence of negotiations should not be the determining factor in whether countermeasures are permissible; the determination should rather rest on if the negotiation is, objectively measured, likely to produce the equitable solution that the injured state might acquire with the prospective countermeasures. If yes, countermeasures might be precluded not because good faith negotiations were taking place but because countermeasures were not necessary.

International jurisprudence and the writings of scholars, as well as the comments of governments do not indicate that there exists a rule of international law prohibiting countermeasures because good faith negotiations are under way. Furthermore, comments of governments indicate that there is no consensus about the progressive development of international law, which the ILC had earlier suggested by limiting countermeasures under said circumstances. Also, it is probably a good policy not to discourage good faith negotiation by laying obstacles, such as a ban on countermeasures, in the way of a state that seeks to solve its disputes through negotiation. If the opening of channels of communication limits the right of the injured states to seek redress through unilateral measures, the injured states might be hesitant to seek such amicable means. Finally, as was hinted at in the *Air Service Agreement Case*, the threat of countermeasures might, in some cases, encourage the offending state to concentrate more seriously on the ongoing negations.[14]

(c) Access to an International Court or Tribunal or Other Effective Dispute Resolution Mechanism

There is disagreement as to which international remedies have to be exhausted before an injured state can resort to countermeasures and under what conditions countermeasures are prohibited or have to be suspended because of such remedies. Even if adjudication of international disputes is largely optional, there are good arguments for conditioning the right to resort to countermeasures to exhaustion of all available effective dispute settlement mechanism. Wheaton argued that because states "acknowledge no common arbiter or judge, except such as are constituted by special compact…Every State has therefore a right to resort to force, as the only means of redress for injuries inflicted upon it by others."[15] Martens' writings are in line with this thought, for he argued that if there would be a judge or a superior authority that could decide on the dispute, the injured state's right to use forcible means is reduced unless the measures in question are authorized by the laws or if the courts cannot decide on the issue.[16]

Modern discussion on nonforcible reprisals has largely been in line with these thoughts, however, with certain variations.[17] On the more flexible side is the decision of the tribunal in the *Air Service Agreement Case*, which did not see that its jurisdiction affected the right of the United States to resort to countermeasures. However, it suggested that an existence of an institutional framework capable of ensuring some level of enforcement could preclude the right to resort to countermeasures.[18] The tribunal did not elaborate on what sort of "institutional framework" could preclude the legality of countermeasures.

The prohibition against countermeasures when dispute settlement procedures, such as described previously, are available cannot be inferred from the *UN Charter*, provided that one agrees with the assumption that countermeasures are generally not likely to threaten international peace and security. Under Article 2(3) and 33(1) of the *UN Charter*, states "shall settle their international disputes by peaceful means in such a manner that international peace and security, and justice, are not endangered,"[19] and when they are a party to a dispute that "is likely to endanger the maintenance of international peace and security, [they] shall, first of all, seek a solution by negotiation, enquiry, mediation, conciliation, arbitration, judicial settlement, resort to regional agencies or arrangements, or other peaceful means of their own choice."[20] However, as previously discussed, there is no consensus among scholars or states that these provisions prohibit countermeasures prior to making use of available judicial procedures to settle the dispute. Countermeasures that, by definition do not include the use of force, are limited by the principle of proportionality and, arguably, other considerations[21] would only, in very limited circumstances, come under scrutiny of the principles expressed in Article 2(3) and 33(1) of the charter.

Under a few pre-UN treaty law provisions, states were obliged to refer their disputes to an international dispute settlement mechanism and not resort to unilateral measures. Among such treaties are the *1925 Locarno Treaties*,[22] the *1928 Briand-Kellogg Pact*,[23] and the *1933 Saavedra Lamas Treaty*.[24] Under these treaties, a limited group of states agreed not to take unilateral actions against each other and to refer their disputes to judicial or political settlement bodies, such as the Permanent Court of International Justice or the Council of the League of Nations. These provisions are, however, limited in scope and mainly dealt with the use of force.[25] They are, therefore, in line with obligations under the *UN Charter* but barely suggest a similar rule with regard to countermeasures.

In 1992, the ILC suggested that access to an effective dispute resolution mechanism should preclude countermeasures prior to resorting to such methods. The ILC proposed that certain elements should guide whether such a mechanism should have the aforesaid effects. They were:

a. the strength of the relevant settlement obligation and the extent of the availability of the procedure contemplated;

b. the degree of effectiveness; and
c. the nature and objective function of the measures envisaged.[26]

In line with these elements, the ILC special rapporteur suggested that the proposed draft articles should contain an obligation for the injured state to exhaust "all of the amicable settlements procedures available under general international law, the *Charter of the United Nations* or any other dispute settlement instrument to which it is a party."[27]

Under Article 48(2) of the *1996 Draft Articles*, an injured state was obliged to make use of available dispute settlement mechanisms and suspend countermeasures that it might have taken if the dispute was referred to such mechanisms. Under Article 58(2) of the same draft articles, a state that countermeasures have been taken against could unilaterally refer the dispute to arbitration provided that prior negotiation and a referral to a conciliation committee had not been successful.[28] Under this approach, the access to a compulsory dispute resolution system does not preclude countermeasures, but when a case has been referred to such mechanisms, the injured state must suspend the countermeasures that it has taken, provided that the initial wrongful act has ceased.[29]

This approach came under attack by various states that believed that such provisions would unduly limit their right to protect their own interest, lead to unreasonable cost for injured states, and delay achieving justice.[30] In its comments on the *1996 Draft Articles*, the United States wrote:

> Compulsory arbitration of this sort is not supported by customary international law, would be unworkable in practice and would establish a novel system whereby an injured State may be compelled to arbitrate a dispute. There is no basis in international law or policy for subjecting the injured State to such a requirement when it pursues countermeasures in response to a wrongful act of another State.[31]

Because of the aforementioned and other criticism to the link between compulsory dispute settlement procedures and countermeasures, the dispute settlement provisions were deleted and not included in the *2000 Draft Articles*. Remaining of this approach was, however, the duty of the injured state to suspend countermeasures when a dispute has been submitted to a court or arbitration.[32] The compulsory jurisdiction of an arbitration, which could be invoked by a state against which countermeasures are directed, was no longer on the table.

There was, however, not a consensus among states that the access to compulsory dispute settlement mechanisms should not affect the right to resort to countermeasures. Denmark, which commented on behalf of the Nordic countries, argued in its comments to the *2000 Draft Articles* that "there is no room for countermeasures where a mandatory system of dispute settlement exists."[33] Other states did not explicitly support this point of view.

Thus, the *2001 Draft Articles* do not contain a link between the existence of compulsory dispute settlement mechanisms and the legality of countermeasures, except for the duty to suspend countermeasures when the dispute in question "is pending before a court or a tribunal which has the authority to make decisions binding on the parties" and the initial illegal act has ceased.[34] This issue is the topic of the following subchapter.

The previous discussion shows that a rule that dictates that access to a compulsory dispute resolution mechanism automatically precludes countermeasures or that such mechanism has to be exhausted prior to resorting to countermeasures does not exist in international law. However, this does not mean that the incentives to resort to countermeasures are not affected by such access. Also, the determination of necessity and the principle of proportionality might be affected if a compulsory dispute settlement mechanism that is capable of ordering provisional measures that can protect the endangered rights of the injured state exists. This will, however, only be decided on a case-by-case basis, as numerous other considerations need to be taken into account.

(D) DISPUTE ALREADY SUBMITTED TO AN INTERNATIONAL COURT OR TRIBUNAL

A distinction must be made between an access to a dispute settlement mechanism and the fact that a dispute has actually been submitted to a court or a tribunal. Article 52(3) and 52(4) of the *ILC 2001 Draft Articles* state:

> 3. Countermeasures may not be taken, and if already taken, must be suspended without undue delay if:
>
>   a. The internationally wrongful act has ceased; and
>   b. The dispute is pending before a court or tribunal which has the authority to make decisions binding on the parties.
>
> 4. Paragraph 3 does not apply if the responsible State fails to implement the dispute settlement procedures in good faith.

According to the *2001 Draft Articles*, the access to a binding tribunal or court is not enough; the dispute actually has to have been submitted to the dispute resolution body, and the wrongful act has to have ceased. Although this approach did not seem to face any widespread objection in the international jurisprudence or by legal authors, there are variations.

The tribunal in the *Air Service Agreement Case* took a more relaxed approach to the effects on the right to countermeasures when a case is already before a court. It said that the injured state would retain its right to countermeasures until the "tribunal is in the position to act,"[35] that is, "to achieve the objectives justifying the counter-measures."[36] This translates into a right for the injured state to resort to countermeasures until the court or the tribunal can order enforceable provisional measures. The tribunal went even further than that and argued that if an order for provisional measures is framed narrowly, the injured state might retain some right to resort to countermeasures with regard to injury or preventative measures not covered by order for provisional measures.[37]

In the ICJ's decision in the *Hostage Case* of 1980, the court criticized the United States' attempt to unilaterally rescue the hostages from Tehran while the case was under deliberation by the court, notwithstanding Iran's continuing violation of the court's prior provisional measures order.[38] It must be noted, however, that the court did not, as did the tribunal in the *Air Service Agreement Case*, address the legality of a unilateral action parallel to judicial proceedings. However, the dissenting opinion by Judge Tarazi and the separate opinion by Judge Lachs addressed the legality of the so-called rescue mission.

Judge Lachs addressed the United States' rescue mission in one sentence. He said that the United States "having instituted proceedings, is precluded from taking unilateral actions, military or otherwise, as if no case is pending."[39] The cut-off time for countermeasures is accordingly not when the court is able to act, as the tribunal in the *Air Service Agreement Case* suggested, but when proceedings are initiated. Judge Tarazi provided a clearer analysis of the legality of unilateral actions parallel to court proceedings. In his dissenting opinion, he opposed the possibility of parallel unilateral actions. He argued that once a state submits a dispute to the ICJ, the dispute as a whole is in the custody of the court. He continued and said, "The applicant State must refrain from taking any decisions on the planes of either domestic or international law which could have the effect of impeding the proper administration of justice."[40] Judge Tarazi cited the freezing of assets, the preparation for distributing them to holders of claims against the Iranian government, and the rescue mission as actions incompatible with submitting the case to the court.[41]

Some writers have tried to draw conclusions related to parallel unilateral actions from the words of the court's majority, as well as the dissenting and separate opinions.[42] It must be pointed out that in the provisional measures order from 15 December 1979, the court expressly prohibited any actions that might aggravate the situation.[43] If such order would not have been issued, the tone of the court might have been different and even without condemnation of the United States' unilateral actions.

In the commentary to the *2001 Draft Articles*, the ILC seemed to qualify its prohibition on countermeasures parallel to judicial proceedings. It wrote that this rule is "based on the assumption that the court or tribunal to which it refers has jurisdiction over the dispute and also the power to order provisional measures."[44] The ILC explained:

> The rationale behind [Article 52(3)] is that once the parties submit their dispute to such a court or tribunal for resolution, the injured

> State may request it to order provisional measures to protect its rights. Such a request, provided the court or tribunal is available to hear it, will perform a function essentially equivalent to that of countermeasures. Provided the order is complied with it will make countermeasures unnecessary pending the decision of the tribunal.[45]

These explanations seem to indicate that a strict textual interpretation of the *2001 Draft Articles* is not an accurate description of the applicable customary international law. Thus, a more teleological interpretation might be appropriate, that is, that the object and purpose of the parallel remedy prohibition should play a role when the legality of countermeasures taken after a dispute that has been submitted to a court or a tribunal is determined. Another, equally important element of the qualification of this restriction on countermeasures can be inferred from the last sentence of the previously cited paragraph: the effects of compliance with the provisional measures order. In case of noncompliance, the need for countermeasures remains, perhaps as the only enforcement tool available. As in the *Hostage Case*, offending states will not, under all circumstances, comply with provisional orders by a court. Arguably, the words of the ILC indicate that in such cases, the right to resort to countermeasures in not restricted. This inference might not contradict the words of Judge Tarazi if his discontent regarding the United States' actions would have been limited to the armed measures taken in order to rescue the hostages. However, Judge Tarazi also believed that attempts to freeze Iraqi assets were incompatible with submitting the case to the court.[46]

Another source for the suggestion that this prohibition of parallel unilateral measures is not absolute is Article 52(4) of the *2001 Draft Articles*, which says that paragraph 3 "does not apply if the responsible State fails to implement the dispute settlement procedures in good faith."[47] Noncompliance with a provisional measures order, arguably, does not meet the test of good faith implementation of the settlement procedures. This argument is supported by the ILC commentary to Article 52(4). The ILC wrote that Article 52(4)

> comprehends various possibilities, ranging from an initial refusal to cooperate in the procedure, for example by non-appearance, through *non-compliance with a provisional measures order*, whether or not it is formally binding, through to refusal to accept the final decision of the court or tribunal.[48]

Paragraphs 3 and 4 of Article 52, read together, suggest a departure from a formalistic rule precluding countermeasures when a case has been submitted to a court or a tribunal. As mentioned before, the tribunal in the *Air Service Agreement Case* suggested that the presence of an "institutional framework" capable of ensuring enforcement might preclude countermeasures. The tribunal wrote:

> Many jurists have felt that while arbitral or judicial proceedings were in progress, recourse to counter-measures, even if limited by the proportionality rule, was prohibited. Such an assertion deserves sympathy but requires further elaboration. If the proceedings form part of an institutional framework ensuring some degree of enforcement of obligations, the justification of counter-measures would undoubtedly disappear, but owing to the existence of that framework rather than solely on account of the existence of arbitral or judicial proceedings as such.[49]

The tribunal concluded with regard to the case at hand that because implementation of the tribunal's order would take time, countermeasures, such as suspending the license to operate flights between Paris and Los Angeles, were permitted. The tribunal's approach, coupled with the rules of paragraphs 3 and 4 of Article 52 of the *2001 Draft Articles* seen in the light of the aforementioned ILC commentary, indicate the existence of what might be called an effective-remedy test, composed of the institutional framework test, as well as the good faith test. Such a test would take into account if the court, to which the case has been submitted, possesses in its arsenal a remedy that is effective in the circumstances of the particular case and if the behavior of the offending state would contribute to the resolution of the dispute. This test would include elements such as if the court or tribunal has a right to order provisional measures, if it is effective in resolving the dispute at hand, if it is competent to render decisions that are binding for all or both parties of the dispute, if its competence is comprehensive enough to include the dispute as a whole, and if it is authoritative enough for the injured state to have a reasonable expectation that the offending state will comply with its decision. Such tests would also take into account the behavior of the offending state, such as nonappearance in court, refusal to accept the courts jurisdiction, refusal to comply with provisional measures order, and if its behavior and declarations make it unlikely that the court proceedings will be effective, in that particular dispute. Although the behavior of the offending state might be a subjective element, it could in many instances be determined by objective factors. If this test is positive, that is, if such an institutional framework exists and the offending state is complying with the process in good faith, the necessity requirement and proportionality requirement, which are the foundations for countermeasures, might not be met.[50]

The provisions in Article 52(3)–52(4) were a compromise from a more extensive nexus between the legality of countermeasures and the duty to settle disputes by negotiation, conciliation, or through a dispute resolution body that had compulsory jurisdiction over an injured state taking countermeasures if the state that the countermeasures are directed against decides to refer the case to such a body.[51] While the provisions on settlements of disputes were not included in the *2000 Draft Articles*, the prohibition of countermeasures when a case had been submitted to a tribunal remained. As previously discussed, the United Kingdom and the United States opposed this restriction on the right to take countermeasures.[52] Their comments might, however, be reconciled with a reasonable interpretation of this restriction on countermeasures set forth previously—an interpretation that focuses more on the object and purpose of countermeasures than the strict textual interpretation.[53]

The United Kingdom was concerned that this restriction would "discourage acceptance of or reference to dispute settlement mechanisms."[54] It also expressed concerns that the good faith exception in Article 53(6) of the *2000 Draft Articles*, equivalent to Article 52(4) of the *2001 Draft*

Articles, would be inadequate as safeguards. The United Kingdom feared that it might "take a good deal of time to establish bad faith; and it cannot be right to insist that the imposition of countermeasures must be suspended while that time elapses."[55] These comments deserve some sympathy, although the United Kingdom's concerns might be unfounded if the interpretation as suggested next is used. If the purpose of the countermeasures is to induce the offending state to return to the legal situation, a court, which has the authority to order provisional measures, might be more likely to restore normal relations between the disputing countries than somewhat hostile unilateral measures. A number of objective observations can indicate whether the offending state is likely to subscribe to the dispute settlement procedures in good faith. One would, therefore, not have to expect a priory, without any objective indications, that the offending state will act in good faith. Thus, if the effective-remedy test would be applied to the consequences of referring the dispute to a dispute resolution body, the concerns that the United Kingdom expressed in its comments might be properly addressed and, therefore, not justified as an argument against Article 52(3).

The United States' arguments in its comments to the *2000 Draft Articles* could receive a similar treatment. The United States did not argue against the principle per se but expressed concern about the strict interpretation that Article 53(5)(b) of the *2000 Draft Articles* seemed to require—"there is no basis for such an absolute rule."[56] The United States further discussed the less strict rule to which the tribunal in the *Air Service Agreement Case* seemed to subscribe. Citing the case, the United States suggested that

> once a dispute is submitted to a tribunal that has the 'means to achieve the objectives justifying the countermeasures,' the right to initiate countermeasures disappears, and countermeasures already initiated '*may*' be 'eliminated' but only to the extent the tribunal provides equivalent 'interim measures of protection.'[57]

The United States interpreted the tribunal in the *Air Service Agreement Case* as limiting the duty to suspend existing countermeasures to instances when the tribunal is ready to order provisional measures to replace the countermeasures.[58] However, the silence of the United States on the right to initiate countermeasures indicates that it is in agreement with the notion that such right might disappear earlier, that is, before a tribunal has, in fact, acted. This would be a correct interpretation of the case. It is worth repeating the words of the tribunal:

> To the extent that the tribunal has the necessary means to achieve the objectives justifying the counter-measures, it must be admitted that the right of the Parties to initiate such measures disappears. In other words, the power of a tribunal to decide on interim measures of protection, ...leads to the disappearance of the power to initiate counter-measures and may lead to an elimination of existing counter-measures to the extent that the tribunal so provides as an interim measure of protection.[59]

The United States' concerns refer to the period from the time when the case is pending before the court or the tribunal and until provisional measures have actually been ordered. Arguably, the tribunal is not entirely correct. The answer to how to treat the duty to suspend countermeasures during the time in question might lie in the basic structures of the international legal system and why states have the right, when another state fails to comply with an international obligation owed to them, to resort to unilateral measures to protect their rights and interests, even if such measures would, in the absence of the initial illegal act, be a violation of international law. Among the important reasons for allowing such behavior of the injured state is the absence of a superior authority that possesses a power to decide on the dispute. When such authority is present and competent to handle the case and the dispute is pending before it, the argument for continuing the countermeasure until they have been replaced by provisional measures ordered by the court seems weak. However, these concerns expressed by the United States cannot be written off without some concessions.

Although not stated in the *2001 Draft Articles* or its predecessors, the duty, under these circumstances, to suspend urgent countermeasures that are necessary to preserve the interests and rights of the injured states might not be compatible with customary international law. Urgent countermeasures have a special status in the *2001 Draft Articles*, as they are permitted before the injured state complies with its obligation to notify the offending states of the prospective countermeasures and offer negotiations.[60] They are, however, not exempt from the suspension duty or the prohibition against new countermeasures in Article 52(3). This discrepancy was criticized in comments of the United States to a comparable article in the *2000 Draft Articles*, where it was suggested that it might be a drafting error.[61] Whatever the cause for this difference, the United States indicated it might be willing to accept the suspension duty and the prohibition against new countermeasures if "urgent countermeasures" were excluded.[62]

The other concern raised by the United States that is worth mentioning here is the possible limits of the competencies of the tribunal or the court before which the dispute is pending to order provisional measures. The United States cited, again, the tribunal in the *Air Service Agreement Case* that wrote, "As the object and scope of the power of the tribunal to decide on interim measures of protection may be defined quite narrowly, however, the power of the Parties to initiate or maintain countermeasures, too, may not disappear completely."[63] This comment is justified. As modern disputes are complex and might touch upon many diverse legal questions, the court or tribunal before which the dispute is pending might not have the competence to decide on all aspects of the dispute. If the superior authority does not have the authority to decide on the question before it, the right to take countermeasures, arguably, is still with the injured states; it has not been transferred to the dispute resolution body. This is in line with what already has been discussed under the institutional framework test; the dispute resolution body has to possess the competence to address the dispute as a whole and have in its arsenal an effective remedy in that particular circumstance.

In line with what has been written previously, the formulation of the *2001 Draft Articles* cannot be fully accepted as a description of customary international law. The international case law, however poor it might be, and the quite reasonably argued comments of states indicate that the rule regarding the effect of a submission of a dispute to a court, which is ready and able to decide on a dispute, on the right to take and continue already taken countermeasures does not correspond to a strict reading of Articles 52(3)–52(4). Instead, this study suggests the use of an effective-remedy test, which might, if applied correctly, address the concerns of the relevant states and be in harmony with the customary international law related to the countermeasure doctrine.

It would be too much of a departure from the main topic of this study to include here a detailed analysis of whether or up to what extent the international system of environmental protection provides effective remedies. However, not touching this issue might leave open the question: is there a system of adjudication and enforcement that might, in general, reduce the right of states to resort to countermeasures? The short answer is that there are, at this point in time, little or no evidence indicating that such a system exists in the field of protection of international environmental rights.

Two points could be mentioned to support this. The first point, applicable in general to the international legal system, is that the acceptance of ICJ jurisdiction is generally voluntary, whether it is by accepting the ICJ's jurisdiction according to Article 36(2) of its statute,[64] a special agreement for each dispute,[65] or as an opt-in clause in the international instrument relevant to the dispute.[66] Through the years, the ICJ has adjudicated only a few international environmental disputes and has "had little opportunity to contribute to the development of this field of law."[67] The jurisdiction of most other international adjudication mechanisms is subject to a similar voluntariness.[68]

In addition to jurisdiction on the merits and, perhaps, more important for the right to resort to countermeasures, the ICJ has "the power to indicate, if it considers that circumstances so require, any provisional measures which ought to be taken to preserve the respective rights of either party."[69] These powers are, of course, subject to the same voluntariness as the jurisdiction of the court under Article 36. Additionally, it has been argued that the word "indicate," instead of "order" or "prescribe," suggests that the ICJ provisional measures might not be legally binding for the parties.[70]

Because of its voluntary jurisdiction, the ICJ system is an inherently weak system for solving international disputes, including environmental disputes, which often require prompt resolution. With both France and the United States having abandoned the system—France after the *Nuclear Test Case* in 1974 and the United States during the *Nicaragua Case* in 1984—and after only 60 judgments in its first 50 years, it has been said the ICJ is only "a minor actor in international relations."[71]

The second point worthy of mentioning is that under *UNCLOS*, the principle of compulsory jurisdiction of a court or arbitration was given significant weight. Under *UNCLOS*, states can chose between three methods of adjudication: ICJ, arbitral tribunal, or the International Tribunal for the Law of the Sea (ITLOS).[72] The compulsory jurisdiction was, therefore, a structural part of *UNCLOS*. It was a clear contrast to the opt-in clauses in most other instruments, a noticeable departure from other treaty-drafting methods of those times, and "a landmark in the evolution of the law of the sea…"[73] However, "the jurisdictional provisions of the Convention are exceedingly complex, with a number of ways the Tribunal can be seised of a dispute, but subject to a wide variety of exceptions and limitations."[74] These complexities and exceptions, mainly found in Articles 281, 282, 297, and 298, negate the effectiveness of the *UNCLOS* adjudication mechanism as a viable alternative to unilateral remedies, such as countermeasures. The effects of these exceptions and other limitation of the scope of the *UNCLOS* adjudication system came to light in the *Southern Bluefin Tuna Cases*[75] and the *MOX Plant Case*,[76] which suggested that the impact of the compulsory jurisdiction under *UNCLOS* for environmental disputes is significantly less than desired.

Regardless of that, the value of international adjudication cannot be discounted and no such attempt is made here. Its effect on the right to resort to countermeasures can, however, not be seen as significant. Nevertheless, the true assessment cannot be accomplished by generalizations; it must be undertaken on a case-by-case basis, evaluating the legal and factual situation present in each dispute.

Endnotes

1. John Westlake, *International Rights of Self-Preservation*, at 112–113.
2. *2000 Draft Articles*, article 53(4).
3. *Air Service Agreement Case*, at 310, para. 4.
4. Ibid., at 340, para. 91.
5. See *1996 Draft Articles*, articles 48(2)–48(3), requiring injured states to enter into good faith negotiations and a number of other amicable dispute settlement procedures.
6. *2000 Draft Articles*, article 53(5).
7. *Restatement of the Law: The Foreign Relations Law of the United States*, vol. 2, American Law Institute Publisher, St. Paul, Minnesota, 1987, p. 381.
8. *State Responsibility: Comments and Observations Received from Governments*, UN doc. no. A/CN.4/488, 25 March 1998, p. 120 and p. 122.
9. Ibid., p. 122.
10. *State Responsibility: Comments and Observations Received from Governments*, UN doc. A/CN.4/515, 19 March 2001, p. 85.
11. Ibid., p. 84.
12. Ibid., p. 83.
13. See, for example, comments from Denmark, the Netherlands, and Spain, *State Responsibility, Comments and Observations Received from Governments*, UN doc. A/CN.4/515, 19 March 2001, pp. 83–84.
14. *Air Service Agreement Case*, at 340, para. 91.
15. Henry Wheaton, *Elements of International Law*, p. 339.
16. Georg Friedrich von Martens, *A Compendium of the Law of Nations*, p. 272.
17. With the important variation, of course, that countermeasures may not violate the prohibition against the threat or use of armed force.
18. *Air Service Agreement Case*, at 340, para. 94.
19. *UN Charter*, article 2(3).
20. *UN Charter*, article 33(1).
21. See chap. 10(a).
22. *Locarno Treaties* of 6 October concluded at Locarno, 6 October 1925, entered into force 14 September 1926, 54 LNTS 289, 303, 315, 327, 341, 353 and 359, reprinted in *World Peace Foundation Pamphlets*, vol. IX, 1926, World Peace Foundation, Boston, Massachusetts, pp. 54–75.
23. *General Treaty for Renunciation of War as an Instrument of National Policy*, concluded at Paris 27 August 1928, entered into force 24 July 1929, 46 Stat. 2343.

24. *Anti-War Treaty of Nonaggression and Conciliation*, concluded at Rio de Janeiro 10 October 1933, entered into force 13 November 1935, 49 Stat. 3363; Treaty Series 906.
25. See *Fourth Report 1992 (Arangio-Ruiz)*, p. 14, para. 25.
26. Ibid., pp. 19–20, para. 45.
27. Ibid., p. 22, para. 50.
28. *1996 Draft Articles*, article 56 and 58(2).
29. See *1996 Draft Articles*, article 48(3) and *ILC 1996 Report*, p. 70, para. 11 of the commentary to article 48 of the *1996 Draft Articles*. It is not clear if this suspension also applies to interim measures of protection that a state is, under certain circumstances, permitted to resort to if such measures are necessary in order to preserve the injured state's rights. See *1996 Draft Articles*, article 48(1) and comments of the United States on the *2000 Draft Articles* regarding the irrationality of such conclusion, *State Responsibility: Comments and Observations Received from Governments*, UN doc. A/CN.4/515, 19 March 2001, p. 86.
30. See *Third Report 2000 (Crawford)*, addendum, pp. 7–11, paras. 298–305 and *State Responsibility: Comments and Observations Received from Governments*, UN doc. no. A/CN.4/488, 25 March 1998, pp. 118–124.
31. *State Responsibility: Comments and Observations Received from Governments*, UN doc. no. A/CN.4/488, 25 March 1998, p. 123.
32. See *2000 Draft Articles*, article 53(5)(b).
33. *State Responsibility: Comments and Observations Received from Governments*, UN doc. A/CN.4/515, 19 March 2001, p. 114.
34. *2001 Draft Articles*, articles 52(3)(a)–52(3)(b).
35. *Air Service Agreement Case*, at 340, para. 96.
36. Ibid., at 340, para. 96.
37. Ibid.
38. *United States Diplomatic and Consular Staff in Tehran*, (*United States of America v. Iran*), International Court of Justice, judgment of 24 May 1980, 1980 I.C.J. 3, at 43, para. 93.
39. Ibid., separate opinion of Judge Lachs, at 48.
40. *United States Diplomatic and Consular Staff in Tehran*, dissenting opinion of Judge Tarazi, at 63.
41. Ibid., at 64.
42. See, for example, Oscar Schachter, *International Law in Theory and Practice*, Kluwer Law International, Boston, The Hague, London, 1995, p. 167; Omer Yousif Elagab, *The Legality of Non-forcible Counter-measures in International Law*, pp. 170–171; and John Quigley, "Missiles with a Message: The Legality of The United States Raid on Iraq's Intelligence Head-

quarters," *Hastings International and Comparative Law Review* 18 (1994), at 257.

43. *United States Diplomatic and Consular Staff in Tehran*, order of 15 December 1979, 1979 I.C.J. 7, at 21, para. 47(1)(B).
44. *ILC 2001 Report*, p. 136.
45. Ibid., p. 136–137.
46. *United States Diplomatic and Consular Staff in Tehran*, at 64, dissenting opinion of Tarazi.
47. *2001 Draft Articles*, article 52(4).
48. *ILC 2001 Report*, p. 137, para. 9 of the commentary to article 52, italics added.
49. *Air Service Agreement Case*, at 340, para. 94.
50. See also Omer Yousif Elagab, *The Legality of Non-forcible Countermeasures in International Law*, p. 184, lending some support to this approach.
51. See *1996 Draft Articles*, articles 54–60, in particular article 58(2).
52. See *State responsibility: Comments and Observations Received from Governments*, UN doc. A/CN.4/515, 19 March 2001, pp. 84–87.
53. Such interpretation would in harmony with article 31 of the *Vienna Convention on the Law of Treaties*. ("A treaty shall be interpreted in good faith in accordance with the ordinary meaning to be given to the terms of the treaty in their context and in the light of its object and purpose.")
54. *State Responsibility: Comments and Observations Received from Governments*, UN doc. A/CN.4/515, 19 March 2001, p. 85.
55. Ibid., p. 85.
56. Ibid., p. 86.
57. Ibid., p. 86.
58. Ibid., pp. 86–87.
59. *Air Service Agreement Case*, at 340, para. 96.
60. See *2001 Draft Articles*, article 52(1)(b) and 52(2).
61. *State Responsibility: Comments and Observations Received from Governments*, UN doc. A/CN.4/515, 19 March 2001, p. 86.
62. Ibid., pp. 86–87.
63. *Air Service Agreement Case*, at 340, para. 96 and *State Responsibility, Comments and Observations Received from Governments*, UN doc. A/CN.4/515, 19 March 2001, p. 86.
64. Article 36(2) of the *Statute of the International Court of Justice*, concluded at San Francisco 26 June 1946, entered into force 24 October 1946, 59 Stat. 1055, T.S. 993, 3 Bevans 1179. Sixty-five states currently accept the compulsory jurisdiction of the court based on such a declaration, thereof only one permanent member of the Security Council. See International Court of

Justice: Basis of the Court Jurisdiction, http://www.icj-cij.org/jurisdiction (visited 5 January 2008).

65. Sixteen cases have been brought before the court by means of such agreements. International Court of Justice: Basis of the Court Jurisdiction, http://www.icj-cij.org/jurisdiction (visited 5 January 2008).
66. Several international instruments related to environmental protection contain such a clause. The number of states actually opting for compulsory jurisdiction remains, however, very low. Examples of such instruments are the *Vienna Convention for the Protection of the Ozone Layer of 1985* (out of 191 parties to the convention, 5 have accepted the compulsory jurisdiction provided for in article 11(3)), the *Convention on Biological Diversity* of 1992 (out of 190 parties, 3 have accepted the compulsory jurisdiction provided for in article 27(3)), the *Framework Convention on Climate Change of 1992* (out of 192 parties, 1 [Solomon Islands]) has accepted the compulsory jurisdiction provided for in article 14(2). Article 14 also applies to the dispute settlement under the *Kyoto Protocol to the United Nations Framework Convention on Climate Change, and Convention on Environmental Impact Assessment in a Transboundary Context* (out of 41 parties, 4 have accepted the compulsory jurisdiction provided for in article 15(2)).
67. Nagendra Singh, *The Role and Record of the International Court of Justice*, Martinus Nijhoff Publishers, Dordrecht, Boston, London, 1989, p. 164.
68. The WTO regime, however, provides a strikingly different approach by its dispute resolution rules. Such regime (discussed further in chap. 15 of part III), might well, under the effective remedy test, exclude the right of states to resort to countermeasures against breaches of WTO agreements. See also Joel P. Trachtman, "The WTO Cathedral," *Stanford Journal of International Law* 43 (2007), at 123 and *ILC 2001 Report*, p. 129.
69. *ICJ Statute*, article 41(1).
70. See, for example, Guđmundur Eiríksson, *The International Tribunal for the Law of the Sea*, Martinus Nijhoff Publishers, The Hague, London, Boston, 2000, p. 219.
71. David. P. Forsythe, "The International Court of Justice at Fifty" in *The International Court of Justice: Its Future Role After Fifty Years*, edited by A. S. Muller, D. Raič, and J.M. Thuránsky, Martinus Nijhoff, Cambridge, MA, 1997, p. 402.
72. See *United Nations Convention on the Law of the Sea*, concluded at Montego Bay 10 December 1982, entered into force 16 November 1994, 1833 U.N.T.S. 3, reprinted in 21 I.L.M. 1261 (1982), articles 286–287.

73. E. D. Brown, "Dispute Settlement and the Law of the Sea: The UN Convention Regime," *Marine Policy* 21, no. 1 (1997), at 17.
74. Guđmundur Eiríksson, *The International Tribunal for the Law of the Sea*, Martinus Nijhoff Publishers, The Hague, London, Boston, 2000, p. 111.
75. See *Southern Bluefin Tuna Cases* (provisional measures) (*New Zealand and Australia v. Japan*), International Tribunal for the Law of the Sea, judgment of 27 August 1999, cases nos. 3 and 4 and *Southern Bluefin Tuna Case* (*Australia and New Zealand v. Japan*), award on jurisdiction and admissibility, arbitral tribunal, decided on 4 August 2000, World Bank, International Centre for Settlement of Investment Disputes.
76. See *MOX Plant Case* (provisional measures) (*Ireland v. United Kingdom*), International *Tribunal for the Law of the Sea*, order of 3 December 2001, case no. 10; *MOX Plant Case* (*Ireland v. United Kingdom*), order an arbitral tribunal of 24 June 2003, Permanent Court of Arbitration; *Dispute Concerning Access to Information under Article 9 of the OSPAR Convention*, (*Ireland v. United Kingdom*), arbitral award of 2 July 2003, Permanent Court of Arbitration; and *Commission v. Ireland*, European Court of Justice, case no. C-459/03, judgment of 30 May 2006, 2006 *European Court Reports* I-04635, the last finding Ireland to be in violation of community law by referring the dispute to proceedings under UNCLOS.

Chapter 12

Final Remarks on the Concept of Countermeasures

> A balanced regime of countermeasures is more likely to be of use in controlling excesses than silence on a vitally important subject.
>
> —James Crawford, special rapporteur for the International Law Commission (2000)[1]

There is no doubt that countermeasures can put destructive forces for the international system in motion. Because of the absence of institutional procedures to address many international disputes, unilateral acts of states, such as countermeasures, are, however, an inherent part of the enforcement mechanism of the international system. In its comments on the *1996 Draft Articles on State Responsibility*, Denmark wrote:

> The Nordic countries agree with the Commission in considering countermeasures as a reflection of the imperfect structure of present-day international society, which has not (yet) succeeded

> in establishing an effective centralized system of law enforcement. It is difficult, therefore, to avoid the use of countermeasures which are firmly founded in customary international law. In particular cases, the risk of countermeasures may actually be the only effective deterrent to the commission of internationally wrongful acts.[2]

To prevent the use of countermeasures from leading the contending parties down the slippery slope of escalating conflicts, international law sets a number of obstacles and requirements that need to be overcome or fulfilled before an injured state can resort to countermeasures. What these obstacles and requirements actually comprise is ultimately for the international courts and diplomats to decide.

Nevertheless, this part attempts to clarify the countermeasures doctrine by addressing its individual elements. It submits that the doctrine's primary element is the presence of a prior violation of an international obligation owed to the state taking the countermeasures, attributable to another state or states. This violation has to be actual and proven; a reasonable view of the state taking the countermeasures is not sufficient to justify such measures. Accordingly, anticipatory countermeasures, taken in the face of an imminent breach, cannot be justified under the countermeasures doctrine. It is also suggested that even if the right to take countermeasures is primarily a right belonging to an injured state, countermeasures can also be taken by indirectly injured states. However, in such cases, the legitimate aims are more limited. Thus, countermeasures taken by states that have not suffered a physical injury and are, therefore, not entitled to compensations can only be taken to induce the wrongdoing state to cease the violation and to guarantee it will not be repeated—but not to pay reparations. Similarly, the proportionality principle restricts the measures that such a state is able to take as its injury is presumably of a lesser magnitude than a physical injury of a directly harmed state.

This part suggests that prior to taking countermeasures, the injured state has to comply with certain procedural requirements, such as requesting the wrongdoing state to comply with its obligations and/or pay reparation. The injured state also has, subject to certain exceptions, to notify the responsible state of the prospective countermeasures and offer negotiation. Ongoing good faith negotiations are, however, not an obstacle to the taking of countermeasures.

During the taking of countermeasures, the freedom of the injured state to choose the means and methods to induce the wrongdoing state to comply with its international obligations is not unlimited. First, countermeasures cannot violate certain vital international obligations. Among them are the ban against use of force under the *UN Charter*, fundamental human rights, and prohibition against reprisals against protected persons under humanitarian law, as well as peremptory norms of international law. In addition, countermeasures have to respect rules relating to the inviolability of subjects of diplomatic and consular protection.

The freedom to choose the means and methods of countermeasures is also restricted by the principle of proportionality. This means that the measures taken should be proportionate to the injury suffered and to what is necessary to obtain the legitimate objectives of the measures. This two-point criteria of the principle of proportionality of countermeasures has to be interpreted as a whole. It must also be noted, in line with international jurisprudence and writings of legal scholars, that the determination of proportionality is not a precise science. Therefore, certain approximation is sufficient in order to find countermeasures to be proportionate.

In addition to limitation due to rules regarding prohibited countermeasures and the principle of proportionality, various scholars and governments have suggested that the presence of alternative methods of dispute resolution can eliminate, reduce, or delay the right to resort to countermeasures. However, alternative means of dispute resolution do not generally restrict the right of the injured state to resort to countermeasures. Thus, an ongoing good faith negotiation or access to a binding dispute settlement mechanism does not prevent an injured state from taking countermeasures. However, in the event and to the extent that the dispute settlement mechanism provides an effective remedy for the injured state capable of providing comparable results and guarantees as countermeasures, the injured state might be restricted from taking countermeasures.

The elements of countermeasure are a matter of significant debate and will continue to be so. The right to use countermeasures can be abused by the hawks against the doves and, thus, undermine the rule of law in the international system. They are not, therefore, to be encouraged and have to be subject to reasonable limitation. But in a society of hawks and doves, the absence of a centralized enforcement mechanism cannot be ignored.

Arguably, the international system needs a regime of countermeasure because its ability to resolve international disputes and enforce such settlements is underdeveloped. States still chose to retain a significant part of their sovereignty for various reasons and, even when they are bound by an international obligation, the rule of law is not under all circumstances the most favored approach. It has been argued that under what might be called a new generation of interstate systems, that is, the EU framework, the right to countermeasures is severely diminished if not eliminated.[3] This might be because the states belonging to the community have partly transferred their function as actors in the international arena to community institutions. It must, nevertheless, be noted that the development of the international system does not follow a straight road; it is curvy, broken, and as it is frequently reshaped by previously unthinkable events, the obvious track can be quickly abandoned. When change is the only constant, it is not possible to predict if the development of the international system will follow the European model or any similar methods of transboundary governance. Thus, the end of the exercise of sovereignty and unilateral measures is not immediately visible.

Endnotes

1. *Third Report 2000 (Crawford)*, addendum, p. 4, para. 291.
2. *State Responsibility: Comments and Observations Received from Governments*, UN doc. no. A/CN.4/488, 25 March 1998, p. 114.
3. See for example discussion in *Fourth Report 1992 (Arangio-Ruiz)*, pp. 35–36, paras. 98–99.

Part III

Countermeasures and Environmental Threats: Case Studies

Chapter 13

Introduction

The last part of this book comprises two sets of case studies. They all regard unilateral measures of states taken in order to induce other states to cease behavior that the alleged injured states saw as environmentally threatening. Although the injured states did not explicitly attempt to justify their actions as countermeasures, their arguments often resembled such justification. These cases illustrate the importance of the various issues that states have to take into consideration in order to be able to successfully argue that their unilateral measures can be considered as countermeasures. These issues, the elements of countermeasures, make or break their arguments.

The first set of case studies concerns unilateral measures taken by a coastal state in response to other states' alleged illegal harvesting of fish stocks outside its 200 nm exclusive economic zone (EEZ). They both refer to the harvesting of straddling stocks in that the alleged injured states had vital interest and, therefore, had vital interests in how the management and conservation of the stock was regulated and effectively controlled. The cases included in the first set are the *Már Case*, a dispute between Norway and Iceland regarding fisheries in the Barents Sea, and the *Estai Case*, which was a dispute between Canada and the EC relating to the fisheries of Greenland halibut in the Grand Banks.

The cases in the second set share a commonality in that they were submitted to a GATT or WTO body as a trade dispute. The purpose of the measures, protection of the environment, was referred to as a justification of the measures under Article XX of GATT. The main purpose of the second set is to give examples of the attempt to reconcile the interests of the trade regime and the environmental regime and to discuss how an argument for countermeasures in response to violations of international environmental obligations can survive in a dispute resolution system that seems, at least on its surface, to be predominantly occupied with trade concerns. The cases included in the second set are the tuna cases, disputes between the United States and several tuna-exporting states; the *Shrimp/Turtle Case*, a dispute between the United States and a number of shrimp exporting states; and the *Swordfish Conservation Case*, a case between the European Community and Chile regarding swordfish harvesting in the southeast Pacific.

The review of these cases is not to determine conclusively whether countermeasures in these cases would have been legal; in most of them, they would not. The purpose is, rather, to address how the elements of countermeasures fit with the facts presented in order to ascertain whether the argument of countermeasure would have been a plausible one, as well as to point out the main problems with the applicability of the countermeasures doctrine. Therefore, the discussion in these case studies will not analyze in any detail whether the initial violation has actually occurred, if such behavior can be attributed to a state, if the alleged injured state actually has the right to resort to countermeasures, if the measures taken were in accordance with the required procedures, or if the measures were actually proportional to the injury suffered or what is necessary to induce changes in the offending state's behavior. The purpose of these case studies is, rather, to show how the elements of countermeasures, as they were presented prior in this book, mainly in part II, can be applied in the settings provided by the cases.

Countermeasures, as remedies within the international system, are subject to rules and limitations. They are not a remedy to be taken lightly or to be resorted to without accurate analysis of the underlying situation. The use of such remedies is, therefore, not freely or unimpeded at the disposal of the injured state; they are, as in any other sphere of their international behavior, restricted by the constraints imposed on them by the international system of which international law forms an integral part.

The following review of the cases, when applicable, discusses the main elements of countermeasures and how the behavior of the relevant states, based on the facts presented, positions expressed, and applicable law, corresponds to these elements. The elements referred to are mainly the presence of an internationally wrongful act attributable to the offending state, the presence of an injury, a request from the injured state to the offending state to cease the violation and an offer to negotiate, the subject of the unilateral measures, the purpose of unilateral measures, and, finally, the proportionality of the measures.

Even if the purpose of the following exercise is not to solve the underlying substantive legal issues, such as if a violation has actually taken place, it is, nevertheless, appropriate in order to provide the necessary context and to better understand the nature of the disputes in these cases and to provide an overview of the relevant rules related to the disputes. In order to do so, this part, in relating to the first set of case studies, provides a brief overview of the rules of *UNCLOS* relating to the harvesting of straddling stocks and highly migratory species in the high seas. With regard to the second set, this part discusses the WTO dispute settlement mechanism and how unilateral actions affecting free trade, taken in order to prevent environmental harm, are dealt with by the mechanism. Of particular interest, of course, is the question of whether the argument of countermeasures, as a response to violations of international environmental obligations, is likely to be relevant and applicable before the WTO dispute settlement mechanism.

Chapter 14

Case Studies: Fisheries

(a) Introduction

It must be noted first that the handling of the cases presented here differs somewhat. This is partly resulting from a different level of access to information relating to these cases and to the fact that the handling of these cases before the relevant dispute resolution bodies differs greatly. Although both cases were referred to proceedings before a third party dispute settlement body, neither of them came before such a body as a dispute regarding the legality of countermeasures. The dispute between the EC and Canada was brought before the ICJ by Spain but was dismissed on jurisdictional grounds. Also, the dispute between Iceland and Norway was brought before the EFTA Surveillance Authority (ESA)[1] as a dispute related to free trade in services but not as a dispute related to fisheries. Any comparison between these cases must take this into account.

(B) THE APPLICABLE LAW ON HIGH SEAS FISHERIES

The international instruments governing the legal debate on fisheries in the high seas today are primarily *UNCLOS* and the *Fish Stocks Agreement*.[2] Numerous regional agreements complement those primary instruments. However, as the *Fish Stocks Agreement* was not in force during the periods relevant to the cases discussed in this chapter, the law applicable to the underlying disputes in the following cases is *UNCLOS*. The provisions of the *Fish Stocks Agreement* will, nevertheless, be given due attention as it is intended to implement the relevant provisions of *UNCLOS*.

(i) *UNCLOS*

Under Article 87 of *UNCLOS*, the high seas are open to all states who enjoy numerous rights, including "freedom of fishing, subject to the conditions laid down in section 2..." of part VII of *UNCLOS*.[3] Section 2—Articles 116 to 120—contains provisions on conservation and management of the living resources of the high seas. Under Article 116, the rights of states to fish in the high seas is subject to "their treaty obligations; ...the rights and duties as well as the interests of coastal States provided for, *inter alia*, in article 63, paragraph 2, and articles 64 to 67; and...the provisions of this section."[4] Under Article 117, "All States have the duty to take, or to cooperate with other States in taking, such measures for their respective nationals as may be necessary for the conservation of the living resources of the high seas."[5] Article 117 must be understood as not only requiring states to cooperate but also to take their own measures that may be necessary. Quite arguably, Article 117 contains an obligation for a state whose vessels are fishing from straddling stocks in the highs seas to, in the absence of cooperation, unilaterally decide scientifically sensible quotas for its vessels in the high seas if such measures are necessary for the conservation of the stock.[6]

Article 116 contains a reference to Article 63(2) and Article 64 of *UNCLOS*, which are of relevance to the present set of cases. Under these articles, states that harvest stocks that "occur both within the exclusive economic zone and in an area beyond and adjacent to the zone, ...shall seek…to agree upon measures necessary for the conservation of these stocks in the adjacent area."[7] Similarly, with regard to highly migratory species, Article 64 provides for cooperation between states that harvest migratory species. Unlike Article 63(2), which only provides for cooperation in relation to the harvesting of straddling stocks in the adjacent area for conservation purposes, Article 64 provides for cooperation "with a view to ensuring conservation and promoting the objective of optimum utilization of such species throughout the region, both *within and beyond the exclusive economic zone*."[8] However, this does not mean that the sovereign rights of a coastal state within its EEZ have been eliminated, as paragraph 2 of Article 64 clearly states that the article applies "in addition to the other provisions of this Part…"[9] This includes the rights of a coastal state under Article 56 of *UNCLOS*, giving it sovereign rights to explore, exploit, and manage, as well as conserve natural resources within the EEZ.[10]

Article 63 and 64 differ from Article 117, as the latter not only requires states to cooperate with but also to take measures for their respective nationals to ensure proper conservation. This indicates that, even in the absence of cooperation, states are required to ensure that fishing activities of their nationals in the high seas do not jeopardize the conservation of straddling stocks and highly migratory stocks.

(ii) The *Fish Stocks Agreement*

In 1995, a UN conference adopted the *Agreement for the Implementation of the Provisions of United Nations Convention on the Law of the Sea of 10 December 1982 Relating to the Conservation and Management of Straddling Fish Stocks and Highly Migratory Fish Stocks* (*Fish Stock Agreement*). The agreement, which entered into force on 11 December 2001, was not the applicable law in any of the disputes reviewed in this part.[11] However, as its subject is the implementation of *UNCLOS*, in particular the provisions reviewed previously, it is appropriate to consider its main provisions.

The objective of the agreement is to "ensure the long-term conservation and sustainable use of straddling fish stocks and highly migratory fish stocks through effective implementation of the relevant provision of [*UNCLOS*]."[12] Article 5 of the agreement describes the general principles concerning the conservation and management of straddling and highly migratory fish stocks. Under Article 5, coastal states and states fishing in the high seas area shall adopt measures to ensure the long-term sustainability of straddling stocks and ensure that these measures are based on the best scientific evidence available, and when scientific evidence is incomplete or unreliable, states shall apply the precautionary approach.[13]

Article 7 of the agreement places duties on the relevant coastal states and states whose nationals fish for straddling fish stocks in the adjacent high seas to seek to agree upon measures necessary for the conservation of straddling stocks in the adjacent high seas.[14] In the case of highly migratory fish stocks, the states shall cooperate "with a view to ensuring conservation and promoting the objective of optimum utilization of such stocks throughout the region, both within and beyond the areas under national jurisdiction."[15] As was pointed out in relation to Article 63(2) and 64 of *UNCLOS*, these arrangements apply also to the harvesting of highly migratory fish stocks within the EEZ.

The *Fish Stocks Agreement* provides for a large role of regional and subregional organizations in the conservation and management of harvesting straddling and highly migratory fish stocks. Under the agreement, states that have "real interest in the fisheries concerned may become members of such organization or participants in such arrangement."[16] Such membership or participation is vital for the right of a party to the *Fish Stocks Agreement* because without it a state party can be excluded from "access to the fishery resources to which those measures apply."[17]

The most promising provisions of the agreement concern enforcement of regional or subregional conservation and management measures. Under Article 19 of the agreement, the primary enforcement duty rests on the flag state. First of all, it has a duty to "enforce such measures irrespective of where violations occur..."[18] It has a duty to

> investigate immediately and fully any alleged violation of subregional or regional conservation and management measures...and

> report promptly to the State alleging the violation and the relevant subregional or regional organization or arrangement on the progress and outcome of the investigation...[19]

Under Article 20, other states shall cooperate with the flag state if it so requests. Furthermore, the flag state can authorize a coastal state to inspect or board its vessel in the high seas.[20] Finally, member states of regional or subregional organizations or arrangements

> may take action in accordance with international law, ...to deter vessels which have engaged in activities which undermine the effectiveness of or otherwise violate the conservation and management measures established by that organization or arrangement from fishing on the high seas in the subregion or region until such time as appropriate action is taken by the flag State.[21]

Further enforcement provisions are in Article 21, which give certain enforcement powers to members of regional or subregional organization or participants in regional or subregional arrangement. Under Article 23, a port state is also given powers to enforce regional or subregional conservation or management measures, including the right to "inspect documents, fishing gear, and catch on board fishing vessels, when such vessels are voluntarily in its ports or at its offshore terminals,"[22] as well as to "adopt regulations empowering the relevant national authorities to prohibit landings and transshipments where it has been established that the catch has been taken in a manner which undermines the effectiveness of subregional, regional or global conservation and management measures on the high seas."[23]

(C) Norway/Iceland Loophole Dispute: The *Már Case*

(i) Summary

In early July 1995, Norway refused an Icelandic fishing vessel access to port in northern Norway.[24] The vessel, which had been fishing in international waters adjacent to the Norwegian EEZ from a straddling cod stock that was managed by Norway and Russia, had requested permit to dock to have a net cut out of its propeller.[25] The owner of the vessel claimed that Norway had violated a provision of the *Agreement on the European Economic Area* (*EEA Agreement*),[26] which provides for free trade in services.[27] Norway, which claimed that Iceland had violated provisions of *UNCLOS*,[28] argued that the restrictions on the vessel's right to be serviced in Norway were not in breach of Norway's obligation under the *EEA Agreement*. It also claimed that it had, by restricting access to services, taken defensive measures that, in the light of the fishing activities of the vessels, should be seen as justified.[29] The case was brought before the EFTA Surveillance Authority (ESA) as a dispute over trade in services. The ESA decided not to take action against Norway.[30]

(ii) Facts and Analysis

In August 1993, Icelandic fishing vessels commenced fishing in a disputed area 200 nm north of Norway. At first, the fleet fished mostly within the so-called Spitzbergen fish conservation zone, but after a few and serious confrontations with the Norwegian coast guard, which included shots being fired,[31] the fleet moved to an international area, the so-called Loophole. Norway protested the fisheries along with Russia, which threatened to send warships to stop the Icelandic fishing vessels.[32] Attempted negotiations between Iceland and Norway were not fruitful.[33]

The Loophole, a 24,090 sq. mile (62,400 sq. km) area, is located 200 nm north of the Russian Kola Peninsula, northeast of Norway. Spitzbergen is 200 nm to the northwest. To the east is Novaya Zemlya, a Russian island, and 200 nm to the north is the Russian archipelago Franz Josef Land. The area is indisputably high seas and, therefore, outside the Norwegian and Russian 200 nm EEZ and the conservation zone around Spitzbergen.

The reason for the influx of Icelandic fishing vessels, as well as from numerous other nations, was a straddling cod stock, the Barents Sea cod. This stock spawns within the Norwegian EEZ, then floats north in the larval stage, and then spreads around and enters the Loophole in later stages. The cod stays, however, mostly within the Norwegian and Russian EEZ.[34] Because of the presence of the cod within the Norwegian and Russian EEZ, it is primarily subject to their conservation and management. However, the Barents Sea cod swims without respect for the outer boundaries of these countries' EEZ.

Among the Icelandic vessels fishing in the Loophole was the trawler *Már*. While in the Loophole in July 1995, the captain noticed a problem with the propeller. After a brief examination, the crew concluded that a rope or a net was caught in it. The captain of the trawler, claiming the ship was in distress, decided to head to Norway to have the propeller repaired.[35] The captain explained the situation to the Headquarters Defence Command North Norway and announced its intentions to head to port in northern Norway. Norwegian authorities initially granted access for the vessel to its waters and to port.[36] Before the vessel could dock at the port of Honningsvåg in northern Norway, the Norwegian coast guard withdrew the permit to dock. Instead, the vessel was allowed to anchor inside the territorial sea. The operator of the vessel had already secured a contractor to repair the propeller, but because of the refusal to dock, no work was performed on the propeller.[37] While *Már* was at anchor, it was boarded and inspected by the coast guard, who found that despite that "remnants of the codend, measuring 2–3 metres by 50 cm, were attached to two of the three propeller blades, …the vessel would not be in any imminent danger if it were to sail from Norwegian waters without assistance."[38] Subsequently, it ordered *Már* to leave the territorial waters of Norway.[39] After Icelandic authorities protested and sent a coast guard ship to escort *Már* to Iceland, Norwegian authorities allowed *Már* back into the territorial sea to have the propeller repaired. The coast guard, however, "not to enter into undue competition with private firms," refused to perform the repairs but referred to local contractors in the area.[40] Because of the hostile media coverage in Norway, only one contractor was willing to perform the repairs. However, after being allegedly threatened with boycott from the local fishery industry, he withdrew his offer.[41] Realizing that no one was willing to provide assistance to the vessel, the Norwegian coast guard ordered the vessel out of the territorial sea. After a few days of diplomatic maneuvers, the coast guard finally agreed to repair the propeller. After the repairs, *Már* sailed back to the Loophole and resumed fishing.[42]

The operator of *Már*, a small fishing company on Iceland's west coast, filed a complaint with the ESA, alleging that "the measures taken by Norwegian authorities, with the objective to prevent the trawler *Már* from receiving the services it had repeatedly asked for and was in dire need of, violated Chapter III of the Agreement on the European Economic Area, in particular Article 36 thereof…".[43] Article 36 of the *EEA Agreement*, which is identical in substance to Article 49 of the *EC Treaty* as amended by the Treaty of Amsterdam,[44] provides for prohibition on restriction to provide services within the EEA. The European Court of Justice had interpreted Article 49 of the *Treaty of Rome* as to contain also prohibition against restriction on seeking services within the EC.[45] Article 36(1) of the *EEA Agreement* reads:

> Within the framework of the provisions of this Agreement, there shall be no restrictions on freedom to provide services within the territory of the Contracting Parties in respect of nationals of EC Member States and EFTA States who are established in an EC Member State or an EFTA State other than that of the person for whom the services are intended.[46]

In its response to ESA, Norway argued that Article 36 does not constitute "any obligation to allow Norwegian ports to be used for the provision of services to Icelandic or any other vessels while engaged in contested and unregulated fishing operations."[47] Norway explained that under *Norwegian Regulation No. 1130*, Section 12(2), "except in cases of *force majeure* or distress, access to port may be denied if a fishing vessel is engaged in activities deemed to be contrary to established principles of sustainable resource management."[48] This right granted to the Norwegian authorities was, in Norway's opinion, "in full conformity with general international law."[49] When addressing the alleged breach of Article 36, Norway wrote that it "does not find it necessary to enter into a discussion of the extent to which the principle of freedom to provide services may also constitute a legal basis for a right to access to ports for fishing vessels under Community law."[50] Without discussing further how its actions might or might not have been in contradiction to Article 36, Norway argued that since the *EEA Agreement* does not include fisheries or a fishery policy, the dispute at hand was outside the scope of the EEA institutions.[51] Norway then wrote:

> Consequently, the right of EEA Contracting Parties to take defensive measures in accordance with their rights under general international law cannot be excluded. On the contrary, the restrictions imposed by a coastal State on the free exchange of services by refusing foreign vessels port access when they are engaged in uncontrolled and damaging harvesting of fish stocks of vital interest are to be considered both proportionate and necessary to protect the effective management of fish resources.[52]

The language of this passage clearly resembles an argument for countermeasures. However, Norway left out an important element of the legality of countermeasures. It did not at this stage attempt to establish that Iceland had violated any international obligations, only that the vessel was engaged in contested and unregulated fishing. The arguments were, therefore, related to conservation needs and the apparent uncontrolled fishing of the Barents Sea cod. Nevertheless, as will be discussed next, if Norway had been able to show that Iceland was, in fact, in violation of an international obligation related to fishing in the high seas, a case for countermeasures would have had merits.

In the *Letter of Formal Notice*, addressed to Norwegian authorities, ESA examined Norway's argument that because the underlying dispute concerned the management and harvesting of living marine resources, Article 36 was not applicable and the dispute could not be resolved within the EEA institutional system.[53] After a brief analysis, ESA rejected Norway's suggestions and held that the regulation authorizing Norwegian authorities to effectively prevent the vessel *Már* from seeking services in Norwegian ports constituted an "obstacle to the freedom to receive services in accordance with Article 36 of the *EEA Agreement*."[54]

ESA took notice of Norway's assertion that "the right of EEA Contracting Parties to take defensive measures in accordance with their rights under *general international law* cannot be excluded."[55] ESA's answer to that question did not support this assertion. However, it is not conclusive with regard to countermeasures under the EEA framework. As briefly mentioned before, the European Court of Justice has repeatedly held that the *EC Treaty* precluded the use of countermeasures against a violation that falls within the purview of the treaty.[56] Although the *EEA Agreement* is more limited in scope, ESA might be tempted to use a somewhat similar approach. However, because the *EEA* framework does not include obligations related to responsible fisheries, such approach might be an incorrect interpretation of the court's findings. Nevertheless, ESA wrote:

> The very purpose of the *EEA Agreement* is namely to create and maintain between the Contracting Parties a legal framework within which they renounce using against each other's nationals a number of rights to which they are otherwise entitled to resort under international law. One of the rights that the EEA States have thus given up is the right to obstruct the freedom of nationals of other EEA States—including operators of fishing vessels flying the flag of such a State—to go to that EEA State to receive a service there in accordance with Article 36 or the *EEA Agreement*.[57]

ESA then wrote, "when making cumbersome *Már's* access to repair services in Norway and ordering her out of its territorial waters, Norway breached its obligations under Article 36 of the *EEA Agreement*."[58] ESA continued and wrote, "Norway cannot justify such action by referring to a right to refuse access to ports which it may have under international law."[59]

Under Article 33 of the *EEA Agreement*, states are permitted to derogate from the duty not to obstruct the free flow of services within the EEA, where such derogation is authorized by national law, regulation, or administrative action, "on grounds of public policy, public security or public health."[60] This provision, which seems to leave some room for unilateral measures, has, however, been limited to circumstances where the presence or conduct of the foreign national "constitutes a genuine and sufficiently serious threat to public policy"[61] and where the threat affects "one of the fundamental interests of society."[62] ESA held that these strict requirements are not met when "a foreign fishing vessel which wishes to enter a port has been fishing in the high seas on fish stocks which do not fall under any national jurisdiction or any international regulatory regime."[63]

In accordance with its procedures, ESA gave Norway an opportunity to submit its observations on the content of the *Letter of Formal Notice*. Norway replied with a letter dated 29 November 1996.[64] In its reply, Norway maintained its position that the refusal to provide access to port was justified as a defense measure. However, instead of arguing that the dispute was out the scope of the EEA institutional system, Norway now suggested that the "difference between the scope of the EEA Agreement and that of the EC Treaty with respect to fishery policy, must necessarily influence the *interpretation* of the two agreements."[65] The differences referred to were mainly that since fisheries were within the scope of the *EC Treaty*, and since the EC institutional structure provided resolution of resource management disputes, the need to resort to unilateral measures was less under the EC framework. The situation under the *EEA Agreement* was, however, different as there were not any possibilities to resolve prior resource management conflicts independently or in connection with the resolution of a dispute over violation of Article 36.[66] Since the EEA institutional system was unable to address violation of conservation obligations, the public policy exception in Article 33 should be interpreted differently, making room for unilateral measures in this case. Norway wrote:

> In the absence of a common policy within the EEA Agreement under which such violations could be dealt with, its Contracting Parties must retain their right under general international law *actively* to redress a violation. Otherwise, the EEA Agreement, unlike the EC Treaty, would leave its Contracting Parties in limbo in this respect, unable to honour their obligation to maintain international law in this particular field. Consequently, the

> right to redress in this situation qualifies as valid public policy consideration under Article 33 of the EEA Agreement, regardless of whether this would hold true within the European Community with its common fisheries policy.[67]

Norway's argument can be read as suggesting that the remedy taken should be justified under the public policy exception in the absence of another effective remedy. Norway might be right on point with this passage; because the substantive rules of the *EEA Agreement* do not cover conservation and management of living marine resources, the EEA states have retained their right to resort to countermeasures whether such measures are framed as public policy measures or not, whereas the EC states have surrendered this right, with regard to relations between themselves, to the EC institutions. It is also possible to interpret Norway's position as suggesting that because conservation and management of living marine resources fall outside the *EEA Agreement*, ESA either does not have competence to directly address the underlying alleged violation of the law of the sea. Having in mind ESA's place in a pan-European institutional framework that focuses mainly on trade-related issues, Norway might also have been concerned that if ESA would rule on the dispute, it would not consider an argument based on the countermeasures doctrine or, at least, give conservation interests lower priority than the interests of trade. This concern was the issue of a paper submitted by the EC to the WTO Committee on Trade and Environment in October 2000. The paper suggested that, when in conflict, environmental considerations should not be given lower priority than trade-related issues—otherwise, international efforts to tackle environmental problems would be undermined.[68] Related concerns were expressed by the Chilean representative when the EC's request to convene a panel to settle their swordfish dispute was discussed in the WTO Dispute Settlement Body.[69] For these reasons, that is, the danger that ESA would distance itself from the underlying environmental arguments because of its trade-related preferences, ESA should give Norway a wide margin of discretion and not take actions against it even if the refusal of access to port might have stepped out of what the EC jurisprudence accepts as permissible public policy measures.

ESA's final decision on whether Norway had violated Article 36 of the *EEA Agreement* was taken in the spring of 1998 and announced to the Norwegian authorities in a letter dated 14 May 1998.[70] The conclusion was that Norway's regulation, authorizing it to refuse access to port for vessels engaged in contested fisheries, was applied "in a manner which may have constituted a restriction on the free movement of services."[71] The softened language is immediately noticeable; instead of the firm opinion on the incompatibility of Norway's actions with Article 36, which was expressed in the *Letter of Formal Notice*, ESA no longer seemed to be certain that a violation had occurred. This decision needs explanation. First, ESA noted that *UNCLOS* and the *Fish Stock Agreement*, "which are applicable to both parties,"[72] contain provisions on the conservation of stocks in the highs seas. Then ESA wrote:

> The Authority is of the opinion that by signing the EEA Agreement the Contracting Parties thereto have limited their right to deny access to ports for EEA fishing vessel. The effect of the EEA Agreement is therefore that an EEA State must grant access to its ports by fishing vessels flying the flag of another EEA State, *unless such access can be restricted either on a non-discriminatory and necessary basis in the interest of the general good*, or on grounds recognized by its Article 33.[73]

ESA seemed to have opened the door for reasons justifying Norway's unilateral measures on grounds other than public policy, public security, or public health under Article 33. The passage indicates, therefore, that the alleged violation of the conservation obligation that Iceland owed to Norway had played a role in ESA's final conclusion, indicating that Norway's argument for taking defensive measures was valid even if the measures violated the *EEA Agreement*. Two other passages support this conclusion. First, even though ESA did not determine whether Iceland had, in fact, violated its international obligations or not, the possibility was discussed.[74] Second, in its concluding remarks, ESA wrote the following:

> It is my view that although the case at hand is based on a complaint by the owner of a fishing vessel and concerns access to

> port services, the underlying dispute is one between Norway and Iceland relating to Icelandic fishing in international waters in Barents Sea, for which the authority has no competence.[75]

ESA then suggested that the concerned states resolve their dispute using dispute settlement procedures under *UNCLOS* or other forums within the EEA structures.[76]

(iii) Additional Analysis Related to the Elements of Countermeasures

There is little doubt that the vessel *Már* or its crew did not violate international law or Norwegian law or regulations.[77] Arguably, a captain of a vessel has a moral obligation with regard to his fishing operations and their effects on the conservation of the marine environment. However, such obligations are irrelevant for the legality of countermeasures. Nevertheless, the legality of the act of fishing does not mean that countermeasures cannot be justified or that no violation of an international obligation has occurred. As already mentioned, a state party to *UNCLOS* has "the duty to take…such measures for their respective nationals as may be necessary for the conservation of the living resources of the high seas."[78] As was duly noted by Norway, the Icelandic government did not decide on the limits of the catch of the Icelandic fleet in the Loophole after the fishing there started, although it did adopt some measures to prevent fishing of undersized fish.[79] Because Iceland had failed to take the required measures, Norway argued that Iceland appeared to have breached its obligations under Article 117 of *UNCLOS*.[80]

Norway mentioned that some authors had suggested "that the coastal state is considered authorized to establish conservation measures applicable to the stock as a whole, comprising the high seas portion, and to demand compliance by high seas fishing states."[81] However, instead of building its argument on such stock-oriented scholarly writing, Norway turned to the *Fish Stock Agreement* for further arguments for Iceland's alleged violation of the law of the sea.[82] Since this study does not attempt to determine whether the initial breach justifying countermeasures actually took place, there is no need to go further into Norway's arguments.

It is sufficient to take note that Norway did assert that Iceland had violated its obligation owed to it as a coastal state and that their assertion had merits, at least on its surface.[83]

The question whether Norway has suffered injury that gives it standing to resort to countermeasures is not complex. It is uncontested that the Barents Sea cod stock lives mostly within the jurisdictions of the two coastal states, that is, their EEZs and the Spitzbergen conservation zone. Arguably, the obligation to take conservation measures in the high seas is owed to all states that have interests in the particular stocks in question and even in stocks belonging to the same biosystem. Thus, there is no doubt that if states have an obligation under the *UNCLOS* high seas fishery regime to unilaterally decide on reasonable quotas for their fishing vessels under Article 117, such obligation is, in this case, also owed to Norway.

The debate on whether fisheries above the suggested 700,000 tons of total allowable catch can be harmful for the Barents Sea cod stock and contribute to its decline belongs, rather, to the discipline of marine science than environmental law. Nevertheless, the amount of the total catch of the Icelandic vessels indicates that their fisheries had the potential to negatively affect the Barents Sea cod stock. After the extension of the Norwegian and Russian EEZs in 1977,[84] no third state fishing took place in the Loophole until 1991 when trawlers from Greenland, the Faeroe Islands, and the EC began fishing there.[85] Prior to the fisheries of the Icelandic vessels, the stock had been growing, arguably, as a result of responsible management of the Joint Norwegian Russian Fisheries Commission the years prior to 1995.[86] The total catch of the Icelandic fleet in the Loophole was 4,202 tons in 1993; 32,276 in 1994; and 33,969 in 1995[87] or just under 5% of the total allowable catch. There can, therefore, be little doubt that the unrestricted fisheries of the Icelandic vessels had the potential to affect the stock. It must be noted, however, that in 1997 the total allowable catch was increased to 850,000 tons despite the continued fishing of Icelandic trawlers.[88]

When arguing the purpose of the refusal to allow *Már* to be serviced in the port on Honningsvåg, Norway departed from the structure of an argument for countermeasures, especially by stating that the measures were directed against the vessel "in order to prevent further damage to the stock by that particular vessel, and not in order to deter other vessels."[89] Accordingly, the declared intention was not to induce the wrongdoing state to cease the violation but to prevent that particular private party from engaging in fishing practices that were contrary to Norwegian laws and Norway's international rights and obligations to conserve and manage the Barents Sea cod stock. This departure was to entertain a requirement imposed by the case law of the European Court of Justice for justification for a trade restriction based on public policy under Article 33 or the *EEA Agreement*.[90] This differentiation from the underlying dispute is not, however, in harmony with the remainder of Norway's submissions in this dispute before ESA—in particular its detailed discussion on how Iceland allegedly failed to comply with its obligations to take measures to conserve the Barents Sea cod stock and to cooperate with the interested parties, namely, Norway and Russia.

Arguably, the refusal of port access was a proportionate response to a violation of an international obligation designed to induce Iceland to refrain from permitting uncontrolled fisheries of Icelandic vessels in the Loophole. Norway, however, chose to argue the case within the EEA framework but with an important variation; because the EEA structure did not provide for remedies against alleged violations of international environmental obligations related to the conservation of living marine resources in the high seas, the prohibition against trade restrictions should be interpreted as to give Norway an authority to resort to unilateral measures to protect its interests. Although ESA did not formally agree with Norway, ESA's decision indicates that the facts relating to the underlying dispute were sufficient to convince ESA to adopt a hands-off policy toward Norway's actions.

(D) CANADA/EC HALIBUT DISPUTE: *THE ESTAI CASE*

(i) Summary

On 9 March 1995, Canadian authorities arrested and brought to port a Spanish fishing vessel.[91] The vessel, called *Estai*, was engaged in fishing in the high seas adjacent to the 200 nm Canadian exclusive fishing zone (EFZ) of a straddling fish stock, the Greenland halibut, also called turbot.[92] Spain and the EC—fisheries of EC member states were and still are under the competences of the EC—protested and claimed that Canada had violated a number of provisions of *UNCLOS*.[93] Canada, which had repeatedly claimed that fisheries by EC member states were in violation of their international obligations, justified its action by conservation needs.[94] The vessel was released 6 days later after its owner posted a bond.[95] Canadian and EC officials shortly thereafter began negotiating an increased quota for EC vessels of the Greenland halibut. On 16 April 1995, they reached an agreement, which resulted in an increase of the EC quota and a decrease of the halibut quota allocated to Canada.[96] Spain brought a claim for the alleged illegal arrest of the vessel against Canada before the ICJ. The court held in 1998 that it did not have jurisdiction to adjudicate the dispute brought before it.[97]

(ii) Facts and Analysis

In 1994, Canadian authorities argued for stricter conservation measures for the Greenland halibut in the NAFO[98] convention area, which is comprised of a part of the Canadian EFZ and a high seas area adjacent to their EFZ. One stock was of particular concern, the Greenland halibut, which the Canadian ambassador to the EC, Jacques Roy, later called the "last commercially-viable stock in the North Atlantic..."[99] On 12 May 1994, the Canadian parliament approved an amendment to the 1985 *Coastal Fisheries Protection Act*.[100] The amendment authorized Canadian authorities to enforce Canadian legislation in the NAFO regulatory area, that is, the part of the NAFO convention area that is outside the 200 nm Canadian EFZ.[101] Additionally, Canada made a list of states that were not allowed to fish at all in this area.[102] Shortly thereafter, the Canadian fisheries minister, Brian Tobin, fired what was later called "[t]he warning shot in the turbot war"[103] by announcing that Canada would begin patrolling the fishing grounds outside its 200 nm fishing zone.[104] Two days prior to adopting the said amendment, the Canadian government replaced its prior acceptance of compulsory jurisdiction of the ICJ with a new one that excluded "disputes arising out of or concerning conservation and management measures taken by Canada with respect to vessels fishing in the NAFO Regulatory Area, ...and the enforcement of such measures"[105] from the jurisdiction of the court.

In late 1994, NAFO agreed to reduce the catch of the Greenland halibut from 60,000 tons to 27,000 tons. This decision was supported by Canada, as well as the EC.[106] Initially, in line with prior practice, no allocation of the total allowable catch was made.[107] In January 1995, the Canadian fisheries minister accused fishing vessels from the EC of catching stocks, such as American plaice, yellowtail, and witch flounder, in the Grand Banks despite the NAFO ban against fishing these species in 1994.[108] Canada also claimed that fishing vessels with Spanish or Portuguese crews registered under flags of convenience, such as Panama and the Bahamas, were fishing in the NAFO regulatory area in contravention to NAFO rules.[109] In a meeting in Brussels at the end of January 1995, NAFO decided by a narrow margin of votes to allocate the Greenland halibut total allowable catch to the member states. Instead of allocating 75% of the quota to the EC, in line with what the EC argued was the recent fishing practice,[110] the EC was allocated around 13% or 3,400 tons. Canada, which had in the prior year fished between 6,000 and 7,000 tons, was allocated 16,300 tons of the 27,000-ton quota.[111]

The newly appointed EC Fisheries Commissioner Emma Bonino protested and asked the EC Commission and the Council of Ministers to initiate objection procedures.[112] She said that the dispute was not about conservation or management but about allocation of the total allowable catch,[113] which the commission called "completely unrepresentative of recent turbot fishing trends."[114] On 28 February 1995, the EC Council of Ministers formally adopted objections to the allocation of halibut quotas by NAFO.[115] In response to the reduction in quota, EC unilaterally decided its quota to be 18,630 tons or about 69% of the reduced total allowable catch.[116]

The Canadian foreign minister objected to the unilaterally decided quota and threatened actions.[117] On 3 March, an implementing regulation of the *Coastal Fisheries Protection Act* was amended to effectively allow search and arrest of Spanish and Portuguese fishing vessels outside the Canadian fishery zone.[118] Around the same time, the Canadian press obtained a Canadian foreign affairs document that indicated that Spanish and Portuguese fishing vessels had repeatedly violated NAFO rules by not declaring catches, fishing in closed zones, keeping insufficient logbooks, and so forth.[119]

On 9 March 1995, Canadian coast guard officers unsuccessfully tried to board the Spanish fishing vessel *Estai* outside the Canadian fishery zone.[120] According to Canadian sources, *Estai* threw its boarding ladder overboard, cut its trawl, and "made a run for it."[121] Three Canadian vessels chased *Estai* in the high seas and surrounded it, but the vessel refused to stop until one of the coast guard ships fired warning shots at *Estai* with a machine gun.[122] When *Estai* finally stopped, an armed Canadian crew boarded the vessel and arrested the captain.[123]

The Canadian government believed that "the arrest of the *Estai* was necessary in order to put a stop to the overfishing of Greenland halibut by Spanish fishermen."[124] EC officials objected firmly, calling the arrest "illegal, unacceptable, unjustified, and dangerous"[125] and "a flagrant violation of the law of the sea."[126] Bonino, who later called the arrest "a real act of international piracy,"[127] demanded the "unconditional release of the vessel illegally seized, its captain, its crew and its cargo."[128] Spanish foreign minister Javier Solana also protested and said that Spain intended to refer the case to the ICJ.[129]

Canadian Fisheries Minister Tobin explained the details of the alleged violations committed by *Estai*. He said that 79% of the catch was undersize. The net, which Canadians later recovered from the ocean, had 115 mm mesh size, slightly smaller than the 130 mm minimum required under NAFO regulations. In addition, the net was lined with an 80 mm mesh size filter.[130] EC officials, however, said that the net that Canadians found had no identifying markings and that the net could not have come from the Spanish vessel as the fish size on board *Estai* was compatible to what could have been caught with regular nets.[131] Canada rebutted and said that the net had markings identical to equipment on board of *Estai*[132] and that the police "matched the steel cables attached to the net to the severed cables aboard the *Estai*."[133] Canadian officials also said that inspectors found 15 hidden storage rooms, holding 25 tons of American plaice, a fish that has been under moratorium for some years.[134] EC officials, after examining the vessel, said that no evidence of secret holds were found[135] and that the quantities of American plaice found aboard was no more than ordinary by-catch.[136] Fisheries Minister Tobin said that the captain of *Estai* had been keeping two separate log books with different figures, "one was apparently for the NAFO inspectors, while the other was for the captain's personal use."[137] The EC said that the second logbook was a continuation of the other.[138] On 15 March, the fishing vessel was released after paying a bond of C$500,000.[139]

Spanish trawlers came back to the contested area and Canada threatened to take action again.[140] On 26 March, a Canadian patrol boat cut the nets of a Spanish trawler in the contested nose and tail areas in the Grand Banks.[141] A similar event took place on 5 April.[142]

The EC and Canada commenced negotiations in late March. The EC said its goal was to reassure Canada that catch limits would be enforced and to increase the EC halibut quota in the Grand Banks area.[143] The EC called on Canada to cease its "aggressive attitude"[144] and added that Canada had itself to blame for decline of fish stocks in its fishery zone and the Grand Banks.[145] The EC had already claimed that it had tried to find diplomatic solutions and invited Canada for talks that Canada had refused.[146] EC Commissioner Bonino framed the problem not as a conservation problem by saying, "The real argument is not how much we can fish, but over who can fish it."[147] Similarly, the EC Ambassador to Canada John Beck did not see Canada's actions as conservation measures but "rather a desire to secure exclusive market rights to a natural resource beyond its territorial waters."[148]

Fisheries Minister Tobin, however, said that the dispute was "not an issue about who gets what slice of the pie but rather sustaining the pie, sustaining the resource, preventing the extinction."[149] He also said, "It is not enough to have the most poetic text if there is no means to enforce it."[150]

On 16 April 1995, the EC and Canada reached an agreement on the allocation of the Greenland halibut in the Grand Banks.[151] The parties agreed that in 1995, Canada could catch 10,000 tons of Greenland halibut, thereof 7,000 tons within its own fishery zone. The EC's quota would be 5,013 tons after 16 April 1995,[152] in addition to the previously estimated 6,000 to 8,000 tons it had already caught.[153] During the negotiation, Canada agreed to set this number at 5,000 tons.[154] The parties agreed that Canada would, on the basis of advice from the NAFO Scientific Council, manage the Greenland halibut stock with its 200 nm fishery zone.[155] In the NAFO regulatory area, that is, outside the Canadian fishery zone, the stock would be under NAFO's management. The parties agreed that, aside from allocation to other contracting parties, the stock in the NAFO regulatory area would be divided between the EC and Canada in the ratio of 10:3, respectively.[156] The agreement did not fix the quota that Canada could take within its fishery zone after 1995, but some interpreted the agreement as giving Canada exclusive rights to the 7,000 tons it was allocated for 1995.[157] The parties also agreed to increase the role of observers, set up a system of satellite tracking, and share information.[158]

As Foreign Minister Solana had indicated, Spain brought a case before the ICJ, claiming that Canada had violated international law by pursuing, boarding, and arresting *Estai* outside its 200 nm fishery zone.[159] Canada objected on jurisdictional grounds,[160] making interpretation of the new Canadian acceptance of the jurisdiction of the court the center of the case. Spain argued that the new declaration should be interpreted restrictively. The court, however, rejected this view and wrote it should rather be interpreted "in harmony with a natural and reasonable way of reading the text."[161] The court wrote, "A declaration of acceptance of the compulsory jurisdiction of the Court, whether there are specified limits set to that acceptance or not, is a unilateral act of State sovereignty."[162] Furthermore, because a declaration under Article 36(2) of the ICJ Statute "is a unilaterally drafted instrument, the Court has not hesitated to place a certain emphasis on the intention of the depositing State."[163] The court noted that when Canada sent its declaration from 10 May 1994, it simultaneously repealed an older declaration from 10 September 1985. The only difference between these two declarations was a reservation with regard to disputes related to fisheries in the NAFO regulatory area. The court, therefore, asserted "that this reservation is not only an integral part of the current declaration but also an essential component of it, and hence of the acceptance by Canada of the Court's compulsory jurisdiction."[164] The court also noted that there was a clear connection between the amendment of the *Costal Fisheries Protection Act* and the declaration, as the declaration was intended to "preclude any challenge which might undermine Canada's ability to protect the stocks."[165] The court also cited a statement given by the Canadian minister of foreign affairs to the Senate, stating that the reservation in the declaration was intended to protect the integrity of the amendment.[166] The court accordingly held that a natural and reasonable reading of the reservation in the declaration that precluded ICJ jurisdiction over the dispute between Canada and Spain.[167]

(iii) Additional Analysis Related to the Elements of Countermeasures

Canadian officials did not explicitly justify Canada's actions as countermeasures. Their arguments were, rather, in line with the extension of jurisdiction to protect a fish stock endangered by irresponsible and uncontrolled fishing. The declared purpose of extending the jurisdiction of both conservation laws and the penal code was to conserve the Greenland halibut and to provide the tools necessary to prosecute violations of Canadian laws. Thus, at first glance, the primary element of countermeasures, the presence of a violation of an international obligation, does not seem to have played a large role in Canada's decision making relating to the dispute. First of all, NAFO's allocation of Greenland halibut quota was not binding for the EC since it formally objected to it. Therefore, Canada's assertion that Spain or the EC was in violation of NAFO rules because Spanish fishing vessels were fishing above the allocated quota does not seem to have merits. Second, even if it was proven that *Estai* had been fishing undersized fish, with illegal mesh size, and species under moratorium, such actions do not necessarily invoke state responsibility. The vessel is a private entity and not, in itself, an extension of the Spanish government or EC institutions. Under *UNCLOS*, states "have the duty to take, or to cooperate with other States in taking, such measures for their respective nationals as may be necessary for the conservation of the living resources of the high seas."[168] In this case, the said duty rests on Spain and the EC.[169] According to EC sources, EC ships had been under sufficient surveillance. In 1994, EC inspectors boarded 45 EC ships in the NAFO regulatory area 430 times.[170] Additionally, Canadian authorities boarded EC ships 200 times in 1994.[171] EC Ambassador to Canada Beck said that in the 2 months preceding the taking of *Estai*, the vessel had been inspected three times but no illegal nets were found.[172] Unlike the dispute between Iceland and Norway, where Iceland did not set unilateral quotas for its fishing vessels in the Loophole, the EC decided unilaterally its maximum catch of Greenland halibut in the NAFO regulatory area. The unilateral quota was less than a half of what it had taken the year before and was also a smaller portion of the significantly reduced total allowable catch.[173] Therefore, the EC's claim that it had not violated international law seems to have merits.

As a last point on the possible violation by the EC of its international obligations, one might argue that, with regard to protection of the Greenland halibut, the implementation of the EC fishery policy did not meet *UNCLOS* requirement of responsible conservation and management of straddling stocks. Christoper Joyner and Alejandro Alvarez von Gustedt wrote:

> [F]isheries policy within the European Community generally is complicated by its intimate connection to serious domestic economic pressures and political problems, especially in Spain where unemployment is already extremely high. Generally speaking, Western Europe's fishing industry is burdened by an overwhelming excess of fishing capacity relative to the actual availability of stocks in the Atlantic for harvest.[174]

The EC's track record of conservation arguably indicates that the system and its implementation may have failed to fulfill the EC's obligations under *UNCLOS*, for example, by sacrificing the weight of scientific evidence and conservation needs for economic pressures. Such argument, which will not be further explored here, would require a thorough analysis of the requirements of the *UNCLOS* regime, as well as of the EC fisheries policy, its implementation, and the possible systemic failures, which partially might be the cause for decline of fish stocks in many areas under the EC's jurisdiction or where EC vessels fish.[175]

Although the primary element of countermeasures here has largely been deemed absent and the justification for the action will accordingly not be the countermeasures doctrine, there are two issues that, if raised, might add value to the analysis of the legality of countermeasures in the context of the Canada/EC dispute: first, whether the actions were proportionate to the "injury suffered, taking into account the gravity of the internationally wrongful act and the rights in question,"[176] and, second, although outside the scope of countermeasures, Canada's unilateral actions might possibly be justified under the state of necessity doctrine.[177]

It was suggested earlier that countermeasures had to be proportionate to the injury suffered and what is needed to induce a state to cease the alleged illegal situation, including paying reparation. This case study does not present any scientific evidence proving a causal connection between the alleged illegal fisheries of the EC in the Grand Banks and the harm caused to the fish stock and, therefore, Canadian interests. However, it is quite plausible that the means and methods allegedly used by Spanish trawlers in the area, such as undersized meshes, intentional catch of species under moratorium, and underreporting of the catch, have the potential to contribute to the decline of the Greenland halibut stock. Seen in isolation, the taking of *Estai* and the cutting of the nets of two other Spanish fishing vessels do not seem to be disproportionate to the injury suffered. On the other hand, asserting jurisdiction over the part of the high seas is arguably disproportionate to other rights in question, that is, the long-standing principle of the freedom of the high seas. As was already discussed, the ICJ in the *Gabcikovo-Nagymaros Project* found that Slovakia by:

> depriving Hungary of its right to an equitable and reasonable share of the natural resources of the Danube—with the continuing

> effects of the diversion of these waters on the ecology of the riparian area of the Szigetkoz—failed to respect the proportionality which is required by international law.[178]

The court, citing the Permanent Court of International Justice in the *River Oder Case*, which emphasized the principle of equal rights of riparian states to use navigable rivers,[179] seemed to conclude that a wholesale depravation of such an important right could not be proportional to the harm resulting in Hungary's noncompliance to the agreement on the *Gabcikovo-Nagymaros* project.

This approach might not be, however, appropriate in this case. It must be noted that Canada's actions to assert jurisdiction in the NAFO regulatory area did not constitute a general prohibition of the use of the high seas. The actions were intended to be much more targeted—address vessels engaged in the harvesting of a fish stock believed to be at risk. Furthermore, the effects on the physical rights that Hungary enjoyed as a riparian state by the Danube included the adverse ecological effects on the Szigetkoz area, such as a fall of groundwater levels and reduced water quality, as well as eutrophication.[180] As such, the actions of Slovakia would have had widespread negative effects on interests and rights largely unrelated to the alleged violation of Hungary. The effects of Canada's actions, although affecting a long-standing principle, is much narrower in scope and directly related to the value that the measures are purported to protect. Therefore, the measures taken by Canada seem to have been in compliance with the principle of proportionality.

In relation to the Loophole dispute, Norway did not argue that the Barents Sea cod stock was in danger of extinction or in any danger at all. In fact, a high level official in the Norwegian fishery ministry stated that the stock was in excellent condition.[181] In contrast, the status of the Greenland halibut was dire. Both parties agreed that the stock was in decline and were ready to react to it by reducing the total allowable catch. Therefore, the emergency circumstances of this case raise the question of whether Canada could not have justified the taking of *Estai* and the cutting of the nets of the two other Spanish trawlers under the state of necessity doctrine.[182] The decline in the stocks and the alleged aggressive fisheries by vessels that Canada had no or only questionable jurisdiction over might indicate that the actions were necessary "to safeguard an essential interest against a grave and imminent peril."[183] In the earlier stages of the debate on state responsibility, the ILC suggested that among a situation that could justify state of necessity is "a grave danger to…the ecological preservation of all or some of [the] territory [of a state]."[184] Further, in the 1997 *Gabcikovo-Nagymaros Project*, the ICJ accepted ILC's suggestions that environmental interest can constitute essential interests of a state.[185] There are, however, a few problems facing the one who intends to argue Canada's actions under the necessity doctrine. Canada would have to show that no other measures were sufficient to reach the legitimate aim and that it had not contributed to the situation.[186] It would also have to show that its methods were not in contradiction to the ban against the use of force under Article 2(4) of the *UN Charter*.[187]

It is submitted here that Canada's actions do not have the appearance of being in compliance with its international obligations. Also, the withdrawal of the acceptance of the jurisdiction of the ICJ with regard to fishery disputes related to the NAFO regulatory area indicates that the Canadian government knew that the legality of its actions might not have been well founded.

Endnotes

1. ESA was established by a side agreement, the *Agreement Establishing the EFTA Surveillance Authority and the EFTA Court*, concluded at Oporto 2 May 1992, entered into force 1 January 1992, O.J. 1994 L344/1. ESA's role is mainly to monitor the compliance of the EFTA states with the *EEA Agreement.*
2. *Agreement for the Implementation of the Provisions of the United Nations Convention on the Law of the Sea of 10 December 1982, Relating to the Conservation and Management of Straddling Fish Stocks and Highly Migratory Fish Stocks*, concluded at New York 4 August 1995, entered into force 11 December 2001, UN doc. A/CONF.164/37 (hereafter referred to as the *Fish Stocks Agreement*).
3. *UNCLOS*, article 87(1)(e).
4. Ibid., article 116.
5. Ibid., article 117.
6. See also suggestions by Norway in the *Már Case* in part III, chap. 14 and endnote 80 of this chapter, and Chile in the *Swordfish Conservation Case* next, in part III, chap. 15.
7. *UNCLOS*, article 63(2).
8. Ibid., article 64(1), italics added.
9. Ibid., article 64(2).
10. Ibid., article 56. See also Ellen Hey, *The Regime for the Exploitation of Transboundary Marine Fisheries Resources*, Martinus Nijhoff Publishers, Dordrecht, Boston, London, 1989, p. 59.
11. In addition, Spain, the European Community, and Chile are not parties to the agreement. Spain and the European Community have, however, signed the agreement. For further information about the possible future development of the *Fish Stock Agreement*, see *Report of the Review Conference on the Agreement for the Implementation of the Provisions of the United Nations Convention on the Law of the Sea of 10 December 1982 Relating to the Conservation and Management of Straddling Fish Stocks and Highly Migratory Fish Stocks*, UN doc. A/CONF.210/2006/15, 5 July 2006, in particular pp. 9–29.
12. *Fish Stocks Agreement*, article 2.
13. *Fish Stocks Agreement*, article 5. Article 6 of the agreement elaborates further on the content of the precautionary approach.

14. Ibid., article 7(1)(a).
15. Ibid., article 7(1)(b).
16. Ibid., article 8(3).
17. Ibid., article 8(4).
18. Ibid., article 19(1)(a).
19. Ibid., article 19(1)(b).
20. Ibid., article 20(6).
21. Ibid., article 20(7).
22. Ibid., article 23(2).
23. Ibid., article 23(3).
24. See *Letter of Formal Notice on the Failure to Comply with Article 36 or the EEA Agreement*, a letter from the EFTA Surveillance Authority to the Norwegian government, 3 September 1996, doc. no. 96-4652-D, decision no. 109/96/COL (hereafter referred to as *Letter of Formal Notice*), p. 2, para. 5.
25. Ibid., p. 2. para. 5.
26. *Agreement on the European Economic Area*, concluded in Oporto 2 May 1992, entered into force 1 January 1994, *Official Journal of the European Communities* (O.J.) 1994 L1/3. The European Economic Area comprises of the European Community, Iceland, Norway, and Lichtenstein.
27. The *EEA Agreement* expands the European Community law related to the so-called four freedoms (goods, services, penple, and capital) and certain horizontal areas, to Iceland, Lichtenstein, and Norway.
28. *Letter from the Norwegian Royal Ministry of Foreign Affairs to ESA in Reply of Letter of Formal NotIce*, 29 November 1996, doc. no. 95/02762-31 VII/DM (hereafter referred to as *Reply to Letter of Formal Notice*), p. 12, para. 55.
29. *Letter from the Norwegian Royal Ministry of Foreign Affairs to ESA*, 8 October 1995, doc. no. 95/02762-VII (hereafter referred to as *Norway's letter to ESA*), on file with the author, p. 11, para. 6.
30. *ESA's Letter to Ambassador Einar Bull, Norwegian Mission to the European Union*, 14 May 1998, doc. no. 98-3393-D, (hereafter referred to as *ESA's Decision*), p. 3.
31. See, for example, Hugh Carnegy, "Trawler Held After Clash," *Financial Times* (London), 8 August 1994, p. 2.
32. Paul Pivcevic, "Environment: Iceland at Loggerheads Over Last Atlantic Cod," *Inter Press Service*, 23 September 1993.
33. See Robin R. Churchill, "The Barents Sea Loophole Agreement: A "Coastal State" Solution to a Straddling Stock Problem," *International Journal of Marine and Coastal Law* 14 (1999), at 471.

34. See ibid., at 468–470.
35. See *Violation by Norwegian Authorities of Chapter II of the Agreement on the European Economic Area*, a letter from the attorney of the operator of Már to the EFTA Surveillance Authority (ESA) initiating procedures before ESA, 17 July 1995 (hereafter referred to as *Complaint to ESA*) and *ESA's Decision*. Both documents are on file with the author.
36. See *Letter from the Norwegian Royal Ministry of Foreign Affairs to ESA*, 8 October 1995, doc. no. 95/02762-VII (hereafter referred to as *Norway's Letter to ESA*), on file with the author, pp. 6–7, para. 4.
37. See *Complaint to ESA*, 17 July 1995.
38. *Norway's Letter to ESA*, p. 8, para. 4.
39. See Ibid., pp. 8–9, para. 4.
40. Ibid., p. 9, para. 4.
41. *Complaint to ESA*, 17 July 1995.
42. *Norway's Letter to ESA*, p. 9, para. 4.
43. *Complaint to ESA*, 17 July 1995.
44. Article 49 of the *EC Treaty*, as amended by the *Treaty of Amsterdam*, was formerly article 59 of the *EC Treaty*. See *Consolidated Versions of the Treaty on the European Union and of the Treaty Establishing the European Community*, O.J. 2002 C 325/1.
45. *Luise & Carbone v. Ministro del Tesero*, European Court of Justice, case nos. 286/82 and 26/83, judgment of 31 January 1984, 1984 European Court Reports 377. Under article 6 of the *EEA Agreement*, provisions of the agreement that are identical in substance to the *EC Treaty* shall be interpreted in conformity with the relevant rulings of the European Court of Justice.
46. *EEA Agreement*, article 36(1).
47. *Norway's Letter to ESA*, p. 1, para. 1.
48. Ibid., p. 3, para. 2.
49. Ibid., p. 6, para. 3.
50. Ibid., p. 10, para. 6.
51. Ibid., p. 11, para. 6.
52. Ibid.
53. *Letter of Formal Notice*, see supra endnote 24 of this chapter, p. 8, para. 28.
54. Ibid., p. 11, para. 49. See also Ibid., p. 14, para. 63.
55. Ibid., p. 8, para. 28.
56. See *Commission v. Luxemburg and Belgium*, case nos. 90 and 91/63, judgment of 13 November 1964, 1964 European Court Reports 625, at 631; *Commission v. Italy*, case no. 52/75, judgment of 26 February 1976, 1976 European Court Reports 277, at 284; *Commission v. France*, case no. 232/78,

judgment of 25 September 1979, 1979 European Court Reports 2729, at 2739; and, somewhat, *The Queen v. Ministry of Agriculture, Fisheries and Food, ex parte Hedley Lomas (Ireland) Ltd.*, case no. C-5/94, judgment of 23 May 1996, 1996 European Court Reports I:2553.

57. *Letter of Formal Notice*, p. 12, para. 51.
58. Ibid., p. 12, para. 52.
59. Ibid.
60. *EEA Agreement*, article 33. The article is in a chapter concerning the right to establishment, but according to article 39, article 33 also applies to the freedom to provide services.
61. *Roland Rutili v. Minster for the Interior*, case no. 36/75, judgment of 28 October 1975, 1975 European Court Reports 1219, at 1231.
62. *Regina v. Pierre Bouchereau*, case no. 30/77, judgment of 27 October 1977, 1977 European Court Reports 1999, at 2014.
63. *Letter of Formal Notice*, p. 14, para. 61.
64. *Letter from the Norwegian Royal Ministry of Foreign Affairs to ESA in reply of Letter of Formal Notice*, 29 November 1996, doc. no. 95/02762-31 VII/DM (hereafter referred to as *Reply to Letter of Formal Notice*).
65. *Reply to Letter of Formal Notice*, p. 2, para. 9.
66. Ibid., pp. 2–3, paras. 10–11.
67. Ibid., p. 15, para. 70.
68. *Resolving the Relationship Between WTO Rules and Multilateral Environmental Agreements*, submission by the European Community, 19 October 2000, WTO doc. WT/CTE/W/170 (hereafter referred to as *EC Paper on WTO and MEAs*), p. 2, para. 5, see also discussion on this issue on in part III, chap. 15 (b) next.
69. *Minutes of the Meeting*, held in the Centre William Rappart, 17 November 2000, WTO doc. WT/DSB/M/92 (15 January 2001) (hereafter referred to as *Minutes of Meeting on 17 November 2000*), p. 21, para. 109.
70. *ESA's Decision.*
71. Ibid., p. 2, italics added.
72. Ibid., p. 2. ESA did not seem to be concerned about the fact that at the time of the events, which are the subject of the dispute, the *Fish Stock Agreement* had not been concluded. Nor was it concerned about the fact that the *Fish Stock Agreement* was not in force when the decision in this case was taken.
73. Ibid., p. 2 (italics added).
74. ESA wrote, "Norway alleges that Iceland, for its part, has breached its obligation under international law by not introducing for 1995 such catch limits for Icelandic fishing vessels that might have been necessary to preserve the

stocks concerned. However, it is disputable whether Iceland, by its omission in the situation at hand, did breach international law, and whether the restrictions on access to port was in fact necessary." See *ESA's Decision*, p. 2.

75. *ESA's Decision*, p. 3. The use of first person in this passage is explained by the fact that formally this decision is taken by a single person acting as a member of the so-called College. See *Rules of Procedure of the EFTA Surveillance Authority*, adopted 7 January 1994, *ESA* doc. dec. no. 1/94 as amended, in particular article 15. Available at http://www.eftasurv.int/about/col/dbaFile801.html (visited 11 January 2008).
76. *ESA's Decision*, p. 3.
77. This was contested by Norway in the *Reply to Letter of Formal Notice*, where it argued that "while the primary subjects of the norms of international law concerning fishing are States, vessels are also bound by those norms, even if they have not been incorporated into domestic law…" See *Reply to Letter of* Formal *Notice*, p. 11, para. 50.
78. *UNCLOS*, article 117. At the time when the events took place, Norway had not ratified *UNCLOS*. It did so on 24 June 1996. Iceland, however, had ratified *UNCLOS* on 21 June 1985, see *Multilateral Treaties Deposited with the Secretary-General*. Despite that *UNCLOS* itself was not the applicable law between the parties to this dispute, Iceland never officially contested Norway's reference to *UNCLOS*.
79. *Reply to Letter of Formal Notice*, p. 11, para. 51. A proposal to unilaterally decide on a reasonable limit of the catch was aired by a small group of fishing operators in Iceland but lacked support from the industry or the government.
80. Ibid., p. 12, para. 55.
81. Ibid., p. 16, para. 75. See thoughts on this issue in William T. Burke, *The New International Law of Fisheries: UNCLOS 1982 and Beyond*, Clarendon Press, Oxford, 1994, p. 134 and Barbara Kwiatkowska, "The High Seas Fisheries Regime: At a Point of No Return?", *International Journal of Marine and Coastal* Law 8, no. 3 (1993), at 330.
82. Norway's approach is interesting as the *Fish Stocks Agreement* was not in force when the vessel *Már* was refused access to port. In fact, the *Fish Stocks* Agreement did not enter into force until 2001—3 years after ESA took its decision on the dispute.
83. R*eply to Letter of Formal Notice*, p. 14, para. 64. For literature related to the Loophole dispute, see, for example, Robin R. Churchill, "The Barents Sea Loophole Agreement: A "Coastal State" Solution to a Straddling Stock Problem," *International Journal of Marine and Coastal Law*

14 (1999): 467–490; Olav Schram Stokke, "The Loophole of the Barents Sea Fisheries Regime," in *Governing High Seas Fisheries: The Interplay of Global and Regional Regimes*, edited by Olav Schram Stokke, Oxford University Press, Oxford, 2001, p. 273; and Olav Schram Stokke, Lee G. Anderson, and Natalia Mirovitskaya, "The Barents Sea Fisheries," in *The Effectiveness of International Environmental Regimes: Causal Connection and Behavioral Mechanism*, edited by Oran R. Young, MIT Press, Cambridge, Massachusetts, London, England, 1999, p. 91.

84. See Robin R. Churchill, "The Barents Sea Loophole Agreement: A "Coastal State" Solution to a Straddling Stock Problem," *International Journal of Marine and Coastal Law* 14 (1999), at 468.
85. Ibid., at 470. Greenland, Faroe Islands, and the EC were given quotas in the *Barents Sea Cod* in 1991 by agreement with Norway and Russia.
86. Ibid., at 470. The Joint Norwegian Russian Fisheries Commission was established by the 1975 *Treaty on Co-operation in the Fishing Industry Between Norway and the Soviet Union*, 983 U.N.T.S. 3.
87. Information from Fiskistofa, the Icelandic Directorate of Fisheries, on file with the author. Norwegian Coast Guard estimated the 1995 catch to be 32,386 tons, see *Reply to Letter of Formal Notice*, p. 11, para. 51. Thus, there seems to be agreement on the approximate total catch.
88. See *Reply to Letter of Formal Notice*, p. 12, para. 52.
89. Ibid., p. 15, para. 69.
90. The court seemed to indicate that when restricting trade in services based on public policy consideration, states must "base the measures adopted exclusively on the personal conduct of the individuals concerned", see *Rutili v. Minster for the Interior*, supra endnote 61 of this chapter, at 1231.
91. John Carvel, "Canada Arrests Spanish Captain as Fish War with Europe Looms," *The Guardian*, 10 March 1995, p. 13.
92. Ibid., p. 13.
93. *Commission Statement on Canadian Seizure of European Fishing Vessel*, RAPID, 9 March 1995, Press Release, IP:95-230.
94. *Fisheries Jurisdiction Case* (*Spain v. Canada*), International Court of Justice, judgment of 4 December 1998, 1998 I.C.J. 432, at 443–444, para. 20.
95. John Carvel, "Trawler Freed as Truce Declared in Fish War," *The Guardian*, 16 March 1995, p. 3 and "Release of Spanish Trawler Raises Hopes of Settlement to Fish Row," *European Report*, 15 March 1995, no. 2025.
96. "EU and Canada Celebrate Easter Deal on Fishing Rights," *European Report*, 19 April 1995, no. 2034.
97. *Fisheries Jurisdiction Case*, at 468, para. 89.

98. Northwest Atlantic Fisheries Organization was established by a convention on 24 October 1978, see *Convention of Future Mulilateral Co-operation in the North-West Atlantic Fisheries*, O.J. L 378, 30 December 1978 and *Canada Treaty Series* 1979, no. 11.
99. "Fisheries: EU and Canada on the Brink of a Fish War," *European Report*, 7 March 1995, no. 2022.
100. *Coastal Fisheries Protection Act* amendment of 12 May 1994, Statutes of Canada (S.C.) 1994, chap. 14.
101. Ibid., section 4, amending section 7 of the *Coastal Fisheries Protection Act.*
102. Jose A. de Yturriaga, *The International Regime of Fisheries—From UNCLOS 1982 to the Presential Sea*, pp. 239–240.
103. Claire Trevena, "No More Mr. Nice Guy as Canada Bites in the Turbot War," *The Observer*, 19 March 1995, p. 21.
104. Ibid., p. 21.
105. International Court of Justice, *Declarations Recognizing the Jurisdiction of the Court as Compulsory, Declaration of Canada*, 10 May 1995, http://www.icj-cij.org/jurisdiction/ (visited 14 January 2008) and *Fisheries Jurisdiction Case*, at 439, para. 14. See also Jose A. de Yturriaga, *The International Regime of Fisheries—From UNCLOS 1982 to the Presential Sea*, p. 239.
106. *Commission Statement on Canadian Seizure of European Fishing Vessel*, RAPID, 9 March 1995, Press Release, IP:95-230 and "Canada Renews Calls for Fisheries Restraint," *European Report*, 1 February 1995, no. 2012.
107. See *Statement by Mrs. Bonino on the Resolution Adopted by the European Parliament Regarding the Objection to NAFO's Decision Allocating the 1995 TAC for Greenland Halibut*, RAPID, 17 February 1995, Press Release, IP: 95-144.
108. "Canada Calls for End to Illegal Fishing in Grand Banks," *European Report*, 14 January 1995, no. 2007.
109. Ibid.
110. "Fisheries: EU Formally Objects to NAFO Turbot Quota as Canada Warns Against", *European Report*, 3 March 1995, no. 2021. The EU also claimed that its average catch of Greenland halibut for 1991–1993 was 37,000 tons, see *Background Note—EU—Canada/Fisheries*, RAPID, 10 March 1995, memo: 95-38. Canada claimed that 5 years earlier the EU only caught 20% of the Greenland halibut total allowable catch, but the EU catch grew up to 80% in 1994 or around 50,000 tons, see "Fisheries: EU and Canada on the Brink of a Fish War," *European Report*, 7 March 1995, no. 2022.

111. Jose A. de Yturriaga, *The International Regime of Fisheries—From UNCLOS 1982 to the Presential Sea*, p. 241.
112. *Statement by Mrs. Bonino on the Resolution Adopted by the European Parliament Regarding the Objection to NAFO's Decision Allocating the 1995* TAC *for Greenland Halibut*, RAPID, 17 February 1995, Press Release, IP: 95-144. Under the NAFO regime, a member state that formally objects to NAFO's decision regarding allocation of quota or stocks under NAFO management is not bound by such decision.
113. Ibid.
114. "Fisheries: EU Formally Objects to NAFO Turbot Quota as Canada Warns Against," *European Report*, 3 March 1995, no. 2021.
115. Ibid.
116. Ibid.
117. Ibid.
118. "Fisheries: EU and Canada on the Brink of a Fish War," *European Report*, March 7, 1995, no. 2022 and *Commission Calls on Canada to Negotiate in Good* Faith, RAPID, 29 March 1995, Press Release, IP: 95-313.
119. Eoin Kenny, "Fish War Looms: Canada Prepared for Tough Measures Against Foreign Trawlers that Threaten Endangered Species," *The Record* (Kitchener-Waterloo, Ontario), 9 March 1995, p. A1.
120. John Carvel, "Canada Arrests Spanish Captain as Fish War with Europe Looms," *The Guardian*, 10 March 1995, p. 13 and "Canada Seizes Spanish Trawler," *Canada Newswire*, 9 March 1995, Domestic News.
121. Edison Steward, "Canadians Seize Spanish Trawler: Warning Shots Fired in Turbot War Escalation," *Toronto Star*, 10 March 1995, p. A1.
122. Ibid.
123. John Carvel, "Canada Arrests Spanish Captain as Fish War with Europe Looms," *The Guardian*, 10 March 1995, p. 13.
124. *Fisheries Jurisdiction Case*, at 443, para. 20.
125. Dave Todd, "Both Sides Stand Firm in Fish War," *Montreal Gazette*, 11 March 1995.
126. *Commission Statement on Canadian Seizure of European Fishing Vessel*, RAPID, 9 March 1995, Press Release, IP:95-230.
127. "Tensions Rise Again Over Fish in North Atlantic," *European Report*, 29 March 1995, no. 2028.
128. *NAFO/Canada: Mrs. Bonino Demands Release of European Vessel*, RAPID, 12 March 1995, Press Release, IP: 95-235.
129. Dave Todd, "Risk of Conflicts on High Seas Escalates," *Hamilton Spectator* (Ontario), 13 March 1995, p. A1.

130. "Release of Spanish Trawler Raises Hopes of Settlement to Fish Row," *European Report*, 15 March 1995, no. 2025.
131. John Carvel and Claire Trevena, "Talks Start on Fish Dispute Amid Raging War of Words," *The Guardian*, 30 March 1995, p. 12 and *"Estai" Found to Comply with NAFO Rules—Canadian Assertion Not Proven*, RAPID, 26 March 1995, Press Release, IP: 95-295.
132. Stephen Thorne, "Seized Spanish Trawler Released: Net Recovered from Ocean Supports Allegation of Illegal Fishing," *The Record* (Kitchener-Waterloo, Ontario), 16 March 1995, p. A3.
133. "Grand Banks Turned into "Wild West": EU Commissioner Suggests Net May Not Be from Estai," *Hamilton Spectator* (Ontario), March 28, 1995, p. A3.
134. "Release of Spanish Trawler Raises Hopes of Settlement to Fish Row," *European Report*, 15 March 1995, no. 2025.
135. John Carvel and Claire Trevena, "Talks Start on Fish Dispute Amid Raging War of Words," *The Guardian*, 30 March 1995, p. 12 and *"Estai" Found to Comply with NAFO Rules—Canadian Assertion not Proven*, RAPID, 26 March 1995, Press Release, IP: 95-295.
136. "Tensions Rise Again Over Fish in North Atlantic," *European Report*, 29 March 1995, no. 2028.
137. "Release of Spanish Trawler Raises Hopes of Settlement to Fish Row," *European Report*, 15 March 1995, no. 2025 and Eoin Kenny, "Fish War Looms: Canada Prepared for Tough Measures Against Foreign Trawlers that Threaten Endangered Species," *The Record* (Kitchener-Waterloo, Ontario), 9 March 1995, p. A1.
138. *Commission Calls on Canada to Negotiate in Good Faith*, RAPID, 29 March 1995, Press Release, IP: 95-313.
139. "Release of Spanish Trawler Raises Hopes of Settlement to Fish Row," *European Report*, 15 March 1995, no. 2025.
140. Dave Todd and Joan Bryden, "They're Back: Defiant Spaniards Fish near Grand Banks," *Hamilton Spectator* (Ontario), 15 March 1995, p. A1.
141. Eoin Kenny, "Canada Wasn't Bluffing: Spanish Trawler Has Its Nets Cut," *The Record* (Kitchener-Waterloo, Ontario), 27 March 1995, p. A1 and "Tensions Rise Again over Fish in North Atlantic," *European Report*, 29 March 1995, no. 2028.
142. "EU Divided on How to Tackle Fish Row with Canada," *European Report*, 8 April 1995, no. 2031.
143. John Carvel and Claire Trevena, "Talks Start on Fish Dispute Amid Raging War of Words," *The Guardian*, 30 March 1995, p. 12.

144. *Commission Calls on Canada to Negotiate in Good Faith*, RAPID, 29 March 1995, Press Release, IP: 95-313.
145. Ibid.
146. *Commission Statement on Canadian Seizure of European Fishing Vessel*, RAPID, 9 March 1995, Press Release, IP: 95-230.
147. "Release of Spanish Trawler Raises Hopes of Settlement to Fish Row," *European Report*, 15 March 1995, no. 2025.
148. Dave Todd, "First Fish Battle Settles Nothing: Canada is Paying for Years of Neglect of Its Responsibility for all of the Grand Banks Fishery," *Hamilton* Spectator (Ontario), 18 March 1995, p. A8.
149. "Fisheries: Bonino Condemns Canadian Attack as an Act of Piracy," *European Report*, 10 March 1995, no. 2023.
150. Canadian Fishery Minister Brian Tobin, January 1995, cited in "Canada Calls for end to Illegal Fishing in Grand Banks," *European Report*, 14 January 1995, no. 2007.
151. "EU and Canada Celebrate Easter Deal on Fishing Rights," *European Report*, 19 April 1995, no. 2034.
152. *Canada-European Community: Agreed Minute on the Conservation and Management of Fish Stocks*, Brussels, 20 April 1995, 34 I.L.M. 1260 (1995) (hereafter referred to as *Agreed Minute*), annex II, sections I–II.
153. "EU and Canada Celebrate Easter Deal on Fishing Rights," *European Report*, 19 April 1995, no. 2034.
154. Joan Bryden, "Gunboat Diplomacy: In the Final Analysis, Force was the Only Thing that Ended Canada's Turbot War," *The Record* (Kitchener-Waterloo, Ontario), 18 April 1995, p. A9.
155. *Agreed Minute*, annex II, section III(b).
156. Ibid., section III(c).
157. See, for example, "EU and Canada Celebrate Easter Deal on Fishing Rights," *European Report*, 19 April 1995, no. 2034.
158. *Agreed Minute*, annex I, section II.
159. *Fisheries Jurisdiction Case*, at 433, para. 1.
160. Ibid., at 435, para. 3.
161. Ibid., at 453, para. 47, citing *Anglo-Iranian Oil Co. (preliminary objection) (United Kingdom v. Iran)*, International Court of Justice, judgment of 22 July 1952, 1952 I.C.J. 93, at 104.
162. Ibid., at 453, para. 46.
163. Ibid., at 454, para. 48.
164. Ibid., at 457, para. 59.

165. "New Release from the Canadian Government," 10 May 1994, cited in *Fisheries Jurisdiction Case*, at 457, para. 60.
166. *Fisheries Jurisdiction Case*, at 457, para. 60.
167. This dispute was later settled between Canada and the EU with substantially more quota for the EU and by allowing fishing vessels from Spain and Portugal to fish the Greenland halibut in the area. See Jose A. de Yturriaga, *The International Regime of Fisheries—From UNCLOS 1982 to the Presential Sea*, p. 244.
168. *UNCLOS*, article 117.
169. Inasmuch as EU member states have transferred powers regarding fisheries to the EU, the EU has, in fact, taken a role of a state regarding the exercise of these powers. A duty assigned to a state with regard to their nationals therefore arguably now rests on the EU.
170. *Background Note—EU—Canada/Fisheries*, RAPID, 10 March 1995, memo: 95-38.
171. *Commission Calls on Canada to Negotiate in Good Faith*, RAPID, 29 March 1995, Press Release, IP: 95-313.
172. Allan Thompson, European Union, "Canada Set for Negotiation of Fish Stocks: Truce on East Coast Allows Talks to Begin," *The Toronto Star*, 6 March 1995, p. A12.
173. The unilaterally decided quota was 69% of the 27,000 total allowable catch, down from about 75% of the 60,000 total allowable catch of 1994.
174. Christopher Joyner and Alejandro Alvarez von Gustedt, "The Turbot War of 1995: Lessons for the Law of the Sea," *International Journal of Marine and Coastal Law* 11, no. 4 (1996), at 438, endnotes omitted.
175. Canadian Ambassador to the EU Jacques Roy said that the EU fleet "had contributed heavily to the collapse of every other fish stock in the Northwest Atlantic…" see "Fisheries: Bonino Condemns Canadian Attack as an "Act of Piracy," *European Report*, 10 March 1995, no. 2023.
176. See *2001 Draft Articles*, article 51.
177. See part I, chap. 3 (e).
178. *Gabcikovo-Nagymaros Project* (*Hungary v. Slovakia*), International Court of Justice, judgment of 25 September 1997, 1997 I.C.J. 7, at 56, para. 85.
179. See *Territorial Jurisdiction of the International Commission of the River Oder*, Permanent Court of International Justice, judgment of 10 September 1929, 1929 P.C.I.J. Series A, no. 23.
180. See *Gabcikovo-Nagymaros Project*, 1997 I.C.J. 7, at 35, para. 40. Eutrophication is water pollution caused by excessive plant nutrients.

181. Jon Henley, "Fish Loopholes Heats Tempers in Frozen Sea," *The Guardian* (London), 3 August 1996, p. 14.
182. See part I, chap. 3 (e) previously. See also such suggestion in Yves Le Bouthillier, "High Seas, Fishy Tactics," *The Guardian*, 4 April 1995, p. 10 and "Legality of Arrests in Doubt: Canada Insists it has the Right to Protect the Fish Stocks," *The Record* (Kitchener-Waterloo, Ontario), 15 March 1995, p. A2.
183. See *2001 Draft Articles*, article 25.
184. *ILC 1980 Report*, p. 35, para. 3.
185. *Gabcikovo-Nagymaros Project*, at 41, para. 53.
186. See, for example, *2001 Draft Articles*, article 25(1)(a) and 25(2)(b).
187. EU claimed that the measures did violate article 2(4) of the *UN Charter*, see *Commission Calls on Canada to Negotiate in Good Faith*, RAPID, 29 March 1995, Press Release, IP: 95-313.

Chapter 15

Case Studies: Trade-Related Countermeasures

(a) Introduction

In this interdependent world, almost any measure a state takes in relation to another state affects free trade, whether it be in goods, services, or intellectual property, in one way or another. Countermeasures are no exception. As was apparent in the *Már Case*, refusal to serve a trawler that is allegedly engaged in illegal fisheries can have trade effects even though the dispute is predominantly not trade related. With the use of force excluded from the pool of permissible countermeasures, trade measures or measures with trade-related effects are probably the largest remaining category of measures suitable to induce other states to alter their alleged illegal actions. However, such measures are bound to collide with the regime of free trade, which not only has clearer substantive rules than does the environmental regime, but also it has an effective dispute settlement mechanism that is able to render enforceable decisions within a strictly limited time period. Such collision is, therefore, bound to be problematic for trade-related countermeasures that are aimed against violations of international environmental obligations.

In the present chapter, this book discusses four cases where states took unilateral measures to counter environmental threats. These cases are the two tuna cases and the *Shrimp/Turtle Case*, where claims were brought against the United States for violations of its obligations under GATT, and the *Swordfish Conservation Case* between the EC and Chile. Although the first three are not taken in response to an alleged violation of an international obligation and for this reason do not qualify as countermeasures, they all illustrate certain disparity between the trade regime and the environmental regime. In the fourth case, the country taking the measures claimed that a violation of an international obligation had occurred. That case was submitted to a WTO panel, as well as to the *UNCLOS* adjudication mechanism but, unfortunately for the legal debate, was suspended due to a provisional settlement between the parties.

Before discussing these cases, it is appropriate to examine how the WTO dispute settlement mechanism operates and how a case involving the taking of countermeasures could come before it. The issue at hand is not that countermeasures that violate WTO obligations are less justifiable than other countermeasures but, rather, whether the underlying dispute justifying the countermeasures and the presence of the primary element of countermeasures will receive sufficient attention by the WTO dispute settlement mechanism. If not, the countermeasures argument, although sufficient under other circumstances, might be set aside to entertain the interests of a predictable, secure, and impermeable regime of international trade. The conclusions of this chapter suggest the opposite—that the countermeasures argument might be applicable in a dispute before the WTO panel and that WTO rules do not automatically have priority over environmental considerations. Instead, the WTO legal framework contains provisions that, if applied properly, can strike a fair balance between these two different and sometimes conflicting regimes.

(B) The World Trade Organization and Dispute Settlements

(i) General Overview

In stark contrast to the limited existence of a compulsory jurisdiction of a court or an arbitral tribunal over disputes regarding international environmental obligations, the trade regime has established a relatively strong dispute settlement mechanism. Under the GATT system, prior to the establishment of the WTO, parties to GATT could refer their disputes to a panel for resolution. The panel, which had replaced an earlier system of working parties "consisting of representatives of states and always including the parties to the dispute,"[1] did not have the authority to render a binding decision; its conclusions had to be adopted by all contracting parties. This meant that the panel was, in fact, a mediation or conciliation body, and its conclusions could be rejected by the losing party if it chose so.[2] Under the WTO system, a comprehensive dispute resolution mechanism was established under one hat, the Dispute Settlement Body (DSB), with "the authority to establish panels, adopt panel and Appellate Body reports, maintain surveillance of implementation of rulings and recommendations, and authorize suspension of concessions and other obligations under the covered agreements."[3]

If consultations under Article 4 of the *Dispute Settlement Understanding (DSU)*[4] between parties to a dispute regarding WTO rights are not successful within the strict time limits provided, the complaining party can request a panel to be established.[5] Panelists are nominated by the WTO secretariat from a roster of individuals with the relevant expertise.[6] If parties to a dispute do not agree on the panelists, the WTO director-general in consultation with the chairman of the DSB and the chairman of the relevant council or committee will select the most appropriate nominees.[7] Unlike the prior system of adoption by consensus of panel reports, the DSB can only refuse to establish a panel or adopt its finding by consensus.[8]

A WTO panel shall examine the matter referred to it and "make such findings as will assist the DSB in making the recommendations or in giving the rulings provided for in [the relevant covered agreements]."[9] The panel shall "address the relevant provisions in any covered agreement or agreements cited by the parties to the dispute."[10] Under Article 11, the function of the panel "is to assist the DSB in discharging its responsibilities under [*DSU*] and the covered agreements..." and to

> make an objective assessment of the matter before it, including an objective assessment of the facts of the case and the applicability of and conformity with the relevant covered agreements, and make such other findings as will assist the DSB in making the recommendations or in giving the rulings provided for in the covered agreements.[11]

Thus, formally, a WTO panel does not make the final decision on the dispute; it only concludes a report that is submitted to the DSB. However, because of the negative consensus rules of Article 16(4) and 17(14), in the case of an appellate body report, a report would almost always be adopted by the DSB.

As an important addition to the prior GATT system, the WTO system includes an appellate body to which panel decisions can be appealed.[12] The appellate body only reviews "issues of law covered in the panel report and legal interpretations developed by the panel."[13] New facts can, therefore, not be presented to the appellate body. The dispute resolution process is subject to a strict time limit that is, when the report is not appealed, generally 9 months from the establishment of the panel to the time when the DSB considers the report and 12 months when it is appealed.[14]

Article 20(1) of the *DSU* emphasizes that "[p]rompt compliance with recommendations or rulings of the DSB is essential in order to ensure effective resolution of disputes to the benefit of all members."[15] Accordingly, a vital component of the WTO dispute resolution mechanism is the implementation and enforcement of panel or appellate body reports. If the respondent state loses, it must "inform the DSB of its intentions in respect of implementation of the recommendations and rulings of the DSB..." at a DSB meeting held within 30 days from the adoption of the report.[16] Certain extensions of the time limit are permitted if it is "impracticable to comply immediately with the recommendations and rulings..."[17]

If the respondent state, which the panel or appellate body report goes against, does not, within a reasonable time limit, defined in Article 21 of *DSU*, implement the recommendations and rulings of the DSB, the state invoking the dispute settlement procedures can, if negotiations are not fruitful, request authorization from the DSB to resort to unilateral measures referred to as a suspension of concessions.[18] Such authorization would sometimes be preceded by another panel report under Article 21(5) or arbitration under Article 22(6) by the panel initially charged with resolving the dispute, which, in the case of Article 22(6), arbitration can "determine whether the level of such suspension is equivalent to the level of nullification or impairment..." and if certain procedures have been followed.[19] Without the authorization of the DSB, the state that initiated the dispute settlement proceedings can generally not take unilateral measures against the losing party that affect WTO obligations of the former.[20] Additionally, unilateral measures will generally have to be related to the same sector as the initial violation[21] and are subject to what seems to be a strict proportionality criterion, that is, "the level of the suspension of concessions or other obligations authorized by the DSB shall be equivalent to the level of the nullification or impairment."[22] The logic behind such limitation on unilateral measures is understandable as such measures, despite being "effective means of encouraging compliance with rulings and recommendations, ...also have the potential to disrupt international trade very seriously, which plainly runs counter to the aims of the *DSU*."[23]

In the *United States Trade Act Case*,[24] the EC argued that the *Uruguay Round Agreements*

> consists of a trade-off between, on the one hand, the practical certainty of adoption by the [DSB] of panel and Appellate Body reports and of authorization for Members to suspend concessions—in the EC's view, an explicit U.S. request—and, on the other hand, the complete and definitive abandoning by the U.S. of its long-standing policy of unilateral action.[25]

The dispute concerned an authorization given to the United States trade representative under United States laws to determine whether a foreign state is denying the United States its rights under trade agreements and to take unilateral trade measures if it is determined that such rights have in fact been denied.[26] The panel wrote that "Article 23.2 clearly…prohibits specific instances of unilateral conduct by WTO Members when they seek redress for WTO inconsistencies in any given dispute."[27] The panel also found that legislation could be inconsistent with Article 23, even if no determination of denial of rights or unilateral measures had been taken.[28] The panel, however, found that the discretionary powers of the trade representative had been sufficiently limited by an administrative act, linking the determination of denial of rights to decisions of a WTO panel or the appellate body in cases concerning a WTO member state.[29]

This case illustrates the sensitivity of the WTO system for unilateral measures and how enforcement of a panel decision is, in general, subject to authorization of the *DSU*. This sensitivity is present even in cases where no enforcement decision has been made, but domestic legislation authorizes such enforcement to the detriment of the predictability of the system. It is, therefore, safe to conclude that under the *DSU* and the WTO system, member states may have largely surrendered the right to resort to countermeasures against violations of obligations under WTO-covered agreements without authorization by the DSB in exchange for an effective dispute settlement mechanism.[30]

It must be emphasized that the *DSU* does not limit the right of states, under customary international law, to take trade-related countermeasures in response to violations of international environmental obligations of states. However, the dispute settlement mechanism will not apply to such disputes, at least not until they become WTO-related issues, that is, when the trade-related countermeasures have already been taken. This abolishment of countermeasures in response to WTO-related violations raises questions regarding the fate of the argument, before a WTO panel, of trade-related countermeasures that are taken in response to non-WTO violations and mainly if the countermeasures restriction will lead to a presumption against such measures beyond what one is to expect if the dispute was before another body, such as the ICJ. What we have is a system that regulates and restricts trade-related countermeasures in response to a trade-related violation, determining whether unilateral measures taken in response to violations outside the regulatory framework of WTO could be justified as countermeasures. The challenge facing the state taking the countermeasures would be to make a WTO panel, or the appellate body, distinguish between the primary purpose of the measures as countermeasures and their secondary effects as interrupting international trade, apply the countermeasures doctrine, and find that no WTO violation has occurred and no actions should be taken. As is suggested next, there are strong arguments in support of such a treatment of the countermeasures doctrine by the WTO panel or an appellate body.

This brief review of the WTO dispute settlement mechanism suggests that the said mechanism and enforcement of the decisions taken within it is on a level very different from what one can generally expect from the international environmental regime. Although the WTO dispute resolution mechanism does not deal directly with environmental issues, it can and has dealt with the legality of trade-related unilateral measures taken by a member state with the aim to induce another state or a group of states to change an environmentally harmful policy or practice or to cease a possible violation of their international environmental obligations. Since many countermeasures are likely to have trade implications, it is possible that the WTO dispute resolution mechanism will not only coincidentally have to examine such disputes, but also the mechanism might become a magnet for resolution of disputes related to countermeasures. Within this context, Joost Pauwelyn wrote,

> [A] state wanting to enforce compliance, for example, with most environmental rules has no recourse to international jurisdiction. In the alternative, trade sanctions can be imposed, but there again the victim of the sanctions (i.e., the alleged violator of the environmental rule) may complain to the WTO. The state imposing the sanctions cannot in most instances resort, say, to UNEP for judicial settlement. All of these factors increase the potential and importance of interplay between the WTO and other rules of international law in WTO dispute settlement.[31]

The access to an effective remedy against trade violations increases the risk, which also might be seen as an opportunity, that disputes that are predominantly of environmental nature will be high jacked by the trade regime.

A number of cases where trade has allegedly been restricted for environmental reasons have come before WTO panels and the appellate body. The respondent state has rarely tried to justify the trade restrictions as countermeasures as the concept is used in this study.[32] Instead, the states taking the measures have relied on Article XX of GATT 1994. Article XX contains a list of authorized derogations from WTO obligations that states can apply in order to protect certain interests. The provisions of Article XX relevant to environmental protection read:

> Subject to the requirement that such measures are not applied in a manner which would constitute a means of arbitrary or unjustifiable discrimination between countries where the same conditions prevail, or a disguised restriction on international trade, nothing in this Agreement shall be construed to prevent the adoption or enforcement by any contracting party of measures:
>
> ...
>
> b. necessary to protect human, animal, or plant life or health;
>
> ...
>
> g. relating to the conservation of exhaustible natural resources if such measures are made effective in conjunction with restrictions on domestic production or consumption;
>
> ...[33]

It must be noted that Article XX does not address the right to resort to countermeasures against alleged violations of international environmental obligations when such measures do not fulfill the conditions laid down in the article. On one hand, the article authorizes measures otherwise contrary to other WTO obligations, which could not be justified as countermeasures for example, because the primary element of prior violation of an international environmental obligation is lacking. On the other hand, the article can arguably prohibit measures, which might be justified as countermeasures, because they do not fall into the categories of paragraphs (b) and (g) or do not fulfill the conditions laid down in the chapeau of Article XX. In such cases, the argument for trade-related countermeasures might have to be taken one step further, beyond Article XX, and rely solely on customary international law, that is, the doctrine of countermeasures.

Three issues seem to be of primary relevance for analysis if such a step is plausible. The first issue is whether a WTO panel would have jurisdiction to consider disputes in which a rule of customary international law would play such a predominant role or whether a panel can exercise its discretion and refrain from addressing such a case. Second, the issue is whether a rule of customary international law, such as the countermeasures doctrine could be deemed applicable to a dispute within the WTO system. And the third issue is whether international trade obligations would have priority over the international environmental obligation allegedly violated, so that despite recognizing the violation of an international environmental obligation, countermeasures outside the realm of Article XX would not be permitted.

(ii) Jurisdiction

There is a presumption, true or not, that WTO panels have a tendency to focus more on trade-related aspects of a dispute than environmental aspects. A state that has taken countermeasures in response to a violation of an international environmental obligation and has been summoned before a WTO panel by the initial wrongdoing state might, therefore, want to avoid such proceedings and the unleashing of the power of the

WTO DSB if it is to lose its case. The question is, therefore, can such an injured state claim that the WTO panel does not have jurisdiction over the case because the dispute is predominantly related to a violation of environmental obligation and not WTO rights? The short answer to that question is no. Here is a somewhat longer answer.

Unlike the ICJ statute or part XV of *UNCLOS*, which describe the parameters of the jurisdiction of the ICJ and the *UNCLOS* adjudication mechanism, *DSU* or other WTO rules do not contain a clear description of the jurisdiction of the WTO panels. Instead, the jurisdiction of WTO panels has to be deducted from several articles of *DSU*, mainly Articles 7(1), 7(11) and, arguably, Articles 3(2) and 23(1). Article 7(1) contains the standard terms of reference for a WTO panel. It suggests that a panel should

> examine, in the light of the relevant provisions in (name of the covered agreement(s) cited by the parties to the dispute), the matter referred to the DSB by (name of party) in document...and to make such findings as will assist the DSB in making the recommendations or in giving the rulings provided for in that/those agreement(s).[34]

Under these terms of reference, the panel seems to have a wide authority to review complaints of breach of obligations under the covered agreements. However, the standard terms of reference do not seem to limit the authority of the panel to refer to non-WTO rules for purposes of applying and interpreting WTO rights or determine if they have, in fact, been breached. Article 11 of the *DSU* describes the functions of the panels, which includes making "an objective assessment of the facts of the case and the applicability of and conformity with the relevant covered agreements, and *make such other findings* as will assist the DSB in making the recommendations or in giving the rulings provided for in the covered agreements."[35] The core role of the panel is, therefore, to address allegations of violations of a right under WTO-covered agreements, but it also extends to making other findings relevant to the case. It must, however, be emphasized that the panels can only address a violation of a WTO right under the covered agreements listed in Appendix 1 of *DSU*, that is, if the complainant claims that non-WTO rights have been violated, the panel can only address such violations inasmuch as they also constitute a violation of covered agreements. This was illustrated in the *Oilseeds Agreement Case* between the EC and Brazil.[36] In this case, Brazil claimed that it had certain rights under an agreement, the *Oilseeds Agreement*, whose substantive rules had been incorporated into a WTO-covered agreement.[37] The appellate body held that Brazil could only claim rights under the covered agreement but not the *Oilseeds Agreement* and based its legal analysis on the relevant covered agreement.[38]

Within these parameters, the jurisdiction of a WTO panel is quite wide. Pauwelyn wrote that the degree of proof for jurisdiction might be slightly lower than would be expected from many other international adjudication bodies, such as the ICJ, in the fact that it amounts "to a *presumption* (in favor of jurisdiction) not sufficiently rebutted by the defendant."[39] Articles 7(1), 11, and 23(1) of the *DSU* might support such an argument; as long as the dispute is related to a violation of a provision in covered agreements under Appendix 1 of the *DSU*, jurisdiction is presumed to be sufficient. Thus, as long as the claim brought by the complaining state genuinely concerns a WTO rule, this suggestion is "notwithstanding the fact that the wider dispute underlying the claim also or even predominantly involves other rules of international law."[40] The same author also argued that the implied or incidental jurisdiction of WTO panels includes "jurisdiction to decide all matters linked to the exercise of substantive jurisdiction and inherent in the judicial function…"[41] including issues related to state responsibility.[42]

There are clear and convincing arguments for the assertion that the panels have jurisdiction over claims even if non-WTO rules are at issue, as long as the claim itself is based on a WTO-covered agreement. The injured state taking countermeasures would accordingly not be able to argue that a WTO panel does not have jurisdiction to decide a case because it is predominantly of an environmental nature.

Having said that, one must ask whether a WTO panel has discretion to refrain from adjudicating a dispute before it because the underlying dispute involves a claim that the panel does not have jurisdiction to decide on. In the *Már Case*, ESA appeared to have applied such a principle,[43] but the WTO Appeallate Body, agreeing with the panel, held that WTO panels do not have discretion to decline to exercise its jurisdiction[44] unless there are legal impediments to the exercise of the panel's jurisdiction.[45]

The real issue here, then, is not of jurisdiction but, rather, about the applicable law that the panel will consider. If a dispute is properly brought before a panel, let's say, for a violation of Article V of GATT 1994, the panel has jurisdiction. When the panel has asserted jurisdiction, what laws will it apply? Will WTO rules be read in isolation from general international law or will the panel see WTO rules as a part of the international legal system and take notice of rules of customary international law, such as the countermeasures doctrine?

(iii) Applicable Law

Under Article 3(2), WTO rights shall be interpreted "in accordance with customary rules of interpretation of public international law."[46] This has often been seen as a reference to the *Vienna Convention on the Law of Treaties* and its rules of interpretation. The reference to such rules, however, opens up the possibilities to include a wide range of international law applicable between the parties for the purposes of interpreting the WTO rights in question, including taking into account "[a]ny relevant rules of international law applicable in the relations between the parties."[47] David Palmeter and Petros C. Mavroidis suggested that the WTO legal system

> is an important part of the larger system of public international law, as reflected not only by the interpretive principles that are brought to bear on its texts, which are explicitly those of public international law, but also by its increasing recourse to the other traditional sources of public international law: custom, the teachings of publicists, general principles of law, and other international

> instruments, particularly those incorporated by reference into the WTO and its agreements.[48]

Pauwelyn expressed a similar line of though by suggesting that although the "*DSU* limits the jurisdiction of WTO panels and the appellate body…, [i]t does not limit the potentially applicable law before them."[49] Pauwelyn continued and wrote that the repeated references to WTO rules in relation to the competence of the panels "relate to the jurisdiction or substantive mandate of WTO panels to judicially enforce only WTO covered agreements, not to the law that may be applied in doing so."[50]

It has been noted that the standard terms of reference only mention the relevant provisions of WTO-covered agreements as provisions to be examined by the panel. The WTO panel in *Korea—Measures Affecting Government Procurement* wrote:

> The purpose of the terms of reference is to properly identify the claims of the party and, therefore, the scope of a panel's review. We do not see any basis for arguing that the terms of reference are meant to *exclude* reference to the broader rules of customary international law in interpreting a claim properly before the Panel.[51]

Other WTO jurisprudence supports this line of thought that the WTO system is created within an international legal system, and its rules cannot be interpreted in a vacuum, disregarding its foundations.[52] Accordingly, WTO rules are "not to be read in clinical isolation from public international law…"[53] On the contrary, "Such international law applies to the extent that the WTO treaty agreements do not 'contract out' from it."[54] As was discussed before, even if WTO members have "contracted out" from resorting to countermeasures in response to violations of the covered agreements,[55] they have not explicitly done so with regard to countermeasures in response to non-WTO related violations, such as violations of international environmental obligations.

A WTO panel acting as arbitration under Article 22(6) of the *DSU* referred to the principle of proportionality of countermeasures in relation with cumulative compensation and suspension of concessions.[56]

Furthermore, arbitrators in a case between Canada and Brazil departed from the parties' interpretation of countermeasures. They wrote,

> While the parties have referred to dictionary definitions for the term 'countermeasures,' we find it more appropriate to refer to its meaning in general international law and to the work of the International Law Commission (ILC) on state responsibility, which addresses the notion of countermeasures. We note that the ILC work is based on relevant state practice, as well as on judicial decisions and doctrinal writings, which constitute recognized sources of international law.[57]

Quite arguably, the jurisprudence can be interpreted as an indication that the international law that states may use in defense of alleged violations of WTO obligations "potentially includes all rules of international law. In practice, this inclusiveness means that a defendant should be allowed to invoke non-WTO rules as a justification for breach of WTO rules, even if the WTO treaty itself does not offer such justification."[58]

Not all authors support this suggestion that WTO panels can apply substantive non-WTO law in their decisions. Joel P. Trachtman argued, "The mandate to WTO dispute resolution panels, to the Appellate Body, and to the Dispute Settlement Body is clear: apply (directly) only WTO law."[59] Trachtman sought support for his argument from the provision of the *DSU*, namely, Articles 3(2), 7 and 11. Article 3(2) states that the dispute settlement system "serves to preserve the rights and obligations of Members under the covered agreements, and to clarify the existing provisions of those agreements in accordance with customary rules of interpretation of public international law."[60] The role of the system to preserve rights does, however, not exclude non-WTO rules as applicable for the respondent state. The provision, read in the context of Article 3(2), refers to the functions of the dispute settlement system to provide a forum where violations are addressed and remedies provided in order to provide security and predictability of the system as a whole. Trachtman's statement—that the reference to international law in relation to interpretation of WTO rules is not an implicit reference to non-WTO substantive law apart from rules on interpretation—can be accepted. Nevertheless,

Article 3(2) does not exclude such rules. Trachtman also argued that the last sentence of Article 3(2)[61] confirms that non-WTO international law is not applicable in panel proceedings. As Trachtman admitted, the WTO system, like civil law systems, does not recognize *stare decisis*.[62] The WTO dispute settlement system can, therefore, not change the rights or obligations of parties as a judicial body within a common law system, which incorporates the *stare decisis* doctrine, could do. In other words, the WTO dispute settlement system does not have the role of a quasi-legislator; its role is merely to decide on whether a WTO party has violated its obligations under covered agreements.[63] Article 3(2), *in fine*, confirms this approach but cannot be interpreted as a far-reaching exclusion of the applicability of non-WTO international law. Pauwelyn supports this interpretation, but he argued that Article 3(2) of the *DSU* does

> not address the jurisdiction of panels, the applicable law before them, or the relationship between WTO covered agreements and all past and future law. Rather, they deal with the inherent limits a WTO panel must observe in interpreting WTO covered agreements. In exercising this judicial function of interpretation, WTO panels may clarify the meaning of WTO covered agreements, but they may not 'add to or diminish the rights and obligations provided in the covered agreements.' To put it differently, as judicial organs, WTO panels may not create new rights and obligations; they must apply those that WTO members agreed to.[64]

Trachtman's reference to Article 7 is similarly tempting for criticism. First of all, Article 7, which sets the default terms of reference, does not explicitly exclude non-WTO rules. The authority to examine a matter "in the light of the relevant provisions"[65] in the covered agreements and a duty to "address the relevant provisions in any covered agreement or agreements cited by the parties to the dispute..." does not explicitly restrict the review to those provisions. The question, whether non-WTO rules are applicable, is simply not answered in the article.

Similarly, Article 11 of the *DSU* provides that the functions of the DSB and WTO panels include "an objective assessment of the facts of the case and the applicability of and conformity with the relevant covered agreements…"[66] The article does not provide, explicitly or implicitly, that in the process of such assessment, the panel is precluded from applying non-WTO rules that might affect the application of WTO rules relevant to the case at hand.

Trachtman cited two WTO cases as a support for his arguments against applying non-WTO rules, the *Oilseed Agreement Case* and the *Argentina-Footwear Case*. He wrote that the former suggests that "a tariff agreement settling a matter between two WTO members does not constitute WTO law applicable by a panel."[67] It is suggested here that Trachtman's analysis, as far as it goes, is correct and the appellate body applied the law correctly. However, in this case, Brazil claimed rights agreed on in an agreement that was not a WTO-covered agreement, that is, the so-called *Oilseed Agreement*.[68] It was, therefore, asking the panel, and later the appellate body, to adjudicate on and eventually enforce rights it alleged it had under non-WTO rules, thus, to use the power of the WTO system for purposes for which it was not intended. It must be noted that the EC did, however, not argue before the appellate body that the *Oilseeds Agreement* was not an applicable law because it was a non-WTO law. Rather, it argued that *Schedule LXXX* was later in time, and if it differed from the *Oilseeds Agreement* the former should, under Article 59(1) and 30(3) of the *Vienna Convention on the Law of Treaties*, take precedence.[69] After examining the relations between the *Oilseeds Agreement* and *Schedule LXXX*, which incorporated most of the *Oilseeds Agreement*, the appellate body concluded that whereas the *Oilseed Agreement* was a bilateral agreement between Brazil and the EC, it was, unlike *Schedule LXXX*, not a covered agreement in the meaning of the *DSU*.[70]

This conclusion is to be interpreted as confirming that the WTO dispute settlement system cannot be used to enforce rights that are not included in the covered agreements. However, it says nothing about the use of non-WTO rules in order to show that the rights claimed under covered agreements have not been violated or that they are not applicable, that is, that the panel should not enforce WTO rights because of non-WTO rules.

The other reference Trachtman offered as support for his argument of the non-applicability of non-WTO rules is to a case against Argentina regarding the import of footwear, textiles, apparel, and other items. Unlike the *Oilseed Agreement Case*, the non-WTO rules were in this case used for the defense in arguing that because of a special agreement between the International Monetary Fund (IMF) and Argentina, the latter did not violate its WTO obligations. The issue was, therefore, the content of this agreement and, eventually, what to do if obligations under the IMF agreement were in conflict with a WTO obligation. It is argued here, as has been somewhat suggested before,[71] that the IMF rules were actually applied but because of lack of clarity of their content and because of rules of conflicts of law, Argentina's obligations under WTO rules were not affected by them. The said IMF agreement was entitled a *Memorandum on Economic Policy between Argentina and the IMF*.[72] Argentina contended that "its agreement with the IMF includes an undertaking to impose a tax in the form of a statistical tax."[73] Argentina further argued that "by its acquiescence, the United States helped to create Argentina's obligation with the IMF, and the United States cannot now deny the binding nature, [that is,] its legal effects with regard to Article VIII of the GATT 1994, of that obligation."[74] The panel did not agree with Argentina's argument that the agreement between the IMF and Argentina affected Argentina's obligation under GATT. The panel provided explanation as to why, not because the agreement was not applicable but that "in the situation before the Panel, there is no evidence that Argentina was requested by the International Monetary Fund (IMF) to impose an import tax that would violate the provisions of the WTO Agreement."[75] The appellate body agreed with this conclusion.[76] In addition, the appellate body wrote that "there is nothing in the *Agreement Between the IMF and the WTO*, the *Declaration on the Relationship of the WTO with the IMF* or the *Declaration on Coherence* which justifies a conclusion that a member's commitments to the IMF shall prevail over its obligations under Article VIII of the GATT 1994."[77] Thus, the agreement between Argentina and IMF was considered, but the conclusion was that it did not contain an obligation to impose the tax in question, and even if it had, it would, under conflict of law rules, not have had priority over WTO obligations.[78] Pauwelyn wrote on this conclusion:

> If the Appellate Body had thought that the IMF memorandum could not possibly cure the violation of GATT Article VIII simply because the memorandum is not part of WTO-covered agreements, it could have said so. But it did not. Rather, it assessed whether the IMF memorandum conflicts with GATT rules and considered which of the two rules should prevail in case a conflict arises.[79]

Similar considerations should prevail if the non-WTO rule was in the field of environmental law, that is, the appellate body

> should not confine itself to the WTO covered agreements but apply the environmental rule as a possible defense and in the event of conflict between it and WTO rules..., apply the relevant conflict rules of general international law... . Should the applicable conflict rule determine that the environmental rule prevails (e.g., as *lex specialis*), the Appellate Body would then be obliged not to apply the contradictory WTO rule and the complainant would lose. However, it would not have jurisdiction to hear claims of violation of the environmental rule.[80]

The appellate body in *Mexico Soft Drinks* appears to state an opinion that would question this non-WTO law inclusive approach on its surface. It said that it saw "no basis in the *DSU* for panels and the Appellate Body to adjudicate non-WTO disputes"[81] and that the DSU did not intend the panels and the appellate body to "become adjudicators of non-WTO disputes."[82] The EC expressed its concerns about the language in the report and cautioned against a broad reading of this statement, as well as suggested that the term "adjudicating" should be understood as not referring to interpretation and application of "non-WTO law and ruling on non-WTO obligations, where this was legally relevant for deciding a WTO dispute."[83] Further, the case dealt with interpretation of Article XX (d) of GATT 1994, which authorizes a state to secure compliance with domestic laws, not paragraphs (b) or (g) of Article XX (health and environment), which are clearly not restricted to domestic measures only. It is, therefore, only marginally applicable to such cases, as pointed out by the appellate body.[84]

The previous discussion on the applicable law before a WTO panel suggests that panels can only address rights and obligations under the WTO-covered agreements, that is, the case has to be brought before that panel as a violation of WTO rights. It cannot go beyond that and enforce rights that the complaining state enjoys under non-WTO agreements. However, in determining whether the complaining state actually has the rights it claims, or if it has, in fact, been violated, the panel's review is not limited to WTO rules only. Thus, the respondent state can argue, based on non-WTO rules, that the rights claimed are more limited than the claimant states, or they have, in fact, not been violated. If the respondent state could not refer to such non-WTO rules, the WTO system would be taken out of its context and the panel decision would be in isolation from the international legal system under which the WTO system is created. Such theory, arguably out of sync with its context, would need to be supported by a clear and explicit provision in the WTO agreements, excluding non-WTO rules and, therefore, detaining the whole system in an ivory tower of a tunnel-visioned trade regime. That was, however, barely the intention of the member states, which have the protection of a wide spectrum of interests reaching far beyond pure trade interests within their mandate. Additionally, it would not be in line with the WTO jurisprudence. It is, therefore, submitted that a WTO panel can, if the issue is raised and followed through by the respondent state, address the question of countermeasures and whether a non-compliance to a WTO obligation can be justified under the countermeasures doctrine.

(iv) Priority and Proportionality

Even if one agrees that the countermeasures doctrine can be considered before a WTO panel and, therefore, it would be theoretically possible that the wrongfulness of a violation of a WTO obligation would be precluded based on the said doctrine, it does not necessarily follow that it will happen in reality. Among the questions that come up in this context is how this paradox will be resolved and what rules will be there to guide the panel. Would the panel follow the tenets of conflict-of-law rules? Would it have to assess if either regime, in this case the trade regime or the environmental regime, has inherent priority over the other? Or, are there other principles that would provide the steering force for such decision? First, it is suggested here that the first option should be ruled out; there are no conflicts between the right to take countermeasures and WTO obligations. Second, it is suggested WTO obligations do not have inherent priority over the enforcement of environmental law.

It might at first sound strange to argue that the countermeasure doctrine is not in conflict with WTO obligations when the doctrine is used to justify a violation of such obligation. However, the explanation is fairly simple and straight forward. The countermeasures doctrine does not simply mean that a state is entitled to take action against other states that otherwise might be unlawful. The right to take countermeasures has to be seen in the context of the obligation that is violated by the measures, but because of countermeasure doctrine, the wrongfulness of that act is precluded. This means that if the conditions for the taking of countermeasures are present, the state can choose, within the limits prescribed by the principle of proportionality and with a few other limitations, which obligation of the ones it owes the offending state it will not comply with in their relations. Under such circumstances, the injured state, after making that determination, is precluded from international responsibility for not complying with that obligation, that is, if it does not have it, the obligation has vanished up to the extent and for the duration of the time while the countermeasures are permitted. For example, if state A violates obligation X that it owes to state B, and given that other elements of countermeasures are present, state B decides to violate obligation Y it owes to state A and justify it as countermeasures, obligation Y has temporarily vanished. Therefore, there is no conflict between obligation Y and the right to take countermeasures; at the moment the countermeasures are taken and during the period they can be legally sustained, obligation Y has ceased to exist.

This suggestion has to be qualified. First, the measures taken have to comply with the principle of proportionality, and second, the measures chosen by the injured state cannot be among prohibited countermeasures. I first elaborate on the latter.

The very nature of countermeasures suggests that they will always upset a rule of international law. Inherent in many, if not most, rules of international law is that under specific circumstances, derogations are permitted, that is, states are allowed to act in noncompliance with such rules without being held responsible for that act. This study has already discussed that certain measures can, however, not be justified under the countermeasures doctrine. Among them is a violation of the *UN Charter* prohibition against the use of force. Same goes probably for violations of fundamental human rights, humanitarian law, and peremptory norms of international law.[85] As previously mentioned, one state suggested that measures that cause "widespread, long-term and severe damage" to the environment should be included on the list of prohibited countermeasures.[86] WTO obligations have, however, not been included on such a list.

This leads us closer to a conclusion that the question whether the countermeasure doctrine will be applied by a WTO panel is not a question of jurisdiction, not of applicable law, not of conflict-of-law rules, not of any inherent priority of free trade principles over environmental principles, but a question of proportionality between the harm done and the measures taken. The question of proportionality is, however, in this context, really a question about priority of regimes, that is, are the principles of free trade so sacred that a violation of them in order to induce a state to comply with an international environmental obligation can never be justified as countermeasures because the measure taken—the trade restrictions—are inherently out of proportion to the harm done?

Pauwelyn pointed out that the WTO system does not, unlike, for example, the *UN Charter*, include a hierarchy clause, giving WTO obligations priority over other rules of international law or excluding the latter altogether.[87] However, as was pointed out several years ago, the GATT/WTO system has a tradition of operating "with only moderate regard to substantive principles of international or national environmental policy and law."[88] Nevertheless, there are hints that this might be changing, favoring respect for the environmental regime.[89]

For example, in *Tuna II*, the United States argued that "in becoming contracting parties to the General Agreement, countries did not agree to surrender their ability to take affective action to protect the environment, including the global commons."[90] In a paper submitted by the EC to the WTO Committee on Trade and Environment, the issue of finding a balance between trade rules and multilateral environmental agreements (MEAs) was addressed:

> The relationship between WTO rules and MEAs in general is unclear. If MEAs were deemed to justify discriminatory and protectionist action, it could set a damaging precedent for the Multilateral trading system. Similarly, subordinating MEAs to the WTO would undermine international efforts to tackle environmental problems and would fuel the arguments of those opposed to the WTO.[91]

The EC was suggesting a balance between environmental rules and trade rules, that coexistence is the preferred state of interaction between these rules and not dominance of one over the other. The paper also reaffirmed that "WTO rules should not be interpreted in clinical isolation of complementary bodies of international law, including MEAs"[92] and that MEAs should not be subordinate to WTO rules; the bodies are "separate but equal."[93] The EC also declared it was considering whether the burden of proof in Article XX of GATT 1994 should be reversed, "so that the country challenging the measure would...have to prove the measures imposed by the other party do not meet the conditions of Article XX."[94] WTO panels or the appellate body have, however, not gone quite that far. Nevertheless, after the United States had shown *prima facie* that its unilateral actions complied with the chapeau of Article XX, the panel in the second phase of the *Shrimp/Turtle Case* transferred the burden to show otherwise to the state claiming that the actions were incompatible to GATT 1994.[95]

(v) A Fusion of Article XX and the Countermeasures Doctrine?

Despite a number of hints that the balance has been changing to favor the environmental regime, and the fact that the WTO appellate body has upheld unilateral trade restrictions justified under the environmental exception in Article XX of GATT 1994, it remains to be seen if a panel will, in fact, recommend to the DSB that no action should be taken in the face of a violation of a WTO obligation justified as countermeasures outside Article XX, that a panel will set aside a WTO obligation to entertain an argument brought in from the cold, outside the comfort zone of international trade principles. It is possible that there is a way out, taking into consideration the right to respond to violations of international obligation while allowing the WTO system to keep face as a complete framework for world trade. A panel could avoid having to refer to an outside principle, such as the countermeasures doctrine, by interpreting Article XX to permit the countermeasures in question, a sort of "shoehorning" the countermeasures principle into Article XX. This may look like an attempt to use the law of countermeasures without actually saying it, and, up to a certain extent, it is. Thus, instead of coming to the conclusion that the application of the countermeasures doctrine was required to justify the noncompliance of the injured states with its WTO obligations, a panel might be less rigid or strict on the determination of whether the countermeasures are in conformity with the requirements in the chapeau of Article XX. This would not require the panel to "add to or diminish the rights and obligations provided in the covered agreements…"[96] as Article 3(2) of *DSU* would prevent, but would require it to interpret Article XX in a manner consistent with the countermeasures doctrine.

It is submitted here that such an interpretation would be possible under some circumstances, in particular when the measures taken fall within the relevant subparagraphs, whether it be subparagraph (b) or (g), but the manner in which the measures are applied might not fully comply with the current interpretation of the chapeau of Article XX. The variable that would make a relaxed interpretation of justifiable discriminatory or arbitrary means possible would be the presence of a violation of international environmental obligation—the same element as the countermeasures doctrine requires. The presence of a violation of an international obligation could justify discriminatory means that could not be justified if the purpose of the measures is merely to enforce an environmental policy for purposes of conservation or protection of natural living resources.

It must be noted that measures under Article XX can be permissible under the article, even if they are applied in a discriminatory manner, so long as such a manner can be justified. A reference to the countermeasures doctrine, in particular the presence of a prior violation of an international obligation, might provide such justification. There is, however, no such thing as justified arbitrary discriminatory manner under Article XX of GATT 1994. However, if the countermeasures are directed against the wrongdoing state only, if their purpose is to induce that state to comply with its international obligations, if the measures are proportionate and preceded by a warning and an offer to negotiate, then the manner in which the measures are applied is arguably not arbitrary discrimination, even if the manner in which similar measures, taken without a prior violation of an international obligation, might be. A problem might arise when there are many offending states and the injured state decides to resort to countermeasures against some of them but not all of them. To answer that question, recourse might be had to Article 47 of the *2001 Draft Articles* that suggests that in the case where "several States are responsible for the same internationally wrongful act, the responsibility of each State may be invoked in relation to that act"[97] without indicating that the injured state is bound by a nondiscrimination rule. Such interpretation could be supported by Article 3(2) of *DSU*. This point will, however, have to be analyzed on a case-by-case basis.[98]

The conclusion is, therefore, that it is possible to use the countermeasures doctrine to interpret Article XX, permitting measures that otherwise would not be permissible. It remains, however, to be seen how such an argument would play out in the hands of a panel or the appellate body.

(c) *The Tuna Dolphin Case of 1991* (*Tuna I*)

(i) Summary

The Tuna Dolphin Case of 1991, (hereafter referred to as *Tuna I*) concerned an import ban that the United States imposed on yellowfin tuna products from Mexico. The U.S. prohibited the imports because Mexico allegedly did not comply with U.S. laws, whose purpose was to limit the by-catch of dolphins resulting from tuna fishing.[99] Mexico brought the dispute to a GATT panel in January 1991.[100] The panel held that the measures taken by the United States were not in compliance with Article III[101] and XI of GATT 1947.[102] The United States argued that despite the inconsistencies with said articles, the measures were authorized under Article XX of GATT, paragraphs (b) and (g).[103] The panel disagreed and held that Article XX did not, in this case, excuse noncompliance with Articles III and XI.[104]

(ii) Facts and Analysis

According to the United States law, the *Marine Mammal Protection Act* (*MMPA*),[105] the secretary of treasury should "ban the importation of commercial fish or products from fish which have been caught with commercial fishing technology which results in the incidental kill or incidental serious injury of ocean mammals in excess of United States standards."[106] Mexico, and a few other states,[107] did not fulfill these requirements according to United States authorities. On 28 August 1990, the United States

> imposed an embargo, pursuant to a court order, on imports of commercial yellowfin tuna and yellowfin tuna products harvested with purse-seine nets in the [eastern tropical Pacific Ocean] until the Secretary of Commerce made positive findings based on documentary evidence of compliance with the *MMPA* standards.[108]

The embargo was shortly thereafter lifted but then imposed again.[109] Mexico believed this import ban was a violation of GATT 1947, mainly Articles III and XI.[110] In addition to Mexico's claim, a number of other states exporting tuna products to the United States were affected by the ban as intermediary nations if they did not prohibit imports of tuna from states whose direct tuna import to the United States was prohibited under *MMPA*.[111]

The relevant provisions of Article III:1 provide that internal taxes, laws and regulations, and requirements affecting internal sale or distribution should not be applied as to afford protection to domestic production. Furthermore, the same requirement applies to internal quantitative regulations requiring processing or use of products in specific amounts or proportions.[112] Article III:4 provides that a product from a contracting state must be "accorded treatment no less favourable than that accorded to like products of national origin in respect of all laws, regulations and requirements affecting their internal sale, offering for sale, purchase, transportation, distribution or use."[113] The limits on the by-catch, which the United States applied both to domestic and Mexican fishing vessels, could not, according to the panel, "be regarded as being applied to tuna products as such because they would not directly regulate the sale of tuna and could not possibly affect tuna as a product."[114] It was, rather, directed at the harvest of tuna, that is, at the process, in an attempt to reduce the dolphin by-catch. The panel accordingly found that the import ban was not a permitted internal regulation under Article III.[115]

The panel also found that the United States was in violation of Article XI. Article XI:1 states that no "prohibition or restriction...whether made effective through quotas, import or export licenses or other measures, shall be instituted or maintained by any contracting party on the importation of any product of the territory of any other contracting party."[116] Not surprisingly, the direct import ban of yellowfin tuna products was found to be inconsistent with Article XI.[117]

The defenses set forward by the United States, most relevant to this study, were based on Article XX, subparagraphs (b) and (g) of GATT 1947. The panel began by stating that since Article XX contains exceptions from the general obligations, it was to be interpreted narrowly. Also, the burden to justify invocation of Article XX was to be placed with the party invoking the exceptions.[118] The panel first discussed Article XX(b), especially whether it covered measures that were directed at protection of animals outside the jurisdiction of the contracting party taking the measures.[119] The panel cited the drafting history of Article XX(b) from the draft charter of the International Trade Organization and concluded that it was the intention of the drafters that the provision only applies to protection measures inside the jurisdiction of the importing country.[120]

Furthermore, the panel held that if the broad interpretation of extrajurisdictional effects of Article XX(b) were to be upheld, "each contracting party could unilaterally determine the life or health protection policies from which other contracting parties could not deviate without jeopardizing their rights under [GATT]." Then GATT would no longer be the multilateral framework for trade, "but would provide legal security only in respect of trade between a limited number of contracting parties with identical internal regulations."[121]

The panel also held that the necessity requirement in Article XX(b) was not met because the

> United States had not demonstrated to the Panel—as required of the party invoking an Article XX exception—that it had exhausted all options reasonably available to it to pursue its dolphin protection objectives though measures consistent with [GATT], in particular through the negotiation of international cooperative arrangements, which would seem to be desirable in view of the fact that dolphins roam the waters of many states and the high seas.[122]

This point suggests that the country taking measures under Article XX(b) has to show that it has already attempted to resolve the issues on a multilateral level if the issues at hand are of such nature. While not taking a position on whether this analysis is correct, it must be stressed that in this case the United States did not argue that Mexico had violated international obligations; rather, the focus was on incompatibility with requirements for imports of tuna, that is, a United States imposed obligation. Under the countermeasures doctrine, the situation would have been different. Then, the focus would have been on the prior violation of the wrongdoing state and the injury to the state taking the countermeasures, whether it is material or legal. Under such circumstances, the injured state would not have been required to "exhaust all options reasonably available to it;"[123] it would be sufficient to initiate communications with the wrongdoing states, requesting the wrongdoing state to cease the illegal situation and offer negotiation, and in case the illegal situation is prolonged, proportionate countermeasures might be taken. When the prior violation of international obligation is lacking, such relatively lax restrictions of unilateral measures are not possible. Then, the state whose interests have been adversely affected by undesirable behavior—but not illegal—of another state is not as free from its obligation to resolve the dispute, which at this stage is rather a political dispute than a legal one, in a peaceful cooperative manner in accordance with the rules of the relevant game.

The panel added to its argument regarding the necessity requirement that "even assuming that an import prohibition were the only resort reasonably available to the United States, the remedy taken could not have been deemed necessary."[124] The panel wrote that the

> United States linked the maximum incidental dolphin taking rate...to the taking rate actually recorded for United States fishermen during the same period. Consequently, the Mexican authorities could not know whether, at a given point of time, their policies conformed to the United States' dolphin protection standards.[125]

The panel placed this argument under the hat of necessity, but it also has links to the proportionality principle, that is, the measures might not be proportionate to what is necessary to achieve the goals of the legislation. Arguably, if the measures were genuinely intended to induce Mexican authorities to comply with standards set by the United States, the measures taken go too far as they do not give the Mexican authorities a reasonable opportunity to comply with the requirement. Furthermore, they fail to provide predictability; even if Mexico would take measures in order to comply, it could never be sure that these measures would provide market access for yellowfin tuna products in the United States. The nature of the measures would, therefore, have been another obstacle for the argument of countermeasures. The panel then held that the import ban could not be justified under Article XX(b).[126]

The panel then went on to discuss Article XX(g) and noted the requirement of the paragraph that the measures taken had to be "made effective in conjunction with restriction on domestic production or consumption."[127] Based on a decision of a previous panel,[128] the panel in this case held that the exception in Article XX(g) "could only be considered to have been taken 'in conjunction with' production restriction 'if it was primarily aimed at rendering effective these restrictions'."[129] This was interpreted as to only include measures that were aimed at "rendering effective restrictions on production or consumption within their jurisdiction."[130] This line of arguments indicates that the measures restricting the trade of a particular product must be related to the conservation of the source of that particular product. The measures taken by the United States were related to the preservation of dolphins but were directed against import of tuna. The panel, therefore, refused to link the trade restriction to the process of harvesting tuna and the effects that the trade restrictions are likely to have on such a process. Under the countermeasures doctrine, this link would not at all have to be this strict. If it would be established that the methods Mexico used to harvest tuna were incompatible with their international obligations to preserve dolphins, a reasonable trade restriction of tuna would not be seen as too distantly related to the subject of the alleged violation; in fact, there is generally no need for such a link, as countermeasure may be directed against interests unrelated to the violation.

Two of the arguments already mentioned in relation to the application of Article XX(b) were also used by the panel to reject application of Article XX(g). First, the arguments that the panel used to reject extrajurisdictional effect of Article XX(b) also were applicable with regard to Article XX(g), that is, one contracting party could not be allowed to adopt a unilateral conservation policy that other parties could not deviate from without risking their rights under GATT.[131] Second, the panel cited the link to the incidental by-catch of United States fisherman to the rate Mexico had to meet, and because of that link, Mexican authorities could never know if their conservation policy would at any given time be in compliance with the standards adopted by the United States. As with regard to Article XX(b), these conditions were found too unpredictable to be "regarded as being primarily aimed at the conservation of dolphins."[132] The panel accordingly held that Article XX(g) could not be used to justify the yellowfin tuna import ban.[133]

(iii) Concluding Remarks

The tuna cases' import bans were not argued as countermeasures but rather as permissible under Article XX of GATT. According to the facts presented, justifying the measures as countermeasures before the panel would have been unsuccessful. First of all, in 1991 the intrusion of environmental considerations into the realm of trade disputes had not grown anywhere close to the level on which it presently is. It is, therefore, quite possible that the countermeasures doctrine would not have received the attention it would need to prevail. Second, even if the panel would have considered the customary international law related to countermeasures, it would have had to determine that Mexico, as well as the intermediary states whose imports of yellowfin tuna into the United States market was affected, had violated an international obligation by failing to protect dolphins while fishing for tuna. That determination would probably not have been favorable for an argument for countermeasures.

(D) *The Tuna Dolphin Case of 1994* (*Tuna II*)

(i) Summary

In June and July 1992, the European Economic Community and the Netherlands brought a case before a GATT panel against the United States claiming that an import ban on tuna from their territories violated GATT 1947.[134] As in *Tuna I*, the United States claimed that the trade restrictions were related to conservation measures of dolphins and, therefore, permissible under Article XX of GATT.[135] The main difference between *Tuna I* and *Tuna II* is that the United States did not claim that the complainants had harvested tuna with methods incompatible to United States' policy, but that they had not shown that they had not imported tuna from countries that did.[136] The panel held that the measures violated United States' obligations under GATT 1947 and that they could not be justified under Article XX of GATT.[137]

(ii) Facts and Analysis

Tuna II was brought to a GATT panel by the European Economic Community and the Netherlands on 5 June 1992 and 14 July 1992, respectively, after consultations had failed.[138] Unlike *Tuna I*, which mainly concerned primary nation embargo,[139] *Tuna II* was brought by parties whose tuna exports to the United States were restricted because they had not shown that they had not imported tuna from primary embargoed nations. The complainants alleged that the United States' import restrictions on tuna were not compatible with GATT 1947, in particular Article III and XI. It is notable that the United States "did not refute these claims, other than to state that the EEC and the Netherlands, as the complainants, bore the burden of proof."[140] Instead, it concentrated most of its defense on justifying the measures under Article XX.[141] The panel quickly came to the conclusion that the measures were not compatible with Articles III and XI:1 of GATT 1947.[142]

The United States discussed the obligation of states to protect the environment, and that by agreeing to the provisions of GATT 1947, they had not abandoned this obligation.[143] The United States argued that this dispute should be distinguished from typical trade disputes. It asserted that the dispute

> was not an instance, for example, where one contracting party was concerned about actions by another party to protect its market. ...In this case, there had been no suggestion that the challenged measures were motivated by a desire to restrict imports or to protect domestic production. Indeed, all sides agreed that the United States' restrictions on tuna imports were based on conservation concerns shared by governments, including the parties to this dispute, non-governmental organizations, and private citizens around the world.[144]

The United States argued that, although it was not under an obligation under international treaties to maintain an embargo such as the one at hand,[145] the "measures at issue were consistent with and directly furthered the objectives of an international environmental agreement...,"[146] namely, the *Convention on International Trade in Endangered Species of*

Wild Fauna and Flora, which provided for " 'stricter domestic measures' in order to further the objectives of that agreement."[147]

The panel suggested a three-step method of determining whether Article XX(g) could justify the measures taken. First, "it had to be determined whether the policy in respect of which these provisions were invoked fell within the range of policies to conserve exhaustible natural resources."[148] Second, it had to be determined whether the trade measures in question were " 'related to' the conservation of exhaustible natural resources, and whether it was made effective 'in conjunction' with restrictions on domestic production or consumption."[149] Third, the panel suggested that it had to be determined whether the application of the measures was in conformity with the preamble to Article XX—mainly that the measures were not applied in an arbitrary or unjustifiably discriminatory manner, or that they were not a disguised restriction on international trade.[150]

After confirming that dolphins were exhaustible natural resources under Article XX(g), the panel discussed in some length the issue of extrajurisdictional nature of the measures. The United States brought the panel's attention to other provisions of Article XX that were clearly intended to authorize trade restriction due to conditions outside the jurisdiction of the country taking the measures and argued that Article's XX silence on this issue does not mean that extrajurisdictional measures are precluded.[151] Citing the drafting history of Article XX, the United States argued that "the negotiators had contemplated a country applying measures outside its jurisdiction."[152]

The panel noted that states have authority to regulate the conduct of their nationals outside their territory, including vessels flying its flag[153] and, as the United States suggested, that Article XX(g) does not explicitly limit its applicability to conservation measures taken within the territory of the states taking the measures.[154] The panel then concluded that it saw "no valid reason supporting the conclusion that the provisions of Article XX(g) apply only to policies related to the conservation of exhaustible natural resources located within the territory of the contracting party invoking the provision."[155] Nevertheless, it qualified its conclusion by limiting the extraterritorial application to "jurisdiction over its nationals and vessels..."[156]

The panel then came to the second step of its analysis and found that the link between the measures and the policy pursued was not sufficiently close. The panel adopted an argument from the EEC, which had been confirmed by a previous panel,[157] and interpreted this link as requiring the measures to be primarily aimed at the conservation of dolphins and primarily aimed at rendering effective the domestic restriction on production or consumption of dolphins. The panel explained the phrase "primarily aimed at" as referring "not only to the purpose of the measure, but also to its effect on the conservation of the natural resource."[158] The panel found that the trade measures were not directly linked to the conservation of dolphins, instead they were intended to force states to change their policies regarding tuna fisheries; such changes would then have positive effects on the conservation of dolphins.[159] The panel noted that Article XX(g) did not give clear answers as to if this indirect link between the measures and the conservation policy was sufficient, and that Article XX(g), as an exception from obligation under GATT 1947, should be interpreted narrowly.[160] It then wrote that if

> Article XX were interpreted to permit contracting parties to take trade measures so as to force other contracting parties to change their policies within their jurisdiction, including their conservation policies, the balance of rights and obligations among contracting parties, in particular the right of access to markets, would be seriously impaired. Under such an interpretation, the General Agreement could no longer serve as a multilateral framework for trade among contracting parties.[161]

The panel then concluded that the link between the measures and the conservation policy was too weak for Article XX(g) to be applicable. Accordingly, there was no need to determine if the requirements in the preamble of Article XX were met.[162]

For the analysis of if Article XX(b) could justify the trade measures taken by the United States, the panel, again, suggested a three-step method: first, to determine whether the United States' policy in question "fell within the range of policies referred to in these provisions, that is policies to protect human, animal or plant life or health..."[163] second, if the measures were necessary to protect the life and health of dolphins; and third, if they were compatible with the preamble of Article XX.[164]

Although both parties agreed that the protection of the life or health of dolphins could fall under Article XX(b), the EEC argued that the article did not apply to animals outside of the jurisdiction of the state taking the measures.[165] Similarly to its analysis of this issue in relation to Article XX(g), the panel found that nothing in Article XX(b) limited the application of measures to animals located within the jurisdiction of the states taking the measures. Accordingly, it concluded that "the policy to protect the life and health of dolphins in the eastern tropical Pacific Ocean, which the United States pursued within its jurisdiction over its nationals and vessels, fell within the range of policies covered by Article XX(b)."[166]

The second step in the panel's methodology of resolving the question of compatibility of the measures taken by the United States with Article XX(b) was the question of necessity. Citing a report of a previous panel,[167] the panel determined that a state could not justify its measures as necessary unless no other measures consistent with GATT 1947 were reasonably available to it and that among the measures reasonably available, the measure selected is the one that "entails the least degree of inconsistency with other GATT provisions."[168] The panel, therefore, saw the necessity requirement as a proportionality requirement, requiring states to take the least illegal measure among those reasonably available. The panel, however, did not build on this analysis in its remaining arguments where it rejected the link between the measures taken and the policy to protect the life or health of dolphins. The panel did not indicate what other measures were reasonably available. It, rather, questioned the measures' effectiveness, as they would not directly result in protecting dolphins; for them to be effective, they had to be "followed by changes in policies or practices, not in the country exporting tuna to the United States, but in third countries from which the exporting country imported tuna."[169] Consequently, the panel rejected the United States' argument that the measures were justified under Article XX.[170]

(iii) Concluding Remarks

Unlike *Tuna I*, this case was mainly about intermediary nation embargo, meaning against states that exported tuna to the United States that could have originated from a state against which a primary nation embargo was directed. Even if measures in the form of a primary nation embargo, as in *Tuna I*, could have been justified under Article XX, an intermediary nations' embargo was one link farther away from such justification. The panel wrote that

> measures taken under the intermediary nation embargo prohibited imports from a country of any tuna, whether or not the particular tuna was harvested in a manner that harmed or could harm dolphins, and whether or not the country had tuna harvesting practices and policies that harmed or could harm dolphin, as long as it was from a country that imported tuna from countries maintaining tuna harvesting practices and policies not comparable to those of the United States.[171]

Furthermore, the United States made no attempt to argue the action or inaction of the secondary embargoed nations as a violation of their international obligations. As the facts of the dispute were presented in the case before the panel, such attempt would probably have been futile. The measures taken by the United States in this case could accordingly not have been justified under the countermeasures doctrine as the primary element of countermeasures, the presence of a prior violation of an international obligation, is lacking.

(E) The *Shrimp/Turtle Case of 1998 and 2001*

(i) Summary

This *Shrimp/Turtle Case* was initially brought before a WTO panel by Malaysia, Thailand, Pakistan, and India in January and February 1997.[172]

At issue was an import ban on shrimp that the United States imposed on certain nations. By imposing the embargo, the United States was enforcing domestic legislation that required all United States' fishermen to use turtle-friendly equipment while hunting shrimps. The legislation had been extended to require an import ban on shrimps from nations that were allegedly hunting shrimps with methods that put at risk endangered species of sea turtles.[173] The complainants argued that the import ban violated Articles XI:1 and XIII:1 of GATT 1994.[174] The United States argued in defense that the import ban was justified under Article XX, as measures necessary to conserve an exhaustible natural resource. The panel, and later the appellate body, found that the measures violated the United States' obligations under GATT 1994 and that they were not justified under Article XX.[175] The shrimp/turtle dispute did not end there. In October 2000, Malaysia requested the DSB to establish a panel to find that the United States had not complied with its obligation to lift the import ban.[176] The panel then found that the import ban, as implemented under amended guidelines, was justified under Article XX of GATT 1994.[177] The panel's finding was later confirmed by the appellate body.[178]

The United States did not claim that the complainants had violated international obligations or that the import ban was in response to such violation.

(ii) Facts and Analysis: *Shrimp/Turtle I*

The *Shrimp/Turtle Case* was in many ways similar to the previously discussed tuna cases. It concerned a violation of the general WTO obligations, which the responsible state tried to justify as authorized measures under Article XX. The relevant facts of this case are that in 1987 the United States adopted a regulation requiring all United States shrimp trawl vessels to use certain types of sea turtle-friendly devices, so called turtle excluder devices or TEDs, in all areas where it was likely that shrimp trawling would threaten sea turtles.[179] The TED consists of grid of bars, fitted into the neck of the shrimp trawl. It has an opening either on the top or the bottom. Whereas small animals, such as shrimps, slip through the bars and into the trawl, large animals, such as sea turtles, do not but are instead ejected through the opening of the TED. While "incidental capture and drowning of sea turtles by shrimp trawlers was the most significant source of mortality of sea turtles…"[180] the National Marine Fisheries Service has said that 97% of them could be excluded from the trawls by the use of TEDs.[181]

As in the tuna cases, the United States, in order to increase the effectiveness of the measures taken with regard to domestic fishermen, enacted in November 1989 the so-called Section 609,[182] which imposed an import ban on shrimp harvested with commercial fishing technology that may adversely affect sea turtles.[183] To avoid the import ban, states had to get a certification confirming either that their shrimp trawling did not threaten sea turtles or, if sea turtles lived in the area, confirming that the state had enacted a regulatory program designed to prevent incidental killings of sea turtles, similar to the one of the United States.[184] In addition, the average incidental killings of sea turtles had to be comparable to that of United States' vessels.[185] All seven recognized species of sea turtles were, at the time the measures were taken, listed in Appendix I of the 1973 *Convention on International Trade in Endangered Species of Wild Fauna and Flora.*[186] There was no dispute among the parties as to the "endangered nature of…sea turtles…as well as the need to protect them…"[187]

On 15 May 1998, a WTO panel instigated by Malaysia, Thailand, Pakistan, and India found the measures to be in violation of GATT 1994.[188] It did not accept U.S. arguments that the import ban was authorized under Article XX of GATT 1994. Despite the loss on the panel level, there were certain hints that environmental concerns were getting increased attention. Gregory Shaffer pointed at, as an early sign that the panel intended to take the environmental issues seriously, the WTO panel's appointment of a five-member group of experts in conservation biology to evaluate the environmental concerns in the case. They all agreed that sea turtles were endangered species but did not agree on what measures were appropriate. A second issue Shaffer pointed at was the fact the even though the panel did not accept amicus briefs from two NGOs that attempted to influence the case, the panel, however, accepted the factual part of the briefs as an exhibit to a United States submission.[189]

On 13 July 1998 the United States appealed the panel report to the WTO Appellate Body.[190] The issue under appeal relevant to this study was if the shrimp embargo was justified under Article XX of GATT 1994.[191]

The appellate body, citing its decision in the *Gasoline Case*,[192] adopted a two-tier analysis of Article XX.[193] The method constituted of "first, provisional justifications by reason of characterization of the measure under XX(g); second, further appraisal of the same measure under the introductory clause of Article XX."[194] In other words, if the measure taken by the United States would fit the description of permitted measures under paragraph (g), the appellate body would look at the introductory provisions of Article XX, the chapeau, to examine whether the manner in which the measures were applied "would constitute a means of arbitrary or unjustifiable discrimination between countries where the same conditions prevail, or a disguised restriction on international trade…"[195] The panel, however, never discussed whether the characteristics of the measure could fall under any of the exceptions in the subparagraphs. It discussed only the chapeau and whether the design or the nature of the measure taken by the United States constituted unjustifiable discrimination between countries where the same conditions prevail.[196] The appellate body suggested that the panel had looked at the object and the purpose of GATT 1994 as a whole and described it "in an overly broad manner."[197] The appellate body continued and stated, "[T]he Panel arrived at the very broad formulation that measures which 'undermine the WTO multilateral trading system' must be regarded as 'not within the scope of measures permitted under the chapeau of Article XX'."[198]

In examining Article XX(g), the appellate body addressed four main issues. First, it addressed whether sea turtles, which the measures where intended to protect, were "exhaustible natural resources" in the meaning of the article. Second, the question whether Article XX(g) applied to migratory species that might predominantly live outside the jurisdiction of the state taking the measures was addressed. Third, the appellate body addressed whether the measures were relating to the conservation of such species, and fourth, they addressed whether the measures were "made effective in conjunction with restrictions on domestic production or consumption."[199]

On the issue of whether sea turtles were exhaustible natural resources, India, Thailand, and Pakistan argued that Article XX(g) only applied to nonliving natural resources. The appellate body, however, did not agree. It examined the preamble of the *WTO Agreement*, where parties stated their concern for the environment and then looked at how the phrase "natural resources" is used in other international treaties for living and nonliving resources. Among them were treaties that were not applicable as such between the parties to the dispute at hand, such as *UNCLOS* and the 1979 *Convention on Conservation of Migratory Species of Wild Animals*.[200] After citing two adopted GATT panel reports that found that fish were exhaustible natural resources[201] and noting that all of the seven species of sea turtles are listed in Appendix 1 of the CITES, the appellate body concluded that sea turtles were "exhaustible natural resources."[202]

In *Tuna I*, the panels held that Article XX(g) did not have extra-jurisdictional effect, and in *Tuna II*, the panel did not come to a precise conclusion. Clearly this was a problem for the present case, but the appellate body did not answer the question directly. Instead, it concluded that there was enough nexus between the United States' conservation interests and the sea turtles by pointing out the migratory nature of the species and implying that a part of the world population of sea turtles might migrate to or traverse waters under United States jurisdiction.[203] Although the appellate body made it clear that these findings relating to the jurisdictional problem only applied in the "specific circumstances of the case before us,"[204] it seems obvious that it has implications for other migratory species, such as marine mammals and migratory birds. Furthermore, these findings imply that it is not necessary for the application of Article XX(g) to prove that the object of the conservation measures, sea turtles in this case, ever enter the jurisdiction of the state taking the action, only that it is possible under the circumstances.

The third issue was whether the measures taken by the United States were "relating to the conservations of exhaustible natural resources," as required in Article XX(g). The appellate body defined its task as to look into "the relationship between the measure at stake and the legitimate policy of conserving exhaustible natural resources"[205] by examining "the relationship between the general structure and design of the measure here at stake, Section 609, and the policy goal it purports to serve, that is, the conservation of sea turtles."[206] In the *Gasoline Case*, the appellate body held that the relationship between the so-called baseline establishment rules and the measures of prohibiting the import of gasoline not produced under such rules could not "be regarded as merely incidental or inadvertently aimed at the conservation of clean air in the United States for the purposes of Article XX(g)."[207] The appellate body in that case, consequently, concluded that the rules were primarily aimed at the conservation of clean air.[208] The appellate body in the *Shrimp/Turtle I Case* held that the structure and design of the measures taken in accordance with the implementing guidelines of Section 609 were "fairly narrowly focused"[209] and that the exemptions from the import ban were clearly and directly related "to the policy goal of conserving sea turtles."[210] Furthermore, the appellate body agreed that the TEDs were an effective tool in sea turtle conservation[211] and that the measures were "in principle, reasonably related to the ends."[212] Therefore, the appellate body concluded that "Section 609 is a measure 'relating to' the conservation of an exhaustible natural resource within the meaning of Article XX(g) of the GATT 1994."[213]

Arguably, this conclusion departs significantly from the ones presented by the GATT panels in the tuna cases. In the *Shrimp/Turtle Case*, the United States had implemented a policy to preserve sea turtles, not shrimp, and conditioned the import of shrimps to implementation of comparable policies where necessary. As in the *Gasoline Case*, the appellate body accepted that restriction of import of one product in order to protect unrelated values—gasoline versus clean air and shrimp versus sea turtles—was sufficiently related to its aim if the production of the former adversely affected the latter.

The appellate body lastly addressed whether the requirement of Article XX(g) that the measures had to be "made effective in conjunction with restriction on domestic production or consumption" was met. Whereas the panel in *Tuna II* interpreted the exception in Article XX(g) narrowly, the appellate body in this case referred to a doctrine of even handedness that it had previously developed in the *Gasoline Case*, where it said that the requirement causing the import restriction should also apply to domestic production.[214] The appellate body, however, noted that the domestic production of shrimp that did not fulfill the requirements was not subject to the distribution ban. Instead, the government relied "on monetary sanctions and civil penalties for enforcement..."[215] and, in egregious cases, seizure of shrimp catch.[216] Nevertheless, the appellate body concluded that the measures were even handed and, therefore, "made effective in conjunction with the restriction on domestic harvesting of shrimps..."[217]

This conclusion confirms the global nature of environmental threats by not strictly limiting the territorial scope of the measures taken under the exception in Article XX(g) to the jurisdiction of the acting state. Furthermore, it rejects the holistic approach adopted by the panel in this case, an approach that made a presumption, rarely rebuttable, that trade restriction as a measure to protect the environment was an abuse of the exceptions in Article XX that would devastate the predictable and effective system of free international trade under the WTO.[218]

As discussed before, the appellate body applied a two-tier analysis in determining whether the measures taken by the United States could be justified under Article XX. After the analysis of the first tier had produced a positive resolution for the United States, the latter resulted in a different conclusion. The introductory provision of Article XX requires that protection measures that are, because of its nature and design, justified by subparagraphs (a) to (j) of Article XX cannot be applied "in a manner which would constitute a means of arbitrary or unjustifiable discrimination between countries where the same conditions prevail, or a disguised restriction on international trade…"[219] The appellate body held that the import restrictions imposed by the United States did not meet this requirement and that the manner in which the measures were applied constituted both unjustifiable and arbitrary discrimination between countries where same conditions apply.[220]

The appellate body believed that the measures, as applied, were too strict and rigid, even beyond what was required by the United States Congress.[221] Although they were enforced in a unified manner in the United States despite different circumstances in the various states within the country, the United States could not require all states to adopt a system that was not merely a comparable regulatory program but essentially the same,[222] irrespective of the different conditions in the multicolored flora of WTO members.[223]

The appellate body also noted with displeasure that if a state was not certified, as required by Section 609, shrimp harvested in its waters was excluded from import into the United States, even though the vessels used the TEDs.[224] Furthermore, it was apparent that the United States did not negotiate effectively with all countries affected by the import ban. Some WTO member states were included in negotiations but others, such as the parties to the present case, were not. The appellate body cited numerous international instruments indicating that environmental problems and issues of conservation should not be resolved by unilateral measures; on the contrary, concerted and coordinated efforts should be undertaken to address such transboundary problems.[225]

The appellate body also noticed that while certain Caribbean and Latin American countries were given a 3-year phase-out time from 1991 to 1994, the parties to the present case were only given 4 months, from 29 December 1995 to 1 May 1996, to adjust to the TEDs requirement.[226] The appellate body saw the length of the adjustment period as affecting the burden that the measures placed upon countries that had to comply with the requirements and did not accept the United States' arguments justifying the different adjustment periods.[227] Lastly, the appellate body noted the lower level of efforts put into a technology transfer to countries, such as the complainants, than to countries of the Caribbean and Latin America.[228]

The appellate body then concluded that when the differences in the means of application of the import ban are considered in their cumulative effect, "those differences in treatment constitute 'unjustifiable discrimination' between exporting countries desiring certification in order to gain access to the United States shrimp market within the meaning of the chapeau of Article XX."[229]

Although the appellate body found that one of the requirements in the introductory provisions of Article XX was not met and did not have to examine if the other requirements were met, it, nevertheless, decided to seek an answer to the question if the manner of applying the measures also constituted arbitrary discrimination. In short, the appellate body found that they did.[230] The certification process was found to be nontransparent and unpredictable. Furthermore, the appellate body said, about the certification process, that there was

> no formal opportunity for an applicant country to be heard, or to respond to any arguments that may be made against it, in the course of the certification process before a decision to grant or to deny certification is made. Moreover, no formal written, reasoned decision, whether of acceptance or rejection, is rendered on applications for either type of certification…[231]

The appellate body also noted that there was no review and no appeal procedure available for countries that were denied certification.[232] This lack of transparency and basic due process rights led the appellate body to conclude that the measures were applied in an arbitrary discriminating manner.[233]

(iii) Facts and Analysis: *Shrimp/Turtle II*

The appellate body report in *Shrimp/Turtle I* was adopted by the DSB on 6 November 1998.[234] On 25 November, the United States declared it intended to comply with the recommendations and rulings of the DSB,[235] and later agreed to a 13-month reasonable period of time to implement them.[236] In July 1999, the United States issued revised guidelines for the implementation of Section 609.[237] The guidelines were, according to the United States, designed to "increase the transparency and predictability of the certification process and to afford foreign governments seeking certification a greater degree of due process."[238] The United States also claimed that it had significantly increased its effort to negotiate an agreement of the conservation of sea turtles in the Indian Ocean region and had approached several governments in the region with a view to reaching an agreement on the issue. Finally, the United States pointed out that it had offered and organized technical training to the governments in the Indian Ocean region on the design, construction, installation, and use of TEDs.[239] The United States claimed that these measures addressed the concerns raised by the appellate body, making the restrictions compliant with Article XX of GATT 1994.[240]

Malaysia, in its request to establish a panel under Article 21(5) of *DSU*,[241] argued that the measures taken by the United States were not in compliance with the recommendations and rulings of the DSB and that the United States, consequently, continued to violate its obligations under GATT 1994.[242] The panel, however, found that

> in light of the recommendations and rulings of the DSB, Section 609…, as implemented by the Revised Guidelines of 8 July 1999 and as applied so far by the US authorities, is justified under Article XX of the GATT 1994 as long as the conditions stated in the findings of this Report, in particular the ongoing serious good faith efforts to reach a multilateral agreement, remain satisfied.[243]

Malaysia appealed the findings of the panel, arguing that the panel erred in finding that the United States was in compliance with its GATT 1994 obligations.[244] The arguments set forth by Malaysia were mainly twofold. First, the United States could not continue the disputed unilateral measures without first concluding an international agreement on the conservation of sea turtles. Second, because of the unilateral nature of the measures taken, they could not be compatible with the chapeau of Article XX even if the revised guidelines on the implementation of

Section 609 were flexible enough to allow certification of countries that had enacted measures comparable in effectiveness to the United States' measures.[245]

The appellate body upheld the findings of the panel.[246] It agreed with the panel that Article XX of GATT 1994 did not require the state justifying its measures under Article XX to conclude an agreement on the issue; it was sufficient to show that the state had engaged in a good faith negotiation with a view to concluding such an agreement. The appellate body recalled that among the reasons for concluding in *Shrimp/Turtle I* that the manner in which the disputed measures were applied constituted unjustifiable discrimination was that the United States

> had adopted a cooperative approach with WTO Members from the Caribbean/Western Atlantic region, with whom it had concluded a multilateral agreement on the protection and conservation of sea turtles, namely the Inter-American Convention. Yet the United States had not, we found, pursued the negotiation of such a multilateral agreement with other exporting Members, including Malaysia and the other complaining WTO Members in that case.[247]

The appellate body explained that the United States had to "make good faith efforts to reach international agreements that are comparable from one forum of negotiation to the other."[248] However, it was unreasonable to demand that the state taking the measures had to conclude an agreement. That would "mean that any country party to the negotiations with the United States, whether a WTO Member or not, would have, in effect, a veto over whether the United States could fulfill its WTO obligations."[249] As to whether the United States had, in fact, engaged in good faith negotiation, the panel and the appellate body compared efforts to negotiate a sea turtle conservation agreement with states in the Indian Ocean and the Southeast Asia region to the attempts to negotiate with states in the Caribbean/western Atlantic region,[250] a process that resulted in the *Inter-American Convention for the Protection and Conservation of Sea Turtles*.[251] The appellate body found that

> the Panel was correct…in concluding that the efforts made by the United States in the Indian Ocean and South-East Asia region constitute serious, good faith efforts comparable to those that led to the conclusion of the Inter-American Convention.[252]

The appellate body found that, in view of the serious good faith negotiation in which the United States was now engaged, the manner in which Section 609 was applied no longer constituted an unjustifiable or arbitrary discrimination.[253]

As to the latter argument set forth by Malaysia, the appellate body had already held in *Shrimp/Turtle I*, "that conditioning access to a Member's domestic market on whether exporting Members comply with, or adopt, a policy or policies unilaterally prescribed by the importing Member may, to some degree, be a common aspect of measures falling within the scope of [the exceptions under Article XX of GATT 1994]."[254] Thus, it was not the unilateral nature of the measures in Shrimp/Turtle I that rendered them incompatible with the chapeau of Article XX but rather their character as a rigid and unbending requirement to adopt "essentially the same policies and enforcement practices as those applied to, and enforced on, domestic shrimp trawlers in the United States."[255]

The appellate body in Shrimp/Turtle II emphasized the important difference between conditioning market access to compliance with essentially the same regulatory system and a system comparable in effectiveness. The latter would give "sufficient latitude to the exporting Member with respect to the programme it may adopt to achieve the level of effectiveness required [and allows it] to adopt a regulatory programme that is suitable to the specific conditions prevailing in its territory."[256] The appellate body noted that under the revised guidelines, a great deal of flexibility had been provided, allowing certification of states that have regulatory programs " 'comparable in effectiveness' to that of the United States…"[257]

Previously, the panel in *Shrimp/Turtle II* had reviewed the text of the revised guidelines and its implementation and concluded that Section 609, as implemented, allowed more flexibility than before, that is, it was an application of a comparable effectiveness test in line with what the appellate body in *Shrimp/Turtle I* had prescribed.[258] This finding of the panel was confirmed by the appellate body.[259]

The panel in *Shrimp/Turtle II* understood the appellate body's report from *Shrimp/Turtle I* as suggesting that the essential reason for concluding that the measures taken by the United States were applied in a manner that constituted unjustifiable discrimination under the chapeau of Article XX of GATT 1994 was that "the application of the measure at issue did not allow for any inquiry into the appropriateness of the regulatory programme for the conditions prevailing in the exporting countries."[260] The panel examined whether the revised guidelines provided for such an inquiry and if they were applied appropriately. The panel noted that the revised guidelines authorized the United States government to consider, for purposes of certification, if regulatory programs other than those that require the use of TEDs offer comparable protection to sea turtles.[261] Although the revised guidelines indicated that no other measures or series of measures to reduce the harmfulness of shrimp trawls were in fact compatible with the use of TEDs, the panel viewed that as a presumption that did not exclude the certification of other regulatory programs, such as a fishing ban.[262] As a support for this assertion, the panel cited the case of Pakistan, which had been granted certification for a program that combined the use of TEDs and shrimp trawling prohibition.[263]

After reviewing the revised guidelines, as well as the practice of the United States, the panel concluded that "the United States has established a *prima facie* case that the implementing measure complies with the findings of the Appellate Body concerning the insufficient flexibility of the 1996 Guidelines."[264]

Furthermore, the panel found that other reasons, which the appellate body in *Shrimp/Turtle I* had referred to while concluding that the measures taken by the United States were unjustifiable discrimination, such as unequal phase-in period and transfer of technology, had been remedied under the revised guidelines and the subsequently adopted practice. Thus, the measures taken by the United States were found to be compatible with the prohibition of unjustifiable discrimination under the chapeau of Article XX of GATT 1994.[265]

For similar reasons, the panel held that the prohibition against arbitrary discrimination under Article XX had been met. In particular, the panel noted that the due process requirement, which the appellate body in *Shrimp/Turtle I* had held was not met, had been sufficiently addressed in the revised guidelines, giving any state applying for certification the opportunity to be heard and have an unfavorable decision reviewed.[266]

Lastly, the appellate body in *Shrimp/Turtle II* addressed Malaysia's claim that the revised guidelines did not specifically address the particular circumstances prevailing in Malaysia. It held that Article XX did not require such specificity[267] and that the revised guidelines were flexible enough to enable the United States to "consider the particular conditions prevailing in Malaysia."[268]

The appellate body, accordingly, upheld the findings of the panel.[269]

(iv) Additional Analysis Relating to the Elements of Countermeasures

Opinions differed as to what the consequences of the *Shrimp/Turtle I* really were for environmental protection. Some were pessimistic, suggesting that the appellate body "closed the door on member countries' abilities to initiate much needed extraterritorial environmental measures."[270] Others wrote it is "a significant step forward, if not an outright victory for...environmental groups..."[271] It is suggested here that the trend that can be extracted from the development from *Tuna I* to *Shrimp/Turtle II* is clearly favorable for the suggestion that trade restrictions can be used to fight environmental degradation.

Arguably, the WTO has made itself subject to rules that are not favorable for free trade in isolation by taking a holistic approach and considering the broader obligations of making the use of the planet sustainable. In *Shrimp/Turtle I*, the appellate body expressed its understanding of these obligations when it said:

> In reaching these conclusions, we wish to underscore what we have *not* decided in this appeal. We have *not* decided that the protection and preservation of the environment is of no significance to the Members of the WTO. Clearly, it is. We have *not* decided

> that the sovereign nations that are Members of the WTO cannot adopt effective measures to protect endangered species, such as sea turtles. Clearly, they can and should. And we have *not* decided that sovereign states should not act together bilaterally, plurilaterally or multilaterally, either within the WTO or in other international fora, to protect endangered species or to otherwise protect the environment. Clearly, they should and do.[272]

The tables have somewhat turned from the time when the GATT panel decided on *Tuna I*. Instead of suggesting that an environmental policy could not be applied in such a manner as to risk the uniformity and predictability of the international trade system, the approach is, rather, that the international trade system has to take into account environmental issues and the sustainability of the planet. As *Shrimp/Turtle II* confirmed, the reason why the United States lost *Shrimp/Turtle I* was not that trade restriction could not be used to protect sea turtles, it was the manner in which the measures were applied that was unacceptable to the appellate body. By adopting a different certification system, more flexible and transparent; containing necessary due process protection for states that requested certification; and by offering and conducting good faith negotiations with all states affected by the import ban, as well as making available to them training on the design and use of TEDs, the shrimp import ban became a successful unilateral measure to protect environmental interests and, more importantly, accepted by the WTO system.

This case has relevance for the question of countermeasures because it indicates that the WTO system has become more susceptible to environmental concerns, meaning that the isolationism somewhat expressed in the tuna cases and certainly in the panel in *Shrimp/Turtle I* is no longer an acceptable method of resolving conflicts between trade and environmental protection. Therefore, the case can be interpreted as increasing the chances that a panel will genuinely consider whether trade restrictions can be justified as countermeasures taken in response of a violation of environmental obligations. The case is, however, not conclusive regarding this issue.

What clearly distinguishes this case from a case of countermeasures, as the doctrine is presented in this book, is that the trade measures were not taken in response of a violation of international obligations. Thus, they were not countermeasures and not justified as such. At the time the measures were taken, there was no clear obligation to conserve sea turtles, which the complainants were bound by in its relations to the United States. The *Shrimp/Turtle Case* has, therefore, in common with the tuna cases that they, apparently, could not have been justified as countermeasures. Nevertheless, there are a few issues that raise the question if the countermeasure doctrine can, at all, get a favorable treatment, that is, being genuinely considered within the WTO dispute resolution system.

In *Shrimp/Turtle I*, the appellate body placed a burden on the United States to negotiate with the complainants and to conduct such negotiation in a nondiscriminatory manner.[273] On its surface, this obligation seemed to be somewhat heavier than the duty to offer negotiation suggested in the *2001 ILC Draft Articles on State Responsibility*[274] but possibly in line with earlier ILC suggestions on demanding good faith negotiations prior to resorting to countermeasures,[275] as well as to prohibit countermeasures while negotiations are being conducted in good faith.[276] In *Shrimp/Turtle II*, Malaysia argued that the appellate body in *Shrimp/Turtle I* had, in fact, held that the United States could not continue its unilateral measures "whilst it engages in negotiations for the conservation of marine turtles."[277] Malaysia went even further and argued that the United States could not resort to unilateral measures under Article XX of GATT 1994 before an agreement on the conservation of sea turtles had been *concluded*.[278]

As previously suggested, the obligation to conduct negotiation in good faith in a nondiscriminate manner would not apply if the measures in question were to be justified as countermeasures, that is, it is not required to conduct negotiations with the offending state prior to taking countermeasures. This contrast reflects the different situation in which the *Shrimp/Turtle Case* was decided from the underlying principles of countermeasure, that is, its primary element—the presence of a prior violation attributable to the offending state. A rule of international law is generally either adopted after significant negotiations or developed through long-standing state practice. Violating it can have legal consequences, such as a duty to pay reparation and a duty to cease the violation if it is ongoing. In some instances, such as under the WTO framework, the wrongdoing state is under an obligation to accept that the dispute be referred to dispute settlement procedures and to accept the decision as binding upon it. These procedures, as well as other less compulsory procedures, do not mean that the legal rule has to be renegotiated. The situation is quite different when there is no substantive rule to be broken. Then, the modalities of conservation have to be worked out between the countries affected, that is, the dispute, which at that stage would generally not be a legal dispute but a political, economic or scientific, has to be addressed by concerted and cooperative methods. Thus, there is no need to interpret the conclusion in the *Shrimp/Turtle I* as requiring states to enter into good faith negotiation prior to taking countermeasures. It must be emphasized that he appellate body in *Shrimp/Turtle II* did not suggest that all cooperative avenues had to be exhausted prior to resorting to unilateral measures but only that good faith negotiations were offered and conducted.[279]

The second question is whether the emphasis on nondiscriminatory means indicates that countermeasures in the form of trade restrictions have to be directed against all WTO-member states that have violated the legal obligation in question, that is, if the trade regime's nondiscrimination tenor adds another requirement into the countermeasures doctrine when it would come before a WTO panel or the appellate body. As was suggested before, the answer might be sought in the solution suggested in Article 47 of the *2001 Draft Articles on State Responsibility*,[280] which "states the general principle that [when more than one state is responsible for a wrongful act] each State is separately responsible for the conduct attributable to it, and that responsibility is not diminished or reduced by the fact that one or more other States are also responsible for the same act."[281] The decision of the ICJ in *Certain Phosphate Lands in Nauru* also indicates that an injured state can choose which of the responsible states it goes against; there is no duty to invoke state responsibility against all responsible states at the same time.[282] As this principle would also apply to countermeasures, a WTO panel would have to take this principle into consideration. This would be true whether or not the countermeasures doctrine is applied directly or through interpretation of Article XX.

(F) HIGHLY MIGRATORY FISH STOCKS: CHILE/EC SWORDFISH DISPUTE

(i) Summary

In 1990 and 1991, Chile imposed restrictions on landings by Spanish fishing vessels that had been harvesting swordfish in the high seas outside the Chilean EEZ. The restriction led to a long-lasting dispute between Chile and the EC.[283] In the summer of 2000, Chile brought a case before an arbitral tribunal under *UNCLOS*, claiming that the EC had violated its obligation under *UNCLOS*.[284] In November 2000, after consultations had failed,[285] the EC brought a case before a WTO panel claiming that the restrictions violated Chile's obligations under WTO, in particular Article V.[286] Both cases were suspended at the request of the parties before memorials or other substantive documents were submitted.[287]

(ii) Facts and Analysis

In the late 1980s, the swordfish stock in the eastern Atlantic was as good as depleted, and in 1990, the International Commission for the Conservation of Tuna declared severe restrictions on its harvesting, effective from July 1991.[288] In the light of the depletion of the stock, the Spanish fishing industry, which had been fishing swordfish in the Atlantic, was by then already exploring whether its vessels could fish swordfish in the southeast Pacific using similar methods, that is, the so-called surface-set long line.[289] Such fisheries commenced in 1990 in the southeast Pacific, including an area adjacent to the 200 nm Chilean EEZ.[290] The EC supported these fisheries with financial aid.[291]

Chile, which at a similar time increased its swordfish fisheries in the same area, initially permitted Spanish ships to use Chilean ports to transship their catch and for other operational needs.[292] However, after an incident that included stoning of a Spanish vessel in 1990, the Chilean government introduced restrictions on transshipment and transit of swordfish. The ban was initially based on a requirement for a zoo-sanitary certificate,[293] but in 1991, the Chilean fishery laws were amended to provide a better legal basis for the restriction.[294] According to European sources, no prior consultation or negotiation took place.[295] Furthermore, the reasons for the restrictions were, according to European sources, not related to violations of international obligations but were related to non-compliance with Chilean laws.[296]

Although Chilean law authorized more extensive measures against Spanish vessels, including prohibition on "landing, supply and any type of direct or indirect service of vessels in Chilean ports and within the exclusive economic zone and territorial sea..."[297] the measures taken were limited to the landing of swordfish. Therefore, Spanish vessels could dock at Chilean ports for "repairing activities or in order to provide medical assistance to the crew, or for refueling."[298] Also, the measures were relatively narrow in scope as they restricted only landing of specific species.[299] Vessels fishing other species could upload and transship their catches.[300]

After 10 years of unsuccessful negotiations, the EC, with a letter to the WTO DSB dated 19 April 2000, invoked the WTO dispute resolution mechanism by requesting consultations with Chile "regarding the prohibition on unloading of swordfish in Chilean ports..."[301] Consultations were not successful, and with a letter dated 6 November 2000, the EC requested establishment of a WTO panel to resolve the issue.[302] Prior to that request, Chile had referred the conservation part of the dispute to an arbitral tribunal under *UNCLOS*.[303] With a letter dated 18 December 2000, Chile, in agreement with the EC, requested that the case be removed from the arbitral tribunal and submitted to a special chamber of ITLOS in accordance with Article 15(2) of the ITLOS Statute.[304]

In line with its alleged policy of giving priority to a dispute settlement mechanism under environmental instruments when a trade dispute's undertone was predominantly of an environmental character, the EC had already considered the possibility of referring the underlying dispute to the *UNCLOS* adjudication mechanism.[305] The explanations given for not choosing this route were threefold. The first reason was that the dispute was, in fact, more related to jurisdiction than to actual environmental concerns.[306] The second explanation was that coastal state jurisdiction over straddling stocks and highly migratory species was sensitive. Thus, referring such an issue to an arbitral tribunal "could be politically unwise, as it could reopen a thorny and vast debate, contribute to block-building and delay the entry into force of the 1995 [*Fish Stocks Agreement*] and the growing international consensus on it because undecided states would wait for the outcome of the dispute before ratifying it..."[307] The third explanation was that the EC was concerned that a "too aggressive attitude towards Chile...could much reduce the possibility of negotiating an agreement."[308] The EC also noted the lack of guarantees for enforcement of *UNCLOS* judgments and that *UNCLOS* procedures would inevitably take more time than WTO dispute settlement procedure.[309] In addition to a lack of enforcement, the EC was concerned that even if a favorable conclusion before an *UNCLOS* arbitral tribunal would make a WTO case easier to pursue, the *UNCLOS* procedure would not address the main concern—the restrictions on landing and transshipment of swordfish in Chilean ports. Finally, a favorable conclusion was not a guarantee that a WTO panel would not hold that Chile's measures were justified under Article XX(g) of GATT 1994.[310]

In the case before the ITLOS special chamber, Chile requested the chamber to decide "whether the European Community [had] complied with its obligations under [*UNCLOS*], especially articles 116 to 119 thereof..." and Article 64.[311] Furthermore, Chile asked the chamber to decide whether the EC had

> challenged the sovereign right and duty of Chile, as a coastal State, to prescribe measures within its national jurisdiction for the conservation of swordfish and to ensure their implementation in its ports, in a non-discriminatory manner, as well as the measures themselves, and whether such challenge would be compatible with the Convention...[312]

The EC requested the chamber to decide whether Chile's unilateral conservation measures were compatible with *UNCLOS*, in particular Article 87, 89 and 116 to 119.[313] Additionally, the EC requested a decision on whether Chile had breached its obligation under *UNCLOS* by failure to negotiate.[314]

Going back to the WTO side of the dispute, at a DSB meeting on 17 November 2000, Chile and the EC explained their arguments. The EC argued that Chile's unilateral acts were incompatible with Article V and Article XI of GATT 1994.[315] The EC emphasized that "the most effective way to deal with international environmental issues…was to do so multilaterally in a negotiated agreement."[316] At the meeting, Chile did not attempt to refute the allegations that the restrictions on landings were incompatible with Articles V and XI. Instead, its representative focused its attention on the need to enact an effective conservation measure with regard to swordfish and that the swordfish was fully exploited so that additional harvesting would not be sustainable.[317] Chile argued that its measures were justified under *UNCLOS*. It pointed out that the right to fish in the high seas was subject to "rights and duties, as well as the interests of coastal states."[318] Furthermore, Chile reminded the DSB that Article 117 of *UNCLOS* "made it the duty of States to adopt, with respect to their nationals, measures for the conservation of the living resources of the high seas."[319]

Chile argued that it had been willing to negotiate a solution of the dispute and that it had proposed a dialogue for that purpose already in 1995. After Chile and the EC had set up a technical committee, Chile had "explained the scientific grounds for its conservation measures, whereas the EC had been unable to provide any information on conservation measures applied by the EC fleet catching swordfish in the Pacific…"[320] Neither had the EC "agreed to supply any information regarding its catches, which was not transmitted to the United Nations Food and Agriculture Organization (FAO), as required by the international obligations incumbent upon all fishing states."[321]

The EC seemed to have expected that Chile would argue that the WTO panel did not have competence because the underlying dispute was outside the jurisdiction of the panel. The EC, nevertheless, believed that such argument would not be victorious as "a GATT panel seized within the realm of its jurisdiction cannot refuse a decision because other international law questions are relevant."[322] At the DSB meeting, Chile argued that the dispute was of an environmental nature and that "the WTO dispute settlement mechanism was not the proper forum for considering and resolving this dispute, which was clearly defined, regulated and mentioned specifically as a matter for dispute settlement under [*UNCLOS*]."[323] Chile, however, did not seem to argue that the WTO did not have competence at all but did suggest that the "environmental dispute on conservation and observance of principles or the precautionary approach could not be placed before any forum other than the dispute settlement mechanism under the Convention on the Law of the Sea."[324]

This suggestion seems to indicate that Chile preferred that the WTO panel would not interfere with the proceedings until after the special chamber under *UNCLOS* had concluded its proceedings and then accept its findings as to the environmental issues underlying the trade dispute. However, it was not an argument against the jurisdiction of a WTO panel but, rather, a suggestion that the panel should exercise its discretion and not, at this point, examine issues that belong to other dispute resolution bodies.

The Chilean representative argued that the EC was, by referring the case to a WTO panel, in contradiction to its own policies to place environmental disputes before environmental bodies. He referred to a visit of an EC commissioner to Chile where the commissioner warned against parallel dispute settlement procedures of this kind, as it could contain "the seeds of a serious potential conflict between the multilateral trading system and the multilateral environmental protection system."[325]

Chile described the behavior of the fishing fleet of "some EC member States" as "repeatedly exceeding the catch limits and minimum size of swordfish in the Atlantic, the Mediterranean and the North Sea, with harmful effects on the marine environment and whose predatory methods of fishing were exacerbated by large amounts of aid and subsidies."[326] The measures taken were to prevent these conditions from happening in the southeast Pacific; they "had a clear environmental purpose and not any trade aims, as claimed by the EC."[327] Finally, Chile argued that the measures, which had not been applied unilaterally or arbitrarily and solidly based on rights and duties under *UNCLOS*, "were fully justified by Article XX of the GATT 1994."[328]

At the meeting, both parties confirmed their interests in the conservation of highly migratory species, such as swordfish, and showed willingness to negotiate a settlement. In fact, the case did not go much further than this because a few months later, the parties decided to suspend their cases pending before the special chamber and the WTO panel. Therefore, on 9 March 2001, the EC and Chile informed ITLOS that they had reached a provisional arrangement concerning the dispute and the process should be suspended.[329] Similar communication was submitted to the DSB on 23 March 2001, with the arrangement enclosed.[330] The arrangement included provisions on a bilateral scientific and technical commission and a joint research fisheries program on swordfish in the southeast Pacific.[331] The research program contained provisions on a maximum catch of 1,000 tons for each party and access to port by the four community vessels participating in the program. Furthermore, the arrangement provided for consultation in order to establish a mechanism for cooperation regarding swordfish stocks in the southeast Pacific, either by establishing a new organization or working trough an existing one.[332]

(iii) Concluding Remarks

It was unfortunate for the legal debate that the *Chile/EC Swordfish Dispute* did not develop further before the WTO panel or ITLOS. The dispute, in particular the parallel dispute settlement proceedings, could have raised a number of interesting legal questions—some of them at the core of the debate on the balance between environmental protection and conservation and free trade. Among such questions is the issue of *res judicata* and if the ITLOS special chamber would reach a conclusion first. Would the WTO panel be obliged to refer in its decision to the legal findings regarding the question raised in the ITLOS wing of the dispute? If the multilateral trading system is not to be viewed in clinical isolation from the international legal system, the WTO panel would have to rely on Article 296(2) of *UNCLOS*, giving the ITLOS decision binding effects as law between the parties. If the answer would be in the affirmative and the special chamber would find that the EC had violated its international obligations under *UNCLOS*, would the WTO decide the case solely on WTO rules, including Article XX? Or, would it rely on other international legal obligations of the parties, including the right to resort to countermeasures under international law? Also, what if the special chamber would hold that the EC was in violation and the WTO panel would, in fact, decide in EC's favor? One would then have to consider the different enforcement mechanisms and whether the relatively effective mechanism under WTO would override the weak regime of enforcement of ITLOS decisions under *UNCLOS*, rendering the ITLOS decision largely ineffective between Chile and the EC. These and many other interesting questions will now remain unanswered, at least for the time being.

The swordfish dispute distinguishes itself from the tuna and shrimp disputes because the state taking the measures claimed that the EC had violated its international obligations by either failing to consult or failing to unilaterally take necessary measures for the conservation of swordfish in the southeast Pacific. As in the *Már Case*, and unlike in the *Estai Case*, the distance-water fishing party, Iceland and the EC, had failed to take measures related to the conservation of the fish stock that their nationals were fishing. Whether such failure is actually a breach of *UNCLOS* will not be decided here; for such a determination, much more scientific input and factual analysis is necessary. Nevertheless, this case could possibly have been argued under the countermeasure doctrine before the WTO panel.

With regard to the proportionality of the measures, one must note that the measures were not a total ban on port access for community vessels. On the contrary, the measures were narrowly tailored to affect landing of swordfish only, not other services and not the harvesting of other species. The access restrictions, having only minimal effects on trade in swordfish, would have to be seen as proportionate.

Although it is not sufficiently clear from the facts of this case, the strength of Chile's arguments for countermeasures might weaken, somewhat, because Chilean authorities did not seem to have demanded compliance with international legal obligation or have initiated communication with the EC prior to taking the measures. The facts indicate, inconclusively though, that Chile did not entertain the idea of serious consultation until 1995 when it

> proposed to the EC a dialogue aimed at evaluating the resources so as to be able to harmonize or agree conservation measures for the high seas in the south-east Pacific and to facilitate access by the Community fleet to Chilean ports, respecting the conservation regime.[333]

Although prior negotiations are not a condition for the legality of countermeasures, the injured state is, in most cases, required to communicate to the wrongdoing states its allegations that the latter is in violation of its international obligation and that cessation of that violation is requested; otherwise, appropriate measures will be taken.

ENDNOTES

1. J.G. Merrils, *International Dispute Settlement*, 3rd ed., Cambridge University Press, Cambridge, New York, 1998, p. 199.
2. See Ibid., p. 200.
3. *Understanding on Rules and Procedures Governing the Settlement of Disputes*, annex 2 to the *Marrakesh Agreement Establishing the World Trade Organization*, concluded at Marrakesh 15 April 1994, entered into force 1 January 1995, 1869 U.N.T.S. 401, reprinted in 33 I.L.M. 114 (1994) (hereafter referred to as *Dispute Settlement Understanding* or *DSU*), article 2(1). Covered agreements are listed in Appendix 1 to *DSU*.
4. Ibid.
5. *DSU*, articles 4 and 6(1).
6. *DSU*, articles 8(1)–8(6).
7. *DSU*, article 8(7).
8. *DSU*, article 16(4).
9. *DSU*, article 7(1).
10. *DSU*, article 7(2).
11. *DSU*, article 11.
12. J.G. Merrils, *International Dispute Settlement*, p. 200 and *DSU*, article 17.
13. *DSU*, article 17(6).
14. Ibid., article 20.
15. Ibid., article 20(1).
16. Ibid., article 21(3).
17. Ibid., article 21(3).
18. Ibid., articles 22(1) and 22(2).
19. See Ibid., articles 21(5), 22(6), and 22(7).
20. Ibid., article 23.
21. Ibid., article 22(3).
22. Ibid., article 22(4).
23. J.G. Merrils, *International Dispute Settlement,* p. 213.
24. *United States—Sections 301–310 of the Trade Act of 1974*, World Trade Organization, report of a WTO panel, 22 December 1999, WTO doc. WT/DS152/R, adopted by the DSB on 27 January 2000.
25. Ibid., p. 300, para. 7.2.
26. Ibid., pp. 2–6, paras. 2.1–2.20.
27. Ibid., p. 312, para. 7.39.

28. Ibid., pp. 311–314, paras. 7.35–7.46.
29. Ibid., pp. 329–337, paras. 7.109–7.136.
30. See, for example, *ILC 2001 Report*, p. 129.
31. Joost Pauwelyn, "The Role of Public International Law in the WTO: How Far Can We Go?" *American Journal of International Law* 95, no. 3 (2001), at 538.
32. See a rather poor attempt by Mexico in *Mexico—Tax Measures on Soft Drinks and Other Beverages,* World Trade Organization, report of the appellate body, 6 March 2006 (hereafter referred to as *Mexico Soft Drinks*), WTO doc. WT/DS308/AB/R. Mexico's main argument before the appellate body was, however, article XX(d) of GATT 1994.
33. *General Agreement on Tariffs and Trade*, annex 1A to the *Marrakesh Agreement Establishing the World Trade Organization*, concluded at Marrakesh 15 April 1994, entered into force 1 January 1995, 1867 UNTS 154, reprinted in 33 ILM 15 (1994). The *General Agreement on Tariffs and Trade* was initially opened for signature on 30 October 1947, 55 UNTS 187 (hereafter referred to as GATT 1994 or GATT 1947 in a context prior to the establishment of the WTO), article XX.
34. *DSU*, article 7(1).
35. Ibid., article 11, italics added.
36. *European Communities—Measures Affecting the Importation of Certain Poultry Products*, World Trade Organization, report of the appellate body, 13 July 1998 (hereafter referred to as the *Oilseeds Agreement Case*), WTO doc. WT/DS69/AB/R.
37. The *Oilseeds Agreement Case* had been incorporated into *Schedule LXXX.* Under the *Marrakesh Protocol* (*Marrakesh Protocol to the General Agreement on Tariffs and Trade 1994*, 1867 U.N.T.S. 237), *Schedule LXXX* was annexed to GATT 1994. Under GATT 1994, article 2(7) annexed schedules form and integral part of GATT 1994. Thus, *Schedule LXXX* was a covered agreement under *DSU.*
38. *Oilseeds Agreement Case*, p. 29, para. 79.
39. Joost Pauwelyn, "The Role of Public International Law in the WTO," at 556–557. See also Joost Pauwelyn, "Evidence, Proof and Persuasions in WTO Dispute Settlement: Who Bears the Burden," *Journal of International Economic Law* 1, no. 2 (1998), at 227.
40. Joost Pauwelyn, "The Role of Public International Law in the WTO," at 557 and 558. See also *United States Diplomatic and Consular Staff in Tehran*, 1980 I.C.J. 3, in particular at 19, para. 36. This case was discussed in part I, chap. 5 (d). The handling of the *Már Case* by ESA arguably differs from this suggestion.

41. Joost Pauwelyn, "The Role of Public International Law in the WTO," at 555.
42. Ibid.
43. See part III, chap. 15 (c) previously.
44. *Mexico Soft Drinks*, p. 24, para. 57.
45. *Mexico Soft Drinks*, p. 21–23, para. 54. See also case from a GATT 1947 panel, *U.S.—Sugar Quota*, between the United States and Nicaragua, panel report adopted on 13 March 1984, B.I.S.D. 31S/67, paras. 3.10–3.11.
46. *DSU*, article 3(2).
47. *Vienna Convention on the Law of Treaties*, concluded at Vienna 23 May 1969, entered into force 27 January 1988, 1155 U.N.T.S. 331, article 31(3)(c).
48. David Palmeter and Petros C. Mavroidis, "The WTO Legal System: Sources of Law," *American Journal of International Law* 92, no. 3 (1998), at 413.
49. Joost Pauwelyn, "The Role of Public International Law in the WTO," at 561.
50. Ibid.
51. *Korea—Measures Affecting Government Procurement*, report of a WTO panel, 1 May 2000, WTO doc. WT/DS163/R, adopted by the DSB on 19 June 2000, p. 184, para. 7.101, note 755.
52. See Joost Pauwelyn, "The Role of Public International Law in the WTO," at 562–563.
53. *United States–Standards for Reformulated and Conventional Gasoline*, World Trade Organization, report of the appellate body, 29 April 1996, WTO doc. WT/DS2/AB/R, p. 14, reprinted in 35 I.L.M. 603 (1996), at 621. See also *Resolving the Relationship Between WTO Rules and Multilateral Environmental Agreements*, submission by the European Community, WTO doc. WT/CTE/W/170 (19 October 2000), p. 3, para. 13, where the European Community reaffirmed that "WTO rules should not be interpreted in clinical isolation of complementary bodies of international law, including MEAs." (MEAs refer to multilateral environmental agreements).
54. *Korea—Measures Affecting Government Procurement*, p. 183, para. 7.96.
55. See *DSU*, article 23(2)(c).
56. *European Communities—Regime for the Importation, Sale, and Distribution of Bananas,* decision by arbitrators under article 22(6), 9 April 1999, WTO doc. WT/DS27/ARB, p. 38, para. 6.16.
57. *Brazil—Export Financing Programme for Aircraft*, decision by arbitrators under article 22(6) of *DSU* and article 4(11) of the *SCM Agreement*

(*Agreement on Subsidies and Countervailing Measures*), 28 August 2000, WTO doc. WT/DS46/ARB, pp. 14–15, para. 3.44 (endnotes omitted).
58. Joost Pauwelyn, "The Role of Public International Law in the WTO," at 577.
59. Joel P. Trachtman, "The Domain of WTO Dispute Resolution," *Harvard International Law Journal* 40 (1999), at 342.
60. *DSU*, article 3(2).
61. *DSU*, article 3(2), ("Recommendations and rulings of the DSB cannot add to or diminish the rights and obligations provided in the covered agreements.").
62. Joel P. Trachtman, "The Domain of WTO Dispute Resolution," at 339.
63. This seems to have been the understanding of the United States in *Tuna II*, citing a comparable provision in the 1982 *Ministerial Declaration* on dispute settlement, see *United States—Restrictions on Imports of Tuna* (hereafter referred to as *Tuna II*), report of a GATT panel, 20 May 1994, GATT doc. DS29/R, para. 3.11, reprinted in 33 I.L.M. 839 (1994), at 853.
64. Joost Pauwelyn, "The Role of Public International Law in the WTO," at 564.
65. *DSU*, article 7(1).
66. *DSU*, article 11.
67. Joel P. Trachtman, "The Domain of WTO Dispute Resolution," at 342–343.
68. See supra endnote 37 of this chapter.
69. *Oilseed Agreement Case*, see supra endnote 36 of this chapter, para. 40.
70. Ibid., para. 79.
71. Joost Pauwelyn, "The Role of Public International Law in the WTO," at 568–569.
72. *Argentina—Measures Affecting Imports of Footwear, Textiles, Apparel, and Other Items*, World Trade Organization, report of the appellate body, 27 March 1998, WTO doc. WT/DS56/AB/R, (hereafter referred to as *Argentina—Footwear*), para. 13.
73. Ibid., para. 13.
74. Ibid., para. 13.
75. *Argentina—Measures Affecting Imports of Footwear, Textiles, Apparel, and Other Items*, World Trade Organization, report of a WTO panel, 25 November 1997, WTO doc. WT/DS56/R, para. 5.3.
76. Ibid., para. 69.
77. Ibid., para. 70.
78. See Ibid., para. 74.

79. Joost Pauwelyn, "The Role of Public International Law in the WTO," at 569.
80. Ibid.
81. *Mexico Soft Drinks*, p. 23, para. 56.
82. Ibid., p. 33, para. 78. It should be noted that the appellate body carefully and correctly avoided phrasing its comments as its opinion on whether it or the WTO panel could, regardless of the *DSU*, entertain an argument for setting aside a WTO obligation based on the countermeasures doctrine.
83. *Minutes of the Meeting*, held in the Centre William Rappart, 24 March 2006, WTO doc. WT/DSB/M/208 (28 April 2006), p. 2, para. 7.
84. *Mexico Soft Drinks*, p. 32, para. 76.
85. See part II previously, chap. 10 (a).
86. *State Responsibility: Comments and Observations Received from Governments*, UN doc. A/CN.4/515, 19 March 2001, pp. 79–80.
87. Joost Pauwelyn, "The Role of Public International Law in the WTO," at 565.
88. Benedict Kingsburry, "Environment and Trade: The GATT/WTO Regime in the International Legal System," in *Environmental Regulation and Economic Growth*, edited by Alan E. Boyle, Clarendon Press, Oxford, 1994, p. 189, at 221.
89. One of those hints is the *Shrimp/Turtle Case* discussed in the next section in chap. 15 (e) of this part.
90. *United States—Restrictions on Imports of Tuna,* (*Tuna II*), report of a GATT panel, 20 May 1994, GATT doc. DS29/R, para. 3.10, reprinted in 33 I.L.M. 839 (1994), at 852.
91. *EC Paper on WTO and MEAs*, see supra endnote 68 of chap. 14, p. 2, para. 5.
92. Ibid., p. 3, para. 13. See also *United States—Standards for Reformulated and Conventional Gasoline*, report of the appellate body, WTO doc. WT/DS2/AB/R, 29 April 1996, p. 14, reprinted in 35 I.L.M. 603 (1996), at 621.
93. *EC Paper on WTO and MEAs*, p. 3, para. 14. The phrase "separate but equal" is rather unfortunate as it served as a mantra for racial discrimination in the United States from the 1896 case of *Plessy v. Ferguson* (163 U.S. 537, 16 S. Ct. 1138, 41 L Ed. 256), until the 1954 case of *Brown v. Board of Education* (347 U.S. 483; 74 S. Ct. 686; 98 L. Ed. 873).
94. *EC Paper on WTO and MEAs*, p. 3, para. 15.
95. See chap. 15 (e) of this part and *United States—Import Prohibition of Certain Shrimp and Shrimp Products*, recourse to article 21.5 by Malaysia, report of the panel, 15 June 2001 (hereafter referred to as *Shrimp/Turtle* panel II), WTO doc. WT/DS58/RW, p. 70, para. 5.19 and p. 99, para. 5.137.

96. *DSU*, article 3(2).
97. *2001 Draft Articles*, article 47.
98. In *Mexico Soft Drinks* (see endnote 32 of this chapter), Mexico argued that its actions were, in fact, countermeasures. Mexico did not get very far with that argument for various reasons. Since that case dealt with interpretation of para. (d) of article XX (not (b) or (g)), it provides little guidance here.
99. *United States—Restrictions on Imports of Tuna*, report of a GATT panel, 16 August 1991, not adopted, (hereafter referred to as *Tuna I*), para. 2.7, GATT doc. DS21/R, reprinted in 30 I.L.M. 1594 (1991), at 1599.
100. *Tuna I*, para. 1.1, at 1598 (page numbers refer to pages in I.L.M.).
101. *Tuna I*, para. 5.14, at 1618.
102. *Tuna I*, para. 5.19, at 1618.
103. *Tuna I*, para. 3.6, at 1601.
104. *Tuna I*, para. 5.29, at 1620 and para. 5.34, at 1621.
105. Marine Mammal Protection Act, P.L. 92–522, 86 Stat. 1027 (1972), as amended, mainly by P.L. 100–711, 102 Stat. 4755 (1988) and later by P.L. 101–627 at 104 Stat. 4467 (1990). Partly codified at 16 U.S.C. 1361ff.
106. *Marine Mammal Protection Act*, section 101(a)(2).
107. These other states were Venezuela, Vanuatu, Panama, and Ecuador. They later proved their compliance to the rules and were only affected briefly by the ban.
108. *United States—Restrictions on Imports of Tuna*, report of a GATT panel, 16 August 1991, (*Tuna I*), para. 2.7, GATT doc. DS21/R, reprinted in 30 I.L.M. 1594 (1991), at 1599.
109. *Tuna I*, para. 2.7, at 1599–1600.
110. *Tuna I*, para. 3.1, at 1601.
111. *Tuna I*, para. 2.10, at 1600.
112. GATT 1947, article III:1.
113. Ibid., article III:4.
114. *Tuna I*, para. 5.14, at 1618, italics added.
115. *Tuna I*, para. 5.14, at 1618.
116. GATT 1947, article XI(1).
117. *Tuna I*, para. 5.18, at 1618.
118. *Tuna I*, para. 5.22, at 1619.
119. *Tuna I*, para. 5.25, at 1619.
120. *Tuna I*, para. 5.26, at 1620.
121. *Tuna I*, para. 5.27, at 1620.

122. *Tuna I*, para. 5.28, at 1620.
123. See quote peviously from *Tuna I*, 30 I.L.M. 1594 (1991), at 1620.
124. *Tuna I*, para. 5.28, at 1620.
125. *Tuna I*, para. 5.28, at 1620.
126. *Tuna I*, para. 5.29, at 1620.
127. GATT 1947, article XX(g).
128. *Canada—Measures Affecting Exports of Unprocessed Herring and Salmon*, report of a GATT panel, adopted 22 March 1988, B.I.S.D. 35S/98/112, p. 114, para. 4.6.
129. *Tuna I*, para. 5.31, at 1620–1621
130. *Tuna I*, para. 5.31, at 1621.
131. *Tuna I*, para. 5.32, at 1621.
132. *Tuna I*, para. 5.33, at 1621.
133. *Tuna I*, para. 5.34, at 1621.
134. *United States—Restriction on Imports of Tuna*, Report of a GATT panel, 20 June 1994 (hereafter referred to as *Tuna II*), GATT doc. DS29/R, para. 1.1, reprinted in 33 I.L.M. 839 (1994), at 844.
135. Ibid., para. 3.2, at 850–851.
136. Ibid., paras. 2.12–2.15, at 849–850.
137. Ibid., para. 6.1, at 899.
138. Ibid., para. 1.1, at 844.
139. Embargo of nations that are engaged in tuna fishing in violation of United States standards regarding regulatory framework to prevent dolphin by-catch and implementation of such framework. See Ibid., paras. 2.9–2.11, at 847–848.
140. Ibid., para. 5.7, at 889. See also para. 3.6 at 851–852.
141. See Ibid., paras. 3.7–3.34, at 852–861.
142. Ibid., paras. 5.9–5.10, at 889–890.
143. Ibid., para. 3.10, at 852.
144. Ibid., para. 3.11, at 853.
145. Ibid., para. 3.13, at 853.
146. Ibid., para. 3.14, at 853.
147. Ibid., para. 3.14, at 853.
148. Ibid., para. 5.12, at 890.
149. Ibid.
150. Ibid., para. 5.12, at 891.
151. Ibid., para. 3.16, at 854.
152. Ibid., paras. 3.27–3.29, at 859–860. See opposite conclusion of the panel in *Tuna I*, based on the drafting history of article XX(b) in *Tuna I*, para. 5.26, 30 I.L.M. 1594 (1991), at 1620.

153. *Tuna II*, para. 5.17, at 892.
154. Ibid., para. 5.16, at 891.
155. Ibid., para. 5.20, at 893.
156. Ibid., para. 5.20, at 893.
157. *Canada—Measures Affecting the Exports of Unprocessed Herring and Salmon*, report of a GATT panel, adopted 22 March 1988, B.I.S.D. 35S/98/112, at 114, para. 4.6.
158. *Tuna II*, para. 5.22, at 893.
159. Ibid., paras. 5.23–5.24, at 893–894.
160. Ibid., para. 5.26, at 894.
161. Ibid., para. 5.26, at 894.
162. Ibid., paras. 5.26–5.27, at 894.
163. Ibid., para. 5.29, at 895.
164. Ibid., para. 5.29, at 895.
165. Ibid., para. 5.30, at 895.
166. Ibid., para. 5.33, at 896.
167. *United States—Section 337 of the Tariff Act of 1930*, report of a GATT panel, adopted 7 November 1989, L/6439, B.I.S.D. 36S/345.
168. *United States—Section 337 of the Tariff Act of 1930*, para. 5.26, at 392, cited in *Tuna II*, para. 5.35, at 896–897.
169. *Tuna II*, para. 5.36, at 897.
170. See Ibid., paras. 5.36–5.38, at 897.
171. Ibid., para. 5.36, at 897.
172. *United States—Import Prohibition of Certain Shrimp and Shrimp Products*, report of the WTO appellate body, 12 October 1998 (hereafter referred to as *Shrimp/Turtle I*), WTO doc. WT/DS58/AB/R, pp. 1–2, para. 1, reprinted in 38 I.L.M. 118 (1999).
173. Ibid., pp. 2–.3, para. 3, 38 I.L.M. 118 (1999), at 124.
174. *United States—Import Prohibition of Certain Shrimp and Shrimp Products*, World Trade Organization, report of the panel, 15 May 1998 (hereafter referred to as *Shrimp/Turtle panel I*), WTO doc. WT/DS58/R, p. 7, para. 3.1.
175. Ibid., p. 306, para. 8.1 and *Shrimp/Turtle I*, p. 76, para. 187, at 175.
176. See *United States—Import Prohibition of Certain Shrimp and Shrimp Products*, recourse to article 21.5 by Malaysia, report of the panel, 15 June 2001 (hereafter referred to as *Shrimp/Turtle panel II*), WTO doc. WT/DS58/RW.
177. Ibid., p. 100, para. 6.1.
178. *United States—Import Prohibition of Certain Shrimp and Shrimp Products*, recourse to article 21.5 by Malaysia, report of the appellate body,

22 October 2001, (hereafter referred to as *Shrimp/Turtle II*), WTO doc. WT/DS58/AB/RW, p. 50, para. 153.

179. *Shrimp/Turtle panel I*, p. 4, para. 2.6.
180. Ibid., p. 3, para. 2.5.
181. National Marine Fisheries Service, see http://www.nmfs.noaa.gov/pr/species/turtles/teds.htm (visited 13 January 2008).
182. Section 609, P.L. 101–1026, 16 U.S.C. § 1537.
183. *Shrimp/Turtle panel I*, p. 4, para. 2.7.
184. *Shrimp/Turtle panel I*, pp. 5–6, paras. 2.12–2.15.
185. *Shrimp/Turtle panel I*, p. 6, para. 2.14.
186. *Convention on International Trade in Endangered Species of Wild Fauna and Flora* (CITES), concluded at Washington 3 March 1973, entered into force 1 July 1975, 993 U.N.T.S. 243, reprinted in 12 I.L.M. 1085 (1973) and 5A Weston V.H.10. See also *Shrimp/Turtle panel I*, p. 3, para. 2.3.
187. *Shrimp/Turtle panel I*, p. 304, para. 7.58.
188. *Shrimp/Turtle panel I*, p. 306, para. 8.1.
189. Gregory Shaffer, "International Trade—WTO—Quantitative Restriction-Environmental Protection-Endangered Species—U.S. Import Ban on Shrimps," *American Journal of International Law* 93 (1999), at 509.
190. *Notification of an Appeal by the United States*, 13 July 1998, WTO doc. WT/DS58/11.
191. *Shrimp/Turtle I*, p. 34, para. 98, 38 I.L.M. 118 (1999), at 145.
192. *United States—Standards for Reformulated and Conventional Gasoline*, World Trade Organization, Report of the appellate body, 29 April 1996, WTO doc. WT/DS2/AB/R (hereafter referred to as the *Gasoline Case*).
193. Similar to the panel decision in *Tuna II*, except that the panel found that the measures taken did not meet the requirements of the relevant subparas. of article XX so there was no need to address the second tier, the preamble of the article. See *Tuna II*, para. 5.27 at 894 and para. 5.39, at 897.
194. *Gasoline Case,* p. 22, cited in *Shrimp/Turtle I*, p. 44, para. 118, at 152.
195. GATT 1994, article XX.
196. See *Shrimp/Turtle I*, p. 42, para. 115, 38 I.L.M. 118 (1999), at 151.
197. Ibid., p. 43, para. 116, 38 I.L.M. 118 (1999), at 151.
198. Ibid., p. 43, para. 116, 38 I.L.M. 118 (1999), at 151.
199. See GATT 1994, article XX(g).
200. *Convention on Conservation of Migratory Species of Wild Animals*, concluded at Bonn 23 June 1979, entered into force 1 November 1983, 1651 U.N.T.S. 333, reprinted in 19 I.L.M. 15 (1980).

201. *United States—Prohibition of Imports of Tuna and Tuna Products from Canada*, report of a GATT panel adopted 22 February 1982, B.I.S.D. 29S/91, para. 4.9 and *Canada—Measures Affecting Exports of Unprocessed Herring and Salmon*, report of a GATT panel, adopted 22 March 1988, B.I.S.D. 35S/98/112, para. 4.4.
202. *Shrimp/Turtle I*, p. 50, para. 133, 38 I.L.M. 118 (1999), at 157.
203. Ibid., p. 51, para. 134, 38 I.L.M. 118 (1999), at 157.
204. Ibid., p. 51, para. 134, 38 I.L.M. 118 (1999), at 157.
205. Ibid., p. 51, para. 135, 38 I.L.M. 118 (1999), at 157.
206. Ibid., p. 52, para. 137, 38 I.L.M. 118 (1999), at 158.
207. *Gasoline Case,* p. 19, cited in *Shrimp/Turtle Case I*, p. 52, para. 136, 38 I.L.M. 118 (1999), at 158.
208. Ibid.
209. *Shrimp/Turtle I*, p. 52, para. 138, 38 I.L.M. 118 (1999), at 158.
210. Ibid., p. 52, para. 138, 38 I.L.M. 118 (1999), at 158.
211. Ibid., p. 53, para. 140, 38 I.L.M. 118 (1999), at 159.
212. Ibid., p. 53, para. 141, 38 I.L.M. 118 (1999), at 159.
213. Ibid., p. 54, para. 142, 38 I.L.M. 118 (1999), at 159.
214. See *Gasoline Case,* pp. 20–21.
215. *Shrimp/Turtle I*, p. 54, para. 144, 38 I.L.M. 118 (1999), at 160.
216. Ibid., p. 55, para. 145, 38 I.L.M. 118 (1999), at 160.
217. Ibid., p. 55, para. 145, 38 I.L.M. 118 (1999), at 160.
218. See *Shrimp/Turtle panel I*, pp. 297–299, paras. 7.44–7.49.
219. GATT 1994, article XX.
220. *Shrimp/Turtle I*, p. 75, para. 184, 38 I.L.M. 118 (1999), at 174.
221. Ibid., p. 63, para. 161, 38 I.L.M. 118 (1999), at 166.
222. Ibid., p. 64, para. 163, 38 I.L.M. 118 (1999), at 167.
223. Ibid., p. 65, para. 164, 38 I.L.M. 118 (1999), at 167.
224. Ibid., p. 65, para. 165, 38 I.L.M. 118 (1999), at 167.
225. Ibid., pp. 67–69, paras. 168–169, 38 I.L.M. 118 (1999), at 169–170.
226. Ibid., p. 71, para. 173, 38 I.L.M. 118 (1999), at 171.
227. Ibid., pp. 71–72, para. 174, 38 I.L.M. 118 (1999), at 172.
228. Ibid., p. 72, para. 175, 38 I.L.M. 118 (1999), at 172.
229. Ibid., p. 72, para. 176, 38 I.L.M. 118 (1999), at 172.
230. Ibid., pp. 73–74, para. 177, 38 I.L.M. 118 (1999), at 172–173.
231. Ibid., pp. 73–74, para. 180, 38 I.L.M. 118 (1999), at 173.
232. Ibid., p. 74, para. 180, 38 I.L.M. 118 (1999), at 173.
233. Ibid., p. 75, para. 184, 38 I.L.M. 118 (1999), at 174.

234. *Minutes of Meeting*, held in the Centre William Rappart on 6 November 1998, WTO doc. WT/DSB/M/50 (14 December 1998) p. 18, para. 1(a).
235. *Minutes of Meeting*, held in the Centre William Rappart on 25 November 1998, WTO doc. WT/DSB/M/51 (22 January 1999) p. 7, para. 3(a) and *Shrimp/Turtle panel II*, p. 6, para. 2.19.
236. *Shrimp/Turtle panel II*, p. 6, para. 2.20.
237. *Revised Guidelines for the Implementation of Section 609 of Public Law 101–162 Relating to the Protection of Sea Turtles in Shrimp Trawl Fishing Operations*, U.S. Department of State, Federal Register vol. 64, no. 130, 8 July 1999, Public Notice 3086, pp. 36946–36952.
238. *United States—Import Prohibition of Certain Shrimp and Shrimp Products*, status report by the United States, 15 July 1999, WTO doc. WT/DS58/15, p. 1.
239. See *United States—Import Prohibition of Certain Shrimp and Shrimp Products*, status reports by the United States, 15 July 1999, 8 September 1999, 15 October 1999, 9 November 1999, and 17 January 2000, WTO doc. WT/DS58/15, and addendums 1–4.
240. *Shrimp/Turtle panel II*, p. 17, para. 3.46.
241. *United States—Import Prohibition of Certain Shrimp and Shrimp Products*, recourse by Malaysia to article 21.5 of the *DSU*, 13 October 2000, communication from Malaysia, WTO doc. WT/DS/58/17.
242. *Shrimp/Turtle II*, p. 3, para. 8.
243. *Shrimp/Turtle panel II*, p. 100, para. 6.1.
244. *United States—Import Prohibition of Certain Shrimp and Shrimp Products*, notification of an appeal by Malaysia, 23 July 2001, WTO doc. WT/DS/58/20.
245. *Shrimp/Turtle II*, p. 32, para. 113.
246. Ibid., p. 50, para. 153.
247. Ibid., p. 35, para. 119.
248. Ibid., p. 36, para. 122.
249. Ibid., p. 37, para. 123.
250. Ibid., pp. 39–42, paras. 128–133. See also *Shrimp/Turtle panel II*, pp. 81–86, paras. 5.69–5.88.
251. *Inter-American Convention for the Protection and Conservation of Sea Turtles,* concluded at Caracas, 1 December 1996, entered into force 2 May 2001.
252. *Shrimp/Turtle II*, p. 42, para. 133.
253. Ibid., pp. 42–43, para. 134.
254. *Shrimp/Turtle I*, p. 45, para. 121, cited in *Shrimp/Turtle II*, p. 44, para. 137.
255. *Shrimp/Turtle II*, p. 45, para. 140.

256. Ibid., p. 46, para. 144.
257. Ibid., p. 46, para. 142.
258. *Shrimp/Turtle panel II*, pp. 88–89, para. 5.94.
259. *Shrimp/Turtle II*, p. 46, para. 144.
260. *Shrimp/Turtle panel II*, p. 88, para. 5.92.
261. Ibid., pp. 89–90, para. 5.96–5.97.
262. Ibid., p. 90, para. 5.98.
263. Ibid., p. 90, para. 5.100.
264. Ibid., p. 91, para. 5.104.
265. Ibid., pp. 93–95, paras. 5.112–5.120.
266. Ibid., pp. 96–98 , paras. 5.126–5.136.
267. *Shrimp/Turtle II*, p. 49, para. 149.
268. Ibid., p. 48, para. 148.
269. Ibid., p. 50, para. 153.
270. Bret Puls, "The Murky Waters of International Environmental Jurisprudence: A Critique of Recent WTO Holding in the Shrimp/Turtle Controversy," *Minnesota Journal of Global Trade* 8 (1999), at 376.
271. Brett Grosko, "Just When Is It That a Unilateral Trade Ban Satisfies the GATT: The WTO Shrimp and Shrimp Products Case," *Environmental Lawyer* 5 (1999), at 819.
272. *Shrimp/Turtle I*, p. 75, para. 185, 38 I.L.M. 118 (1999), at 174.
273. See *Shrimp/Turtle I*, pp. 65–70, paras. 166–172, 38 I.L.M. 118 (1999), at 168–171.
274. *2001 Draft Articles on State Responsibility*, (hereafter referred to as *2001 Draft Articles*), report of the International Law Commission, fifty third session (23 April–1 June and 2 July–10 August 2001), UN doc. A/56/10, Yearbook of the International Law Commission, (hereafter referred to as *ILC 2001 Report*), p. 26 et seq., article 52(1)(b).
275. *1996 Draft Articles on State Responsibility*, report of the International Law Commission on the work of its forty eighth session, 6 May to 26 July 1996, UN doc. A/51/10, p. 125 et seq., article 48(1).
276. *2000 Draft Articles on State Responsibility*, report of the Drafting Committee, UN doc. A/CN.4/600, 21 August 2000, article 53(4).
277. *Shrimp/Turtle panel II*, p. 26, para. 3.99. See also *Shrimp/Turtle II*, p. 7, para. 20.
278. *Shrimp/Turtle II*, p. 34, para. 116.
279. See *Shrimp/Turtle II*, pp. 42–43, para. 134. This conclusion is implied in the appellate body's decision to accept as sufficient, for the purposes of article XX, ongoing good faith negotiation.
280. *2001 Draft Articles*, article 47.

281. *ILC 2001 Report*, p. 124, para. 1 of the commentary to article 47.
282. *Certain Phosphate Lands in Nauru* (preliminary objections) (*Nauru v. Australia*), International Court of Justice, judgment of 26 June 1992, 1992 I.C.J 240, at 258–259, para. 48.
283. Spain is a member of the European Community, which has competence over fisheries of its member states.
284. Andrew Serdy, "See You in Port: Australia and New Zealand as Third Parties in the Dispute Between Chile and the European Community over Chile's Denial of Port Access to Spanish Vessels Fishing for Swordfish on the High Seas," *Melbourne Journal of International Law* 3, no. 1 (2002), at 85 and footnote 31. The case was later removed from the arbitral tribunal and resubmitted to an ITLOS special chamber under article 15 of the ITLOS Statute, see *Conservation and Sustainable Exploitation of Swordfish Stock in the South-Eastern Pacific Ocean* (*Chile v. the European Community*), International Tribunal for the Law of the Sea, case no. 7, order of 20 December 2000, p. 2, para. 2 (hereafter referred to as *Swordfish Conservation Case*).
285. The European Community requested consultation in April 2000, see *Chile—Measures Affecting the Transit and Importation of Swordfish*, request for consultation by the European Communities, 26 April 2000, WTO doc. WT/DS193/1.
286. *Chile—Measures Affecting the Transit and Importation of Swordfish*, request for the establishment of a panel by the European Communities, 7 November 2000, WTO doc. WT/DS193/2.
287. *Chile—Measures Affecting the Transit and Importation of Swordfish*, arrangement between the European Communities and Chile, 6 April 2001, WTO doc. WT/DS193/3 and latest suspension from 17 December 2007, WT/DS193/3/Add.4 (hereafter referred to as the *Chile/EC Arrangement*) and *Swordfish Conservation Case*, order of 15 March 2001, and the latest order of this kind, order of 30 November 2007, suspending the case until 1 January 2009.
288. *TBR Proceedings Concerning Chilean Practices Affecting Transit of Swordfish in Chilean Ports, Report to the Trade Barriers Regulation Committee*, European Commission, March 1999, p. 9, para. 3.1, http://trade.ec.europa.eu/doclib/docs/2004/october/tradoc_112193.pdf (visited 13 January 2008), (hereafter referred to as the *TBR Report*).
289. *TBR Report*, pp. 9–10, para. 3.1.
290. Ibid., p. 10, para. 3.1 and p. 16, para. 4.1.
291. Ibid., p. 10, para. 3.1, and note 6.

292. Ibid., p. 10, para. 3.1.
293. Mark Clough, "The WTO Dispute Settlement System: A Practitioner Perspective," *Fordham International Law Journal* 24, no. 1–2 (2000), at 258.
294. *General Law of Fisheries and Aquaculture*, law no. 18.892 1989, (Ley General de Pesca y Acuicultura) consolidated with amendments by presidential decree no. 430 (28 September 1991), article 165. See also *TBR Report*, p. 10, para. 3.1, and note 7.
295. *TBR Report*, pp. 10–11, para. 3.1.
296. Ibid., p. 33, para. 5.1.1.5.
297. *General Law of Fisheries and Aquaculture*, article 165(3).
298. *TBR Report*, p. 29, para. 5.1.1.
299. Swordfish and horse-eye jack, see *TBR Report*, p. 29, note 27.
300. *TBR Report*, p. 33, para. 5.1.1.5.
301. *Chile—Measures Affecting the Transit and Importation of Swordfish,* Request for consultation by the European Communities, 26 April 2000, WTO doc. WT/DS193/1.
302. *Chile—Measures Affecting the Transit and Importation of Swordfish*, Request for the Establishment of a Panel by the European Communities, 7 November 2000, WTO doc. WT/DS193/2.
303. Andrew Serdy, "See You in Port: Australia and New Zealand as Third Parties in the Dispute Between Chile and the European Community over Chile's Denial of Port Access to Spanish Vessels Fishing for Swordfish on the High Seas," at 85.
304. *Swordfish Conservation Case*, order of 20 December 2000, p. 2, para. 2.
305. *TBR Report*, p. 42, para. 5.1.2.2.
306. Ibid., p. 42, para. 5.1.2.2.
307. Ibid., p. 42, para. 5.1.2.2.
308. Ibid., p. 42, para. 5.1.2.2.
309. Ibid., p. 43, para. 5.1.2.2.
310. Ibid., p. 43, para. 5.1.2.2.
311. *Swordfish Conservation Case*, p. 2–3, para. 3(a) and (b).
312. Ibid., p. 3, para. 3(c).
313. Ibid., p. 3, para. 3(e).
314. Ibid., p. 3, para. 3(f) and 3(g).
315. *Minutes of Meeting on 17 November 2000*, p. 19, paras. 101–102.
316. Ibid., p. 19, para. 101.
317. Ibid., pp. 19–20, para. 103.
318. Ibid., p. 20, para. 104.
319. Ibid.

320. Ibid., p. 20, para. 106.
321. Ibid.
322. *TBR Report*, p. 43, para. 5.1.2.2. The report of the appellate body in *Mexico Soft Drinks* would support this argument, see *Mexico Soft Drinks*, p. 24, para. 57. See also on this issue Andrew Serdy, "See You in Port: Australia and New Zealand as Third Parties in the Dispute Between Chile and the European Community over Chile's Denial of Port Access to Spanish Vessels Fishing for Swordfish on the High Seas," at 90.
323. *Minutes of Meeting on 17 November 2000*, p. 21, para. 109.
324. Ibid., p. 21, para. 109.
325. Ibid., p. 21, para. 111.
326. Ibid., p. 21, para. 112.
327. Ibid.
328. Ibid.
329. *Swordfish Conservation Case*, order of 15 March 2001, p. 2, para. 4. See also *Swordfish Conservation Case*, order of 30 November 2007, suspending the proceeding until 1 January 2009.
330. *Chile/EC Arrangement*, see supra endnote 287 of this chapter.
331. Ibid., p. 2.
332. Ibid., p. 3.
333. *Minutes of Meeting on 17 November 2000*, p. 20, para. 106.

Chapter 16

Conclusions on Case Studies

The case studies examined in this part reveal not only a number of problems but also a few opportunities for the application of the countermeasures doctrine. One problem that stands out in particular is the lack of clear substantive legal obligation to conserve and protect the environment. Without an obligation not to harvest tuna in a way harmful for dolphins, or not to harvest shrimp in a manner dangerous for sea turtles, the argument of countermeasures will be futile. It is notable that the cases that seem most compatible to the countermeasures doctrine involve the law of the sea, that is, high seas fisheries. Even though the limits on the right to fish in the high seas are not its clearest parts, the law of the sea regime has developed further than most other regimes related to environmental protection.

The absence of the argument of countermeasure from these cases is apparent. The reasons might be many. First, out of six cases reviewed in this part, five of them are argued in a legal framework that seems on the surface not particularly susceptible to the countermeasures doctrine, that is, the WTO framework and the EEA framework. The only case that never entered that sphere was the halibut dispute between Canada and the EC, a dispute that was short and brutal but had a fortunate ending, at least for a while. As was suggested in relation to that dispute, the only argument for countermeasures would have to be based on the analysis of the systemic inability of the EC fisheries policy to comply with obligations under *UNCLOS*, an argument that would require political and legal preparation of mammoth proportions.

Another reason why the countermeasures doctrine was not more visible in the reviewed cases might be the lack of clarity of the doctrine. Legal advisers might find themselves on more solid legal grounds by taking a more traditional path, grounded in the treaty law and jurisprudence of the relevant regime. The conclusion of the *ILC Draft Articles on State Responsibility* and the possible codification of the document in the distant future might bring the countermeasurses doctrine closer to the surface and make it more acceptable, even for the more conservative and cautious legal advisers.

On a more positive note for the countermeasures doctrine, it was suggested earlier in this book that the WTO panels probably have to take into consideration, when analyzing the applicability of and compliance with WTO rules, whether a violation of obligations under WTO-covered agreements can be justified with reference to the countermeasures doctrine. Therefore, states taking countermeasures in the form of trade restrictions otherwise prohibited under WTO rules should be able to refer to the doctrine before a WTO panel or the appellate body, either independently or through an interpretation of Article XX that, due to the presence of an international violation, might be more amenable to accept measures that would, in the absence of such violation, not be justifiable under Article XX. Although this suggestion is, however, untested as of yet, the countermeasures doctrine is already present in the house of the WTO and has been invited to the table when the use of measures under Article XX are discussed. It remains to be seen whether it will be allowed to speak or if its status is of an observer only.

General Conclusions

Although this book is structured as to spell out the relevant conclusions at its earlier pages—and leaving the reader here with the taste of shrimp and swordfish in the mouth would not be such a bad idea—a few concluding remarks might, nevertheless, be appropriate.

Countermeasures are a tricky tool of international relations. They can be disruptive and affect international goodwill, trade relations, and cultural and educational relations. Further, they can lead state relations down a spiral of hostilities that may be painful to exit. There is, therefore, no surprise that states have preferred more cooperative methods in resolving its disputes. The predominance of such methods in the international system is not that different from the domestic legal system. Individuals and legal persons also have strong tendencies to prefer nonconfrontational methods of dispute resolution; the other tracks are time consuming, expensive, and often not good for business. And this it true regardless of the access to courts or arbitration with compulsory jurisdiction and the subsequent enforcement mechanism of a developed domestic legal system.

The lack of a compulsory adjudication and enforcement system in the international legal system leaves states with fewer options than an individual has in its domestic legal system. When consultations, negotiations, and one-on-one lunches at the UN cafeteria have turned fruitless, or when the domestic political situation requires immediate action, this lack of options will direct states toward unilateral measures despite the flaws of such a method as a tool to resolve disputes. The countermeasures doctrine does not create this method; it is an attempt by customary international law to tame this animal, prevent abuses, and to ensure that unilateral measures, such as countermeasures, are truly a last resort but, nevertheless, are still available when the dire need arises.

No one really denies the fact that the political importance of environmental protection is rising. Robert D. Kaplan wrote in his provocative book, *The Coming Anarchy*, that it was "time to understand 'the environment' for what it is: *the* national-security issue of the early twenty-first century."[1] Kaplan was not the first one to view environmental threats through the security prism. When the end of the Cold War was approaching, the Soviet foreign minister gave a speech at the UN General Assembly about a new concept of security. He said:

> It is perhaps for the first time that we have seen the stark reality of the threat to our environment—a second front fast approaching and gaining an urgency equal to that of the nuclear-and-space threat. For the first time, we have clearly realized that in the absence of any global control man's so-called peaceful constructive activity is turning into a global aggression against the very foundations of life on Earth.[2]

With the Soviet Army still in Afghanistan, work on the Strategic Defense Initiative, often called Star Wars, underway, and the Cold War not yet being over, a statement like this coming from the Soviet foreign minister was quite remarkable. Richard N. Gardner[3] called it "unprecedented Soviet proposals," and although he was suspicious about anything with a Soviet label, he thought it "may be shaped into outcomes in the interest of both superpowers and all U.N. members."[4]

In the academic sphere, the concept of environmental security was not a novelty in 1988. Already in 1977, Lester Brown had argued that the defense of a nation must focus on preserving the biological systems. After all, nature is the resource for the economic well-being of a nation and should be of concern to all and not only the environmentalists.[5] Awarding the 2007 Nobel Peace Prize to Al Gore and the Intergovernmental Panel on Climate Change (IPCC) is a clear indicator of the elevation of the importance of environmental protection above and beyond science and grass root activism; and, even more importantly, it is evidence of its link to conflict prevention. There can be many reasons for such elevation. One of them could be the increased usage of the planet's resources, such as its fossil fuels, forests, fish stocks, water, and arable land. Another could be the improved scientific data predicting the slippery slope down that this increased usage could lead mankind. A third reason might be the increased influence of environmental NGOs on the political decision-making process, for example, through electronic media. This change should not just been seen as an opportunity for states whose international environmental rights have been violated, but it is also something states should have in mind when they consider policies or actions that are less concerned about the future of our planet.

Natural resources can also be identified as values relevant to the human existence or level of civilization, both the opportunity to exploit the resources and the need to keep them unspoiled. Depletion of fish stocks can cause significant disruption in the social fabric of a country; air pollution can cause serious health problems and increase premature mortality. Water pollution and water scarcity causes deaths and undermines political stability. When these values of such importance are threatened, the variety of politically viable options changes and patience for consultation and negotiation might be diminished. This does not mean that a state is entitled to, in response to other states' violation of their international environmental obligations, exercise its right to "exhaust its resources, and nobly shed the last drop of its blood,"[6] as Vattel's words were once so elegantly translated. However, states might be inclined to address environmental threats caused by another state's violation of their international environmental obligations as they would deal with security threats; the decision makers might lean toward realist approaches and prefer unilateral remedies over cooperation to resolve an imminent problem threatening important environmental interests.

All of this suggests increased chances that the protection of environmental rights will not just be on the agenda but will be there with higher priority than in the last 50 years. Its political value has increased; its importance for humanity has become clearer. To refer again to the words of Louis Henkin quoted at the beginning of part I; as any law, the countermeasures doctrine is politics[7] and should be designed and allowed to promote a political value we cherish—the environment.

Endnotes

1. Robert D. Kaplan, *The Coming Anarchy: Shattering the Dream of the Post Cold War*, Random House, New York, 2000, p. 19.
2. "Text of Remarks Prepared for Delivery by Soviet Foreign Minister Eduard A. Shevardnadze before the 43rd Session of the United Nations," September 27, 1988, *Federal News Service*, Section: News Makers & Policy Makers.
3. Richard N. Gardner was, at that time, a professor of international law at Columbia University and the U.S. co-chairman of a newly established Soviet-American working group on the strengthening of the United Nations.
4. Richard N. Gardner, "All That Soviet Activity at the UN Is Something U.S. May Need to Match," *Los Angeles Times*, 29 September 1988, Section: Metro; part 2; p. 7; column 3; Op-Ed Desk.
5. Lester Brown, *Redefining National Security*, Worldwatch paper no. 14. Washington, D.C.: Worldwatch Institute, 1977, p. 7.
6. Emmerich de Vattel, *Le Droit des Gens* or *Principes de la Loi Naturelle, Appliqués à la Conduite et aux Affaires des Nations et des Souverains* (1758), book II, chap. xviii, as cited in Lauterpacht, *The Function of Law in the International Community*, p. 9.
7. Louis Henkin, *International Law: Politics and Values*, Martinus Nijhoff Publishers, Dordrecht, Boston, London, 1995, p. 4.

Bibliography

Treaties and International and Domestic Documents (Chronological Order)

(a) Multilateral Instruments

Locarno Treaties of 16 October, concluded at Locarno, Switzerland 16 October 1925, entered into force 14 September 1926, 54 L.N.T.S. 289, 303, 315, 327, 341, 353, and 359.

General Treaty for Renunciation of War as an Instrument of National Policy, concluded at Paris, France 27 August 1928, entered into force 24 July 1929, 46 Stat. 2343.

Anti-War Treaty of Non-Aggression and Conciliation, concluded at Rio de Janeiro, Brazil 10 October 1933, entered into force 13 November 1935, 49 Stat. 3363, T.S. 906.

Charter of the United Nations, concluded at San Francisco, California 26 June 1946, entered into force 24 October 1946, 59 Stat. 1031, T.S. 993, 3 Bevans 1153.

Statute of the International Court of Justice, concluded at San Francisco, California 26 June 1946, entered into force 24 October 1946, 59 Stat. 1055, T.S. 993, 3 Bevans 1179.

General Agreement on Tariffs and Trade signed in Geneva, Switzerland 30 October 1947, entered into force on 1 January 1948, 55 U.N.T.S. 187.

Inter-American Treaty of Reciprocal Assistance, concluded at Rio De Janeiro, Brazil 2 September 1947, entered into force 3 December 1948, *OAS Treaty Series*, nos. 8 and 61, 21 U.N.T.S. 93.

Treaty on Social and Cultural Collaboration and Collective Self-Defence, concluded at Brussels, Belgium 17 March 1948, entered into force 25 August 1948, Department of State Publication 6446.

Charter of the Organization of American States, concluded at Bogota, Colombia 30 April 1948, entered into force 13 December 1951, 119 U.N.T.S. 3.

International Convention on the Intergovernmental Maritime Consultative Organization, concluded at Geneva, Switzerland 6 March 1948, entered into force on 17 March 1958, 289 U.N.T.S. 3.

North Atlantic Treaty, concluded at Washington, D.C., 4 April 1949, entered into force 24 April 1949, 63 Stat. 2241, T.I.A.S. 1964, 4 Bevans 824.

Convention for the Amelioration of the Condition of the Wounded and Sick in Armed Forces in the Field (First Geneva Convention), concluded at Geneva, Switzerland 12 August 1949, entered into force 21 October 1950, 75 U.N.T.S. 31.

Convention for the Amelioration of the Condition of Wounded, Sick, and Shipwrecked Members of Armed Forces at Sea (Second Geneva Convention), concluded at Geneva, Switzerland 12 August 1949, entered into force 21 October 1950, 75 U.N.T.S. 85.

Convention Relative to the Treatment of Prisoners of War (Third Geneva Convention), concluded at Geneva, Switzerland 12 August 1949, entered into force 21 October 1950, 75 U.N.T.S. 135.

Convention Relative to the Protection of Civilian Persons in Time of War (Fourth Geneva Convention), concluded at Geneva, Switzerland 12 August 1949, entered into force 21 October 1950, 75 U.N.T.S. 287.

European Convention for the Protection of Human Rights and Fundamental Freedoms, concluded at Rome, Italy 4 November 1950, entered into force 3 September 1953, 213 U.N.T.S. 221.

International Convention for the Prevention of Pollution of the Sea by Oil, concluded at London, U.K. 12 May 1954, entered into force 26 July 1958, 327 U.N.T.S. 3.

Convention on the Territorial Sea and the Contiguous Zone, concluded at Geneva, Switzerland 29 April 1958, entered into force 10 September 1964, 516 U.N.T.S. 205.

Convention on the High Seas, concluded at Geneva, Switzerland 29 April 1958, entered into force 30 September 1962, 450 U.N.T.S. 11.

Convention on Fishing and Conservation of the Living Resources of the High Seas, concluded at Geneva, Switzerland 29 April 1958, entered into force 20 March 1966, 559 U.N.T.S. 285.

Convention on the Continental Shelf, concluded at Geneva, Switzerland 29 April 1958, entered into force 10 June 1964, 449 U.N.T.S. 311.

Convention on Third Party Liability in the Field of Nuclear Energy, concluded at Paris, France 29 July 1960, entered into force 1 April 1968, 956 U.N.T.S. 251.

Vienna Convention on Diplomatic Relations, concluded at Vienna, Austria 18 April 1961, entered into force 24 April 1964, 500 U.N.T.S. 95.

International Covenant on Civil and Political Rights, concluded at New York, U.S. 16 December 1966, entered into force 23 March 1976, 999 U.N.T.S. 171.

Vienna Convention on the Law of Treaties, concluded at Vienna, Austria 23 May 1969, entered into force 27 January 1988, 1155 U.N.T.S. 331.

American Convention on Human Rights, concluded at San Jose, Costa Rica, 22 November 1969, entered into force 18 July 1978, O.A.S. Official Records OEA/Ser. K/XVI/1.1, doc. 65, rev. 1, corr. 1, reprinted in 9 I.L.M. 101 (1970).

International Convention Relating to Intervention on the High Seas in Cases of Oil Pollution Casualties, concluded at Brussels, Belgium 29 November 1969, entered into force 6 May 1975, 26 U.S.T. 765, T.I.A.S. 8068.

International Convention on Civil Liability for Oil Pollution Damage, concluded at Brussels, Belgium 29 November 1969, entered into force 19 June 1975, 973 U.N.T.S. 3.

Montreal Convention for the Suppression of Unlawful Acts Against the Safety of Civil Aviation, concluded at Montreal, Canada on 23 September 1971, entered into force on 26 January 1973, 974 U.N.T.S. 177.

Convention Relating to Civil Liability in the Field of Maritime Carriage of Nuclear Material, concluded at Brussels, Belgium 17 December 1971, entered into force 15 July 1975, 974 U.N.T.S. 255.

Stockholm Declaration of the United Nations Conference on the Human Environment, adopted by the *UN Conference on the Human Environment* at Stockholm, Sweden 16 June 1972, UN doc. A/CONF.48/14/Rev. 1 (1973), reprinted in 11 I.L.M. 1416 (1972).

Convention on the Prevention of Maritime Pollution by Dumping of Wastes and Other Matter, concluded at Washington, D.C., U.S., London, Mexico City, and Moscow 29 December 1972, entered into force 30 August 1975, 1046 U.N.T.S. 120.

Convention on International Trade in Endangered Species of Wild Fauna and Flora (*CITES*), concluded at Washington, D.C., 3 March 1973, entered into force 1 July 1975, 993 U.N.T.S. 243, reprinted in 12 I.L.M. 1085 (1973) and 5A Weston V.H.10.

International Convention for the Prevention of Pollution from Ships, concluded at London 2 November 1973, enacted by *Protocol Relating to the International Convention for the Prevention of Pollution from Ships*, (MARPOL 73/78) concluded at London, U.K. 17 February 1978, entered into force 2 October 1983, I.M.C.I. doc. TSPP/CONF/11, 1341 U.N.T.S. 3.

Convention for the Prevention of Marine Pollution from Land-Based Sources, concluded at Paris, France 4 June 1974, entered into force 6 May 1978, reprinted in 13 I.L.M. 352 (1974) and Weston V.F.18.

Additional Protocol to the Geneva Conventions of 12 August 1949, and Relating to the Protection of Victims of International Armed Conflicts, (*Protocol I*) concluded at Geneva, Switzerland 8 June 1977, entered into force 7 December 1978, 1125 U.N.T.S. 3.

Convention of Future Multilateral Co-operation in the Northwest Atlantic Fisheries, *Official Journal of the European Communities*, L 378, 30 December 1978, and *Canada Treaty Series 1979*, No. 11.

Convention on Conservation of Migratory Species of Wild Animals, concluded at Bonn, Germany 23 June 1979, entered into force 1 November 1983, 1651 U.N.T.S. 333, reprinted in 19 I.L.M. 15 (1980).

Convention on Long-Range Transboundary Air Pollution, concluded at Geneva, Switzerland 13 November 1979, entered into force 16 March 1983, 1302 U.N.T.S. 217, reprinted in 18 ILM 1442 (1979).

United Nations Convention on the Law of the Sea, concluded at Montego Bay, Jamaica 10 December 1982, entered into force 16 November 1994, 1833 U.N.T.S. 3, reprinted in 21 I.L.M. 1261 (1982).

Convention for the Protection and Development of Marine Environment of the Wider Caribbean Region, concluded at Cartagena, Colombia 24 March 1983, entered into force 11 October 1986, T.I.A.S. 11085.

Vienna Convention for the Protection of the Ozone Layer, concluded at Vienna, Austria 22 March 1985, entered into force 22 September 1988, 1513 U.N.T.S., UNEP doc. IG.53/5323, T.I.A.S. 11097, reprinted in 26 I.L.M. 1529 (1987), 5 Weston V.E.5.

Protocol to the 1979 Convention on Long-Range Transboundary Air Pollution on the Reduction of Sulphur Emission or Their Transboundary Fluxes by at Least 30 Per Cent, concluded at Helsinki, Finland 8 July 1985, entered into force 2 September 1987, 1480 U.N.T.S. 215.

Montreal Protocol on Substances That Deplete the Ozone Layer, concluded at Montreal, Canada 16 September 1987, entered into force 1 January 1989, reprinted in 26 I.L.M. 1550 (1987) and 5 Weston V.E.9.

Protocol to the 1979 Convention on Long-Range Transboundary Air Pollution Concerning the Control of Emission of Nitrogen Oxides or Their Transboundary Fluxes, concluded at Sofia, Bulgaria 31 October 1988, entered into force 14 February 1991, 1593 U.N.T.S. 287.

Protocol to the 1979 Long-Range Transboundary Air Pollution Concerning the Control of Emission of Nitrogen Oxides or Their Transboundary Fluxes, concluded at Sofia, Bulgaria 31 October 1988, entered into force 14 February 1991, reprinted in 28 I.L.M. 212 (1989) and Weston V.E.10.

Convention for the Prohibition of Fishing with Long Driftnets in the South Pacific, concluded at Wellington, New Zealand 23 November 1989, entered into force 17 May 1991, reprinted in 29 I.L.M. 1454 (1990).

Basel Convention on the Control of Transboundary Movements of Hazardous Wastes and Their Disposals, concluded at Basel, Switzerland 22 March 1989, entered into force 5 May 1992, 1673 U.N.T.S. 57.

Convention on the Protection and Use of Transboundary Watercourses and International Lakes, concluded at Helsinki, Finland 17 March 1992, entered into force 6 October 1996, doc. ENVWA/R.53 and add.1.

Agreement Establishing the EFTA Surveillance Authority and the EFTA Court, concluded at Oporto, Portugal 2 May 1992, entered into force 1 January 1994, *Official Journal of the European Communities*, 1994 L344/1.

Agreement on the European Economic Area, concluded in Oporto, Portugal 2 May 1992, entered into force 1 January 1994, *Official Journal of the European Communities*, 1994 L1/3.

United Nations Framework Convention on Climate Change, concluded at Rio De Janeiro, Brazil 9 May 1992, entered into force 21 March 1994, 1771 U.N.T.S. 107, reprinted in 31 I.L.M. 849 (1992).

Convention on Biological Diversity, concluded at Rio De Janeiro, Brazil 5 June 1992, entered into force 29 December 1993, 1760 U.N.T.S. 79, reprinted in 31 I.L.M. 818 (1992).

Convention for the Protection of the Marine Environment of the North-east Atlantic, concluded at Paris, France 22 September 1992, entered into force 25 March 1998, reprinted in 32 I.L.M. 1069 (1993).

Convention for the Protection of the Marine Environment of the North-east Atlantic (*OSPAR*), concluded at Paris, France 22 September 1992, entered into force 25 March 1998, reprinted in 32 I.L.M. 1069 (1993).

Convention for the Conservation of Southern Bluefin Tuna, concluded at Canberra, Australia 10 May 1993, entered into force on 8 April 1994 (Japan), 9 May 1994 (New Zealand), and 20 May 1994 (Australia), 1819 U.N.T.S. 359.

Agreement to Promote Compliance with International Conservation and Management Measures by Fishing Vessels on the High Seas, concluded at Rome, Italy 24 November 1993, entered into force 24 April 2003, reprinted in 33 I.L.M. 968 (1994).

Marrakesh Agreement Establishing the World Trade Organization, concluded at Marrakesh, Morocco 15 April 1994, entered into force 1 January 1995, 1867 U.N.T.S. 3, reprinted in 33 ILM 15 (1994).

Understanding on Rules and Procedures Governing the Settlement of Disputes, annex 2 to the *Marrakesh Agreement Establishing the World Trade Organization*, concluded at Marrakesh, Morocco 15 April 1994, entered into force 1 January 1995, 1869 U.N.T.S. 401, reprinted in 33 I.L.M. 114 (1994).

Marrakesh Protocol to the General Agreement on Tariffs and Trade 1994, concluded at Marrakesh, Morocco 15 April 1994, entered into force 1 January 1995, 1867 U.N.T.S. 237.

Protocol to the 1979 Convention on Long-Range Transboundary Air Pollution on Further Reduction of Sulphur Emissions, concluded at Oslo, Norway 14 June 1994, entered into force 5 August 1998, UN doc. EB.AIR/R.84.

Agreement for the Implementation of the Provisions of the United Nations Convention on the Law of the Sea of 10 December 1982 Relating to the Conservation and Management of Straddling Fish Stocks and Highly Migratory Fish Stocks, concluded at New York 4 August 1995, entered into force 11 December 2001, UN doc. A/CONF.164/37.

Inter-American Convention for the Protection and Conservation of Sea Turtles, concluded at Caracas, Venezuela 1 December 1996, entered into force 2 May 2001, 2164 U.N.T.S. 29.

Convention on the Law of the Non-Navigational Uses of Watercourses, adopted 8 July 1997 by a United Nations General Assembly Resolution, UN doc. A/RES/51/229. Not yet in force.

Kyoto Protocol to the United Nations Framework Convention on Climate Change, concluded at Kyoto, Japan 10 December 1997, entered into force 16 February 2005, FCCC/CP/1997/7/add. 1, reprinted in 37 I.L.M. 32 (1998).

Convention on Access to Information, Public Participation in Decision Making and Access to Justice in Environmental Matters, concluded in Århus, Denmark 25 June 1998, entered into force 30 October 2001, doc. ECE/CEP/43.

Rome Statute of the International Criminal Court, concluded at Rome, Italy 17 July 1998, entered into force 1 July 2002, UN doc. A/CONF.183/9.

(b) Other Treaties

Treaty of Amity, Commerce, and Navigation, concluded at London, U.K. 19 November 1794, proclaimed 29 February 1796 (United States—United Kingdom), 1 Malloy 590.

Treaty of Peace and Amity, concluded at Ghent, Belgium 24 December 1814, proclaimed 18 February 1815 (United States—United Kingdom), 1 Malloy 612.

Air Service Agreement (United States—France), concluded 27 March 1946, 139 U.N.T.S. 253, T.I.A.S. 1507, amended by an Exchange of Notes of 5 April 1960, 458 U.N.T.S. 292, T.I.A.S. 5135.

Treaty Concerning the Construction and Operation of the Gabcikovo-Nagymaros System of Locks, signed at Budapest, Hungary on 16 September 1977, entered into force on 30 June 1978 (Hungary—Czechoslovakia), 1109 U.N.T.S. 235.

Agreement Between the Government of the Czechoslovak Socialist Republic and the Government of the Hungarian People's Republic Concerning Mutual Assistance in the Construction of the Gabcikovo-

Nagymaros System of Locks, signed on 16 September 1977, entered into force on 30 June 1978 (Hungary—Czechoslovakia), 1724 U.N.T.S. 119.

Protocol Amending the Agreement Between the Government of the Czechoslovak Socialist Republic and the Government of the Hungarian People's Republic Concerning Mutual Assistance in the Construction of the Gabcikovo-Nagymaros System of Locks, signed on 10 October 1983, entered into force on 7 February 1984 (Hungary—Czechoslovakia), 1724 U.N.T.S. 124.

Protocol Amending the Agreement Between the Government of the Czechoslovak Socialist Republic and the Government of the Hungarian People's Republic Concerning Mutual Assistance in the Construction of the Gabcikovo-Nagymaros System of Locks, concluded and entered into force on 9 February 1989 (Hungary—Czechoslovakia), 1724 U.N.T.S. 128.

(c) International Courts or Arbitration

(i) Permanent Court of International Justice, 1920–1946

Status of Eastern Carelia, advisory opinion of 23 July 1923, P.C.I.J. Series B, no. 5.

S.S. Lotus (*France v. Turkey*), judgment of 7 September 1927, P.C.I.J. Series A, no. 10.

Territorial Jurisdiction of the International Commission of the River Oder (Germany, Denmark, France, Great Britain, Sweden, Czechoslovakia, and Poland), judgment of 10 September 1929, 1929 P.C.I.J. Series A, no. 23.

(ii) International Court of Justice, 1946–

Fisheries Case (*United Kingdom v. Norway*), judgment of 18 December 1951, 1951 I.C.J. 116.

Anglo-Iranian Oil Co. (preliminary objection) (*United Kingdom v. Iran*), judgment of 22 July 1952, 1952 I.C.J. 93.

Barcelona Traction, Light and Power Company, Limited (*Belgium v. Spain*), judgment of 5 February 1970, 1970 I.C.J. 3.

Fishery Jurisdiction Case (*United Kingdom v. Iceland*), judgment of 25 July 1974, 1974 I.C.J. 3.

Nuclear Tests Case (*New Zealand v. France*), judgment of 20 December 1974, 1974 I.C.J. 253.

United States Diplomatic and Consular Staff in Tehran (*United States of America v. Iran*), order of December 15, 1979, 1979 I.C.J. 7.

United States Diplomatic and Consular Staff in Tehran (*United States of America v. Iran*), judgment of 24 May 1980, 1980 I.C.J. 3.

Military and Paramilitary Activities in and Against Nicaragua (jurisdiction) (*Nicaragua v. United States*), judgment of 26 November 1984, 1984 I.C.J. 392.

Frontier Dispute (provisional measures) (*Burkina Faso v. Republic of Mali*), order of 10 January 1986, 1986 I.C.J. 3.

Military and Paramilitary Activities in and Against Nicaragua (merits) (*Nicaragua v. United States*), judgment of 27 June 1986, 1986 I.C.J. 14, 25 I.L.M. 1023 (1986).

Questions of Interpretation and Application of the 1971 Montreal Convention Arising from the Aerial Incident at Lockerbie (*Libyan Arab Jamahiriya v. United States*), order of 14 April 1992. 1992 I.C.J. 114.

Certain Phosphate Lands in Nauru (preliminary objections) (*Nauru v. Australia*), judgment of 26 June 1992, 1992 I.C.J 240.

Application of the Convention on the Prevention and Punishment of the Crime of Genocide (provisional measures) (*Bosnia and Herzegovina v. Yugoslavia*), order of 8 April 1993, 1993 I.C.J. 3.

East-Timor (*Portugal v. Australia*), judgment of 30 June 1995, 1995 I.C.J. 90.

Land and Maritime Boundary Between Cameroon and Nigeria (provisional measures) (*Cameroon v. Nigeria*), order of 15 March 1996, 1996 I.C.J. 13.

Legality of the Threat or Use of Nuclear Weapons, advisory opinion of 8 July 1996, 1996 I.C.J. 226.

The Gabcikovo-Nagymaros Project (*Hungary v. Slovakia*), judgment of 25 September 1997, 1997 I.C.J. 7.

Questions of Interpretation and Application of the 1971 Montreal Convention Arising from the Aerial Incident at Lockerbie (preliminary objections) (*Libyan Arab Jamahiriya v. United States*), judgment of 27 February 1998, 1998 I.C.J. 115.

Fisheries Jurisdiction Case (jurisdiction) (*Spain v. Canada*), judgment of 4 December 1998, 1998 I.C.J. 432.

Application of the Convention on the Prevention and Punishment of the Crime of Genocide (*Bosnia and Herzegovina v. Serbia and Montenegro*), judgment of 26 February 2007.

(iii) International Tribunal for the Law of the Sea, 1997–

The M/V "SAIGA" (no. 2) Case (*Saint Vincent and the Grenadines v. Guinea*), request for provisional measures, order of 11 March 1998, case no. 2.

Southern Bluefin Tuna Cases (provisional measures) (*New Zealand and Australia v. Japan*), judgment of 27 August 1999, case nos. 3 and 4.

Conservation and Sustainable Exploitation of Swordfish Stocks in the Southeastern Pacific Ocean (*Chile v. the European Community*), order of 15 March 2001 and order of 16 December 2003, case no. 7.

MOX Plant Case (provisional measures) (*Ireland v. United Kingdom*), order of 3 December 2001, case no. 10.

Land Reclamation by Singapore in and around the Straits of Johor (provisional measures) (*Malaysia v. Singapore*), order of 8 October 2003.

(iv) GATT Panel Decisions, WTO Panel, and Appellate Body Decisions

United States—Prohibition of Imports of Tuna and Tuna Products from Canada, report of a GATT panel, adopted 22 February 1982, B.I.S.D. 29S/91.

Canada—Measures Affecting Exports of Unprocessed Herring and Salmon, report of a GATT panel, adopted 22 March 1988, B.I.S.D. 35S/98/112.

United States—Section 337 of the Tariff Act of 1930, report of a GATT panel, adopted 7 November 1989, L/6439, B.I.S.D. 36S/345.

United States—Restrictions on Imports of Tuna, report of a GATT panel, 16 August 1991, not adopted, GATT doc. DS21/R, reprinted in 30 I.L.M. 1594 (1991).

United States—Restrictions on Imports of Tuna, report of a GATT panel, 20 May 1994, GATT doc. DS29/R, not adopted, reprinted in 33 I.L.M. 839 (1994).

United States—Standards for Reformulated and Conventional Gasoline, report of the appellate body, 29 April 1996, WTO doc. WT/DS2/AB/R, reprinted in 35 I.L.M. 603 (1996).

Argentina—Measures Affecting Imports of Footwear, Textiles, Apparel, and Other Items, report of a WTO panel, 25 November 1997, WTO doc. WT/DS56/R.

Argentina—Measures Affecting Imports of Footwear, Textiles, Apparel, and Other Items, report of the appellate body, 27 March 1998, WTO doc. WT/DS56/AB/R.

United States—Import prohibition of certain shrimp and shrimp products, report of the panel, 15 May 1998, WTO doc. WT/DS58/R.

European Communities—Measures Affecting the Importation of Certain Poultry Products, report of the appellate body, 13 July 1998, WTO doc. WT/DS69/AB/R.

United States—Import Prohibition of Certain Shrimp and Shrimp Products, report of the WTO appellate body, 12 October 1998, WTO doc. WT/DS58/AB/R, reprinted in 38 I.L.M. 118 (1999).

European Communities—Regime for the Importation, Sale, and Distribution of Bananas, decision by arbitrators under article 22(6), 9 April 1999, WTO doc. WT/DS27/ARB.

United States—Sections 301–310 of the Trade Act of 1974, report of a WTO Panel, 22 December 1999, WTO doc. WT/DS152/R, adopted by the DSB on 27 January 2000.

Korea—Measures Affecting Government Procurement, report of a WTO panel, 1 May 2000, WTO doc. WT/DS163/R, adopted by the DSB on 19 June 2000.

Brazil—Export Financing Programme for Aircraft, decision by arbitrators under article 22(6) of *DSU* and article 4(11) of the *SCM Agreement* (*Agreement on Subsidies and Countervailing Measures*), 28 August 2000, WTO doc. WT/DS46/ARB.

United States—Import Prohibition of Certain Shrimp and Shrimp Products, recourse to article 21.5 by Malaysia, report of a WTO panel, 15 June 2001, WTO doc. WT/DS58/RW.

United States—Import Prohibition of Certain Shrimp and Shrimp Products, recourse to article 21.5 by Malaysia, report of the appellate body, 22 October 2001, WTO doc. WT/DS58/AB/RW.

Mexico—Tax Measures on Soft Drinks and Other Beverages, report of a WTO panel, 7 October 2005, WTO doc. WT/DS308/R.

Mexico in Mexico—Tax Measures on Soft Drinks and Other Beverages, report of the appellate body, 6 March 2006, WTO doc. WT/DS308/AB/R.

(v) European Court of Justice

Commission v. Luxemburg and Belgium, case nos. 90 and 91/63, judgment of 13 November 1964, 1964 European Court Reports 625.

Roland Rutili v. Minster for the Interior, case no. 36/75, judgment of 28 October 1975, 1975 European Court Reports 1219.

Commission v. Italy, case no. 52/75, judgment of 26 February 1976, 1976 European Court Reports 277.

Regina v. Pierre Bouchereau, case no. 30/77, judgment of 27 October 1977, 1977 European Court Reports 1999.

Commission v. France, case no. 232/78, judgment of 25 September 1979, 1979 European Court Reports 2729.

Luise & Carbone v. Ministro del Tesero, case nos. 286/82 and 26/83, judgment of 31 January 1984, 1984 European Court Reports 377.

The Queen v. Ministry of Agriculture, Fisheries, and Food, ex-parte Hedley Lomas (Ireland) Ltd., case no. C-5/94, judgment of 23 May 1996, 1996 European Court Reports I-2553.

Commission v. Ireland, case no. C-459/03, judgment of 30 May 2006, 2006 European Court Reports I-4635.

(vi) International Arbitration (Various Sources)

The Naulilaa Case (*Portugal v. Germany*), arbitral decision of 31 July 1928, 2 UNRIAA 1011 (1928).

Cysene Case (*Portugal v. Germany*), arbitral decision of 30 June 1930, 2 UNRIAA 1035 (1930).

Trail Smelter Case (*United States v. Canada*), arbitral decision of 11 March 1941, 3 UNRIAA 1911 (1941).

Air Service Agreement of 27 March 1946 (*United States v. France*), arbitral decision of 9 December 1978, 54 I.L.R. 304, 18 UNRIAA 417, *Report of Arbitral Awards*, vol. XVIII.

Southern Bluefin Tuna Case (*Australia and New Zealand v. Japan*), award on jurisdiction and admissibility, arbitral tribunal, decided on 4 August 2000. World Bank, International Centre for Settlement of Investment Disputes.

MOX Plant Case (*Ireland v. United Kingdom*), order an arbitral tribunal of 24 June 2003, Permanent Court of Arbitration.

Dispute Concerning Access to Information Under Article 9 of the OSPAR Convention (*Ireland v. United Kingdom*), arbitral award of 2 July 2003, Permanent Court of Arbitration.

(d) Other International Decisions or Documents

(i) International Law Commission Documents

Report of the International Law Commission on the Work of Its Thirty Second Session, 5 May–25 July 1980, Yearbook of the International Law Commission 1980, vol. II, (part 2), UN doc. A/35/10.

Fourth Report on the Content, Form, and Degrees of International Responsibility by Mr. Willem Riphagen, Special Rapporteur, Yearbook of the International Law Commission 1983, vol. II (part 1), UN doc. A/CN.4/366 and add.1.

Third Report on State Responsibility by Mr. Gaetano Arangio-Ruiz, Special Rapporteur, Yearbook of the International Law Commission 1991, vol. II (part 1), UN doc. A/CN.4/440 and add. 1.

Fourth Report on State Responsibility by Mr. Gaetano Arangio-Ruiz, Special Rapporteur, Yearbook of the International Law Commission 1992, vol. II (part 1), UN doc. A/CN.4.444.

Report of the International Law Commission of the Work of Its Forty Fourth Session, 4 May–24 July 1992, International Law Commission Yearbook 1992, vol. II (part 2), UN doc. A/47/10.

State Responsibility: Comments and Observations Received from Governments, International Law Commission, fiftieth session, Geneva, Switzerland 20 May–12 June 1998, and New York 27 July–14 August 1998, UN doc. A/CN.4/488, 25 March 1998.

Draft Articles on State Responsibility, report of the Drafting Committee, International Law Commission, fifty second session, Geneva, Switzerland, 1 May–9 June and 10 July–18 August 2000, UN doc. A/CN.4/600, 21 August 2000.

Third Report on State Responsibility by Mr. James Crawford, Special Rapporteur, International Law Commission, fifty second session, Geneva, Switzerland, 1 May–9 June and 10 July–18 August 2000, UN doc. A/CN.4/507, add. 1, add. 2, and add. 3, 18 July 2000.

2001 Draft Articles on State Responsibility, report of the International Law Commission of the Work of its fifty third session, 23 April–1 June and 2 July–10 August 2001, UN doc. A/56/10.

Fourth Report on State Responsibility by Mr. James Crawford, Special Rapporteur, International Law Commission, fifty third session, Geneva, Switzerland, 23 April–1 June and 2 July–10 August 2001, UN doc. A/CN.4/517, 2 April 2001.

State Responsibility: Comments and Observations Received from Governments, International Law Commission, fifty third session, Geneva, Switzerland, 23 April–1 June and 2 July–10 August 2001, UN doc. A/CN.4/515, 19 March 2001.

(ii) WTO Documents

Marrakesh Decision on Trade and Environment, adopted at Marrakesh, Morocco, 14 April 1994, reprinted in 33 I.L.M. 1267 (1994).

WTO Decision on Trade in Services and the Environment, adopted 1 March 1995, WTO doc. S/L/4 (4 April 1995).

Notification of an Appeal by the United States, 13 July 1998, WTO doc. WT/DS58/11.

Chile—Measures Affecting the Transit and Importation of Swordfish, request for consultation by the European Communities, 26 April 2000, WTO doc. WT/DS193/1.

Resolving the Relationship between WTO Rules and Multilateral Environmental Agreements, submission by the European Community, 19 October 2000, WTO Doc. WT/CTE/W/170.

Chile—Measures Affecting the Transit and Importation of Swordfish, request for the establishment of a panel by the European Communities, 7 November 2000, WTO doc. WT/DS193/2.

Minutes of the Meeting, held in the Centre William Rappart, 17 November 2000, WTO doc. WT/DSB/M.92 (15 January 2001).

Chile—Measures Affecting the Transit and Importation of Swordfish, arrangement between the European Communities and Chile, 6 April 2001, WTO docs. WT/DS193/3 and WT/DS193/3/add. 1.

(iii) Other Documents From International Organizations

L'Institut de Droit International, "Le Régime de Représailles en Temps de Paix," *Annuaire de l'Institute de Droit International*, Brussels, Belgium, 1934, p. 710.

Security Council Resolution no. 83 (1950), UN doc. S/1511, 27 June 1950.

Final Act of the Conference on Security and Co-operation in Europe, 1 August 1975, 14 I.L.M. 1292 (1975).

Agenda 21, approved by the UN Conference on Environment and Development (UNCED) at Rio de Janeiro, Brazil 13 June 1992, UN doc. A/CONF.151/26, vols. I, II, and III, 1992.

Rio Declaration on Environment and Development, adopted by the *UN Conference on Environment and Development* (*UNCED*) at Rio de Janeiro, Brazil 13 June 1992, UN doc. A/CONF.151/26, vol. I, 1992, reprinted in 31 I.L.M. 874 (1992).

Boutros-Gali, Boutros, *An Agenda for Peace: Preventive Diplomacy, Peacemaking, and Peace-Keeping*, UN doc. A/47/277-S/24111, 17 June 1992.

International Court of Justice, Press Communiqué, 93/20, 19 July 1993.

Security Council Resolution no. 883 (1993), UN doc. S/RES/883 (1993), 11 November 1993.

Canada-European Community: Agreed Minute on the Conservation and Management of Fish Stocks, Brussels, Belgium 20 April 1995, 34 I.L.M. 1260 (1995).

Violation by Norwegian Authorities of Chapter II of the Agreement on the European Economic Area, a letter from the attorney of the operator of *Már* to the EFTA Surveillance Authority initiating procedures before *ESA*, 17 July 1995.

Letter from the Norwegian Royal Ministry of Foreign Affairs to ESA, a letter from Norwegian Authorities to the EFTA Surveillance Authority, 8 October 1995, doc. 95/02762–VII.

Letter of Formal Notice on the Failure to Comply with Article 36 or the EEA Agreement, a letter from the EFTA Surveillance Authority to the Norwegian government, 3 September 1996, doc. 96–4652-D, decision no. 109/96/COL.

International Tribunal for the Law of the Sea, press release, ITLOS/ Press 4, November 1, 1996.

Letter from the Norwegian Royal Ministry of Foreign Affairs to ESA in Reply of Letter of Formal Notice, a letter from Norwegian Authorities to the EFTA Surveillance Authority, 29 November 1996, doc. 95/02762–31 VII/DM.

International Tribunal for the Law of the Sea, press release, ITLOS/ Press 8, 13 November 1997.

Report of the Conference of the Parties on its Third Session, Held in Kyoto from 1 to 11 December 1997, Addendum: Part 2: Action Taken by the Conference of the Parties at Its Third Session, UN doc. FCCC/ CP/1997/7/Add.1, 18 March 1998.

ESA's Letter to Ambassador Einar Bull, Norwegian Mission to the European Union, a letter from the EFTA Surveillance Authority to Norwegian authorities, 14 May 1998, doc. 98–3393-D.

International Court of Justice, Press Communiqué, 98/28, 3 September 1998.

TBR Proceedings Concerning Chilean Practices Affecting Transit of Swordfish in Chilean Ports, Report to the Trade Barriers Regulation Committee, European Commission, March 1999.

Martin Coulson, *NATO-CCMS Achievements in Defence-Related Environmental Studies 1980–2001*, March 2001, report no. A-2001/02.

State Parties to Law of the Sea Convention Open Current Session, United Nations press release, doc. SEA/1772, 9 June 2003.

Report of the Review Conference on the Agreement for the Implementation of the Provisions of the United Nations Convention on the Law of the Sea of 10 December 1982 Relating to the Conservation and Management of Straddling Fish Stocks and Highly Migratory Fish Stocks, UN doc. A/CONF.210/2006/15, 5 July 2006.

Responsibility of States for Internationally Wrongful Acts, report of the Sixth Committee, UN doc. A/62/446, 21 November 2007.

Responsibility of States for Internationally Wrongful Acts, resolution adopted by the General Assembly, UN doc. A/RES/62/61, 8 January 2008.

(e) Domestic Decisions and Documents

(i) Domestic Judicial Decisions (U.S. Courts)

Marbury v. Madison, 5 U.S. (1 Cranch) 137 (1803).

Fong Yue Ting v. United States, 149 U.S. 698 (1893); 13 S.Ct. 1016.

Plessy v. Ferguson, 163 U.S. 537 (1896); 16 S Ct 1138; 41 L Ed 256.

Brown v. Board of Education, 347 U.S. 483 (1954); 74 S. Ct. 686; 98 L. Ed. 873.

Baker v. Carr, 369 U.S. 186 (1962); 82 S.Ct. 691.

(ii) Domestic Legislation

General Law of Fisheries and Aquaculture (*Ley General de Pesca y Acuicultura*), law no. 18.892 1989, consolidated with amendments by Presidential Decree no. 430 (28 September 1991).

Coastal Fisheries Protection Act Amendment of 12 May 1994, Statutes of Canada (S.C.) 1994, Chapter 14.

Marine Mammal Protection Act, P.L. 92–522, 86 Stat. 1027 (1972), as amended mainly by P.L. 100–711, 102 Stat. 4755 (1988), and, later, P.L. 101–627 at 104 Stat. 4467 (1990). Partly codified at 16 U.S.C. 1361ff.

Section 609, P.L. 101–1026, 16 U.S.C. § 1537.

Revised Guidelines for the Implementation of Section 609 of Public Law 101–162 Relating to the Protection of Sea Turtles in Shrimp Trawl Fishing Operations, U.S. Department of State, Federal Register vol. 64, no. 130, 8 July 1999, Public Notice 3086, pp. 36946–36952.

Books, Journals, Reports, and News (Alphabetical Order)

(a) Newspapers and News Services

Auster, Bruce B. "Enviro-Intelligence: The CIA Goes Green." *U.S. News & World Report*, 11, section: World Report, p. 34, March 1998.

Bouthillier, Yves Le. "High Seas, Fishy Tactics." *The Guardian*, p. 10, 4 April 1995.

Bryden, Joan. "Gunboat Diplomacy: In the Final Analysis, Force Was the Only Thing that Ended Canada's Turbot War." *The Record* (Kitchener-Waterloo, Ontario, Canada), p. A9, 18 April 1995.

"Canada Calls for End to Illegal Fishing in Grand Banks." *European Report*, no. 2007, 14 January 1995.

Canada Newswire. "Canada Seizes Spanish Trawler." *Domestic News*, 9 March 1995.

"Canada Renews Calls for Fisheries Restraint." *European Report*, no. 2012, 1 February 1995.

Carnegy, Hugh. "Trawler Held After Clash." *Financial Times* (London), p. 2, 8 August 1994.

Carvel, John. "Canada Arrests Spanish Captain as Fish War with Europe Looms." *The Guardian*, p. 13, 10 March 1995.

———. "Trawler Freed as Truce Declared in Fish War." *The Guardian*, p. 3, 16 March 1995.

Carvel, John, and Trevena, Claire. "Talks Start on Fish Dispute Amid Raging War of Words." *The Guardian*, p. 12, 30 March 1995.

"*Estai*," *Hamilton Spectator* (Ontario, Canada), p. A3, 28 March 1995.

"EU and Canada Celebrate Easter Deal on Fishing Rights." *European Report*, no. 2034, 19 April 1995.

"EU Divided On How to Tackle Fish Row with Canada." *European Report*, no. 2031, 8 April 1995.

Federal News Service. "A New Framework for Multilateral Development Policy." Text of remarks to be delivered by Treasury Secretary Lawrence H. Summers to the Council on Foreign Relations, section not identified, 20 March 2000.

———. "An Alliance for Global Water Security in the 21st Century." A speech by U.S. Secretary of State Madeleine Albright, given at Fort McNair, Washington, D.C., section: State Department Briefing, 10 April 2000.

———. "Current and Projected National Security Threats to the United States." Hearing before the Senate Intelligence Committee, prepared statement by Toby T. Gati, assistant secretary of state for intelligence and research, section: In the News, 5 February 1997.

———. "Defense Department Regular Briefing." 20 May 1992, briefing by Bob Hall.

———. "Environmental Defense Fund Symposium." Remarks by Senator Al Gore, section: Commerce or Trade Speeches or Conferences, 17 May 1991.

———. "Environmental Security—Defending our Future." Hearing before the Subcommittee on Installations and Facilities and the Subcommittee on Readiness, prepared testimony of Sherri W. Goodman, deputy undersecretary of defense, section: In the News, 24 March 1995.

———. "Environmental Security Policy." Remarks by Secretary of Defense William Perry at the Society of American Engineers Luncheon, section: In the News, 20 November 1996.

———. "FY97 Defense Appropriations." Joint hearing before the military procurement and military readiness subcommittees of the House National Security Committee, testimony of Sherri W. Goodman, deputy undersecretary of defense, section: In the News, 21 March 1996.

———. "Hearing in Connection with H.R. 1141, *Sikes Act* Amendments." Hearing before the House Resources Subcommittee on Fisheries, Wildlife and Oceans, prepared statement of Sherri W. Goodman, deputy undersecretary of defense, section: In the News, 17 March 1995.

———. "Peace in Northern Ireland." Remarks by National Security Advisor Anthony Lake at Georgetown University, 8 October 1996.

———. "Remarks by Senator Tim Wirth, D-Co Democratic National Convention." A speech by Tim Wirth before the Democratic National Convention, section: In the News, 16 July 1992.

———. "Remarks by U.S. Defense Secretary William Cohen and General Zhang Wannian of China After Signing of Joint Statement of Cooperation on Environmental Security." Defense Department Briefing, 18 September 1998.

———. "Text of Remarks Prepared for Delivery by Soviet Foreign Minister Eduard A. Shevardnadze Before the 43rd Session of the United Nations." A speech by Eduard A. Shevardnadze before the United Nation General Assembly, section: News Makers & Policy Makers, 27 September 1988.

———. "The Kyoto Protocol: Problems with U.S. Sovereignty and the Lack of Developing Country Participation." Hearing before The House Committee on International Relations, prepared testimony of Frank J. Gaffney, jr. director of The Center for Security Policy, section: In the news, 13 May 1998.

———. "The Urgency of a Massive Effort Against Infectious Diseases." Hearing before the House Committee on International Relations, prepared testimony of David F. Gordon, national intelligence officer for economics and global issues, National Intelligence Council, Section: Prepared Testimony, 29 June 2000.

"Fisheries: Bonino Condemns Canadian Attack as an 'Act of Piracy'." *European Report*, no. 2023, 10 March 1995.

"Fisheries: EU and Canada on the Brink of a Fish War." *European Report*, no. 2022, 7 March 1995.

"Fisheries: EU Formally Objects to NAFO Turbot Quota as Canada Warns Against." *European Report*, no.2021, 3 March 1995.

Gardner, Richard N. "All That Soviet Activity at the U.N. Is Something U.S. May Need to Match." *Los Angeles Times*, section: Metro, part 2, page 7, column 3, Op-Ed Desk, 29 September 1988.

Gellman, Barton. "Aids Is Declared Threat to Security; White House Fears Epidemic Could Destabilize World." *Washington Post*, p. A1, 30 April 2000.

Graham Whitfield. "Mox Plant Set To Start." *The Journal* (Newcastle, U.K.), p. 9, 18 September 2002.

"Grand Banks Turned into 'Wild West': EU Commissioner Suggests Net May Not Be from Estai." *Hamilton Spectator* (Ontario, Canada), p. A3, 28 March 1995.

Henley, Jon. "Fish Loopholes Heats Tempers in Frozen Sea." *The Guardian* (London, U.K.), p. 14, 3 August 1996.

Kenny, Eoin. "Canada Wasn't Bluffing: Spanish Trawler Has Its Nets Cut." *The Record* (Kitchener-Waterloo, Ontario), p. A1, 27 March 1995.

———. "Fish War Looms: Canada Prepared for Tough Measures Against Foreign Trawlers That Threaten Endangered Species." *The Record* (Kitchener-Waterloo, Ontario, Canada), p. A1, 9 March 1995.

"Legality of Arrests in Doubt: Canada Insists It Has the Right to Protect the Fish Stocks." *The Record* (Kitchener-Waterloo, Ontario, Canada), p. A2, 15 March 1995.

Pivcevic, Paul. "Environment: Iceland at Loggerheads Over Last Atlantic Cod." *Inter Press Service*, 23 September 1993.

RAPID. "Background Note–EU–Canada/Fisheries," Memo: 95–38, 10 March 1995.

———. "Commission Calls on Canada to Negotiate in Good Faith," IP: 95-313, 29 March 1995.

———. "Commission Statement on Canadian Seizure of European Fishing Vessel," IP: 95-230, 9 March 1995.

———. "*Estai* Found to Comply with NAFO Rules–Canadian Assertion Not Proven," IP: 95-295, 26 March 1995.

———. "NAFO/Canada: Mrs. Bonino Demands Release of European Vessel," IP: 95-235, 12 March 1995.

———. "Statement by Mrs. Bonino on the Resolution Adopted by the European Parliament Regarding the Objection to NAFO's Decision Allocating the 1995 TAC for Greenland Halibut," IP: 95-144, 17 February 1995.

"Release of Spanish Trawler Raises Hopes of Settlement to Fish Row," *European Report*, no. 2025, 15 March 1995.

Shabecoff, Philip. "Washington Talk: Environment." *New York Times*, section 1, p. 24, 29 May 1989.

Steward, Edison. "Canadians Seize Spanish Trawler: Warning Shots Fired in Turbot War Escalation." *Toronto Star*, p. A1, 10 March 1995.

"Tension Rise Again over Fish in North Atlantic." *European Report*, no. 2028, 29 March 1995.

Thompson, Allan. "European Union, Canada Set for Negotiation of Fish Stocks: Truce on East Coast Allows Talks to Begin." *The Toronto Star*, p. A12, 6 March 1995.

Thorne, Stephen. "Seized Spanish Trawler Released: Net Recovered from Ocean Supports Allegation of Illegal Fishing." *The Record* (Kitchener-Waterloo, Ontario), p. A3, 16 March 1995.

Todd, Dave. "Both Sides Stand Firm in Fish War." *Montreal Gazette*, 11 March 1995.

———. "First Fish Battle Settles Nothing: Canada is Paying for Years of Neglect of Its Responsibility for All of the Grand Banks Fishery." *Hamilton Spectator* (Ontario, Canada), p. A8, 18 March 1995.

———. "Risk of Conflicts on High Seas Escalates." *Hamilton Spectator* (Ontario, Canada), p. A1, 13 March 1995.

Todd, Dave, and Bryden, Joan, "They're Back: Defiant Spaniards Fish Near Grand Banks." *Hamilton Spectator* (Ontario, Canada), p. A1, 15 March 1995.

Trevena, Claire. "No More Mr. Nice Guy as Canada Bites in the Turbot War." *The Observer*, p. 21, 19 March 1995.

(b) Books and Journals

Abel, William T. "Fishing for an International Norm to Govern Straddling Stocks: The Canada-Spain Dispute of 1995." *University of Miami Inter-American Law Review* 27 (1996): 553.

Abramovitz, Janet N. *Imperiled Waters, Impoverished Future: The Decline of Freshwater Ecosystem*, Worldwatch paper no. 128. Washington, D.C.: Worldwatch Institute, 1996.

Adede, A. O. *The System for Settlement of Disputes Under the United Nations Convention on the Law of the Sea: A Drafting History and a Commentary*. Dordrecht, Boston, Lancaster: Martinus Nijhoff Publishers, 1987.

Allain, Jean. *A Century of International Adjudication: The Rule of Law and Its Limits*. The Hague: T.M.C. Asser Press, 2000.

Alvarez, Jose E. "Judging the Security Council," *American Journal of International Law* 90 (1996): 1.

The American Law Insitute. *Restatement of the Law: The Foreign Relations Law of the United States*. Vol. 2. St. Paul: American Law Institute Publisher, 1987.

Ando, Nisuke, Edward Mcwhinney, and Rüdiger Wolfrum (eds.). *Liber Amicorum Judge Shigeru Oda*. Vols. I–II. The Hague, London, New York: Kluwer Law International, 2002.

Annan, Kofi. *We the Peoples, the Role of the United Nations in the 21st Century*. New York: United Nations, 2000.

Ashley, Richard K. "The Poverty of Neorealism." In *Neorealism and Its Critics*, 255. New York: Columbia University Press, 1986.

Bagley, Bruce M., and Sergio Aguayo Quezada (eds.). *Mexico: In Search of Security*. Coral Gables: North-South Center, 1993.

Baldwin, David A. (ed.). *Neorealism and Neoliberalism: The Contemporary Debate*. New York: Columbia University Press, 1993.

Bedeman, David J. "Counterintuiting Countermeasures." *American Journal of International Law* 96 (2002): 817.

Bevans, Charles I. (ed.). *Treaties and Other International Agreements of the United States of America, 1776–1949*. Vol. II. Washington, D.C.: U.S. GPO, 1968.

Bilder, Richard B. Adjudication, International Arbitral Tribunals, and Courts. In *Peacemaking in International Conflicts*, 155. (2nd printing.) Washington, D.C.: United Institute of Peace Press, 1999.

Birnie, Patricia W. and Alan E. Boyle. *International Law and the Environment*. Oxford, New York: Clarendon Press, Oxford University Press, 1992.

Blackwell, A. "The Human Society and Italian Driftnetters: Environmental Activists and Unilateral Actions in International Environmental Law." *North Carolina Journal of International Law and Commercial Regulation Association* 23 (1998): 313.

Blake, Gerald H. (ed.). *Maritime Boundaries*. London, New York: Routledge, 1994.

Bodin, Jean. *On Sovereignty, Four Chapters from The Six Books of the Commonwealth*. Franklin, H. Julian, trans. England: Cambridge, 1992.

Bos, Adriaan and Hugo Siblesz (eds.). *Realism in Law Making: Essays on International Law in Honour of Willem Riphagen*. Dordrecht, Boston, Lancaster: Martinus Nijhoff Publishers, 1986.

Bostian, Ida L. "Flushing the Danube: The World Court's Decision Concerning the Gabcikovo Dam." *Colorado Journal of International Environmental Law and Policy* 9 (1998): 401.

Boulding, Elise. "States, Boundaries, and Environmental Security." In *Conflict Resolution Theory and Practice: Integration and Application*, 194. Manchester, New York: Manchester University Press, 1993.

Boyle, Alan E. (ed.). *Environmental Regulation and Economic Growth*. Oxford: Clarendon Press, 1994.

Briggs, Herbert W. *The International Law Commission*. Ithaca: Cornell University Press, 1965.

Brown, Elizabeth F. "In Defense of Environmental Rights in East European Constitutions." *University of Chicago Law School Roundtable* 1 (1993): 191.

Brown, E. D. "Dispute Settlement and the Law of the Sea: The UN Convention Regime." *Marine Policy* 21, no. 1 (1997): 17–43.

Brown, Lester R., *Redefining National Security*, Worldwatch paper no. 14. Washington, D.C.: Worldwatch Institute, 1977.

Brown, Michael E., Owen R. Coté Jr., Sean M. Lynn-Jones, and Steven E. Miller (eds.). *Theories of War and Peace*. Cambridge, London: The MIT Press, 1998.

Brunnee, Jutta, and Stephen J. Toope. "Environmental Security and Freshwater Resources: Ecosystem Regime Building." *American Journal of International Law* 91, no. 1 (1997): 26–59.

Brus, Marcel M.T.A. *Third Party Dispute Settlement in an Interdependent World: Developing a Theoretical Framework*. Dordrecht, Boston, London: Martinus Nijhoff Publishers, 1995.

Bull, Hedley. *The Anarchical Society: A Study of Order in World Politics*. 2nd ed. New York: Colombia University Press, 1995.

Burke, William T. *The New International Law of Fisheries: UNCLOS 1982 and Beyond*. Oxford: Clarendon Press, 1994.

Buzan, Barry, Ole Wæver, and Japp de Wilde. *Security: A New Framework for Analysis*. Boulder, London: Lynne Rienner Publishers, 1997.

Byers, Michael. *The Role of Law in International Politics: Essay in International Relations and International Politics*. New York: Oxford University Press, 2000.

Caminos, Hugo. "The Jurisdiction of the International Tribunal for the Law of the Sea: An Overview." In *Oceans Policy: New Institutions, Challenges, and Opportunities*, 93. The Hague, Boston, London: Martinus Nijhoff Publishers, 1999.

Cardwell, Paul J., and Duncan French. "Who Decides? The ECJ's Judgment on Jurisdiction in the MOX Plant Dispute." *Journal of Environmental Law* 19, no. 1 (2007): 121–129.

Carius, Alexander, and Kurt M. Lietzmann (eds.). *Environmental Change and Security: A European Perspective*. Berlin, New York, London: Springer, 1999.

Carr, E. H. *The Twenty Years' Crisis, 1919–1939: An Introduction to the Study of International Relations*. London: Macmillan and Co., 1939.

Carter, Jimmy. *Negotiation: The Alternative to Hostility*. Macon: Mercer University Press, 1984.

Cashman, Greg. *What Causes War: An Introduction to Theories of International Conflict*. Lanham, Boulder, New York, Oxford: Lexington Books, 1993.

Cheng, Bin. *General Principles of Law: As Applied by International Courts and Tribunals*. London: Stevens & Sons Limited, 1953.

Churchill, Robin R. "The Barents Sea Loophole Agreement: A 'Coastal State' Solution to a Straddling Stock Problem." *International Journal of Marine and Coastal Law* 14, no. 4 (1999): 467–490.

———. *EEC Fisheries Law*. Dordrecht, Boston: Nijhoff, 1987.

Churchill, Robin R., and A.V. Lowe. *The Law of the Sea*. Manchester: Manchester University Press, 1999.

Churchill, Robin R., and Geir Ulfstein. *Marine Management in Disputed Areas—The Case of the Barents Sea*. London, New York: Routledge, 1992.

Clingan, Thomas A. "Compulsory Settlement of Fisheries Disputes." In *Fisheries Conflict in the North Atlantic, Law of the Sea Institute Workshop*, 169. Cambridge: Ballinger Publishing Company, 1974.

Clough, Mark. "The WTO Dispute Settlement System: A Practitioner Perspective." *Fordham International Law Journal* 24, no. 1–2 (2000), 252–274.

Colbert, Evelyin Speyer. *Retaliation in International Law*. New York: King's Crown Press, 1948.

Conca, Ken. "In the Name of Sustainability: Peace Studies and Environmental Discourse." In *Green Security or Militarized Environment*, 7. Dartmouth: Aldershot, 1994.

Crawford, James, "The Continuing Debate on a UN Convention on State Responsibility." *International and Comparative Law Quarterly* 54, no. 4 (2005): 959–972.

———. *The International Law Commission's Articles on State Responsibility: Introduction* (text and commentaries). Cambridge: Cambridge University Press, 2002.

———. "The ILC's Articles on Responsibility of States for Internationally Wrongful Acts: A Retrospect." *American Journal of International Law* 96 (2002): 874–890.

Cronin, Bruce. "Changing the Norms of Sovereignty and Multilateral Intervention." In *Collective Conflict Management and Changing World Politics*, 161. New York: State University of New York Press, 1998.

Dalby, Simon. "Ecopolitical Discourse: 'Environmental Security' and Political Geography." *Progress in Human Geography* 16, no. 4 (1992): 503–522.

———. "The Politics of Environmental Security." In *Green Security or Militarized Environment*, 25. Dartsmouth: Aldershot, 1994.

Damrosch, Lori Fisler. "Retaliation or Arbitration—Or Both? The 1978 United States—France Aviation Dispute." *American Journal of International Law* 74, no. 4 (1980): 785–807.

Davies, John L., and Ted Robert Gurr (eds.). *Preventive Measures: Building Risk Assessment and Crisis Early Warning Systems*. Lanham, Boulder, New York, Oxford: Rowman & Littlefield Publishers Inc., 1998.

Dinstein, Yoram. *War, Aggression, and Self-Defense*. 2nd ed. Cambridge, New York: Grotius Publication, Cambridge University Press, 1994.

Dycus, Stephen, Arthur L. Berney, William C. Banks, and Peter Raven-Hansen. *National Security Law*. 2nd ed. Boston, New York, Toronto, London: Little, Brown, and Company, 1997.

Eiriksson, Gudmundur. *The International Tribunal for the Law of the Sea*. The Hague, London, Boston: Martinus Nijhoff Publishers, 2000.

Elagab, Omer Yousif. *The Legality of Non-forcible Counter-measures in International Law*. Oxford: Clarendon Press, 1988.

Elise Boulding. "States, Boundaries, and Environmental Security." In *Conflict Resolution Theory and Practice: Integration and Application*, 194. Manchester, New York: Manchester University Press, 1993.

———. "Greening the United Nations: Future Conditional." In *Between Sovereignty and Global Governance: The United Nations, the State, and Civil Society*, 135. New York: St. Martin's Press, 1998.

Elliot, Lorraine. *The Global Politics of the Environment*. New York: New York University Press, 1998.

Evans, Malcolm D. (ed.). *Remedies in International Law: The Institutional Dilemma*. Oxford: Hart Publishing, 1998.

Falk, Richard. *Law in an Emerging Global Village: A Post-Westphalian Perspective*. New York: Transnational Publishers, Inc., 1998.

Finnemore, Martha. "Constructing Norms of Humanitarian Intervention." In *The Culture of National Security: Norms and Identity in World Politics*, 153. New York: Columbia University Press, 1996.

———. *National Interests in International Society*. New York: Cornell University Press, 1996.

Forsythe, David P. "The International Court of Justice at Fifty." In *The International Court of Justice: Its Future Role After Fifty Years*, 385. Cambridge: Martinus Nijhoff, 1997.

Francioni, Francesco and Tullio Scovazzi (eds.). *International Responsibility for Environmental Harm*. London: Graham & Trotman, 1991.

Gamble, John King Jr. and Dana R. Fisher. *The International Court of Justice: An Analysis of a Failure*. Lexington, MA, Toronto, London: Lexington Books, 1976.

Gardiner, Richard A. *Design for Safe Neighborhoods: The Environmental Security Planning and Design Process*. Washington, D.C.: Department of Justice, Law Enforcement Assistance Administration, National Institute of Law Enforcement and Criminal Justice, 1978.

Gebrehana, Teklewold. *Duty to Negotiate: An Element of International Law*. Uppsala: Svenska Institutet för Internationell Rätt, 1978.

Genest, Marc A. *Conflict and Cooperation: Evolving Theories of International Relations*. New York, Montreal, London, Tokyo: Harcourt Brace College Publishers, 1996.

Gilpin, Robert. "The Richness of the Tradition of Political Realism." In *Neorealism and Its Critics*, 301. New York: Colombia University Press, 1986.

Gooch, George P., and Harold W. V. Temperly (eds.). *British Documents on the Origin of the War, 1898–1914*. Vol. 3. London: His Majesty's Stationery Office, 1926–1938.

Gordon, Ruth E. "Intervention by the United Nations: Iraq, Somalia, and Haiti." *Texas International Law Journal* 31, no. 1 (1996): 43–56.

Gore, Al. "SEI: A Strategic Environmental Initiative," *SAIS Review* 10 (1990): 60.

Grieco, Joseph M. "Anarchy and the Limits of Cooperation: A Realist Critique of the Newest Liberal Institutionalism." *International Organization* 24, no. 3 (1988): 485–507.

Grier, Peter. "Clinton Doctrine? What Clinton Doctrine?" *Air Force Magazine*, 1999, 12.

Grosko, Brett. "Just When Is It That a Unilateral Trade Ban Satisfies the GATT?: The WTO Shrimp and Shrimp Products Case." *Environmental Lawyer* 5 (1999): 817.

Grotius, Hugo. *The Rights of War and Peace* (originally published in 1625, translated from Latin). London: W. Innys and R. Manby, J. and P. Knapton, D. Brown, T. Osborn, and E. Wicksteed, 1738.

———. *The Rights of War and Peace* (originally published in 1625 as *De Jure Belli Ac Pacis*). A. C. Campell, trans. London, New York: M. Walter Dunne Publisher, 1901.

Großmann, Harald. "Unilateral Actions by the EC Against Unfair Trade Practices," *Intereconomics* 28, no. 6 (1993): 263–268.

Grunawalt, Richard, John E. King, and Ronald S. McClain (eds.). *Protection of the Environment During Armed Conflict*. Rhode Island: Naval War College, 1996.

Haas, Ernst B., and Allen S. Whiting. *Dynamics of International Relations*. New York, Toronto, London: McGraw-Hill Book Company, Inc., 1956.

Haas, Peter M., Robert O. Keohane, and Marc A. Levy (eds.). *Institutions for the Earth: Sources of Effective International Environmental Protection*. Cambridge: MIT Press, 1993.

Haftendorn, Helga. "The Security Puzzle: Theory-Building and Discipline-Building in International Security." *International Studies Quarterly* 35, no. 1 (1991): 3–17.

Haftendorn, Helga, Robert O. Keohane, and Celeste A. Wallander (eds.). *Imperfect Unions: Security Institutions over Time and Space*. Oxford: Oxford University Press, 1999.

Hall, William E. *A Treatise on International Law*. 6th ed. Oxford: Clarendon Press, 1909.

———. *A Treatise on International Law*. 8th ed. Oxford: Clarendon Press, 1924.

Hasenclever, Andreas, Peter Mayer, and Volker Rittberger. *Theories of International Regimes*. New York: Cambridge University Press, 1997.

Heinze, Eric, and Malgosia Fitzmaurice (eds.). *Landmark Cases in International Law*. London, The Hague, Boston: Kluwer Law International, 1998.

Henkin, Louis. *How Nations Behave; Law and Foreign Policy*. 2nd ed. Published for the Council on Foreign Relations. New York: F. A. Praeger, 1979.

———. *International Law: Politics and Values*. Dordrecht, Boston, London: Martinus Nijhoff Publishers, 1995.

Henkin, Louis, Richard Crawford Pugh, Oscar Schachter, and Hans Smit. *International Law, Cases, and Materials*. 3rd ed. St. Paul, MN: West Publishing Co., 1993.

Herz, John H. "Idealist Internationalism and the Security Dilemma." *World Politics*, no. 2 (1950): 157–180.

Hey, Ellen. *The Regime for the Exploitation of Transboundary Marine Fisheries Resources*. Dordrecht, Boston, London: Martinus Nijhoff Publishers, 1989.

——— (ed.). *Developments in International Fisheries Law*. The Hague, London, Boston: Kluwer Law International, 1999.

Hobbes, Thomas. *The Leviathan*. Oxford: Oxford University Press, 1996.

Hogan, Albert E. *Pacific Blockade*. Oxford: Clarendon Press, 1908.

Holland, Thomas Erskine. *Lectures on International Law*. London: Sweet & Maxwell, 1933.

Homer-Dixon, Thomas F. (ed.). *Ecoviolence: Links Among Environment, Population, and Security*. Lanham, Boulder, New York, Oxford: Rowman & Littlefield Publishers Inc., 1998.

———. *Environment, Scarcity, and Violence*. Princeton: Princeton University Press, 1999.

———. "Threshold of Turmoil: Environmental Scarcities and Violent Conflicts." In *Contested Grounds: Security and Conflicts in the New Environmental Politics*, 63. New York: State University of New York Press, 1999.

Hovi, Jon. *Games, Threats, and Treaties: Understanding Commitments in International Relations*. London, Washington, D.C.: Printer, 1998.

Hutchinson, Mark R. "Restoring Hope: UN Security Council Resolutions for Somalia and an Expanded Doctrine of Humanitarian Intervention." *Harvard International Law Journal* 34 (1993): 624–640.

International Law Commission, *Yearbook of the International Law Commission, 1979–2001*. New York, Geneva: United Nations Publishing, 1980–2006.

Jackson, John H. *The World Trade Organization: Constitution and Jurisprudence*. London: Royal Institute of International Affairs, 1998.

Jasentuliyana, Nandasiri (ed.). *Perspectives on International Law*. London, The Hague, Boston: Kluwer Law International, 1995.

Jarvis, Darryl S. L. *International Relations and the Challenge of Postmodernism: Defending the Discipline*. South Carolina: University of South Caroline Press, 2000.

Jervis, Robert. *Perception and Misperception in International Politics*. Princeton, NJ: Princeton University Press, 1976.

Jessup, Philip C. *A Modern Law of Nations: An Introduction*. New York: The Macmillan Co., 1948.

———. *The Use of International Law*. Ann Arbor: The University of Michigan Law School, 1959.

Jonsson, Hannes. *Friends in Conflict: The Anglo-Icelandic Cod Wars and the Law of the Sea*. London: C. Hurst & Company and Conneticut: Archon Books, 1982.

Jordan, Andrew (ed.). *Environmental Policy in the European Union, Actors Institutions, and Processes*. London: Earthscan Publications Limited, 2002.

Jouvenel, Bertrand De. *Sovereignty: An Inquiry into the Political Good*. J. F. Huntington, trans. Chicago: University of Chicago Press, 1957.

Joyner, Christopher. "On the Borderline? Canadian Activism in the Grand Banks." In *Governing High Seas Fisheries: The Interplay of Global and Regional Regimes*, 207. Oxford: Oxford University Press, Oxford, 2001.

Joyner, Christopher, and Alejandro Alvarez von Gustedt. "The Turbot War of 1995: Lessons for the Law of the Sea." *International Journal of Marine and Coastal Law* 11, no. 4 (1996): 425–458.

Kaikobad, Kaiyan Homi. *The International Court of Justice and Judicial Review: A Study of the Court's Powers with Respect to Judgments of the ILO and UN Administrative Tribunals*. The Hague, London, Boston: Kluwer Law International, 2000.

Kalshoven, Frits. *Belligerent Reprisals*. Leyden: A. W. Sijthoff, 1971.

Kant, Immanuel. *Perpetual Peace*. New York: Colombia University Press, 1939.

Kapteyn, P. J. G., and P. VerLoren van Themaat. *Introduction to the Law of the European Communities: From Maastricht to Amsterdam*. 3rd ed. London, The Hague, Boston: Kluwer Law International, 1998.

Kaplan, Robert D. *The Coming Anarchy: Shattering the Dream of the Post Cold War*. New York: Random House, 2000.

Katzenstein, Peter J. (ed.). *The Culture of National Security: Norms and Identity in World Politics*. New York: Columbia University Press, 1996.

Kaye, Stuart B. *International Fisheries Mangement*. The Hague, London, Boston: Kluwer Law International, 2001.

Käkönen, Jyrki (ed.). *Green Security or Militarized Environment*. Dartmouth: Aldershot, 1994.

Kelsen, Hans. *Principles of International Law*. 2nd ed. New York, Chicago, San Francisco, Toronto, London: Holt Rinehart and Winston, Inc., 1966.

Kennedy, David. *International Legal Structures*. Baden-Baden: Nomos Verlagsgesellschaft, 1987.

Keohane, Robert O. *After Hegemony: Cooperation and Discord in the World Political Economy*. Princeton: Princeton University Press, 1984.

———. "Institutionalist Theory, Realist Challenge After the Cold War." In *Neorealism and Neoliberalism: The Contemporary Debate*, 269. New York: Columbia University Press, 1993.

——— (ed.). *Neorealism and Its Critics*. New York: Columbia University Press, 1986.

———. "The Demand for International Regimes." In *International Regimes*, 141. New York, London: Cornell University Press, 1983.

Keohane, Robert O., and Marc A. Levy (eds.). *Institutions for Environmental Aid: Pitfalls and Promise*. Cambridge: MIT Press, 1996.

Kingsbury, Benedict. "Environment and Trade: The GATT/WTO Regime in the International Legal System." In *Environmental Regulation and Economic Growth*, 189. Oxford: Clarendon Press, 1994.

Kiss, Alexandre, and Dinah Shelton. *International Environmental Law*. 2nd ed. Ardsley: Transnational Publishers, 2000.

Klare, Michael T. (ed.). *World Security: Trends and Challenges at Century's End*. New York: St. Martin's Press, 1991.

Knight, Gary, and Hungdah Chiu. *The International Law of the Sea: Cases, Documents, and Readings*. London, New York: Elsevier Applied Science and UNIFO Publishers, Inc., 1991.

Knorr, Klaus. "National Security Studies: Scope and Structure of the Field." In *National Security & American Society: Theory, Process, and Policy*, 5. Lawrence, Manhattan, Wichita: University Press of Kansas, 1973.

———. "Threat Perception." In *Historical Dimensions of National Security Problems*, 78. Lawrence, Manhattan, Wichita: University Press of Kansas, 1975.

Krasner, Stephen (ed.). *International Regimes*. Ithaca, London: Cornell University Press, 1983.

——— (ed.). *Problematic Sovereignty: Contested Rules and Political Possibilities*. New York: Columbia University Press, 2000.

———. *Sovereignty: Organized Hypocrisy*. Princeton: Princeton University Press, 1999.

Kwiatkowska, Barbara. *Decisions of the World Court Relevant to the UN Convention on the Law of the Sea: A Reference Guide*. The Hague, London, New York: Kluwer Law International, 2002.

———. "The High Seas Fisheries Regime: At a Point of No Return?" *International Journal of Marine and Coastal Law* 8, no. 3 (1993): 327–358.

———. "The Ireland v. United Kingdom (Mox Plant) Case: Applying the Doctrine of Treaty Parallelism." *International Journal of Marine and Coastal Law* 18, no. 1 (2003): 1–58.

Lamy, Pascal. "The Place of the WTO and Its Law in the International Legal Order." *European Journal of International Law* 17, no. 5 (2006): 969–984.

Lauterpacht, H. *The Function of Law in the International Community*. Oxford: Clarendon Press, 1933.

Lawrence, T. J. *The Principles of International Law*. 4th ed. London: Macmillan and Co., 1911.

Levy, Marc A. "Is the Environment a National Security Issue?" *International Security* 20, no. 2 (1995): 35–62.

Lynn-Jones, Sean M., and Steve E. Miller (eds.). *Global Dangers: Changing Dimensions of International Security*. Cambridge: The MIT Press, 1995.

Lyons, Gene M., and Michael Mastanduno (eds.). *Beyond Westphalia? State Sovereignty and International Intervention*. Baltimore: John Hopkins University Press, 1995.

Malloy, William M. (ed.). *Treaties, Conventions, International Acts, Protocols, and Agreements Between the United States of America and Other Powers, 1776–1909*. Vol. I. Washington, D.C.: U.S. GPO, 1910.

Martens, Georg Friedrich von. *A Compendium of the Law of Nations* (originally published in 1795). William Cobbet, trans. London: Cobbet and Morgan, Pall-Mall, 1802.

Mathews, Jessica T. "Redefining Security." *Foreign Affairs* 68, no. 2 (1989): 162–177.

McLaughlin, Richard J. "UNCLOS and the Demise of the United States' Use of Trade Sanctions to Protect Dolphins, Sea Turtles, Whales, and Other International Marine Living Resources." *Ecology Law Quarterly* 21 (1994): 1–78.

McNeil, Frank. *Making Sense of Environmental Security*. North South Agenda paper no. 39. Coral Gables: North-South Center, 2000.

McSweeney, Bill. *Security, Identity, and Interests: A Sociology of International Relations*. Cambridge: Cambridge University Press, 1999.

Mearsheimer, John F. "The False Promise of International Institutions." In *Theories of War and Peace*, 329. Cambridge, London: The MIT Press, 1998.

Merrils, J.G. *International Dispute Settlement*. 3rd ed. Cambridge, New York: Cambridge University Press, 1998.

Miles, Edward L. *Environmental Regime Effectiveness: Confronting Theory with Evidence*. Cambridge: MIT Press, 2002.

Moore, James W. *The Changing Environment*, New York, Berlin, Heidelberg: Springer-Verlag, 1986.

Moore, John Norton. "Enhancing Compliance with International Law: A Neglected Remedy." *Virginia Journal of International Law* 39 (1999): 881.

Morgenthau, Hans. *Politics Among Nations, The Struggle for Power and Peace*. 6th ed. New York: Knopf, 1985.

Myers, Norman. *Ultimate Security: The Environmental Basis of Political Stability*. New York: W.W. Norton, 1993.

Neuzil, Mark. *Mass Media & Environmental Conflict: America's Green Crusades*. Thousand Oaks: Sage Publications, 1996.

Nincic, Djura. *The Problem of Sovereignty in the Charter and the Practice of the United Nations*. The Hague: Martinus Nijhoff Publishers, 1970.

Nordquist, Myron H., and John Norton Moore (eds.). *Current Fisheries Issues and the Food and Agriculture Organization of the United Nations*. The Hague, Boston, London: Martinus Nijhoff Publishers, 2000.

——— (eds.). *Current Marine Environmental Issues and the International Tribunal for the Law of the Sea*. The Hague, London, New York: Martinus Nijhoff Publishers, 2001.

——— (eds.). *Oceans Policy: New Institutions, Challenge and Opportunities*. The Hague, Boston, London: Martinus Nijhoff Publishers, 1999.

O'Connor, J. F. *Good Faith in International Law*. Brookfield: Dartmouth, 1991.

Oellers-Frahm, Karin, and Norbert Wühler. *Dispute Settlement in Public International Law*. Vol. I–II, 2nd ed. Berlin, Heidelberg, New York, Tokyo: Springer Verlag, 2001.

Oppenheim, L. *International Law*. Vol. I, 8th ed. New York: David McKay Company Inc., 1955.

———. *International Law*. Vol. II, 7th ed. New York: David McKay Company Inc., 1952.

——— (ed.). *The Collected Papers of John Westlake on Public International Law*. Cambridge: Cambridge University Press, 1914.

Organisation for Economic Co-operation and Development. "The Economics of Environmental Security: Introduction." In *OECD Working Papers*. Vol. 7, no. 13. Paris, 1999.

Oxman, Bernard H. "Complementary Agreements and Compulsory Jurisdiction." *American Journal International Law* 95, no. 2 (2001): 277–312.

Paolini, Albert J., Anthony P. Jarvis, and Christian Reus-Smit (eds.). *Between Sovereignty and Global Governance: The United Nations, the State, and Civil Society*. New York: St. Martin's Press, 1998.

Pangle, Thomas L. "The Moral Basis of National Security: Four Historical Perspectives." In *Historical Dimensions of National Security Problems*, 307. Lawrence, Manhattan, Wichita: University Press of Kansas, 1975.

Palmeter, David, and Petros C. Mavroidis. "The WTO Legal System: Sources of Law." *American Journal of International Law* 92, no. 3 (1998): 398–413.

Pauwelyn, Joost. "Evidence, Proof, and Persuasions in WTO Dispute Settlement: Who Bears the Burden." *Journal of International Economic Law* 1, no. 2 (1998): 227–258.

———. "The Role of Public International Law in the WTO: How Far Can We Go?" *American Journal of International Law* 95, no. 3 (2001): 535–578.

Petersmann, Ernst-Ulrich. "Constitutionalism and International Adjudication: How to Constitutionalize the UN Dispute Settlement System." *New York University Journal of International Law and Policy* 31 (1999): 753.

Phillips, Harlan B. (ed.). *Felix Frankfurter Reminisces*. London: Secker & Warburg, 1960.

Plant, Glen (ed.). *Environmental Protection and the Law of War*. London, New York: Belhaven Press, 1992.

Porter, Gareth, et. al. *Global Environmental Politics*. 2nd ed. Boulder: Westview Press, 1996.

Postel, Sandra. *Dividing the Waters: Food Security, Ecosystem Health, and the New Politics of Scarcity*, Worldwatch paper no. 132. Washington, D.C.: Worldwatch Institute, 1996.

Powell, Robert. "Absolute and Relative Gains in International Relations Theory." *The American Political Science Review* 85, no. 4 (1991): 1303–1320.

Price, Thomas L. and Ryan S. Lester. "The OSCE's Economic Dimension on the Eve of the 21st Century." In *Yearbook on the Organization for Security and Co-operation in Europe (OSCE)*, 2. Vol. 4. Baden-Baden: Institute for Peace Research and Security Policy at the University of Hamburg/IFSH, 1999.

Pufendorf, Samuel Freiherr von. *Of the Law of Nature and Nations*. Oxford: L. Lichfield, 1703.

Puls, Bret. "The Murky Waters of International Environmental Jurisprudence: A Critique of Recent WTO Holding in the Shrimp/Turtle Controversy." *Minnesota Journal of Global Trade* 8 (1999): 343–379.

Quante, Volker R. "Environmental Threats and International Security: Action Potential for NATO." In *Environmental Change and Security: A European Perspective*, 234. Christopher Hay, trans. Berlin, Heidelberg, New York: Springer Verlag, 1999.

Quigley, John. "Missiles with a Message: The Legality of The United States Raid on Iraq's Intelligence Headquarters." *Hastings International and Comparative Law Review* 18 (1994): 241–274.

Ramcharan, B. G. *The International Law and Practice of Early-Warning and Preventive Diplomacy: The Emerging Global Watch*. Dordrecht, Boston, London: Martinus Nijhoff Publisher, 1991.

Rao, P. Chandrasekhara, and Rahmatullah Khan (eds.). *The International Tribunal for the Law of the Sea: Law and Practice*. The Hague, London, Boston: Kluwer Law International, 2001.

Rao, P. K. *Environmental Trade Disputes and the WTO*. Lawrenceville: Pinninti Publishers, 2001.

Reisman, W. Michael. "Peacemaking." *Yale Journal of International Law* 18 (1993): 415.

Renner, Michael. *Fighting for Survival: Environmental Decline, Social Conflict, and the New Age of Insecurity*. New York, London: W.W. Norton & Company, 1996.

———. *National Security: The Economic and Environmental Dimensions*, Worldwatch paper no. 89. Washington D.C.: Worldwatch Institute, 1989.

Revesz, Richard L., Philippe Sands, and Richard B. Steward. *Environmental Law, the Economy, and Sustainable Development: The United States, the European Union, and the International Community*. Cambridge: Cambridge University Press, 2000.

Rockwell, Richard C. and Richard H. Moss. "Reconceptualizing Security: A Note About Research." In *Mexico: In Search of Security*, 31. Coral Gables: North-South Center, 1993.

Romm, Joseph J. *Defining National Security; Non-Military Aspects*. New York: Council on Foreign Relations Press, 1993.

———. *The Once and Future Superpower: How to Restore America's Economic, Energy, and Environmental Security*. New York: William Morrow and Company, Inc., 1992.

Rosenne, Shabtai, and Louis B. Sohn (eds.). *United Nations Convention on the Law of the Sea 1982: A Commentary*. Vol. V. Dordrecht, Boston, London: Martinus Nijhoff Publishers, 1989.

Sachs, Wolfgang (ed.). *Global Ecology: A New Arena of Political Conflict*. London, Atlantic Highlands: Zed Books and Halifax: Fernwood Pub., 1993.

Sandole, Dennis J. D., and Hugo van der Merwe (eds.). *Conflict Resolution Theory and Practice: Integration and Application*. Manchester, New York: Manchester University Press, 1993.

Sands, Philippe (ed.). *Greening International Law*. New York: New Press, 1994.

Schacter, Oscar. *International Law in Theory and Practice*. Student ed. Boston, The Hague, London: Kluwer Law International, 1995.

———. *Sharing the World's Resources*. New York: Columbia University Press, 1977.

———. "United Nations Law." *American Journal of International Law* 88 (1994): 1–23.

Schoenbaum, Thomas J., Junji Nakagawa, and Linda C. Reif (eds.). *Trilateral Perspectives on International Legal Issues: From Theory to Practice*. Ardsley: Transnational Publishers, Inc., 1998.

Serdy, Andrew. "See You in Port: Australia and New Zealand as Third Parties in the Dispute Between Chile and the European Community over Chile's Denial of Port Access to Spanish Vessels Fishing for Swordfish on the High Seas." *Melbourne Journal of International Law* 3, no. 1 (2002): 79–119.

Shaffer, Gregory. "International Trade–WTO–Quantitative Restriction–Environmental Protection-Endangered Species–U.S. Import Ban on Shrimps." *American Journal of International Law* 93 (1999): 507.

Singh, Nagendra. *The Role and Record of the International Court of Justice*. Dordrecht, Boston, London: Martinus Nijhoff Publishers, 1989.

Sjolander, Claire Turenne, and Wayne S. Cox (eds.). *Beyond Positivism: Critical Reflections on International Relations*. Boulder, London: Lynne Rienner Publishers, 1994.

Stokke, Olav Schram (ed.). *Governing High Seas Fisheries: The Interplay of Global and Regional Regimes*. Oxford: Oxford University Press, 2001.

———. "The Loophole of the Barents Sea Fisheries Regime." In *Governing High Seas Fisheries: The Interplay of Global and Regional Regimes*, 273. Oxford: Oxford University Press, 2001.

Stokke, Olav Schram, Lee G. Anderson, and Natalia Mirovitskaya. "The Barents Sea Fisheries." In *The Effectiveness of International Environmental Regimes: Causal Connection and Behavioral Mechanism*, 91. Cambridge, Massachusetts, London, England: MIT Press, 1999.

Stotzky, Irwin P. *Silencing the Guns in Haiti*. Chicago: The University of Chicago Press, 1997.

Strange, Susan. "Cave! Hic Dragones: A Critique of Regime Analysis." In *International Regimes*, 337. Ithaca, London: Cornell University Press, 1983.

Susskind, Lawrence E. *Environmental Diplomacy: Negotiating More Effective Global Agreements*. Oxford: Oxford University Press, 1994.

Susskind, Lawrence, William Moomaw, and Kevin Gallagher (eds.). *Transboundary Environmental Negotiation: New Approaches to Global Cooperation*. San Francisco: Jossey-Bass Publishers, 2002.

Teece, David R. "Global Overfishing and the Spanish-Canadian Turbot War: Can International Law Protect the Highs-Seas Environment?" *Colorado Journal of International Law & Policy* 8 (1997): 89.

The Independent Commission on Disarmament and Security Issues. *Common Security: A Blueprint for Survival*. New York: Simon and Schuster, 1982.

Tolba, Mostafa K., and Osama A. El-Kholy. *The World Environment: 1972–1992: Two Decades of Challenge*. London: Chapman & Hall, 1992.

Trachtman, Joel P. "The Domain of WTO Dispute Resolution." *Harvard International Law Journal* 401 (1999): 333.

Trager, Frank N. and Frank L. Simone. "An Introduction to the Study of National Security." In *National Security & American Society: Theory, Process, and Policy*, 35. Lawrence, Manhattan, Wichita: University Press of Kansas, 1973.

Treves, Tullio. "The Jurisdiction of the International Tribunal for the Law of the Sea." In *The International Tribunal for the Law of the Sea: Law and Practice*, 111. The Hague, London, Boston: Kluwer Law International, 2001.

Trolldalen, Jon Martin. *International Environmental Conflict Resolution: The Role of the United Nations*. Washington, D.C.: WFED, UNITAR, NIDR, 1992.

Tunkin, G. I. *Theory of International Law*. William E. Butler, trans. Cambridge: Harvard University Press, 1974.

Tzu, Sun. *The Art of War*. (Written in China in the 6th century B.C.) New York: Delacorte Press, 1983.

Udombana, Nsongurua J. "A Question of Justice: The WTO, Africa, and Countermeasures for Breaches of International Trade Obligations." *John Marshall Law Review* 38 (2005): 1153–1199.

Ullman, Richard. "Redefining Security." *International Security* 8 (1983): 1. Reprinted in *Global Dangers, Changing Dimensions of International Security*, 15. Cambridge, London: MIT Press, 1995.

United States Senate Committee on Environment and Public Works. *Environmental Policy and Conflict Resolution Act of 1997*. Washington, D.C., 1997.

Vattel, Emmerich de, *The Law of Nations* or *Principles of the Law of Nature, Applied to the Conduct and Affairs of Nations and Sovereigns*. New York: Messrs. Berry and Rogers, 1787.

———. *The Law of Nations* or *Principles of the Law of Nature, Applied to the Conduct and Affairs of Nations and Sovereigns*. Northhampton: Simeon Butler, 1820.

Viotti, Poul R., and Mark V. Kauppi. *International Relations Theory, Realism, Pluralism, Globalism, and Beyond*. 3rd ed. Boston: Allyn and Bacon, 1999.

Wallace-Bruce, Nil Lante. *The Settlement of International Disputes: The Contribution of Australia and New Zealand*. The Hague, Boston, London: Martinus Nijhoff Publishers, 1998.

Waltz, Kenneth N. *Man, The State, and War: A Theoretical Analysis*. New York: Columbia University Press, 1959.

———. *Theory of International Politics*. New York: McGraw-Hill Inc., 1979.

———. "Anarchical Order and Balances of Power." In *Neorealism and Its Critics*, 98. New York: Columbia University Press, 1986.

———. "Laws and Theories." In *Neorealism and Its Critics*, 27. New York: Columbia University Press, 1986.

———. "Reflections on Theory of International Politics: A Response to My Critics." In *Neorealims and Its Critics*, 331. New York: Columbia University Press, 1986.

Wedgwood, Ruth. "The Enforcement of Security Council Resolution 687: The Threat of Force Against Iraq's Weapons of Mass Destruction." *American Journal of International Law* 92 (1998): 724.

Weiss, Edith Brown. "Invoking State Responsibility in the Twenty-First Century." *American Journal of International Law* 96, no. 4 (2002): 798–816.

Wendt, Alexander. *Social Theory of International Politics*. Cambridge: Cambridge University Press, 1999.

Westing, Arthur H. (ed.). *Global Resources and International Conflict: Environmental Factors in Strategic Policy and Action*. Oxford, New York: Oxford University Press, 1986.

Westlake, John. *Chapters on the Principles of International Law*. Cambridge: Cambridge University Press, 1894.

———. "International Rights of Self-Preservation." In *The Collected Papers of John Westlake on Public International Law*, 111. Cambridge: Cambridge University Press, 1914.

———. "The Equality and Independence of States." In *The Collected Papers of John Westlake on Public International Law*, 86. Cambridge: Cambridge University Press, 1914.

———. "The Principles of International Law." In *The Collected Papers of John Westlake on Public International Law*, 78. Cambridge: Cambridge University Press, 1914.

———. "War." In *The Collected Papers of John Westlake on Public International Law*, 237. Cambridge: Cambridge University Press, 1914.

Wheaton, Henry. *Elements of International Law*. Philadelphia: Lea and Blanchard, 1846.

Williamson, Richard L. "Building the International Environmental Regime." *University of Miami Inter-American Law Review* 21 (1990): 679.

Wise, Mark. *The Common Fisheries Policy of the European Community*. London, New York: Methuen, 1994.

Wolfrum, Rudiger. "Provisional Measures of the International Tribunal for the Law of the Sea." In *The International Tribunal for the Law of the Sea: Law and Practice*, 173. The Hague, London, Boston: Kluwer Law International, 2001.

Woolsey, Theodore D. *Introduction to the Study of International Law*. 5th ed. New York: Charles Scribner's Sons, 1879.

World Commission on Environment and Development. *Our Common Future*. Oxford: Oxford University Press, 1987.

Young, Michael K., and Yuji Iwasawa (eds.). *Trilateral Perspectives on International Legal Issues: Relevance of Domestic Law and Policy*. Irvington: Transnational Publishers, 1996.

Young, Oran R. *Governance in World Affairs*. Ithaca, London: Cornell University Press, 1999.

———. "Regime Dynamics: The Rise and Fall of International Regimes." In *International Regimes*, 93. Ithaca, London: Cornell University Press, 1983.

——— (ed.). *The Effectiveness of International Environmental Regimes: Causal Connection and Behavioral Mechanism*. Cambridge, London: MIT Press, 1999.

Young, Oran R., and Marc A. Levy. "The Effectiveness of International Environmental Regimes." In *The Effectiveness of International Environmental Regimes: Causal Connection and Behavioral Mechanism*, 1. Cambridge, London: MIT Press, 1999.

Young, Oran R., George J. Demko, and Kilaparti Ramakrishna. *Global Environmental Change and International Governance*. Dartmouth College, Hanover: University Press of New England, 1996.

Yturriaga, Jose A. de. *The International Regime of Fisheries—From UNCLOS 1982 to the Presential Sea*. The Hague, Boston, Cambridge: Martinus Nijhoff, 1997.

Zoller, Elisabeth. *Peacetime Unilateral Remedies: An Analysis of Countermeasures*. New York: Traditional Publishers, 1984.

———. *Enforcing International Law Through U.S. Legislation*. New York: Traditional Publishers, 1985.

Index

access to court, 9, 76, 94–95, 109, 193–197, 215, 270, 339
access to port, 229–238, 254n74, 255n82, 319–321
act of war, 25, 72, 123
acts of necessity, 51, 55–62, 80, 99, 104n43, 125, 129, 248, 250
Air Service Agreement Case, 68, 70, 76, 92–96, 105n70, 123–124, 151, 153, 158–159, 162n12, 175–176, 180–181, 190, 193, 197–198, 200, 202, 204
American plaice, 242, 244
anticipatory countermeasures. *See* countermeasures
approximation. *See* proportionality
Arangio-Ruiz, Gaetano, 150–151, 154–155, 172
Argentina-Footwear Case, 278–279
Australia, 138

Bahamas, 242
Baker v. Carr, 38
Barcelona Traction Case, 134–135, 137
Barents Sea, 222, 238
Barents Sea cod, 230–231, 233, 239–240, 249
Beck, John, 244, 247
Belgium, 89, 134–135
Bodin, Jean, 23–24, 44n6
Bonino, Emma, 242–244
Brown, Lester, 341
burden of proof, 94, 105n70, 123, 152, 175, 214, 273, 284, 288, 293

Canada, 222, 225, 240–250, 261n167, 276, 338
Carr, E. H., 15
Certain Phosphate Lands in Nauru, 313
cessation
  constructive demand for cessation, 153
  duty to demand, 136, 150–153, 162n12, 321. *See also* sommation
  right to demand, 136–139
China, 63n2, 130
CITES. *See* Convention on International Trade in Endangered Species of Wild Fauna and Flora
Civil Aeronautics Board, 92
coastal state, 9, 17, 90–91, 137, 221, 226–229, 233, 238–239, 316–317
Cold War, 35, 340
Committee on Economic, Social and Cultural Rights. *See* United Nations
compromi, 33, 36, 126
compensation, 90, 136, 140, 151, 214, 275
compulsory adjudication, 31–32, 36, 340

conciliation, 70, 194–195, 201, 265
consultation, 52, 94, 265, 293, 314–315, 319–321, 340–341
Convention on Conservation of Migratory Species of Wild Animals, 301
Convention on International Trade in Endangered Species of Wild Fauna and Flora (CITES), 293–294, 299, 301
countermeasures
  against private persons, 73, 91, 168–169, 172, 246
  anticipatory countermeasures, 3, 56, 128–129, 214
  collective countermeasures, 129–134, 144n57, 144n61. See also *erga omnes* and self-defense: collective
  definition, 3
  duty to exhaust other means, 70, 136, 146n92, 156, 193, 195–196, 313
  elements of countermeasures, 7–9, 56, 79, 88, 108–109, 113–114, 120, 214, 216, 221–223, 238, 246, 282, 310
  prior internationally wrongful act (primary element), 3, 7–8, 10, 42, 55–56, 67, 69–70, 73–74, 79, 88, 93, 107–109, 113, 121, 123–124, 142n24, 178, 214, 246, 248, 264, 271, 286, 289–290, 297, 312
  prohibited countermeasures, 7–8, 78, 119, 167, 169–173, 207n17, 215, 283
countermeasures (*continued*)
  proportionality of countermeasures. *See* proportionality
  punitive countermeasures, 17, 117–122, 131–132, 141n3
  purpose of countermeasures, 3, 17–18, 73, 117–122, 177–179, 192, 201–202, 223, 239, 269, 286
  reversible, 77, 119–120
  taken by private persons, 4, 69, 139–140
  third party countermeasures, 130, 134
  trade-related countermeasures, 263, 268–269, 271
Crawford, James, 150, 154, 179, 213
Czechoslovakia, 57–58, 64n21, 100–101

Damrosch, Lori Fisler, 124–126, 143n32
Denmark, 141n3, 159, 196, 213
derogation, 2, 76, 172–173, 234, 270, 283
development aid, 52
diplomacy, 2, 36, 54, 72, 128, 173, 232, 244
diplomatic protection, 76–77, 79, 81, 96–99, 105n70, 134, 137, 170, 183n19, 215
directly injured state. *See* injured state
dispute settlement mechanism, 5, 9, 109, 114, 193–196, 201, 215, 223, 263–265, 268–269, 315, 318
distribution of capabilities, 26, 42, 73
draft article. *See* International Law Commission

East-Timor. *See* Timor Leste
EC Treaty, 232, 234–235, 253n45
EC. *See* European Community
ecological necessity, 58–59
EEA Agreement, 230, 232–237, 240, 253n45
effective remedy test, 200, 202, 210n68
EFTA Surveillance Authority (ESA), 225, 230, 232–238, 240, 251n1, 255n75, 274
Elagab, Omer Yousif, 68, 118–119, 121, 125, 131, 153, 176, 178, 181, 187n81
endangered
  fish stocks, 246
  sea turtles, 298–299, 311
enforcement mechanism, 2, 6, 8, 16, 30–31, 95, 213, 216, 320, 339
environmental rights, 5, 205, 341–342
environmental security, 55, 341
erga omnes, 129, 135–138, 147n106, 147n111, 185n45
ESA. *See* EFTA Surveillance Authority
essential rights (interests), 33–34, 36, 56, 59–60, 129, 250
Estai Case, 222, 240–250, 320
European Community (EC), 222, 225, 232, 235–236, 239–248, 251n11, 264, 267–268, 273, 278, 280, 284, 293, 295–296, 314–321, 334n283, 338
European Court of Justice (ECJ), 232, 234, 240, 253n45
European Economic Area (EEA), 10, 47n57, 230, 232–238, 240, 337
European Union, 10, 30–32, 47n56, 52, 216, 261n167, 261n169
exclusive economic zone, 17, 137, 221, 226–228, 230–231, 239, 314–315
exhaustible natural resources, 270, 294, 298, 300–302

Fish Stocks Agreement, 226–228, 237–238, 251n11, 254n72, 255n82, 316
Fishery Jurisdiction Case (*United Kingdom v. Iceland*), 89–92
Fong Yue Ting v. United States, 38
France, 44n6, 92–94, 96, 124, 146n98, 151, 153, 165n64, 175–176, 180, 190, 206
freezing of assets. *See* unilateral measures
fundamental human rights. *See* human rights

Gabcikovo-Nagymaros Project, 57, 99–102, 104n43, 119, 125, 129, 150, 153–154, 159–160, 175–176, 179–180, 248–250
Gardner, Richard N., 340
Gasoline Case, 300, 302–303
General Agreement on Tariffs and Trade (GATT), 17, 222, 264–266, 283–284, 287, 289, 291–293, 295–296, 298–302, 306, 311, 318. *See also* World Trade Organization
  article III, 287–288, 293
  article V, 274, 314, 317
  article VIII, 279–280
  article XI, 287–288, 293, 298, 317

General Agreement on Tariffs and Trade (GATT) (*continued*)
article XX, 17, 222, 270–271, 280, 284–303, 305–310, 312, 314, 316, 319–320, 327n98, 338
chapeau, 271, 284–285, 300, 305–306, 308–309
Geneva Conventions of 1949, 79, 184n39
Germany, 87–88, 103n1
good faith, 9, 123–127, 157–159, 161, 165n64, 190–192, 197, 199–202, 207n5, 209n53, 215, 306–308, 311–313, 333n279. *See also* negotiation: duty to conduct in good faith
Gore, Al, 341
Grand Banks, 222, 242, 244, 248
Greenland halibut, 222, 241–249, 257n110, 258n112, 261n167

Hall, William Edward, 71, 73–75, 131–132, 174
Henkin, Louis, 13, 28–29, 67, 71–74, 342
highly migratory species (fish stocks), 223, 227–228, 251n11, 300–301, 314, 316, 319
Hobbes, Thomas, 23–24
Holland, Thomas Erskine, 71, 74, 174
Hostage Case. *See* United States Diplomatic and Consular Staff in Tehran
Hugo, Grotius, 68, 122–23, 128, 131, 167–168
human rights, 8, 81, 138, 169–172, 215, 283
humanitarian law, 8, 81, 97–98, 169–172, 184n28, 215, 283
Hungary, 57–61, 99–101, 154, 248–249

Iceland, 41, 47n57, 48n78, 89–92, 222, 225, 229–233, 237–240, 247, 254n74, 255nn78–79, 320
India, 297, 299, 301
injured state, 3–5, 8–10, 24, 31, 69–70, 72, 76–78, 80–81, 94, 99, 109, 113, 117–119, 121, 123–124, 126, 129–133, 135–139, 146n98, 149–152, 154–161, 162n12, 165n64, 168–174, 176, 178–182, 186n77, 187n85, 189–193, 195–198, 201, 203–204, 208n29, 214–215, 221–223, 272–273, 282–283, 285–286, 289, 313, 321
indirectly injured, 8, 130–131, 133–135, 138–139, 214
legal injury (juridical injury), 135, 137–138
noninjured states, 129, 136–139, 144n57, 144n60, 146n94, 147n111
Institute of International Law, 151
Inter-American Convention for the Protection and Conservation of Sea Turtles, 307
Intergovernmental Panel on Climate Change (IPCC), 341
International Court of Justice, 33, 39–41, 48n78, 49n91, 54, 57, 59, 79, 87, 89–90, 96, 119, 125, 129, 133–134, 138, 147n106, 150, 153–154, 160, 175, 185n45, 197–198, 205–206, 209n64, 210n65, 225, 241, 243, 245–246, 248, 250, 269, 272–273, 313. *See also* jurisdiction

international development projects, 52, 63n1
international disputes, 9, 16, 31–32, 36, 41, 70, 126, 156, 193–194, 206, 213, 216
international law
  direct domestic effect, 31
  incompleteness of, 32–34, 42–43, 72
  limitation of, 7, 15, 32–34, 43
  self-executing, 31
International Law Association, 171
International Law Commission, 2, 5, 12n2, 56–57, 59–60, 68, 72, 78–81, 82n8, 84n41, 84n52, 86n66, 105n71, 114, 118–119, 125–126, 129, 134–139, 146n92, 146n94, 146n97, 147n107, 150, 153–158, 160–161, 162n12, 169, 171–173, 175–177, 179–181, 183n2, 186n76, 187n81, 187n87, 189–190, 192, 194–195, 197–200, 208n29, 213, 250, 276, 312, 338
  1980 Draft Articles, 59–60
  1996 Draft Articles, 141n3, 146n93, 150, 157, 160, 162n4, 171, 177, 179–181, 186n77, 190–191, 195, 207n5, 208n29, 213
  2000 Draft Articles, 80, 130, 138, 141n3, 144n57, 146n93, 147n107, 147n111, 150, 155, 158, 160, 162n4, 163n33, 170, 179, 189–192, 195–196, 201–202, 204, 208n29
  2001 Draft Articles, 56, 80–81, 86n66, 105n71, 118–120, 126, 129, 136, 138–139, 141n3, 144n57, 146n92, 146n94, 146n98, 147n107, 150, 153, 155–156, 159, 162n12, 169, 171–173, 175–176, 178, 183n2, 190, 196–200, 203–204, 286, 313
  establishment, 79
international regime, 9–10, 31–32, 145n75, 210n68, 213, 222, 235, 239, 248, 258n112, 263–265, 269–270, 281–284, 313, 320, 337, 338
international relations, 1–2, 7, 27–29, 35, 38, 42, 73, 99, 107, 127, 130, 174, 190, 206, 339
International Tribunal for the Law of the Sea (ITLOS), 206, 315–316, 319–320, 334n284
IPCC. *See* Intergovernmental Panel on Climate Change (IPCC)
Iran, 48n74, 76, 96–99, 105n70, 153, 197–198
irreparable harm, 156. *See also* injured state

Japan, 158, 161, 191
Jessup, Philip C., 126–127, 131–132
Joint Norwegian Russian Fisheries Commission, 239
judicial discretion, 38, 271, 274, 318
jurisdiction
  compulsory jurisdiction, 36–37, 190, 195–196, 201, 206, 209n64, 210n66, 241, 245–246, 265, 313, 339–340
  effects on the right to take countermeasures, 193, 196, 198

jurisdiction (*contnued*)
fishery jurisdiction, 89–92, 228, 235, 239, 246, 248–250, 316
International Court of Justice, 33, 36, 39, 41, 48n78, 90, 97, 138, 205–206, 209n64, 210n65, 225, 241–242, 245–246, 250, 272–273
jurisdiction to protect species, 288–289, 291, 294–296, 300–303, 316
of a sovereign, 26, 31
of the international system, 32–33, 205, 270
territorial jurisdiction, 23, 39
to prescribe provisional measures, 205
WTO Dispute Settlement Body, 265, 270–275, 277, 280, 283, 318

Kaplan, Robert D., 340
Korea, Republic of, 63n2, 170
Korea—Measures Affecting Government Procurement, 275
Krasner, Stephen D., 24, 28–30

Lauterpacht, H., 34–35, 40
law of nature, 23, 131
law of war (law of armed conflict), 72, 133
Lawrence, T. J., 26, 74
League of Nations, 35, 132, 194
Legality of the Threat or Use of Nuclear Weapons. See *Nuclear Weapons Case*
letter of marque, 140
Libya, 39–40, 108
Lockerbie Case, 39, 108
Loophole, the, 229–232, 238–240, 247, 249, 255n83

Malaysia, 297–299, 306–308, 310, 312
Már Case, 221, 229–240, 251n6, 263, 274, 320, 323n40
Marbury v. Madison, 40
margin of discretion, 125–126, 236, 268
Marine Mammal Protection Act (MMPA), 287
Martens, Georg Friedrich von, 25–26, 45n19, 69, 131, 140, 168, 174, 193
Mexico, 287, 289–292
Mexico Soft Drinks, 280, 323n32, 327n98, 336n322
Military and Paramilitary Activities in and Against Nicaragua. See *Nicaragua Case*
Montreal Convention of 1971, 39–40
moral damage, 146n98
moral obligation, 12n1, 51, 123, 168, 238
Morgenthau, Hans, 27, 35–36, 47n56
Mox Plant Case, 206
multilateral environmental agreements (MEAs), 284, 306–307, 317–318, 324n53
multilateral trading system, 284, 289, 295, 300, 318–319

NAFO. *See* Northwest Atlantic Fisheries Organization
National Marine Fisheries Service, 299
Naulilaa Case, 87–89, 151, 171, 174, 180

negotiation
as a preferred method of dispute settlement, 91–92, 94, 128, 156–157, 174, 192, 194, 201, 207n5, 267, 289, 307, 312, 316–317, 319, 340–341
duty to conduct negotiation in good faith, 70, 151, 153, 157–158, 160–161, 162n4, 164n38, 165n64, 190–192, 207n5, 267, 304, 306–308, 311–313, 317, 333n279
duty to offer, 3, 8, 81, 92, 114, 150–151, 153–161, 190–191, 204, 215, 223, 286, 289, 312–313, 321
effects of ongoing negotiation, 9, 70, 92, 94–95, 100, 109, 114, 158–159, 161, 189–192, 215, 306, 308, 311–312
Netherlands, 159, 292–293
Nicaragua Case, 36–37, 43, 48n78, 133, 145n77, 177, 186n63, 206
Nobel Peace Prize, 341
nonjusticiable disputes, 32, 34, 36–39, 48n74
non-repetition, right to demand, 136, 138
Northwest Atlantic Fisheries Organization (NAFO), 241–247, 249–250, 257n98, 258n112
Norway, 31, 47n57, 222, 225, 229–240, 247, 249, 254n74, 255nn77–78, 255n82
Nuclear Test Case, 41, 206
Nuclear Weapons Case, 60

offending state, 3–4, 8, 17, 31, 67, 71, 73–74, 76, 81, 88, 109, 114, 117–123, 127, 130–132, 134, 136, 138, 140, 149–152, 154–156, 158–161, 162n4, 167–169, 177–179, 181, 191, 193, 199–202, 204, 214–215, 222–223, 240, 271, 282, 286, 289, 312–313, 321
Oilseeds Agreement Case, 273
Oppenheim, L., 16–17, 23, 35, 71, 73, 131–132, 151–152, 169, 174, 177

Pakistan, 297, 299, 301, 309
Panama, 242, 327n107
Pauwelyn, Joost, 269, 273, 275, 277, 280, 283
peremptory norms, 8, 81, 170–173, 185n45, 215, 283
persona non grata, 98
political disputes, 33–35, 98, 290
political justification, 2, 7, 17, 71, 108
political question doctrine, 38, 40
Portugal, 87–88, 138, 147n106, 261n167
preferential rights, 91–92
principle of noninterference, 24, 42
property rights, 72–73, 103n1, 140, 167–169, 172
proportionality
approximation, 9, 92–94, 175, 180–181, 215
negative or positive formulation, 180–181
of countermeasures, 4, 7–9, 70, 78–79, 81, 88–89, 91–94, 100–101, 109, 113–114, 119–120, 122–133, 136, 173–182, 186n63, 194,

proportionality (*continued*)
200–201, 214–215, 222–223, 249, 267, 275, 281–283, 290, 296, 320
two-point approach, 174, 177, 179
provisional measures, 39–40, 196–206
public policy, 234–237, 240, 256n90
Pufendorf, Samuel Freiherr von, 17, 24, 26, 28

reciprocity. *See* unilateral measures
reconciliation, 33, 157
regional or subregional organizations, 228–229
reparation, 3–4, 8, 17, 24, 68, 88, 117–118, 121, 136, 138–139, 146n98, 150–153, 162n12, 168–169, 174, 177–178, 214, 248, 313
reprisal. *See* unilateral measures
res judicata, 319
Restatement of the Law, 78–79, 180, 190
restitution, 122
retorsion. *See* unilateral measures
riparian rights, 101, 175–176, 249
Riphagen, Willem, 72
River Oder Case, 101, 249
Russia, 169, 230–231, 239–240

S.S. Lotus Case, 16, 22
sea turtles, 298–302, 306–307, 309, 311–312, 337
Section 609, 299, 302, 304, 306–308
security
collective security, 145n75
environmental security, 55, 340–342
security (*continued*)
international security, 16, 34, 53–54, 132, 134, 156, 194, 340
national security, 17, 34, 130, 137, 340–342
public security, 234, 237
Security Council, 7, 16, 22, 35, 39–40, 49n81, 51, 53–55, 63n2, 63n3, 97, 108, 209n64
self-defence, 16–17, 26, 55, 128, 132–134
against environmental threats, 55
collective, 132–134, 145n75
precluding an act from wrongfulness, 80
preemptive, 128
self-help, 5, 17, 73, 78, 113
self-preservation, 5, 27, 111, 174
Shrimp/Turtle I, 222, 264, 297–305, 307–313
Shrimp/Turtle II, 222, 264, 284, 305–313
Slovakia, 59, 99–101, 154, 159–160, 191, 248–249
Solana, Javier, 243, 245
sommation, 150–152, 154–155, 162n4
Southern Bluefin Tuna Cases, 206
sovereignty
absolute sovereignty, 27–28, 33, 42
concept, 7, 15–16, 21–34, 39, 41–43, 44n6, 47n56, 74, 107–108, 189, 216, 227, 245, 311, 316
demi-sovereignty, 25
domestic sovereignty, 24, 29, 31
interdependence sovereignty, 29
international legal sovereignty, 29

sovereignty (*continued*)
relative sovereignty, 28
semi-sovereignty, 27
Westphalian sovereignty, 29
Spain, 134, 159, 225, 240–249, 251n11, 261n167, 314–315, 334n283
Spitzbergen, 230, 239
standing, 134–135, 239
stare decisis, 124, 277
state of necessity. *See* acts of necessity
state responsibility, 2, 12n2, 57, 59, 68, 79–80, 82n8, 98, 114, 126, 129–130, 136–138, 141n3, 150, 172, 213, 246, 250, 273, 276, 312–313, 338
Statute of the International Court of Justice, 33, 36, 97, 205, 209n64, 245, 272
straddling stocks, 9, 221, 223, 226–228, 230, 241, 247, 251n11, 316
Swordfish Conservation Case, 222, 236, 264, 314–321

TEDs. *See* turtle excluder devices
Territorial Jurisdiction of the International Commission of the River Oder. See *River Oder Case*
Thailand, 297, 299, 301
Thirty Year War, 24, 45n18
Timor Leste, 138, 147n106, 185n45
Tobin, Brian, 241, 243–244
Torrey Canyon, 57
total allowable catch, 239, 242, 247, 249, 257n110, 261n173
Trachtman, Joel P., 276–279
Tuna I, 222, 264, 286–293, 297–299, 301–302, 310–312
Tuna II, 222, 264, 284, 292–299, 301–303, 312
turtle excluder devices, 298–299, 302, 304, 306, 309, 311

underlying dispute, 48n74, 97, 101, 189, 226, 233, 236, 238, 240, 264, 273–274, 316–318
unilateral measures
blockade, 16, 70
retorsion, 16, 67, 70–75, 78, 84n44
freezing of assets, 156–157, 198
concept, 1–7, 10–11, 15–18, 22–23, 30–31, 51, 56, 67–68, 70–71, 96, 99–101, 105n70, 107–108, 113, 119, 121, 129, 134, 156–158, 161, 173–174, 192–195, 197–199, 202–203, 206, 213, 216, 221, 223, 234–235, 237, 240, 245, 264, 267–269, 290, 304, 313, 340, 342
for conservation purposes, 2, 9, 55, 91, 100–101, 154, 221, 226, 239, 242, 247–248, 255n79, 261n173, 285, 289, 291, 306, 308, 311–312, 317, 319–320, 342
reciprocity, 16, 48n74, 70–71, 73–78, 84n44, 118–121, 181
reprisals, 4, 8, 12n2, 16, 68–78, 82n8, 84n41, 88–89, 93, 127–128, 130–131, 140, 151–153, 156, 168–172, 174, 180, 184n28, 189, 193, 215

United Kingdom, 57, 89–91, 108, 158–161, 163n33, 191, 201–202
United Nations (UN)
Charter, 16, 78, 169, 195,
article 2, 16, 104n29, 156, 194, 250, 262n187
article 24, 54
article 25, 53, 56, 63n3
article 27, 53, 63n2
article 33, 194
article 39, 54
article 41, 54
article 42, 54
article 51, 55, 132–133
article 94, 54
article 103, 40, 63n3
Committee on Economic, Social and Cultural Rights, 171
General Assembly, 340
purpose and principles, 54
United Nations Convention on the Law of the Sea (UNCLOS), 17, 206, 211n76, 223, 226–228, 230, 237–239, 241, 246–248, 255n78, 264, 272, 301, 314–320, 338
article 63, 226–228
article 64, 226–227, 316
article 116, 226
article 117, 226–227, 238–239, 317
United States Supreme Court, 25, 38
United States Trade Act Case, 267

Variant C, 100–101, 154, 160
Vattel, Emmerich de, 25, 33–34, 36,
Vattel, Emmerich de (*continued*) 73–74, 111, 127, 131, 140, 146n103, 152, 156–157, 168, 174, 341
Vienna Convention on Consular Relations, 96
Vienna Convention on Diplomatic Relations, 96
Vienna Convention on the Law of Treaties, 79, 172, 209n53, 274, 278

Westlake, John, 24, 26–27, 72, 128, 189
Westphalia
state system, 5, 21–23, 29, 42
Treaty of Westphalia, 24
Wheaton, Henry, 25–26, 28, 34, 40, 152, 169, 193
Woolsey, Theodore D., 25, 71, 73–74, 152, 168–169
World Trade Organization (WTO)
applicable law, 274–281
Committee on Trade and Environment, 236, 284
covered agreements, 4–5, 10, 265–266, 268, 272–273, 275–278, 280–281, 285, 338
Dispute Settlement Body (DSB), 12n8, 236, 265–268, 272, 277, 285, 298, 305–306, 315, 317–319
dispute settlement mechanism, 9–10, 12n8, 79, 210n68, 222–223, 264–266, 268–278, 280–284, 297, 299–300, 313–319, 337–338

World Trade Organization (WTO) (*continued*)
  Dispute Settlement Understanding (DSU), 265–268, 272–273, 275–278, 280, 285–286, 306, 326n82
World War II, 35, 103n1, 132
wrongdoing state. *See* offending state

Zoller, Elisabeth, 16, 70–71, 73–77, 118–122, 142n24, 153, 178, 185n58
zoo-sanitary certificate, 315

Made in the USA
Monee, IL
12 November 2026

4ca48ecf-f2cb-4882-97f2-7c59200233feR01